Reliability and Alliance Interdependence

Reliability and Alliance Interdependence

The United States and Its Allies in Asia, 1949–1969

IAIN D. HENRY

Cornell University Press

Ithaca and London

Thanks to generous funding from the Strategic and Defence Studies
Centre at the Australian National University, the ebook editions of
this book are available as Open Access volumes from Cornell Open
(cornellopen.org) and other repositories.

First published 2022 by Cornell University Press

Library of Congress Cataloging-in-Publication Data

Names: Henry, Iain D., 1984– author.
Title: Reliability and alliance interdependence: the United States and
    its allies in Asia, 1949–1969 / Iain D. Henry.
Description: Ithaca [New York]: Cornell University Press, 2022. |
    Series: Cornell studies in security affairs | Includes
    bibliographical references and index.
Identifiers: LCCN 2021040307 (print) | LCCN 2021040308 (ebook) |
    ISBN 9781501763045 (hardcover) | ISBN 9781501765544
    (paperback) | ISBN 9781501763052 (pdf) | ISBN 9781501763069 (epub)
Subjects: LCSH: Alliances—History—20th century. | United
    States—Foreign relations—Asia. | Asia—Foreign relations—
    United States. | United States—Foreign relations—1945–1989.
Classification: LCC JZ1314 .H46 2022 (print) | LCC JZ1314 (ebook) |
    DDC 327.1/16—dc23
LC record available at https://lccn.loc.gov/2021040307
LC ebook record available at https://lccn.loc.gov/2021040308

For Dad:
a loyal and reliable ally

Contents

Acknowledgments

I am deeply indebted to the mentors, colleagues, and friends who helped to make this book a reality. In the project's formative stage, Brendan Taylor, Amy King, and Peter Dean regularly provided encouragement, helpful suggestions, and wise advice. Amy, especially, was beyond generous with her time: she read numerous drafts, and her insightful critiques were always invaluable. Yuen Foong Khong, Mike Green, and David Capie also read the first complete manuscript draft, and their feedback helped to sharpen my ideas and further guide my research. Since then, others have commented on various chapters, papers, or presentations, and I thank Cheng Guan Ang, Timothy Crawford, Yasuhiro Izumikawa, Gregory Miller, Tongfi Kim, Ronald Krebs, Evan Resnick, and Jennifer Spindel. My profound apologies go to anyone I have overlooked.

The Australian National University's Strategic and Defence Studies Centre has been my academic home since 2013. Here, I am indebted to the many colleagues who helped over the years, but special notes of appreciation must go to Hugh White and Brendan Sargeant. During 2014, thanks to the generosity of the Australian-American Fulbright Commission and Princeton University, I was a visiting student at the Woodrow Wilson School of Public and International Affairs. Though I spent much of the year in the Washington, DC, area, conducting archival research, I also benefited from conversations with Aaron Friedberg and Tom Christensen. I thank all those individuals who saw promise in the work, and helped by providing institutional support and/or funding.

At Cornell University Press, Roger Haydon expertly shepherded the book through to the contract signing, before departing for his well-deserved retirement and leaving me in the very capable hands of Michael McGandy.

Along with an anonymous reviewer, Stephen Walt read the entire manuscript and provided invaluable advice during the peer review process. I thank both reviewers, as well as the series editors and Press staff, for their excellent comments and feedback.

Some of the ideas and evidence in this book have previously been published in "What Allies Want: Reconsidering Loyalty, Reliability, and Alliance Interdependence," *International Security* 44, no. 4 (2020): 45–83. I thank the editors and peer reviewers at *International Security* for helping me to refine these ideas throughout 2019. The two maps were produced by staff at CartoGIS Services, College of Asia and the Pacific, the Australian National University, and I am grateful for their permission to use these images in the book.

During months of archival research, the staff at various libraries and archives provided invaluable advice and suggestions. Thank you to the staff at the National Archives and Records Administration (College Park, MD), the Dwight D. Eisenhower Presidential Library (Abilene, KS), the John F. Kennedy Presidential Library (Boston, MA), the Richard M. Nixon Presidential Library (Yorba Linda, CA), and the Seely G. Mudd Manuscript Library (Princeton, NJ).

Two people deserve special notes of appreciation. Since 2013 I have been privileged to know, as a colleague and mentor, Evelyn Goh. Evelyn has been a key influence on my development as a junior scholar and the source of ruthless critiques, wise guidance, and encouragement. The second special thank you goes to my high school history teacher, Andrew Kokic. Andrew piqued my interest in all things international, political, and strategic, and encouraged the pursuit of perfection. Without these two intellectual inspirations, I do not think I could ever have written this book.

Finally, thanks go to my family, who made all this possible.

Abbreviations

ANZUS	Australia–New Zealand–United States
ChiCom	Chinese Communist
CIA	Central Intelligence Agency
ChiNat	Chinese Nationalist
DPRK	Democratic People's Republic of Korea
FRUS	*Foreign Relations of the United States*
GOJ	government of Japan
GRC	government of the Republic of China
JCS	Joint Chiefs of Staff
NARA	National Archives and Records Administration
NATO	North Atlantic Treaty Organization
NCND	neither confirm nor deny
NSC	National Security Council
PATO	Pacific-Asian Treaty Organization
PL	Pathet Lao
PRC	People's Republic of China
ROC	Republic of China
ROK	Republic of Korea
ROKG	Republic of Korea government
SCAP	Supreme Commander for the Allied Powers
SEATO	Southeast Asian Treaty Organization
UN	United Nations
UNSC	United Nations Security Council
USG	United States government
USS	United States Ship
USSR	Union of Soviet Socialist Republics

Reliability and Alliance Interdependence

Introduction

Decision makers have always worried about credibility. They have believed that by failing to follow through on a threat, or by abandoning an ally, their conduct will embolden adversaries or undermine alliance commitments. This is particularly true for decision makers in the United States of America: many lives have been lost in wars fought with the goal of preserving US credibility. Thomas Schelling writes that "We lost thirty thousand dead in Korea to save face . . . and it was undoubtedly worth it," because it established "Soviet expectations about the behavior of the United States."[1] If actions in one situation reveal a national character, which can be used to predict behavior in other situations, then geographically discrete problems are, in fact, interdependent: what happens in Europe could affect Asia and vice versa. At the outbreak of the Korean War, President Harry S. Truman proclaimed that "If aggression were allowed to succeed in Korea, it would be an open invitation to new acts of aggression elsewhere."[2]

During the Cold War, deterrence theorists assumed that commitments were interdependent. These ideas—especially of how an adversary will assess the credibility of Washington's threats—are still immensely influential today. In 2012 President Barack Obama infamously drew a "red line" on the use of chemical weapons in the Syrian civil war, but was excoriated when he later backed down from the threat of force.[3] The controversy about this red line centered on the credibility of a threat issued to an adversary, but recent events have generated interest in the credibility—interdependent or not—of security promises made to allies. Though this concept has not received the same scholarly attention as threats issued to adversaries, wars can also be fought with the goal of preserving trust between allies. US policy throughout the Cold War was often influenced by the belief that disloyalty to one ally would send shockwaves through the system of anti-Communist alliances, tempting allies to either defect or adopt a neutral position between the West and the Communist bloc. President Lyndon B. Johnson said that if the United States were "driven from the field in Viet-Nam, then no nation [could] ever again have the same confidence in American promise or in American protection."[4]

Such ideas persisted even after the Cold War had subsided. Though Washington is no longer formally committed to defend Taiwan through a military alliance, theorists and former US officials have argued that if Washington were to allow Taiwan to be forcibly reunited with mainland China, it would damage Washington's treaty alliances in Asia.[5] The starkest assessment is that of John Mearsheimer, who writes that "If the United States were to sever its military ties with Taiwan or fail to defend it in a crisis with China, that would surely send a strong signal to America's other allies in the region that they cannot rely on the United States for protection. Policy makers in Washington will go to great lengths to avoid that outcome and instead maintain America's reputation as a reliable partner. This means they will be inclined to back Taiwan no matter what."[6]

Nancy Bernkopf Tucker and Bonnie Glaser have also written that "U.S. inconstancy could convince American allies and friends to rely less on Washington, undertake an arms race, and/or bandwagon with China."[7] The consensus among academics and policymakers today appears to be similar to that of the Cold War era: the United States cannot—without calamitous consequences—be disloyal to an ally. If Washington is disloyal to one ally, then other allies will regard the US as unreliable and will look elsewhere for security.

More recently, these ideas of interdependence have again featured in considerations of European and Asian security. When Russia invaded and annexed Crimea in 2014, there were suggestions that Washington's inaction unnerved its allies. Though Ukraine was not a treaty ally, the 1994 Budapest Memorandum pledged that the United States, Russia, and the United Kingdom would "respect the Independence and Sovereignty and the existing borders of Ukraine."[8] Half a world away, in Asia, reports suggested that Washington's decision to not forcefully oppose Russian aggression "caused deep concern among already skittish Japanese officials." According to one "senior American military official," the Japanese "keep asking, 'Are you going to do the same thing to us when something happens?'"[9]

Washington has recently felt the need to reassure its allies in Asia about the strength of its alliances. US treaty allies in the region—Japan, South Korea, Thailand, the Philippines, and Australia—have worried that China's activities in the South China Sea pose a threat to regional security and stability. In addition to seizing disputed territory at the Scarborough Shoal, China has reclaimed land from the sea and placed military equipment on these newly constructed islands. In response, the United States has conducted freedom of navigation operations: military maneuvers in which a US Navy vessel sails within twelve nautical miles of a Chinese-held island. The *New York Times* reported that such operations were intended "to reassure allies . . . that the United States would stand up to China's efforts to unilaterally change facts on the ground."[10]

Today, these Asian allies are heavily reliant on Washington for their security. They are concerned about China's rise and its willingness to threaten and use force. Though Japan, South Korea, and Australia possess advanced military capabilities, all rely on US extended nuclear deterrence. For these nations, reliable alliance promises are of the utmost importance. In 2016, then Republican presidential candidate Donald Trump indicated that he was dissatisfied with the US alliance commitments to South Korea and Japan, which generated speculation that if these allies feared abandonment they might develop their own nuclear weapons.[11] This, in turn, could generate regional security dilemmas and further nuclear proliferation.

The examples, theories, and arguments discussed above are premised on the belief that a state's commitments—whether threats to adversaries or promises to allies—are interdependent. During the Cold War, these beliefs took the form of the *domino theory*, which exercised an immense influence on US behavior. For alliances, this conventional wisdom suggests that interdependence is governed by whether or not a state's conduct demonstrates loyalty to its allies. In both the alliance politics literature and policymaking circles, the belief that interdependence and loyalty are linked is perhaps the most important theory of alliance system management.

It is also wrong.

My Argument in Brief

Working deductively from the existing literatures on alliance politics, deterrence theory, and international reputation, in this book I develop and test three hypotheses which form what I call the *alliance audience effect theory*. My first hypothesis is that US allies monitor Washington's behavior in its other alliances, and these observations influence their perceptions of US reliability. Significantly, reliability is not synonymous with loyalty. An unreliable ally is one that poses a risk of abandonment *or* entrapment. Allies do not want Washington to demonstrate indiscriminate loyalty but instead want their relationship with the US to pose no alliance risks. I show how in some situations, US disloyalty to one ally will be desired—even encouraged—by Washington's other allies.

My second hypothesis is that if these allies assess the United States to be unreliable, they will act to improve their own level of security. If the US is unreliable because it poses risks of entrapment, an ally might attempt to restrain Washington, launch a peace initiative, distance itself from US policy, or even abrogate its alliance. If the US is unreliable because it poses risks of abandonment, an ally might attempt to draw closer to Washington, increase its own military capabilities, seek new allies, or even build nuclear weapons. States will not happily sit idle while their ally's reliability declines.

My third hypothesis expects this prospect of alliance interdependence to affect US policy. Alliance interdependence and concern for credibility are often conceived as limiting Washington's policy freedom and posing severe entanglement risks, but these concerns are not supported by the empirical evidence I examine. Instead of alliance interdependence serving solely to constrain the United States, an awareness of these connections enables policymakers in Washington to manipulate alliance interdependence for their own purposes. This is a remarkably different way of thinking about interdependence. I show that the United States can set the example of acceptable allied behavior in one alliance and this will be observed by—and will influence—other allies. In other cases, the possibly adverse consequences of interdependence can be mitigated if Washington adroitly manages several alliances simultaneously.

Though prominent and influential during the Cold War, deterrence theory's beliefs about the interdependence of commitments have been challenged in recent decades, especially by "reputation skeptic" scholars. My answer to this book's research question—how, if at all, are alliances interdependent?—contributes to this debate between deterrence theory and more recent scholarship on international reputation. Alliance interdependence does exist, but it is not contingent on a moral quality of loyalty: it is instead underpinned by assessments of reliability, which concerns the degree to which shared interests enable allies to cooperate and rely on each other. In expecting alliances to be interdependent based on judgments of loyalty, for decades scholars have been looking in the right place, but for the wrong thing.

The Importance of the Alliance Audience Effect

In developing the alliance audience effect framework, this book makes four important contributions to theories of alliance politics.

The first contribution is to carefully delineate between loyalty and reliability: these are not synonymous. While deterrence theory holds that Washington's disloyalty to an ally will undermine or destroy its other alliances—because these allies will assume the United States to have a national character trait of disloyalty—I demonstrate that states are not always concerned about Washington's general loyalty to its other allies. Instead of focusing on a national character trait of loyalty, each ally focuses on whether the US is likely to be reliable. Reliability, discussed at length in chapter 1, is partially determined by the extent to which allies share convergent interests about an issue on which they expect to cooperate. It is also affected by the military capabilities possessed by each allied state and whether the allies can agree on how to pursue their convergent interests.

Though some reputation skeptics argue that alliances are not interdependent, this book shows that US allies do monitor Washington's conduct in its other alliances in order to better understand US interests, the extent to which they are valued, and the capabilities it can use to pursue these interests. Allies ask: Do US interests align with those of my state? Can and will the US work with my state—using effective military force, if necessary—to achieve those interests? If all the answers are yes, then allies will perceive the US to be reliable. But if Washington's behavior suggests that it does not share the ally's interests and is likely to adopt policies—such as recklessly risking war or reneging on promises of military support—that pose entrapment or abandonment risks, then the ally will regard the US as unreliable.

This might seem more complicated than deterrence theory's rule of thumb that "loyalty matters" or the reputation skeptic conclusion that because commitments are not interdependent states should never worry about their reputations. However, it can be reduced to an even simpler maxim: "national interests matter most." Though decision makers in Washington might worry that disloyalty to one ally will unnerve other allies, those other allies will welcome this instance of disloyalty if it is in their own national interest. Allies do observe how the United States behaves within its other alliances but they are not looking for virtuous moral conduct that exemplifies a national character trait of loyalty, which can then be expected in other alliance interactions. Instead, they look for evidence that Washington's interests remain convergent with their own and that the US therefore remains a reliable ally.

My second contribution is to demonstrate that states do not have a collective or universal alliance reputation. The alliance audience effect theory expects that one ally might regard a specific action as proof that Washington's reliability has declined, while another ally—with different interests—might interpret the same action as positive proof of US reliability. The alliance audience effect framework rejects the idea that universal or collective reputations exist and instead shows that different allies have different interests, and thus they draw different conclusions about US behavior. Because allies do not evaluate US policies against an objective moral standard like loyalty, but instead assess whether US actions further their own interests, a universal and collective belief about a state's reliability cannot form.

The third contribution is to partially rehabilitate one element of deterrence theory. Though some reputation skeptics argue that the United States should not worry about allies doubting its resolve, I demonstrate that it is usually in Washington's interest to maintain an image of alliance reliability. If an ally fears that the US is likely to abandon it in its moment of need, it might increase its own defense capabilities, form new alliances, or conciliate adversaries. If the ally fears that US actions might prompt an unwanted conflict, or even drag the ally into undesired hostilities, it will seek to reduce the likelihood of violence: it will attempt to restrain the US, launch peace efforts, or threaten to stand aside if conflict breaks out. Thus, it is usually—but not always—in Washington's interest for its allies to perceive its commitments as reliable. Declining US reliability can lead to insecurity, which in turn can prompt undesired behavior—such as bandwagoning, adopting a neutral stance, or even the development of nuclear weapons programs—that runs contrary to Washington's goals.

The book's fourth contribution is to show that in some circumstances, alliance interdependence can used to pursue US interests. Because decision makers in Washington have often believed that other allies will react adversely to any instance of disloyalty, alliance interdependence is usually thought of only in negative terms: the need to demonstrate loyalty limits US policy options and entraps Washington in undesired conflicts. But historically, the United States has managed alliance interdependence in two ways: it has avoided undesired system effects through simultaneous alliance management and it has used interdependence to set the example of acceptable allied behavior.

The "set the example" approach enables Washington to use alliance interdependence for its own ends. An example is set when US policymakers choose and/or reject policies based on how they might be perceived by other allies. Washington can adopt a policy in one alliance and expect other allies to observe, and be influenced by, the precedent. For example, Washington might deal harshly with an obstinate ally to publicly demonstrate to other allies—to set the example—that such behavior will not be tolerated. US policymakers can manipulate this interdependence to encourage and discourage certain types of allied behavior.

When Washington expects allies to be worried by developments within another alliance, it can manage this interdependence through "simultaneous alliance management." For example, knowing that some allies will be unnerved by Washington's policy toward another ally, US officials might seek to reassure these allies that this policy does not reduce Washington's reliability. Such reassurance might be provided through closer consultations, additional promises of military support, transfers of equipment, or even the stationing of US forces on the allies' soil.

In summary, the alliance audience effect theory proposes that alliances are interdependent but argues that this is not underpinned by a national character trait that manifests as an international reputation for loyalty. Allies do not judge US policies against a moral yardstick of loyalty or disloyalty. Instead, interdependence is governed by each state's beliefs about its ally's reliability. Counterintuitively, if Washington's disloyalty to an ally reduces the risk of a war that other allies wish to avoid, or if it enhances Washington's ability to keep separate security promises, then this disloyalty might even be welcomed by those other allies.

Research Question and Case Study Selection

This book does not set out to conclusively settle the question of alliance interdependence or to determine under what conditions alliance interdependence is more or less prevalent. Before these can be addressed, a more fundamental question must be answered: How, if at all, are alliance commitments interdependent? To answer this, I use existing literature on alliance politics, credibility, and reputation to deductively generate the three hypotheses which form the alliance audience effect theory. I then test these against Asian alliance interactions during the first twenty years of the Cold War. This period and this region were selected for five reasons.

First, the Asian alliance system between 1949 and 1969 provides case studies that span almost the full spectrum of alliance behavior: alliance formation, alliance politics during a crisis, and peacetime alliance management. The only aspect unexamined is that of alliance abrogation. Thus, if an alliance audience effect is present in all of these varied case studies, it suggests the framework has a higher degree of generalizability. Testing against only a limited subset of alliance interactions—for example, only against cases of abandonment in wartime—would dramatically limit the theory's generalizability. Furthermore, as explained in chapter 1, studies that focus solely on moments of crisis fundamentally misconstrue how alliance trust operates.

Second, these alliances were formed after the advent and use of nuclear weapons. Though many treatments of alliance politics and international reputation note that nuclear weapons may influence interdependence, some consider only pre-1945 case studies. The advent of nuclear weapons meant that the rapid destruction of entire nations became feasible, and so alliances—particularly those that provide extended nuclear deterrence—took on a new importance. Previously, a state may have been able to defend its allies without incurring substantial risk of damage within its own borders, but the Cold War's nuclear balance often removed this possibility. Furthermore, because of the long timeframes involved in developing nuclear weapons, alliance reliability probably became more important. In an age of nuclear weapons, if an ally's promise of extended nuclear deterrence is suddenly shown to be unreliable, this could immediately and drastically render a state insecure and vulnerable to nuclear coercion or attack.[12] Thus, a theory of alliance reliability tested against modern case studies may have greater explanatory power for contemporary situations, where the nuclear element remains influential.

Third, the 1949–1969 period was chosen because several important variables—US capabilities, the global and regional balance of power, the presence of nuclear weapons, the lines of enmity and amity in Asia—can be held as reasonably constant. As a result, the exact reasons for varying levels of allied confidence in US reliability can be more clearly identified. From the late 1960s onward, there was significant uncertainty about the level of Washington's commitment to Asian security. The Guam Doctrine announcement of July 1969—in which President Richard Nixon stated that allies in Asia would continue to receive Washington's support but would have to take primary responsibility for their own defense—recast the US commitment to Asian security. Gradual U.S.-China rapprochement, vacillation, and abrupt decision making concerning troop positioning in South Korea in 1971, as well as President Nixon's visit to China in 1972, also had a significant impact on allies in Asia.[13] As many different events after 1969 cast doubt on the US role in Asia, it would be more difficult to confidently isolate the exact reasons for variance in allied perceptions of US reliability.

Fourth, testing the theory against Asian alliance case studies generates conclusions of significant policy relevance today. Though Taiwan and New Zealand are no longer formal US allies, the overall structure of the Asian alliance network remains intact and it is—depending on who is asked—either the source of, or the possible solution to, contemporary security tensions. Despite the importance of this system, few academic works consider the issue of interdependence between the alliances. The common assumption—that disloyalty to one ally will undermine or destroy the alliance system—is very questionable, but rarely questioned.

Finally, the "hub and spoke" structure of the Asian alliance system facilitates the task of observing and evaluating instances of alliance interdependence.[14] In the period examined, the United States formed bilateral alliances with Japan, South Korea, Taiwan, and the Philippines, and also a trilateral alliance with Australia and New Zealand. There are usually only two actors within the alliance—the United States and its local partner. When interactions within one alliance are observed by other allies, it is easier to identify the cause and result of any reliability concerns. The task of clearly and confidently identifying instances of interdependence within a multilateral alliance, such as the North Atlantic Treaty Organization (NATO) or Southeast Asian Treaty Organization (SEATO), is not impossible, but is necessarily more complicated. With so many states involved, it is far more difficult to precisely identify the reasons for a particular change in defense policy. By examining mainly bilateral alliance case studies, it is possible to mitigate these issues and more precisely identify and evaluate reliability concerns.

Importantly, this is not to say that similar dynamics do not operate within multilateral alliances. In the book's conclusion, I conduct a plausibility probe to determine if the theory can be applied to the multilateral SEATO alliance. However, alliance interdependence can be more clearly observed and process-traced in a bilateral alliance structure. Accordingly, testing the theory in a bilateral setting also sheds light on how such dynamics might operate in a multilateral alliance and thus will aid subsequent investigations of multilateral alliances.

Based on a preliminary analysis of the Asian alliance system in the Cold War, possible case studies were identified. Both the First and Second Taiwan Strait Crises were suitable for testing the theory, but the comparatively short second crisis (1958) was excluded because an examination of the prolonged first crisis (1954–1955) enabled a more thorough investigation of the US policymaking approach. Furthermore, the crisis dynamics, and their influence on alliance interdependence, do not appear to vary significantly across the two situations. The regional reaction to the Guam Doctrine of 1969 was also considered, but ultimately rejected, because Washington's behavior was not confined to a specific alliance relationship. President Carter's plans to withdraw US forces from the Korean Peninsula was another possible case study, but other works have already examined these events and their conclusions support the alliance audience effect.[15]

This process of elimination left a small group of events in which US behavior in one bilateral alliance was (a) observable by other allies and (b) significant for the security of these allies and thus relevant to Washington's reliability. These case studies (outlined below) were selected on the basis that the independent variable of my first hypothesis (i.e., US behavior in one alliance relationship) had to be observable and significant. I do not expect every minor interaction within an alliance to be closely scrutinized by other allies, but *significant* interactions—those that suggest a discrepancy between true interests of the United States and those it publicly professes—provide suitable case studies. The theory expects allies to monitor such interactions closely because they provide opportunities to better understand Washington's interests and thus better assess its reliability. Alliance interdependence is expected only when the ally observing US behavior regards it as *significant* and relevant to Washington's reliability and its own security.

Methodology

I use primary sources, and a process tracing method, to demonstrate how the alliance audience effect operated between 1949 and 1969. Secondary sources are also used, but this book makes a substantial and significant empirical contribution through the use of declassified documents. For the earlier case studies, I use the US government's *Foreign Relations of the United States* (FRUS) series wherever possible.[16] In later chapters, I rely more heavily on documents obtained from the US government's National Archives and Records Administration (NARA) and presidential libraries. The records at NARA—comprising State Department cables, memorandums, letters, intelligence assessments, minutes of meetings, and records of conversation—were especially important for tracing causation in the more recent case studies. They provide accurate information on diplomatic communication between the United States and its allies, as well as the internal deliberations of the US government. I also conducted research at the Dwight D. Eisenhower Presidential Library, the John F. Kennedy Presidential Library, the Richard M. Nixon Presidential Library, the National Archives of Australia, and the archive of John Foster Dulles's personal papers at Princeton University's Seeley G. Mudd Library.

Though data from archives in South Korea, Taiwan, Japan, and the Philippines could have been sought, the decision to focus on US records was made for four reasons. First, US archives contain data on each of the alliances, whereas other national archives contain more limited information specific to that country and its alliance with the United States. Second, language issues would have complicated efforts to obtain declassified documents from Taiwan, South Korea, Japan, or the Philippines. Though such sources would have provided valuable alternative perspectives on certain events, the need to translate such documents would have reduced the overall amount of data that could be collected, collated, and analyzed. As this book focuses on the question of interdependence among several different alliances, it necessarily prioritizes breadth over depth. Third, US archives are the most complete and comprehensive: scholars of Asian alliances typically rely on these sources as some Asian archives are fragmentary or access is restricted.[17] Finally, it was not necessary to go beyond US documents to test the theoretical framework: each of the hypotheses can be satisfactorily tested using these sources.

This reliance on US archival material entails some minor risks but these are not insurmountable. Perhaps the most significant concern is that allies might exaggerate their complaints about Washington's unreliability in an effort to bargain with—and extract greater defense commitments from—the United States. Stephen Walt has suggested that US allies in Asia have been able to "get Uncle Sucker to take on more burdens by complaining that they had doubts about American resolve."[18] If US diplomats or intelligence agencies failed to detect these exaggerations, they would not be reflected in official US documents. However, it is unlikely that this issue could be addressed even with the use of other archives: if allies ever did attempt to manipulate Washington in this manner, they are unlikely to ever declassify material that would reveal such behavior. Furthermore, in the US documents I examined there is often critical examination of, and speculation about, the motives of allied leaders. This increases the likelihood that US diplomats would detect exaggerated complaints made to bolster bargaining positions. Indeed, as shown in chapter 3, Washington sometimes adopted particular alliance policies to set an example that it would not allow its foreign policy to be manipulated by an ally.

Across these institutions, I examined tens of thousands of documents. The availability of such information enables the use of a forensic process tracing methodology that allows causal patterns to be identified, followed, and tested. To empirically test my hypotheses, this approach is best for identifying and contextualizing the factors that influenced reliability perceptions and decision making within alliances. To identify causal patterns, it is necessary to closely trace the evolution of views in Washington and allied capitals, and explain what led to these changes. The only way to demonstrate such causation satisfactorily is through archival research and process tracing methods. Although they do not explain their choice of methodology in these terms, other authors focusing on alliance management have chosen to avoid quantitative approaches in favor of qualitative, historically based process tracing. Two of the most prominent scholars researching alliances in Asia—Victor Cha and Thomas Christensen—have both used historical case studies and process tracing methods.[19] As Alexander George and Andrew Bennett write, process tracing does "not seek to replicate the logic of scientific experimentation . . . [but] to uncover a causal chain coupling independent variables with dependent variables and evidence of the causal mechanisms posited by a theory."[20] Accordingly, this method is well suited to testing and developing the alliance audience effect framework.

Outline of the Book

In chapter 1, I examine the existing literature on credibility, reliability, reputation, and alliances. I further explicate the difference between loyalty and reliability, and develop the three hypotheses that form the alliance audience effect theory.

Chapter 2 examines the creation of Washington's alliances with Japan, the Philippines, Australia, and New Zealand, and how the formation of these security pacts was influenced by US conduct toward the republics of Korea and China. I explain how the US response to the Korean War was critical in influencing the outlook of regional states and their attitude toward security cooperation with the United States.

Chapter 3 considers the formation of the alliances between the United States and the Republic of Korea (ROK) and between the US and the Republic of China (ROC), as well as the initial stages of the First Taiwan Strait Crisis. I show that the ROC's beliefs about US reliability were influenced by how Washington had treated the ROK and how the US used this interdependence to obtain pledges of restraint from Taipei. When these promises were secured, the US concluded an alliance with Nationalist China in late 1954.

The signing of this treaty occurred shortly before an escalation of the First Taiwan Strait Crisis, and this is the focus of chapter 4.[21] This chapter clearly illustrates and firmly justifies my delineation between loyalty and reliability. Washington's excessive loyalty to Taiwan—and the risks of war this posed—caused some allies to assess that US reliability had decreased, so they worked to restrain the United States and reduce the risk of war.

These events had a profound effect on Washington's most important regional ally, Japan, and the revision of the US-Japan alliance is examined in chapter 5. Japanese perceptions of US reliability—which were strongly affected by the First Taiwan Strait Crisis—were key influences on the treaty revision negotiations. The new treaty, signed in 1960, enabled Tokyo to veto some US military operations from bases in mainland Japan and thus improved Japan's opinion of Washington's reliability.

Chapter 6 examines the negotiations to transfer administrative control of Okinawa back to Japan. Okinawa was particularly important for the defense of the ROK and ROC, and these states worried that reversion of the island to Japanese control would reduce US basing rights and thus would imperil their own security. The chapter shows how Washington can simultaneously manage different alliances to prevent or limit undesired consequences.

I conclude the book by examining the case studies against the expectations of the alliance audience effect theory. I consider what events since 1969 might support or challenge the theoretical framework and also examine the framework's relevance to other aspects of alliance theory. A short plausibility probe applies my theory to the failure of a multilateral alliance—SEATO—to uphold a security guarantee it provided to Laos. Finally, I briefly apply my findings to the current security situation in Asia.

Although this is not a history book, because it seeks to identify and examine alliance interdependence—something considered by few authors—it does make a significant contribution to the historical record. Rather than US preferences determining the hub and spoke structure of the US alliance system, as Cha argues, my research supports more recent scholarship which highlights the agency of US allies and the importance of their preferences.[22] It also shows how interdependence between legally discrete alliance commitments both influenced Washington and *was used* by Washington to pursue US interests in the region.

Alliances, Reliability, and Interdependence

In this chapter I review alliance and deterrence theories, and critique their expectations of interdependence. I consider more recent scholarship—the "reputation skeptic" literature—which has argued that commitments are not interdependent, or at least not in the way expected by deterrence theorists. In short, my main critique is that because promises to allies have often been considered as an afterthought to the issue of threats to adversaries, incorrect assumptions about alliance politics have misdirected previous scholarship. Next, I explain why I find both the deterrence and the reputation skeptic arguments unsatisfying. In response, I propose and explain the concept of alliance reliability. This concept is not only more satisfying than resolve or loyalty, but also has greater explanatory power. I conclude the chapter by proposing the three hypotheses which comprise the alliance audience effect theory. This theoretical framework explains how alliance interdependence could operate on assessments of reliability, rather than judgments of resolve or loyalty.

Alliance and Deterrence Theory

Below, I briefly review the basics of alliance politics, including theories about why they form, how they function, and why they dissolve. Then, I examine how Cold War–era alliance and deterrence theories presumed an interdependence between discrete alliance commitments.

WHAT ARE ALLIANCES? WHY DO THEY FORM? HOW DO THEY EVOLVE?

As might be expected, authors have defined alliance in a variety of ways. Stephen Walt defines an alliance as "a formal or informal arrangement for security cooperation between two or more sovereign states."[1] He uses the terms *alliance* and *alignment* interchangeably, while other authors delineate between these concepts. Glenn Snyder defines alliances as "formal associations of states for the use (or non-use) of military force, in specified circumstances, against states outside their own membership," and alignments as "expectations of states about whether they will be supported or opposed by other states in future interactions."[2] For Snyder, "alliances are a subset of alignments—those that arise from or are formalized by an explicit agreement, usually in the form of a treaty."[3] The creators of the Alliance Treaty Obligations and Provisions (ATOP) dataset define alliances as "written agreements, signed by official representatives of at least two independent states, that include promises to aid a partner in the event of military conflict, to remain neutral in the event of conflict, to refrain from military conflict with one another, or to consult/cooperate in the event of international crises that create a potential for military conflict."[4]

Walt's definition is the most expansive, and his inclusion of "informal arrangement[s]" means that many security partnerships, including those not governed by a formal treaty, would be considered as alliances. Though significant security cooperation can occur without a formal alliance, the most solemn alliances are those that are governed by a formal treaty, signed by national governments, endorsed by their elected representatives (if applicable), and publicly proclaimed. The definitions used by Snyder and the ATOP dataset are very restrictive: the absence of a formal treaty or written agreement is enough to see an alliance downgraded to an alignment. But relationships may exhibit decidedly alliance-like activity, even though formal treaties or agreements have not been signed. Accordingly, I adopt Snyder's definition, but modify it to note that an alliance can be epitomized not by a treaty text but by an ongoing pattern of security cooperation.

There are two means of increasing a state's security: the first is internal balancing, which involves "moves to increase economic capability, to increase military strength, to develop clever strategies." The second, external balancing, involves "moves to strengthen and enlarge one's own alliance or to weaken and shrink an opposing one."[5] Many alliances are formed with the primary intent of pooling the military capabilities held by the member states, ensuring that any potential aggressor will have to plan for the possibility of a fight against all the allies.[6] This is called a "capability aggregation" alliance: the military capabilities available to each nation in the alliance exceed their own indigenous forces, and thus the alliance should improve their security.[7] Other states enter alliances to increase their influence or control over other nations. James Morrow has developed a theory of asymmetric alliances, defined as relationships where one ally receives security benefits and the other ally receives autonomy benefits. These benefits might come in the form of political influence over an ally's internal or foreign policies, or perhaps through military bases on an ally's soil. As Morrow notes, an asymmetric alliance "leads to a disproportionate sharing of military expenditures."[8]

Common to both alliance models is the belief that alliances should only form and persist when they provide a net security gain for all members. As Michael Altfield argues, "it can never be rational for a government to form an alliance which does not increase its security."[9] For an alliance to form, and persist, one question—"Do the benefits of this alliance outweigh the cost?"—must be answered in the affirmative. If the answer gradually shifts from "yes" to "no," then the state should withdraw from the alliance, renegotiate its terms, and/or enter into a new alliance. Based on their pursuit of self-interest, states should seek to negotiate (and renegotiate, if necessary) the best alliance deal possible.

ALLIANCE MANAGEMENT: ABANDONMENT AND ENTRAPMENT

Within alliances, two fears are paramount: abandonment and entrapment. Snyder describes abandonment as "the constant worry about being deserted by one's ally. The worry arises from the simple fact that the ally has alternative partners and may opt for one of them if it becomes dissatisfied." Snyder argues that abandonment has two aspects: "the subjective probability that the partner will defect and the cost to oneself if it does." Abandonment can also manifest in a refusal to provide promised military support, or the "failure to support the ally diplomatically in a dispute with its adversary."[10]

According to Snyder, entrapment occurs when one is "dragged into a conflict over an ally's interests that one does not share, or shares only partially . . . when one values the preservation of the alliance more than the cost of fighting for the ally's interests."[11] In contrast to abandonment, which entails "a serious loss of security, the cost of entrapment is an extreme form of lost autonomy," as a state fights in a conflict it would have rather avoided.[12]

Alliances are never free of uncertainty and although the concepts of abandonment and entrapment are usually applied to wartime or security crises, they are also relevant in peacetime. For example, a state may decide that in order to improve its relations with an adversary, which has tense relations with the state's ally, it is necessary to abrogate the alliance. If the state decides that the cost of its alliance (i.e., the preclusion of a more productive relationship with the ally's adversary) is higher than the benefit (e.g., improved security or influence on the ally), then the state will abrogate the alliance. Though this might not occur during wartime, it certainly resembles abandonment. Snyder, too, notes the potential for peacetime abandonment, when he describes the "failure to support the ally diplomatically in a dispute with its adversary, when support was expected," as abandonment.[13]

Extending Snyder's analysis, I argue that there is a need to relax the strictest definitions of abandonment and entrapment. Doing so enables us to more accurately identify and assess how these fears operate in peacetime settings.

I argue that abandonment occurs when a state's ally asks the question "Do the benefits of this alliance outweigh its costs?," answers in the negative, and acts accordingly. In this situation, the ally decides that its interests are best served by reneging on, abrogating, or revising the alliance commitment. This occurs most dramatically in a crisis situation but it can also happen in peacetime: When Washington abrogated the US-ROC Mutual Defense Treaty in 1980, it did so because Beijing made this a condition of establishing diplomatic relations with the People's Republic of China (PRC). Washington's answer to the key question—"Do the benefits of the US-ROC alliance outweigh its costs?"—was negative. Unsurprisingly, this led to the abrogation of the alliance and the abandonment of the ROC.

Entrapment can also be defined in relation to this key question. Entrapment occurs when a state asks itself—"Do the benefits of this alliance outweigh its costs?"—and answers "probably." This requires some explanation. If the answer is an unequivocal "yes," and the benefits clearly outweigh the costs of the alliance, then no real dilemma arises: in peacetime the alliance happily persists, in times of security tension the state moves to signal its support of the ally, in wartime the state moves to fight alongside its ally.

The real issue of entrapment arises when it is difficult to accurately estimate the prospective costs and benefits involved in alliance action. For example, the state may believe that the value of the alliance outweighs the costs of preserving it, but only barely. Because the state cannot confidently predict the exact outcome of the alliance interaction—which may be war, with all of its uncertainties—there is a risk that it will make the wrong decision. It may eventuate that the costs of supporting the ally will be far higher than expected. As the cost/benefit value of the alliance approaches equilibrium, the outcome of the alliance interaction will become more uncertain and the fear of entrapment will increase. Thus, entrapment occurs when the state supports its ally on an issue, even though it is unsure that this is the correct decision and/or would have preferred to avoid the situation altogether.

Snyder writes that "entrapment occurs when one values the preservation of the alliance more than the cost of fighting for the ally's interests."[14] My definition of entrapment—that a state supports its ally's policy despite being unsure whether the value of the alliance will outweigh the costs of this support—maintains Snyder's emphasis on the cost/benefit calculation, but broadens the concept to both crisis and noncrisis situations.[15] It also removes Snyder's implication that abandonment will result in the abrogation of the alliance.[16] For the sake of simplicity, and because my definitions do not differ violently from those offered by other authors, I use the terms abandonment and entrapment throughout the book. That said, the change of emphasis is meaningful. Like my definition of entrapment, my definition of abandonment—that it occurs when a state decides its interests are best served by not supporting an ally's policy—also slightly broadens Snyder's concept by extending it to noncrisis situations.

MANAGING ABANDONMENT AND ENTRAPMENT

Within an alliance, at any time each state will usually have one prevailing fear: either abandonment or entrapment.[17] The fear need not be severe, but most states will regard their ally as either too aggressive or too timid on particular issues. For example, if a state fears that its ally will abandon it if conflict breaks out with an adversary, it is unlikely to fear its ally entrapping it into a conflict with this adversary. However, it may be fearful of its ally entrapping it into a conflict with a different adversary. Fears of abandonment and entrapment will be highest when allies have different adversaries and/or different strategic interests. These fears are less likely to be present at the creation of an alliance agreement because they will complicate—or perhaps prevent—the negotiation of an alliance. However, it may be possible to address some entrapment fears through careful drafting of an alliance treaty. A defensive alliance can guard against some entrapment by specifying that a mutual defense obligation does not apply if one's ally is an aggressor. Abandonment fears can be addressed, at least partially, by the forward stationing of a state's forces to an ally's border with an adversary.[18]

Once in an alliance, a state can try to manage the dangers of abandonment and entrapment as they arise. Faced with a risk of entrapment, a state can attempt to modify its ally's behavior. In a crisis situation, the ally might be restrained by the threat of nonsupport, or it might be reassured and calmed by a strong pledge of support. Faced with the prospect of abandonment, a state might offer to modify its behavior, in the hope of attracting a stronger commitment from its ally. Another method may be to demonstrate greater loyalty to the ally, in the hope that this fidelity will be reciprocated.[19]

In some circumstances, where a state is unable to address the risk of entrapment, it may allow itself to be entrapped. As Victor Cha notes, "the consequences of defecting from a valued partner (i.e. dealignment by that partner) can be more disastrous to one's security than being dragged into the partner's conflict."[20] Abandoning an ally is a risky proposition: the worst-case scenario is that a friend becomes an enemy, but other options—ranging from simple abrogation of the alliance to no retribution at all—are also possible. Faced with the possibility of alliance dissolution as the worst-case scenario, a weak state may decide to fully support its ally's fight against an adversary even if the state does not share the ally's interests at stake. As Snyder notes, "promises are often made and kept even though they are not fully consistent with the parties' interests."[21]

Of course, it is much better to prevent situations in which either alliance promises must be kept in costly ways for uncertain reward (entrapment) or broken (abandonment). Accordingly, states should always keep a close eye on the behavior of their allies. If a state can prevent its ally from behaving in an unreliable fashion, then entrapment and abandonment possibilities might be avoided. It is important to note that these dynamics do not operate solely in their most extreme forms. For example, a state might be partially abandoned by an ally that fails to provide material assistance but offers diplomatic support. Or a state might be entrapped, but following crisis consultations it might be mutually agreed that because of its limited or conflicting interests, the state will provide less military support than the ally might have originally expected.

Having reviewed the basic aspects of alliance politics and slightly modified Snyder's definitions of abandonment and entrapment, I now examine the interdependence expected by deterrence and alliance theory.

WHAT DO DETERRENCE THEORY AND ALLIANCE THEORY SAY ABOUT INTERDEPENDENCE?

During the Cold War, deterrence and alliance theorists often assumed that just as an adversary could assess a state's threats based on its reputation for resolve, a friendly state could assess an ally's promises based on its reputation for loyalty. These ideas are premised on the concept of interdependent commitments. As Thomas Schelling writes, "The main reason why we are committed in many of these places is that our threats are interdependent. Essentially we tell the Soviets that we have to react here because, if we did not, they would not believe us when we say that we will react there."[22] These ideas were operationalized through the domino theory. In 1954, President Dwight Eisenhower suggested that the collapse of Indochina would be analogous to the first domino in a row falling over: it would cause the next domino to fall, which would cause the next to fall, and so on. Thus, the loss of Indochina would result in the loss of Southeast Asia.[23]

These ideas were widely accepted as "conventional wisdom" even though, as Jervis argued in 1979, there was "little evidence for the validity of the propositions" they relied upon.[24] Likewise, Alex Weisiger and Keren Yarhi-Milo note that this theory of reputation and commitment interdependence "gained widespread acceptance on the basis of its clear internal logic and strong policy recommendations rather than on the basis of empirical tests."[25] Memories of the 1939 Munich Crisis led many policymakers to fear that any display of irresolution would invite further challenges, and this mental schema was a significant influence on the domino theory and its proponents.[26]

Alliance theorists argued that as threats to adversaries were interdependent, so too were promises to allies. Glenn Snyder and Paul Diesing write that just "As 'resolve credit' with adversaries can be earned and 'banked' by repeated instances of firmness, so 'loyalty credit' with present or potential allies can be generated and drawn upon in the future by repeated demonstrations of support."[27] Elsewhere, Snyder also refers to a state's interest in "maintaining a reputation for loyalty, since the ally can be expected to keep its promise only if it expects oneself to reciprocate."[28] Snyder and

Diesing extend this beyond a purely reciprocal, bilateral relationship by arguing that allies "have an incentive to stick by their current partners . . . to create a general belief among other states that they are reliable alliance partners."[29] In short, they argue that alliances are interdependent based on loyalty reputations.

Despite the heavy lifting done by this concept of loyalty, it is rarely defined. Most obviously, loyalty could be construed as strictly abiding by the terms of an alliance treaty or as always fighting alongside an ally. But, within an alliance, what is disloyalty? If an ally provokes a conflict over some minor issue, is it disloyal to withhold military support? I return to this important issue later.

Reputation Skeptics

Not all scholars embraced the conventional wisdom on reputation and commitment interdependence. Ted Hopf found that Washington's behavior in the Cold War periphery was not used by Soviet leaders to predict likely US responses in other areas.[30] Robert Jervis also noted that even Eisenhower's famous invocation of the domino theory was not fully representative of his beliefs about commitment interdependence.[31]

But after the fall of the Berlin Wall, these theories received more sustained scholarly attention. Jonathan Mercer examined whether states can develop advantageous reputations for resolve toward adversaries. Premised on the idea that an observer state will explain the behavior of another state based on in-group/out-group dynamics, he argues that observers will attribute a state's desired behavior to situational circumstances but undesired behavior to its character or disposition. For example, if an adversary displays a lack of resolve and retreats on its threat (desired behavior), it is because of situational circumstances. But if it demonstrates resolve and follows through on its threat (undesired behavior), it is because of its national character. If a state abandons its ally (undesired behavior), this is because of a character trait of cowardice or irresolution, whereas if it provides the promised military support (desired behavior), this is only because it was in its interest to do so given the circumstances.[32] Mercer argues that, because of this dynamic, allies can get reputations for disloyalty but not loyalty, whereas adversaries can get reputations for resolve, not irresolution.

Mercer defines resolve as "the extent to which a state will risk war to keep its promises and uphold its threats," but his main finding is that standing firm in one crisis will not convince adversaries that a state is equally likely to stand firm in a future crisis, because "Decision-makers do not consistently use another state's past behavior . . . to predict that state's behavior."[33] The alliance corollary of this is that displaying loyalty in one crisis will not convince allies that similar loyalty is likely in future crises. In his conclusion,

Mercer suggests that a state should not worry about its allies believing that it lacks resolve. Because America's allies will "explain away our efforts to demonstrate resolve by citing the transient situation . . . [and will] assume that our interests and capabilities determine our resolve," Washington cannot gain a reputation for being a loyal ally. Mercer's policy advice—that "fighting to create a reputation for resolution with allies is unwise"—is a bold departure from earlier theories.[34]

Daryl Press extends Mercer's work to argue that even though dispositional judgments may not be made and used to predict future behavior, a state's actions reveal the degree to which certain interests are valued and what capabilities the state can use to pursue those interests. Thus, Press suggests that adversaries will find a state's threats credible if the state "has the power to carry them out, and if the interests at stake justify the likely costs."[35] Together, these two authors tease out the microprocesses through which concepts like credibility and loyalty might manifest: What, exactly, do states observe and judge? Does a state's behavior reveal only its interests and capabilities or something more intangible—like its resolve?

REPUTATION REHABILITATORS

Since the reinvigoration of this debate, other authors have attempted to rehabilitate the concept of reputation, albeit usually in a more limited form. Within the realm of threats to adversaries, Weisiger and Yarhi-Milo convincingly argue that resolve should be examined at the level of general deterrence rather than at moments of security crisis, because in such moments "information gleaned from past action will already have been incorporated into broader estimates of interests."[36] Thus, examining moments of security crisis may stack the deck by selecting case studies where adversaries have already assessed a state's level of interest to be low.

Frank Harvey and John Mitton have produced the most thorough review of the reputation debate to date, and argue that one of the central problems for Press and Mercer is their reliance on interests and capabilities, "as if adversaries have access to all relevant information about these. . . . Interests are not always obvious (or consistent), and Washington's willingness to use force is never unequivocally clear or self-evident."[37] One of Harvey and Mitton's key critiques is that "because . . . adversaries have imperfect information about US interests, commitments, and willingness to use power (resolve) . . . it is wrong to completely dismiss reputations . . . and equally mistaken to assume that reputations are everything."[38]

Gregory Miller has partially rehabilitated the idea of reputation within alliances by positing that a reputation for being a reliable ally might be different from a reputation for being a credible adversary. Miller does not explicitly define reliability, but argues that a state is unreliable if it "Fails to fight when it is obligated to do so," "signs a separate agreement with an enemy," "drags its ally into an unwanted conflict," or "fails to support an ally during a crisis short of war." In so arguing, he implies that alliance reliability is a broader concept than loyalty or resolve. It is not clear whether a state that "drags its ally into an unwanted conflict" would be described by earlier theorists as disloyal, but it could certainly be described as unreliable.[39] Miller's four criteria suggest that allies are unreliable if they present a risk of either entrapment or abandonment.

Miller finds that reliable states will maximize their autonomy within alliances and will be able to ally with states of similar reliability, whereas unreliable states will struggle to attract new allies. Miller finds that an unreliable state will be "more constrained by the design of its alliance," as its allies will modify alliance agreements to compensate for the state's unreliability.[40] He also considers two hypotheses about alliance termination: first, that "An unreliable state will lose the ally that it entrapped or failed to support," and second, "An unreliable state will lose its allies generally."[41] While Miller does not find strong support for these hypotheses, he argues that states should still be concerned about their reputations, because reliable states will be able to "form alliances with other reliable states . . . [and] preserve their freedom of action within their alliances."[42]

Assessing the Literature

Three waves of scholarship have influenced this debate on reputation and interdependence, though scholars have usually focused on how reputations for resolve might be perceived by adversaries. Below, I explore how this scholarship is relevant for the idea of alliance interdependence.

IF STATES OBSERVE AN ALLY, DO THEY JUDGE ITS CHARACTER OR INTERESTS AND CAPABILITIES?

Mercer's conclusions about loyalty reputations among allies raise more questions than they answer. If a state's actions—regardless of whether or not they display resolve—reveal its interests and capabilities, then they are likely to be keenly watched by that state's allies. Observers may be watching the state's actions not to judge its moral character (i.e., its qualities of resolve or loyalty), but to obtain better information about its interests and capabilities. After all, it may be the same capabilities, and similar interests, that determine whether the state will fulfil other alliance commitments. If there are discrepancies between a state's publicly professed interests—expressed through alliances—and those to which its actions attest, then allies might worry about the reliability of the state's other alliance commitments. Alternatively, if once-powerful military capabilities are now obsolete, ineffective, or atrophying, then states might worry not about a divergence of interests, but about the degree to which an ally's military is useful for deterrence and/ or warfighting. As Walt argues, the "litmus test" of an alliance "comes not at annual summit meetings—which are designed for the ritual incantation of unifying rhetoric—but when member-states are called upon to do something for each other."[43] By observing such litmus tests, states can better assess their ally's capabilities, interests, and thus its reliability.

While deterrence theorists and some reputation skeptics expect observing states to make character (dispositional) judgments about their ally's disloyalty, states may instead look for evidence confirming that the interests underpinning their own alliance are still valued by the ally and that the ally has sufficient military capabilities to help defend or pursue those interests.[44] For alliances, Mercer's core argument is that states explain an ally's desired behavior in situational terms, its undesired behavior in character terms, and that only character assessments form reputations (i.e., expectations about future behavior). But what if states conceive of all allied behavior in situational terms—as revelations or proof of capabilities and interests? Mercer hints at this likelihood by concluding his book with the observation that allies will "tend to assume that . . . interests and capabilities determine . . . resolve."[45] If that is the case, then what, exactly, are a state's allies observing? Is it the state's innate moral character or simply new information about its capabilities and interests?[46]

I expect that states will monitor their allies for signs of divergent interests in the same way that they monitor adversaries for signs of hostile intent. Snyder implicitly acknowledges that reliable allies, and strong alliances, are driven by convergent strategic interests: "when allies have a common enemy, the alliance security dilemma is softened by the unlikelihood of abandonment and the low cost of entrapment. . . . When they face different enemies [i.e., have divergent interests], the dilemma is more acute."[47] If an observing state expects its ally's behavior to be determined by capabilities and interests, not some innate national characteristic such as resolve or loyalty, then it is logical for the state to monitor the ally's behavior to confirm that common interests are still valued. Likewise, I expect that a state will monitor the ally for signs that its military power is waxing or waning.

A state's alliance commitments might have been beyond question at the time the treaty was signed, but national interests and capabilities can vary over time: when "conditions change, [alliance] violation becomes more likely. Reassessing policy as incentives change remains important."[48] Knowing this, national leaders and defense planners should constantly monitor their ally, regularly assess the strength of their alliance, and wonder about its future strength as well. An ally's present actions not only attest to its capabilities and interests now but they also hint at the future. For example, if an ally has consistently ordered its preferences in a particular way for some time, and there is no evidence to suggest that this preference ordering is likely to shift, then this will generate expectations of the ally's likely future conduct. An ally's past behavior is not a guarantee of its likely future behavior but if a state can understand how an ally's preferences are shifting or remaining static over time, then it can make more informed assessments of the ally's likely future behavior.

Because states rely on alliances for security, I expect that they should be sensitive to any evidence suggesting variation in an ally's interests or capabilities. If a state believes that its ally's interests or capabilities are changing over time, and therefore that abandonment risks are also likely to increase over time, then the state will probably address the anticipated security deficit by acquiring new defense capabilities or through the drawn-out process of settling old scores and forming new alliances (if new allies are available). Alternatively, if an ally's behavior suggests that abandonment risks are decreasing over time, then a state may wish to reduce its defense spending in favor of health, education, or infrastructure investment. It may seek to free-ride and spend less on its own defense, relaxed in the belief that the ally will protect it. The same dynamic applies to fears of entrapment: if a state believes entrapment risks are growing more acute, it should seek to mitigate these risks through plans to restrain the ally or distance itself from the ally's aggressive stance.

My analysis suggests that a state will observe its ally's behavior, and will do so in an effort to make better assessments of the ally's capabilities and the relative ordering of its interests. This contrasts with Mercer's argument that a state will worry about its ally's character, with the implicit assumption that these concerns will be most influential when the next significant crisis occurs. This focus on crises overlooks the fact that alliance promises are about everyday security, not only emergencies. States might not think too deeply about an adversary's resolve until a showdown, but states need to perpetually monitor an ally's reliability.

In considering issues of alliance management, Mercer's conclusion—that allies will "tend to assume that our interests and capabilities determine our resolve"—is not particularly satisfying.[49] It offers little predictive power about whether—and if so, how and why—a state's actions might influence alliance politics. By contrast, I expect that if a state regards its ally's behavior as proof of its interests and capabilities, then it is likely to carefully observe its ally's behavior—in the ally's other alliance relationships—to better understand the ally's interests and capabilities, and thus better assess whether the ally poses risks of abandonment or entrapment. This would establish clear interdependence between seemingly discrete alliance commitments: what happened within one alliance would affect another. In observing and assessing a state's behavior in one alliance, its other allies would be making assessments about the state's interests and capabilities, not dispositional or character-based judgments about the state's moral qualities.

I am not the first to consider these possibilities. Miller's hypotheses on alliance formation emphasize the value of being perceived as reliable when seeking new allies, but another of his hypotheses—that "an unreliable state will lose its allies generally"—provides a hard test for the concept of reliability in alliance management.[50] Some alliance relationships, once they have commenced and have become institutionalized, are not especially costly.[51] In such circumstances, even if a state believed that its ally would be unlikely to support it in a conflict, is there any advantage to abrogating the alliance? The state could simply allow the alliance to stand but its planning could shift, in that it will intend to renege on the alliance commitment if the ally requests support. Prima facie, the decision to terminate an alliance could only increase the chance of the ally's disloyalty, whereas if the alliance is left intact then some possibility of loyalty might remain. Additionally, the retention of the alliance might pose some deterrent value to possible adversaries. However, having judged that the ally is very likely to prove unreliable in the moment of alliance need, it would be rational for the state to address the likelihood of a sudden security deficit through new balancing behavior.

WHEN DO STATES OBSERVE THEIR ALLY'S BEHAVIOR? DO THEY WANT TO SEE LOYALTY?

In almost all the scholarship reviewed so far, certain assumptions about alliance behavior are common. Because of how the debate progressed from deterrence theory to reputation skepticism, promises to allies have often been considered as an afterthought to—or as an obvious corollary of—threats to adversaries.[52] Two assumptions flow directly from this: The first is that states always want their ally to demonstrate "resolve" and its alliance analogue, "loyalty." The second is that moments of security crisis best illustrate interdependence.

As noted earlier, the idea of loyalty is rarely defined in deterrence, alliance, or reputation theory. Mercer's definition of loyalty—"the extent to which a state will risk war to keep its promises"—suffers from the same flaws as "resolve." What is it that determines "the extent"? If it is capabilities and interests, then is there any point to talking about loyalty (or resolve) at all? At any rate, it is not clear that such a strict definition reflects how alliances actually operate. Snyder's discussion of the alliance "halo" demonstrates that as habits of alliance cooperation form, they create a felt obligation which often goes beyond a strict reading of the alliance text. Allies feel they "ought to give each other mutual support on lesser issues, most especially those that relate somehow to the ultimate military contingency." In his discussion of the alliance halo, Snyder argues that alliances create "an obligation to support, or at least to avoid damaging, the interests of the ally, so far as is possible, on a wide range of peacetime issues."[53]

However, previous scholarship has not adequately considered what loyalty really is and what kind of behavior states actually want from their allies. Because backing down is assumed to be the behavior desired from an adversary, displaying loyalty has been assumed as desired behavior from an ally.[54] However, it is very debatable whether this is true. In looking for alliance interdependence to be underpinned by displays of loyalty, we have been looking in the right place, but for the wrong thing.

I argue that states do *not* want their allies to have a character trait of indiscriminate loyalty. On the contrary, it is easy to conceive of situations in which a state will desperately want its ally to be disloyal to some other ally. For example, consider the alliance structure depicted in figure 1. If state A has two bilateral alliances—with states B and C, which are not allied to each other—and both allies come under simultaneous attack, then state A could be faced with a terrible dilemma. In this scenario, state A's military capabilities are such that it can successfully defend only one of its two allies: if it dispatches half of its military power to state A, and half to state B, then these contributions will not be enough to prevent the defeat of either ally. Thus, state A's rational response is to defend only one of its allies. In this scenario, both allies will earnestly desire state A's loyalty, and will be unperturbed that this would require its *disloyalty* to the other ally.

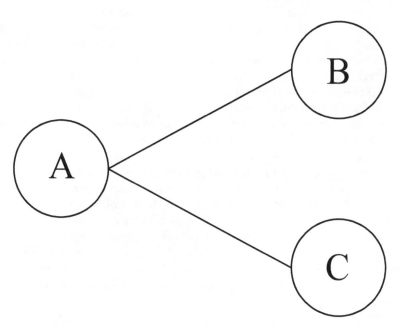

Figure 1. Two bilateral alliances. Courtesy of the author.

The second assumption, concerning the primary importance of security crises, is implicit in the selection of case studies by authors focusing on interdependence: by examining moments of crisis, they have overlooked less dramatic—but no less important—instances of alliance behavior. Because states in alliance rely on their allies for security every day, I expect that they will also be sensitive to all allied behavior. This includes crisis situations, but states will also be attentive to peacetime behavior which suggests that an ally's reliability is changing. Thus, theories of alliance interdependence should be tested not only against moments of security crisis but also against other developments. Within the context of threats to adversaries, other authors have also noted this tendency and have suggested that "the level of general deterrence," rather than "the context of an ongoing crisis," is a "more appropriate place to look for the effect of past actions on future expectations."[55]

What Is Reliability? Does It Differ from Loyalty or Resolve? Do Reputations Exist?

Rather than always desiring that their allies display a character trait of unalloyed loyalty, states want reliable allies. Reliability is determined by the extent to which two allies share convergent interests about an issue on which they expect to cooperate, and whether they have military capabilities useful for pursuing those interests. When a state observes its ally's behavior, it is not looking for displays of character—loyalty or resolve—but proof of interests and capabilities. If an ally shares a state's interests on an issue, and has capabilities that can be used to pursue those interests, then the state will view the ally as reliable. If the ally has divergent interests, or lacks capabilities that can be used to pursue those interests, then it will be viewed as unreliable.

I use the term reliability, instead of possible alternatives such as loyalty or resolve, for four reasons.[56] First, the concept of reliability incorporates the risks of entrapment as well as abandonment. The idea of alliance loyalty is most naturally applied to abandonment: a state was disloyal because it abandoned its ally when it should have fought alongside it. But if the ally launched an unprovoked attack on an adversary, then is it disloyal to not support this aggression? How should the aggressive ally be described? Has it been disloyal by creating the risk of entrapping its alliance partner into a conflict? The idea of loyalty is not a natural fit for such circumstances, but the idea of reliability can be used to describe such behavior. While the idea of loyalty focuses predominantly on abandonment risks, reliability can be used to assess both abandonment and entrapment, and thus a wider range of alliance behavior.

Table 1 illustrates this understanding of reliability during security tensions and wartime. This scenario, depicting how two allies (states A and B) are considering their policy toward an adversary, shows how the idea of re-

Table 1 Alliance reliability during security tensions/wartime

		State A	
		Conciliate	Confront
	Conciliate	Convergent interests Neither A nor B fears abandonment or entrapment Allies are reliable	Divergent interests A fears abandonment B fears entrapment Allies are unreliable

State B	Confront	Divergent interests
		A fears entrapment
		B fears abandonment
		Allies are unreliable
			Convergent interests
			Neither A nor B fears
			  abandonment or
			  entrapment
			Allies are reliable

liability addresses the risks of both abandonment and entrapment. Policy options run along a spectrum from "conciliate" to "confront" (make concessions or go to war). If both A and B desire a conciliatory approach (top left cell) or a confrontational one (bottom right cell), then their interests are aligned and each will be a reliable ally for the other. But if the two allies desire different policies, then each ally will be unreliable to the other because their interests are divergent and thus they pose a risk of either abandonment or entrapment.

Of course, this table is an idealized type—rarely will the interests of two states in alliance be perfectly identical. And even if they agree on a desired outcome, they may disagree on which strategy gives the best chance of realizing it. Snyder and Diesing have described the alliance disagreements that can occur when allies bargain over which strategy the alliance will adopt. In some situations, there may be no sensible equilibrium between two different strategies, and it will be best for both allies if one of them adopts the strategy preferred by the other. In a bilateral alliance between equal powers, either might be able to assume the dominant position and insist on its preferred strategy, while in alliances between strong and weak powers the former will be able to insist that the latter follow its preferred strategy. It is also possible that although both the allies desire the same ends, their disagreement on how to pursue these goals is so severe that no coordinated alliance response is possible. In other cases, there will be some room for negotiation and compromise on how the alliance can cooperate in achieving its shared interests and the two allies will be able to acceptably combine their preferences into a new strategy.[57] States heavily reliant on the alliance for security may have to sacrifice some of their preferences in order to prioritize their most important interests, such as preservation of the alliance and the security it provides.

Second, the concept of loyalty in an alliance relationship has led scholars to focus predominantly on times of conflict. This is unsurprising, as the term applies most naturally to the fear of abandonment in wartime: a loyal ally will provide military support, a disloyal ally will not. But interstate war and conflict occur rarely, so this concept of loyalty establishes an extreme and infrequent test. Moments of security crisis, or warfighting, may be useful for adversaries assessing resolve, but it is not clear that alliances work in the exact same way. Because states depend on reliable allies for security, they should be attentive to behavior suggesting unreliability, no matter when it occurs.

Third, not only does the term reliability deemphasize moments of security tension, but it also demonstrates how the basic calculus of alliance interdependence is the same in times of both peace *and* conflict. Two questions occupy the minds of leaders: Is my ally reliable now, and is there reason to think that it will be more or less reliable in the future? The nature of a peacetime alliance relationship affects these considerations, and does so more frequently than rare moments of security crisis. If two allies work together on defense technology, share intelligence, conduct joint military exercises, have honest exchanges about their national interests, treat each other fairly, and coordinate their diplomatic efforts, then this trend of cooperation is likely to provide a reassuring answer to both questions. An ally can be perceived as reliable even though the ultimate test of alliance loyalty—military support against an enemy—may not have occurred.

But if a state takes a unilateral approach to security affairs—fails to consult, pays little regard to its ally's interests, treats an ally poorly in comparison to other allies, or abruptly changes previous agreements to coordinate policy—then this behavior will be outside the alliance halo expectations. The state is likely to be perceived as an unreliable ally, because its behavior suggests that it does not value the alliance and has interests that diverge from those of its ally. The constancy of a good-faith approach to alliance issues is important, because an inconsistent approach, regular disagreements, or abrupt changes to previously agreed policy, will suggest the ally is unreliable due to divergent interests.

Applying the concept of reliability to peacetime interactions hinges on the slightly broader definition of abandonment that was outlined earlier in this chapter.[58] As shown in table 2, if two allies (states A and B) previously agreed to coordinate their policy on an issue (top left cell), but then A decides that its interests will be best served by changing its own policy and no longer supporting the policy agreed between the two states (the top right cell), then A has abandoned B and is an unreliable ally on this issue. Where states have never agreed to coordinate policy on an issue, or have deliberately agreed to not coordinate their policy (both represented by the lower right cell), there are no expectations of alliance support and reliability is not at issue.

The consequences of peacetime abandonment are unlikely to be as severe as wartime abandonment, but this does not mean they are unimportant. Unreliability in peacetime can generate doubt about an ally's future reliability.

Table 2 Alliance reliability in peacetime

		State A	
		Coordinate policy	Insist on own policy
State B	Coordinate policy	Alliance cooperation: agreed policy on an issue Allies are reliable on this issue	Divergent interests A abandons B A is unreliable on this issue
	Insist on own policy	Divergent interests B abandons A B is unreliable on this issue	No expectations of coordinated policy Reliability not at issue

For example, in 1951 Japan reluctantly accepted America's diktat that Tokyo not recognize, nor trade with, Communist China. Throughout the Cold War, Tokyo feared that the United States would depart from this position and abruptly change policy toward Communist China without first consulting Japan (i.e., Japan feared the United States would abandon it). This is, of course, exactly what happened in the 1970s. The spectrum of policy choices was essentially bounded by "exclude Communist China from the international system" (the agreed policy) at one end, and "normalize relations with Communist China" (America's new policy) at the other. When the United States abruptly changed its policy and worked toward normalization, the abandonment upset Japan and sparked fears as to what further policy reversals might be imminent. Despite the fact that Tokyo had long desired this policy change, the way in which it occurred made Japan worry about US reliability: what other sudden changes of US policy might be made, without prior warning?[59]

Fourth, the idea of reliability deemphasizes the prospect of a state having immutable character traits that will be observed in a uniform fashion by different allies. As explained earlier, in certain situations I expect that a state might actively desire that its ally be disloyal to that ally's other security partners. Consider the alliance structure illustrated in figure 1, where state A has two bilateral alliances (one with state B, and one with state C). If, for example, state A has military capabilities sufficient to defend only one of its two allies and both of these allies come under simultaneous attack threatening national destruction, then each ally will earnestly desire that state A be disloyal to its other ally, so that A's military forces can intervene in their own fight against the enemy.[60] If state A decides to dispatch all of its military forces to defend only one of its allies, then states B and C will come to very different conclusions about its behavior and reliability.

In another scenario, state B might desire that its ally, state A, be disloyal to state C, which has needlessly provoked an unwanted war. From state B's perspective, state C's rogue behavior might justify a decision to abandon it as a way of punishing its adventurism. State B might also be relieved that

29

state A's military capabilities will not be tied up in a defense of the rogue ally, state C.

Because observing states will not observe and assess behavior against an objective standard like loyalty, one important advantage of the reliability concept is that it shifts our analysis away from the idea of reputation, defined by Mercer as "a judgement of . . . character . . . used to predict or explain future behavior."[61] The collective imputation of this word is problematic because it implies that observing states will each judge the ally's behavior in the same manner—against an objective yardstick of loyalty—and that such judgments will create a universal reputation. I do not believe that such reputations exist. Instead, I argue that because states have unique strategic interests, they will each have a different assessment of international events and state behavior.[62] Because they will not judge an ally's behavior against an objective standard like loyalty, two states can observe the same allied behavior but reach opposed conclusions about the ally's reliability. For example, if state A has three allies, as depicted in figure 2, then its decision to abandon state B might be welcomed by state C, but condemned by state D. Because different states have different interests, they will view the behavior of their ally through different lenses.

A key reason for these differing interests is divergent threat perceptions. There is a natural inclination to assume that because states in alliance will have common adversaries, they will automatically agree about the kind and severity of threat an adversary might pose. But allies will often disagree about the risk posed by an adversary: Is it an enemy, a competitor, a neutral state, or perhaps a misunderstood nuisance? Are its activities a minor irritant that can be tolerated or a major threat requiring some kind of reaction? And even if agreement can be reached on these questions, it is entirely possible that allies may not be able to agree on the most appropriate response. For all these reasons, the views of each individual state must be carefully researched and considered. It makes more sense to talk of individual state *assessments* or *beliefs* of reliability rather than a reliability reputation.

Returning to the alliances depicted in figure 2, previous theorists assumed displays of resolve or loyalty to always be desired behavior and would thus incorrectly expect that state A's disloyalty to state B will lead states C and D to both regard state A as an unreliable ally.[63] In contrast, I argue that because observing allies make situational attributions, they will—depending on their own interests—hold different views about what behavior is desirable or undesirable. Further, the ally's behavior is important not because it reveals the nation's moral character, but because it demonstrates its capabilities and reveals its interests. Based on this information, states can better assess not only their ally's likely reaction to future or present conflict scenarios but also its likely alliance reliability. Though leaders might occasionally use value-laden language to describe the conduct of another state, the behavior is important

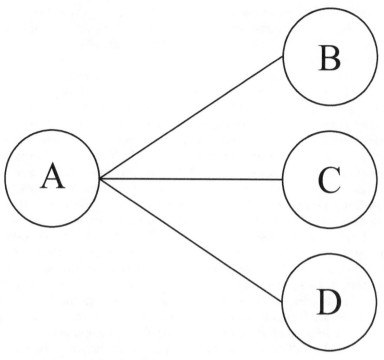

Figure 2. Three bilateral alliances. Courtesy of the author.

primarily for the information it reveals or confirms about interests and/or military capabilities.

This is a significant departure from Mercer's approach, as he argues that only reputations (i.e., character assessments) and not situational judgments (i.e., assessments of capability and interest) govern expectations of future behavior. Mercer defines reputation as "a judgement of someone's character (or disposition) that is then used to predict or explain future behavior," and contrasts this with "a situational attribution [which] has only within-situation validity; it cannot be used to predict or explain behavior in a different situation."[64] If Mercer's reasoning is correct, then a state should never be encouraged nor disturbed by the fact that its ally has displayed loyalty to some other ally, as the state will make a situational attribution: the ally's action in those circumstances is irrelevant to other situations.[65]

I argue that public demonstrations of interest are especially important because the relative ordering of a state's preferences and interests is not simply private information.[66] Rather, it is more accurate to describe the precise ordering of a state's preferences as a known unknown: a state's leaders may have very firm beliefs about how they would behave in a particular crisis situation, but they cannot *know* this is accurate until the actual decisions are made. Other scholars have noted this uncertainty: "Interests are not always obvious . . . and Washington's willingness to use force is never unequivocally clear or self-evident."[67]

In summary, the concept of loyalty is tied to character tests, the most obvious of which is violent conflict and the promise of military support. Whether one's ally is disloyal to its other allies is also likely to matter far less than whether it remains, and is likely to remain, a reliable ally for one's own state: this is determined not by national character or disposition but by interests and capabilities. Further, the term reputation creates the impression of a universal judgment which rarely, if ever, exists. By focusing on how states perceive their ally's reliability, this book emphasizes the importance of convergent strategic interests in determining a state's alliance reliability. So instead of referring to a state's reputation for loyalty, I instead discuss beliefs about allied reliability.

As the above analysis suggests, "I define reliability as the degree to which allies agree on the relative value of particular interests and the manner in which the interests should be pursued."[68] If two states in alliance have convergent or near-convergent interests on an issue, agree on how to pursue these interests, and work cooperatively to achieve their goals, then they will view each other as reliable allies that pose no risk of either abandonment or entrapment. Divergent interests will raise risks of entrapment or abandonment and will result in each ally being unreliable for the other (the first state will pose risks of abandonment to the second, while the second will pose risks of entrapment to the first). Furthermore, in contrast to the idea of loyalty, reliability can describe a broader gamut of alliance behavior and thus be more useful when assessing whether the management of one alliance might affect other alliance relationships.

Although I also expect variation in military capabilities to affect assessments of alliance reliability, in this book I focus predominantly on assessments of allied interests. I do so for two reasons: First, allies often share classified knowledge on their military capabilities and so it is usually easier for a state to assess the military power of its ally. Second, military capabilities are unlikely to change suddenly and without forewarning (unless they are destroyed in conflict), whereas interests and intentions can be revised as governments change or new conceptions of the national interest are embraced. So although military capabilities remain an important influence on assessments of allied reliability, I expect states to more often focus on how allies prioritize their interests.[69]

The Alliance Audience Effect Theory

So far, I have reviewed why policymakers and scholars often assume that a state's loyalty within one alliance will affect other alliances. I also evaluated the existing academic literature on resolve, alliance loyalty, and reliability. In both the theoretical and practical realms, several simple but important questions about alliance politics have not been settled. Do states observe interactions between their ally and its other allies? Do these interactions affect an observer state's beliefs about its ally's reliability and do those beliefs have an impact on the observer state's security fears and defense policy? Do events in one alliance affect other alliances: are alliances *interdependent*? If yes, what governs this interdependence and how do states manage it?

As noted earlier, several authors argue that a state's actions—not its rhetoric—are the truest indication of interests and intent. Considering the alliance system depicted in figure 2, if state A fails to defend its ally, state B, then this reveals previously unknown information about state A's interests: the costs of defending state B were too high relative to the benefits of standing firm alongside it. State A's decision to abandon state B reveals a gap between its publicly proclaimed interests (as expressed through the A-B alliance) and the interests for which state A is actually willing to bleed.[70] This may not even be private information, but rather previously unknown information. It is the revelation of a gap between professed and actual interests—and not the disloyalty itself—that might concern other allies, such as state C.

Given the risks that can be posed by an unreliable ally, state C should monitor state A's behavior in order to better understand its interests and capabilities, and thus its alliance reliability. In this context, the term reliability should not be understood as an innate character trait, like loyalty or resolve. Rather, it is the extent to which state A's actions in the A-B alliance demonstrate that its interests remain convergent with those of state C and that it has adequate capabilities to pursue those interests effectively. Actions that demonstrate convergent interests are evidence of reliability, whereas actions that demonstrate a divergence of interests, or a lack of useful military capabilities, will cause state C to experience fears of abandonment or entrapment, and thus cast doubt on state A's reliability.

My theory's first hypothesis determines whether or not states monitor the actions of their ally, in order to assess the ally's reliability.

> H1: A state will observe its ally's behavior in other alliances. If this behavior reveals that the ally's interests diverge from the observer state's, and thus raises entrapment or abandonment fears, the state will assess the ally as unreliable.

The concept of reliability means that this hypothesis departs significantly from the previous emphasis theorists placed on loyalty and character-based attributions. Deterrence theory, as well as Mercer, would expect observing states to always desire loyalty, whereas my hypothesis is agnostic on whether the observing state wants to see loyal or disloyal behavior.[71] Deterrence theory would expect a demonstration of loyalty to strengthen other alliances and for disloyalty to damage them. Mercer, by contrast, would expect a demonstration of loyalty to have no effect at all and a demonstration of disloyalty to damage other alliances.[72]

This hypothesis would be falsified if an observing state, knowing that its interests would be damaged by a display of allied loyalty, nonetheless desired such behavior due to a belief that the ally's loyalty in this instance would guarantee its loyalty in other alliance interactions. It would also be falsified if an observing state, knowing that its interests would be advanced by an instance of allied *disloyalty*, nonetheless discouraged this behavior due to a belief that the ally's disloyalty in this instance would guarantee its disloyalty in the future. Finally, if observations of disloyal allied behavior *always* damaged other alliance relationships—as expected by deterrence theory and Mercer—this would challenge my conception of reliability and falsify this hypothesis. In short, H1 determines whether my idea of reliability—and its focus on interests and capabilities, rather than ideas of resolve or loyalty—is sound.

At this point, one scope condition should be emphasized: my theory does not expect every minor interaction within an alliance to be intensely monitored by an observing state and to have a tremendous effect on perceptions of reliability. To generate an alliance audience effect, the behavior must be *significant*: it must suggest a discrepancy between an ally's professed interests and those to which its behavior attests. Further, behavior that shows that the ally does not have the capabilities required to defend shared interests will also affect the observing state's perceptions of the ally's reliability.

H1 is only the starting point of the alliance audience effect framework. A number of factors affect security: geography, military capabilities, the disposition of other states, and the military capabilities held by adversaries. Alliances can also provide security but, unlike a state's own military capabilities, the security support promised by an ally cannot be relied upon with absolute certainty: there is always a risk of abandonment. Furthermore, a state will also need to be wary of any evidence suggesting that its alliance poses risks of entrapment. Thus, if a state observes its ally's behavior in another alliance and comes to believe that its ally is now unreliable, then the state's security situation has deteriorated and it should attempt to mitigate the risk posed by its ally's unreliability. If the observing state does react in this way, then the two discrete alliance commitments are, to some degree, interdependent: what happens in one alliance is affecting the other.

But another prospect is also possible: because it is in each state's interest to maximize the benefits and minimize the costs that result from any alliance, states could attempt to manipulate their allies into providing greater benefits by complaining about their unreliability. Walt has worried that America's "credibility obsession" created a situation where US allies could "free-ride . . . because they could always get Uncle Sucker to take on more burdens by complaining that they had doubts about American resolve."[73] Along these lines, Walt criticizes some Asian allies for not doing enough to provide for their own defense: it is "easier to complain about U.S. credibility than to dig deep and buy some genuine military capacity."[74] Expressed another way, the doubts voiced by allies might be just like the promises uttered by allies or the threats issued by adversaries: they might be "the words of people with a powerful motive to deceive."[75]

But if actions do indeed speak louder than words, then any observing state concerned about its ally's reliability will attempt to improve its own security situation. If such a dynamic is observable, it suggests that the observing state's fears are real, influential, and are not duplicitous attempts to free-ride on a gullible ally.

> H2: If a state assesses its ally to be unreliable, it will act to mitigate the specific risk posed.

To support this hypothesis, the observing state's beliefs about allied unreliability must prompt efforts to mitigate the specific risk posed. If, based on its observations of the ally's behavior, the state fears abandonment, it might acquire new arms or increase the size of its defense force. It could introduce conscription or improve the responsiveness of military coordination and decision making. It might attempt to develop closer relations with the ally, in order to better assess its reliability, or the state might seek new alliances. If the observing state fears entrapment, it might diplomatically distance itself from the ally as a way of expressing disapproval. In an effort to restrain the ally, the state might launch a peace plan, threaten to withhold military support, or defect to the opposing side in a conflict.

This hypothesis is less severe than two tested by Miller: that "an unreliable state will lose the ally that it entrapped or failed to support" and "an unreliable state will lose its allies generally."[76] Miller's study does not find strong support for these hypotheses.[77] But my hypothesis does extend beyond another tested by Miller, that "an unreliable state will be more constrained by the design of its alliances."[78] If a state's ally is regarded as unreliable, the state may mitigate the risks of allied unreliability without attempting to revise an alliance treaty text.

H2 may appear, at first glance, to be unfalsifiable: nations are usually modifying their defense policy in some way, whether through acquiring new capabilities or changing defense postures. However, I will consider this hypothesis supported only if detailed process tracing can demonstrate a causal link between a state's observations of allied behavior, its subsequent concerns about the ally's unreliability, and its efforts to mitigate the risks posed by this unreliability. H2 would be falsified if a state feared entrapment or abandonment but did not attempt to mitigate the risk posed by this unreliability. In short, H2 determines whether my idea of reliability has an observable influence on alliance interdependence.

If H1 and H2 are supported, and a state will act to mitigate the risks posed by an unreliable ally, then it would be natural for this possibility to affect the ally's policy deliberations. When the ally's behavior in one alliance could reasonably be expected to influence other alliances, the prospect of interdependence should affect the ally's cost/benefit calculations—and perhaps its ultimate decisions—within any alliance. This is the focus of hypothesis 3:

> H3: A state's actions will be influenced by the possibility that its behavior in one alliance will affect the reliability perceptions of its other allies.

I expect that two forms of behavior could support this hypothesis. First, state A could deliberately adopt a particular policy in the A-B alliance because of how it will be perceived by state C. I describe this as the "set the example" approach. State A might believe that if it abandons one ally, state B, then its other ally, state C, will assess state A as unreliable. As a consequence, state C might then act to mitigate the risk of unreliability: for example, it might decide to build nuclear weapons. But state A might regard this consequence as very undesirable because it could spark an arms race or undermine arms control treaties. The possibility of this response increases the likely costs of state A's decision to abandon state B. State A might have been quite prepared to abandon state B, but only if this didn't prompt state C to develop nuclear weapons. This possible consequence might convince state A that the best course of action is not to abandon state B, but to stand firm alongside it. The prospect of interdependence has influenced state A: because abandoning state B is likely to have important second-order consequences, the costs of abandonment are now too high. This scenario represents one "set the example" approach: state A uses the example of its conduct in the A-B alliance to reassure state C of state A's reliability and thus discourage it from developing nuclear weapons.

Another example-setting approach is also possible, and that is of a state publicly showcasing what behavior it will and will not accept from allies. This comes back to the credibility issue discussed by Stephen Walt. If state A believes that its two alliance commitments are interdependent, then it has a vested interest in not allowing its allies to manipulate it by appealing to this interdependence (by complaining about loyalty or reliability). If state A believes that its behavior in the A-B alliance is observed by, and influences, state C, then state A will be reluctant to grant state B a concession or arrangement that it is not willing to grant state C. For example, during the ANZUS crisis of the mid-1980s—an alliance dispute prompted by New Zealand's refusal to allow port visits from US Navy vessels unless Washington confirmed that they were not carrying nuclear weapons—some US officials wondered "whether it would be better to have New Zealand cast out [of ANZUS], as a useful example of how allies should *not* behave."[79] Media reports noted that Washington's decision to punish Wellington by suspending the alliance obligation was made "primarily because the Reagan administration fear[ed] that the antinuclear policy could spread unless firmly rebuffed."[80]

A second form of behavior could support H3: state A could adopt a policy of "simultaneous alliance management," where it tries to ensure that events in the A-B alliance do not adversely affect the A-C alliance. States with multiple alliances might choose not to avoid the undesired consequences caused by alliance interdependence, but to try and manage them instead. For example: state A might believe that if it abandons state B, then its other ally, state C, will assess state A to be unreliable. But state A might decide that it can still abandon state B if it can prevent any undesired developments in the A-C alliance. State A might be able to abandon state B, but also convince state C that it remains reliable by carefully explaining its policy choice, by demonstrating a strong commitment through troop placements or weapons deals, or through some other measure.[81]

Nations will not want to appear unreliable but neither will they want to appear gullible or susceptible to manipulation. For example, state A might be reluctant to support state B if the latter carelessly provoked an adversary for fear of generating the impression (in the minds of state C's leaders) that state A can be easily manipulated into conflict. Likewise, state A might be reticent to negotiate a particular alliance agreement with state B—such as intelligence sharing, military equipment sales, or a status of forces agreement— unless it is willing to give state C the same deal. Such instances would also support H3 of the alliance audience effect framework.

H3 enables the investigation of an old phenomenon—interdependence— in a new way. If interdependence exists, but is governed by assessments of reliability rather than reputations for loyalty, it would lead states to manage alliance interdependence differently. Specifically, H3 will allow me to determine if interdependence does more than simply constrain decision making by always encouraging loyalty. If I am right, and a state can withhold loyalty to set an example, or withhold loyalty and mitigate the resultant risk of damaging other alliances, then this will shine new light on the dynamics of interdependence. It might be possible to *deliberately manipulate* alliance interdependence to set an example, and/or it might be possible to reduce the undesired consequences of interdependence through simultaneous alliance management.

H3 would be falsified by the absence of evidence showing that the state considered the likely consequences of interdependence or the presence of evidence showing that the state dismissed the likely consequences of this interdependence.

Once the concept of alliance reliability has been proposed and explained, none of these hypotheses is especially demanding or revolutionary. But, taken together with the alliance reliability idea, they facilitate the investigation of what is really at the heart of alliance commitment interdependence. Rival theories, which expect interdependence to be governed by loyalty, or expect interdependence to manifest only when disloyalty occurs, would lead to very different expectations and policy advice. If my theory is correct, it will have greater explanatory power than rival approaches, such as deterrence theory and reputation skepticism. It may also enable policymakers to improve their understanding, analysis, and management of alliance interdependence.

Previous scholarship has assumed that alliance interdependence must be underpinned by loyalty, as an equivalent of deterrence theory's focus on re-solve. However, this equivalence is problematic: the concept of loyalty em-phasizes times of conflict, which are absolute and infrequent tests of an al-liance. Further, it incorrectly assumes that in all circumstances, states will want their allies to demonstrate indiscriminate loyalty. In this chapter, I have explained why states ought to monitor the behavior of their allies not to make character-based judgments but to obtain better information about the allies' capabilities and interests, and thus their alliance reliability.

Based on this analysis, I have proposed the three hypotheses which form the alliance audience effect theory. This framework expects alliance inter-dependence to be underpinned not by a state's loyalty reputation but by whether its actions demonstrate its alliance reliability. What happens in one alliance will affect how other states perceive the common ally's reliability and in turn this will result in changes to their strategic behavior. The pros-pect of interdependence and second-order effects will predispose the com-mon ally to carefully consider their alliance politics. The alliance audience effect means that the common ally may need to simultaneously manage dif-ferent alliances, or it might be able to set the example in one alliance to in-duce or discourage certain behavior from other allies. No alliance is an is-land, and national decisions should consider the possible consequences of interdependence.

In the following chapters, I test the alliance audience effect theory against Asian alliance case studies during the first twenty years of the Cold War. Though my theoretical framework notes how shifts in military capability might affect assessments of reliability, in these case studies the salient issue is more often the question of how US allies might infer US interests and thus assess Washington's reliability. Accordingly, the focus of my research and analysis is the process of how allies observe US behavior to infer Washing-ton's interests and update their assessments of US reliability. To begin, in the next chapter I consider the theory's applicability to the creation of the first three treaty alliances in Asia.

Forming Alliances in Asia, 1949–1951

No single Pacific nation, or any combination of such nations,
can be expected, unless it has reason to believe it will be backed by the
US, to commit itself to a course which might prove futile and even
disastrous.

—Pete Jarman (US ambassador to Australia)

Between 1951 and 1954, the United States formed the hub and spoke system
of alliances in Asia.[1] However inevitable this appears in retrospect, prior to
America's entry into the Korean War there was considerable doubt about the
extent of its security interests in Asia. Although the United States had demonstrated a strong commitment to the security of Western Europe through
NATO in 1949, it was uncertain whether Washington would draw a similar
defensive line in Asia. Within President Harry Truman's administration
there was debate about Asia's importance and disagreement over whether
America needed to play a substantial security role in the region.

Past scholarship has focused on why a system of mainly bilateral alliances,
rather than a multilateral "Asian NATO," formed during this period. Victor
Cha argues that America's desire to maximize control over client state allies led it to prefer bilateral alliances.[2] Christopher Hemmer and Peter Katzenstein write that a lack of collective identity inhibited efforts to realize a
multilateral alliance.[3] Others examine the region's unsuccessful efforts
toward a multilateral "Pacific Pact," and suggest that these efforts were
mainly national attempts to secure bilateral alliances with the United States.[4]
The architect of the alliance system, John Foster Dulles, attributed the mainly
bilateral structure to residual fear of Japan.[5] More recent scholarship, drawing on extensive archival research, has emphasized the interests and agency
of the US allies rather than Washington.[6]

In this chapter I argue that during the creation of alliances with Japan,
the Philippines, Australia, and New Zealand, the alliance audience effect
influenced when and how each alliance was formed. It also ensured that,

with the exception of the US-Japan alliance, the treaty texts were remarkably consistent: interdependence between seemingly discrete commitments meant that the US had to treat each of its allies equitably. In contrast to Cha's argument that the US deliberately constructed a system of bilateral alliances in order to maximize its influence, this chapter emphasizes the historical contingencies which led first to an alliance with Japan and then explains how this development affected negotiation of the subsequent alliances.

During the 1949–1951 period, US military capabilities were never seriously doubted by states in Asia. Instead, the issue was US interests: did Washington intend to keep some of this military power in Asia, and continue to play a regional role? Due to this uncertainty, states monitored how the United States behaved within its other relationships. As expected by H1, these observations influenced assessments of Washington's reliability. Before the Korean War, states observed US policy toward the republics of Korea and China, and concluded that Washington might not be willing to provide security in Asia. States also monitored US conduct toward Japan, and were unnerved by the prospect that the wartime enemy would receive a de facto security guarantee through the presence of US forces, but that wartime allies would not receive any security assurances.

As expected by H2, doubts about US reliability prompted these allies to change their strategic policies: most responded by encouraging Washington to play a greater role in Asia. This involved seeking formal alliances with the United States or offering to host military forces. When their initial efforts failed, states like the ROK and ROC investigated the possibility of an Asian anti-Communist "Pacific Pact" alliance. Finally, as expected by H3, US officials understood that these relationships were interdependent. They sought to prevent developments in one alliance adversely affecting other relationships by either reassuring the concerned ally or avoiding behavior likely to cause concern. In particular, the decision to defend South Korea against Communist attack was strongly influenced—perhaps even determined—by the belief that to not do so would damage regional beliefs about America's reliability. If America "lost" South Korea in the same way that it had "lost" China, it was feared that the subsequent loss of Japan would be a foregone conclusion.[7]

This chapter applies the alliance audience effect framework to a group of states that were not yet formal treaty allies of the United States. However, in 1949 the basic structure of the hub and spoke system existed even though no formal alliances had been signed. By the definition of alliance proposed in chapter 1, Washington's relationships with Australia, New Zealand, the Philippines, Japan, and the republics of Korea and China were informal alliances. Through its colonial relationship and basing arrangements, the US was clearly committed to the defense of the Philippines. Through postwar arrangements and the presence of occupying forces, in 1949 the presence of

US forces guaranteed the security of both Korea and Japan. Previous military cooperation with wartime allies Australia and New Zealand established the bedrock of cooperation that would soon be formalized by an alliance treaty.

In this chapter, I first provide an overview of major events in the 1949–1951 period. Then I consider the alliance audience effect framework against the policies of South Korea, Japan, Australia, the Philippines, and New Zealand. I conclude the chapter with an overall assessment of the framework against the regional security dynamics from 1949 to 1951.

Historical Overview, 1949–1951

At the conclusion of the Second World War, the United States occupied both Japan and South Korea. In 1948, the Korean Peninsula was divided and two separate nations were established: the Republic of Korea (ROK or South Korea), led by President Syngman Rhee, and the Democratic People's Republic of Korea (DPRK or North Korea), led by Kim Il-sung. Following the withdrawal of Soviet forces from North Korea in 1948, the US withdrew its forces from South Korea in 1949.[8]

In Japan, the United States aimed to create a strong nation, anti-Communist in outlook, which could assist Washington's efforts to counter Communist aggression in Asia. Unlike South Korea, US officials considered Japan—with its significant manufacturing capacity, advantageous location, and island geography—to be of immense strategic significance. But in 1949 there was not yet a peace treaty to officially conclude the Second World War, and the Chinese civil war complicated the issue of Chinese representation at any peace conference. Although the US had previously supported the Chinese Nationalists, led by Generalissimo Chiang Kai-shek, in their civil war against the Chinese Communist Party, "By early 1949 the Truman administration had concluded that the United States should disengage from the Chinese civil war and . . . 'let the dust settle'" before formulating a new policy.[9] Truman decided the best strategy was to attempt to prevent Communist domination of Formosa—the island now known as Taiwan, to which the Chinese Nationalists had fled—by providing economic and diplomatic support, but no military aid.[10]

But Washington's policy choices cast doubt on its willingness to play a substantial security role in Asia. In May 1949 the United States withdrew its military forces from South Korea, despite Seoul's pleading for them to stay. This decision was consistent with the Pentagon's view that "Korea was of no long-term strategic interest."[11] In August 1949 the Truman administration published the China White Paper, which "attempted to demonstrate that the United States had done all that it could for the Nationalists . . . [their]

defeat could not . . . be attributed to any lack of aid from Washington . . . but rather was due to [their own] military ineptitude and political corruption."[12] In January 1950, Truman announced that the US would not use military force to intervene in the ongoing Chinese civil war. "Expecting that Taiwan would fall, the administration directed American diplomatic missions worldwide to explain to host governments that the island possessed no strategic significance and that Washington had no responsibility for it."[13]

On January 12, 1950, the secretary of state, Dean Acheson, outlined America's Asia policy in a speech to the National Press Club in Washington. After voicing his firm commitment to the defense of Japan, Acheson described a "defensive perimeter [that] runs along the Aleutians to Japan and then goes to the Ryukyus . . . to the Philippine Islands."[14] The geographical limits of this defensive line were immensely important. South Korea and Formosa were on the wrong side of the line, and this delineation unnerved even those countries explicitly included within the defensive perimeter.[15]

John Lewis Gaddis writes that in 1950 the United States "endorsed, but then almost immediately backed away from, a strategy of avoiding military commitments on the Asian mainland."[16] This policy reversal was prompted by North Korea's invasion of South Korea on June 25, 1950. Within a matter of days, the US decided not only to defend South Korea but also to place the US Navy's Seventh Fleet in the Taiwan Strait. This second measure served two purposes: deterring Communist attacks against the Nationalists and restraining the Nationalists from attacking the mainland and thus widening the Korean War. These two areas—which had been excised from Washington's defensive perimeter in January—were suddenly brought back in.

The Korean War placed renewed emphasis on the negotiation of a peace treaty to conclude the Second World War. In January 1951 John Foster Dulles was appointed as a special representative of President Truman and was instructed to negotiate not only a peace treaty with Japan but also a "mutual assistance arrangement among the Pacific island nations (Australia, New Zealand, the Philippines, Japan, the United States, and perhaps Indonesia)."[17] Some nine months later the Peace Treaty of San Francisco was signed, as were bilateral security pacts with Japan and the Philippines and a trilateral Australia-New Zealand-United States (ANZUS) pact.

As I argue below, events in the 1949–1951 period provide strong support for the alliance audience effect framework: states observed Washington's treatment of other allies and resultant beliefs about US reliability influenced their security policies. Awareness of this interdependence was a strong influence on US policymakers, encouraging them to reconceive their interests and redraw their defensive line in Asia. Gaddis writes that "Korea, hitherto regarded as a peripheral interest, had . . . become vital if American credibility elsewhere was not to be questioned."[18]

South Korea

AMERICA DECIDES TO WITHDRAW FROM
THE KOREAN PENINSULA

From its beginning, South Korea was extremely insecure, and it looked to the United States for assistance. In late 1948 the US ambassador, John Muccio, wrote that only the US military presence provided "minimum Korean external and internal security."[19] Muccio assessed that American support for Korea appeared "to render more secure [the] U.S. position in Japan . . . [and] preserve [a] democratic showcase in northeast Asia . . . and thereby . . . restore [the] faith of Asiatic people in US professions of interest and help."[20] For Muccio, the significance of the American commitment to Korea extended beyond the shores of the Peninsula: it would affect regional perceptions of American reliability.

On February 21, 1949, the secretary of the army, Kenneth Royall, conducted a press conference in Tokyo. He speculated "that in case of war with the Soviet Union . . . Japan is . . . a liability, and that it might be more profitable from the viewpoint of United States policy to pull out all troops from Japan." The American political adviser in Tokyo, William Sebald, thought Royall's words suggested that "even though it was our duty to disarm Japan it is not our responsibility if someone else cuts Japan's throat as a result."[21] Within the US government, there was significant disagreement about the strategic value of various Asian countries. Some policymakers thought the US presence in Asia was a distraction from Europe, while others—particularly General Douglas MacArthur, the Supreme Commander for the Allied Powers (SCAP) in Japan—feared that Asia would be neglected. This uncertainty over US policy was already worrying some states: in February 1949, President Rhee complained that one of the "principal difficulties" of regional security was "the vacillation of the U.S. State Department, which . . . had played a strong part in the loss of China, and might be seriously harmful in Korea."[22]

The National Security Council (NSC) reviewed its Korea policy in March 1949, and defense officials emphasized that the withdrawal of Russian forces from North Korea justified a reciprocal withdrawal of US forces from South Korea. For others—mainly in the State Department—it was essential to increase the ROK's military capacity first. Though some officials were concerned about being entrapped into a conflict in mainland Asia, Muccio noted that President Rhee had specifically promised "that he would refrain from any action that might embarrass the U.S. position in the Far East and that he would not take any offensive military action against north Korea."[23]

The NSC assessed that "abrupt and complete U.S. disengagement could be expected to lead directly" to Soviet domination of Korea and would also "be interpreted as a betrayal by the U.S. of its friends and allies in the Far East."[24] Despite South Korea's lack of strategic importance, the need to avoid reputational damage precluded a complete abandonment of South Korea. As Gaddis notes, "judgements [previously] based on such traditional criteria as geography, economic capacity, or military potential now had to be balanced against considerations of image, prestige, and credibility."[25]

Despite this, the NSC had no intention of entering into a formal alliance with South Korea. This would risk "involvement in a major war in an area in which virtually all of the natural advantages would accrue to the USSR."[26] Such a promise would also be an overcommitment of US policy, given that the Joint Chiefs of Staff (JCS) believed that "the U.S. has little strategic interest in maintaining its present troops and bases in Korea."[27] As Charles Dobbs notes, military leaders considered Korea "a strategic liability, regardless of its symbolic importance."[28] Although "leaders in the Pentagon were inclined to simply write off the Peninsula," Washington could not abandon Korea completely.[29] If US inaction resulted in South Korea following "China along the path of communism [then] the Japanese, responding to prevailing winds, might be difficult to keep in the Western camp."[30]

The NSC split the difference between these two extreme options, and adopted a compromise policy of providing technical, economic, and military support designed to minimize "the chances of south Korea's being brought under Communist domination."[31] Though the United States desired the establishment of a sovereign and democratic Korean state, these objectives were to be pursued in a manner "which would enable the U.S. to withdraw from Korea as soon as possible with the minimum of bad effects."[32] As Gaddis argues, "what American policy-makers sought in Korea was a graceful exit, followed by a 'decent interval' in which the South Korean government could pull itself together as a bulwark against further Soviet expansion."[33] In March 1949 the NSC recommended that the US forces be withdrawn because "withdrawal from Korea at this time would not adversely affect the U.S. position in Japan."[34]

RHEE REACTS TO WITHDRAWAL PLANS BUT ALSO TO US BEHAVIOR TOWARD OTHER STATES

When Rhee was informed of these withdrawal plans, he was reluctant to publicly announce them. Muccio assessed that Rhee was "tarrying, hopeful of more concrete confirmation that the US really intends to carry out assurances of military aid I have given him verbally." Rhee also "expressed hope for some kind of agreement by which the US would guarantee Korean independence and protection in case of attack."[35] Rhee believed "the withdrawal of American troops without such a preliminary undertaking . . . would be open to serious misunderstanding in Korea . . . and in other countries, and might, therefore, have disastrous consequences."[36]

Although Rhee announced the withdrawal plans in April, he continued to push for an explicit US security guarantee, making his case by referring to US policy toward other countries. After Washington suspended military support to the Chinese Nationalists, Rhee told Muccio that "there was a question in the minds of the Korean people whether the United States can be relied upon. The Korean people never thought . . . that the United States would drop China." Despite Muccio's efforts to reassure him, Rhee thought Washington had "decided it is not worth while to try to defend Korea." In particular, he cited Secretary Royall's February 1949 statement on Japan as "indicative of the American position in this respect. If Japan was outside the United States defense line . . . then Korea must be well outside that line."[37]

In May, Rhee attempted to coerce the United States into a more explicit security arrangement. The South Korean press, "unquestionably inspired by governmental circles," began to hint at a "mutual defense agreement," with one paper even reporting that an alliance would be concluded within a month.[38] Rhee also issued "a press release demanding inclusion of the ROK within the American 'first line of defense.'"[39] But these attempts to shame or blackmail Washington into a policy reversal failed to get the desired results. Ambassador Muccio told Rhee that the "US had never entered into [a] mutual defense pact with any single nation, adding constant public reference here was embarrassing and would be productive of no favorable result."[40] The reaction in Washington was even stronger. Acheson cabled Muccio and instructed him to reprimand Rhee for this "grave breach [of] ordinary diplomatic courtesy."[41]

In a meeting with State Department officials, the Korean ambassador to the United States emulated Rhee's approach. He noted that Communist radio broadcasts liked to criticize American policy by arguing that the US had "washed its hands" of China and "was now preparing to do the same thing in Korea." This idea was challenged by American policymakers, who suggested that the Chinese Nationalists had "'put their hands in their pockets' by failing to put up any effective resistance to the Communists." The Korean ambassador was also told that a formal defense pact was "out of the question for the U.S."[42]

Despite Seoul's lack of success, Rhee continued to publicly call for a bilateral security treaty. But he also began to note that a "Pacific Pact similar to the Atlantic Pact" could assist South Korea against the Communist threat.[43] Bruce Cumings writes that "Rhee and his scribes spilled oceans of ink in tracts and speeches calling for a Pacific treaty."[44] In the absence of a solid American commitment to South Korean security, the idea of a Pacific equivalent to NATO had some appeal, but Junghyun Park concludes that "the primary objective of forming the Pacific Pact was not . . . to construct an independent and autonomous regional security system." Rather, it was to "provoke the U.S. into engaging actively in the regional order."[45]

Meanwhile, US policymakers managed these relationships with an awareness of the interdependence between them. In describing the importance of

Korea's continued survival, the acting secretary of state noted that the "abandonment of Korea would raise grave doubts in the minds of those Japanese who are trying to establish a democratic nation . . . regarding our determination to help them do so."[46] For their part, Korean officials continued to regard US policy toward China as having relevance to American reliability. The Korean foreign minister, in a meeting with Rhee and Muccio, "flew into [a] rage, [and] declared [that the] United States had sold China down [the] river and were pursuing [the] same course respecting Korea."[47]

Reluctant to become too involved in Asian security, on May 18, 1949, Acheson released a statement downplaying the prospects of a Pacific Pact. While noting the "serious dangers to world peace existing in the situation in Asia," Acheson's statement claimed that "a Pacific defense pact could not take shape until [the] present internal conflicts in Asia were resolved."[48] Undeterred, Rhee continued to talk up the possibility of such a pact and informed the US embassy that it was the subject of preliminary discussions between the Korean and Filipino governments.[49]

In late May 1949, as US troops withdrew, Muccio was taken aback at the depth of nervousness in South Korea. He reported a "sense of crisis bordering on panic. . . . Among factors responsible are propaganda line espoused by government at retention [of] US troops . . . China debacle, et cetera."[50] Korea continued to request that a final withdrawal be delayed and a firmer security guarantee articulated but these pleas fell on deaf ears in Washington. In place of an explicit security guarantee, on June 8 the State Department issued a tepid statement that claimed that the withdrawal of US troops "in no way indicates a lessening of United States interest in the Republic of Korea, but constitutes rather another step toward the normalization of relations."[51]

In late June, senior Defense officials considered their possible response options to a North Korean invasion of South Korea. Because "Korea is of little strategic value . . . [the] use of military force in Korea would be ill-advised and impracticable in view of . . . the over-all world situation." Though the Truman Doctrine had been applied to Greece and Turkey, it was not fit for Korea: this "would require prodigious effort and vast expenditures far out of proportion to the benefits to be expected."[52] Eager to avoid any recommitment of US forces to South Korea, the JCS recommended that in the event of a North Korean invasion, US citizens be evacuated and the problem referred to the United Nations.

Privately, Washington had decided its position: it had drawn its defensive line, and South Korea was on the wrong side of it.

THE CHINA WHITE PAPER AND ACHESON'S
DEFENSIVE PERIMETER SPEECH

Concurrently, the Chinese Nationalists suffered several defeats at the hands of their Communist foes. In August 1949, the Truman administration issued a

China White Paper, which attributed defeat of the Nationalists not to a lack of US support but to their own "military ineptitude and political corruption."[53] On January 5, 1950, President Truman announced that the United States would no longer provide military assistance to the Nationalists. This official abandonment of Nationalist China further alarmed President Rhee, who raised this issue with Philip Jessup, an American ambassador at large. Jessup considered his discussion "very significant" and he reported "that all of the Koreans were disturbed by the President's recent statement on Formosa and still hope that we may do something to help the Nationalists there."[54]

One week later, on January 12, 1950, Acheson outlined America's Asia policy in a speech to the National Press Club in Washington. He announced a "defensive perimeter [that] runs along the Aleutians to Japan and then goes to the Ryukyus . . . to the Philippine Islands."[55] The speech immediately alarmed Korean officials: "the fact Korea found itself on the other side of that line . . . appeared to raise the serious question as to whether the United States might now be considered as having abandoned Korea."[56] In an interview years later, the Korean ambassador to the United States described Acheson's speech as "sort of an invitation to the Russians or the Communists to come in" and recalled that he "begged them to reconsider that policy."[57] In an April 1950 discussion, he expressed the hope that "the American defense line in the Far East could be extended to include South Korea" and stressed "the importance [to] which the Korean Government and people attached to their apparent exclusion from the defense plans of the United States in the Far East."[58] Downplaying the importance of the defensive line, the new assistant secretary of state for Far Eastern affairs, Dean Rusk, cited the economic and material aid the US was providing as proof of Washington's commitment.

Despite efforts to reassure him, Rhee continued to doubt Washington's reliability. In January 1950, Soviet intelligence reports suggested that Rhee felt South Korea, like Formosa, would not be defended by US forces. According to Thomas Christensen, Korean leaders felt that "the ROK would receive the same treatment as the" Chinese Nationalists. However, Rhee believed that America's conduct toward Korea would be, to some degree, influenced by developments in Japan: the United States "would not write off South Korea entirely . . . until after the issue of Japan was resolved." Importantly, evidence like this suggests that Rhee's pleas to Muccio, Jessup, and others were genuine. A leader like Rhee might, in an effort to secure a greater American commitment, exaggerate the extent to which he was observing, and was influenced by, developments in the US-ROC and US-Japan relationships. But this evidence suggests that Rhee's fears of abandonment were genuinely amplified by US vacillation toward Formosa and inconsistent rhetoric about Japan: what he was saying to his American interlocutors was very similar to what he was saying in private. These Soviet reports also suggest that Rhee's fears were so acute that he was willing to pursue a closer security relationship with Japan: Rhee "was discussing the need for closer collaboration with Japan in the future as a solution to the potential for abandonment by the United States."[59] Given Rhee's own hatred of Japan, such reports emphasize the severity of his concerns about US reliability: he would have considered such an option only if he believed Washington's security reliability to be very poor.

In Seoul, Ambassador Muccio grew more concerned that Korean officials were closely monitoring how the United States was treating other countries in Asia and that these observations were negatively affecting their beliefs about America's reliability. Muccio cabled Rusk to express his concern about public US government statements "from which the name of Korea very frequently is omitted. These omissions are always noted here in Korea, and they add to the sensitivity and fear . . . that the United States Government . . . will abandon Korea at the earliest opportunity."[60] Muccio also expressed concern about the travel plans of senior US officials. The tendency of officials to visit Japan but not Korea gave "credence to [the] Korean fear and suspicion that the United States is more interested in developing and sustaining their recent enemy than their long friends!" After learning that the secretary of defense, Louis Johnson, would visit Tokyo but not Seoul, President Rhee "was much distressed . . . he had become depressed and angered . . . that the U.S. Department of Defense was showing its indifference to the fate of Korea."[61] In the words of Peter Lowe, "the absence of distinguished American visitors seemed to underline [a] lack of interest in the fate of Korea."[62]

On May 18, 1950, Acheson appointed one of his advisers, John Foster Dulles, to investigate a peace settlement with Japan. As part of this process, Dulles visited Korea and met with President Rhee in June. Rhee repeated his familiar pleas for further assistance, and again "expressed deep concern over the fate of Formosa, saying that its loss would be greatly deplored by Korea." Dulles said that the Formosa issue was "under-going constant review within the Department of State" and noted that economic aid was continuing and some military aid would soon resume. Despite Dulles's attempts to reassure Rhee by noting that "formal pacts, alliances or treaties were not necessary prerequisites to common action against a common foe," he could not repair the damage already done.[63] Rhee continued to frantically search around for possible allies and in April 1950 he dispatched a special envoy to Australia, New Zealand, and the Philippines to "sound out some possibility of military alliances . . . something similar to NATO."[64]

Japan

TOKYO UNNERVED BY AMERICA'S TREATMENT OF KOREA AND NATIONALIST CHINA

As noted earlier, during the 1949–1950 period there was significant debate about Washington's commitment to Japan and whether a peace treaty should be concluded. The political adviser in Japan, William Sebald, felt that Royall's comments in February 1949 could not have been "better designed to revive Japanese interest in the possibility or desirability of an orientation towards the Soviets, particularly in the light of recent events on the continent of Asia."[65]

The JCS viewed Soviet aggression as the main threat to Japan, but the State Department assessed the primary threats as internal: "agitation, subversion and *coup d'état*. The threat is that of a conspiracy inspired by the Kremlin, but conducted by the Japanese." The State Department felt that "the early conclusion of a peace settlement" offered the best prospect of cementing Japan's anti-Communist outlook. They were particularly concerned about the Defense Department's desire for military bases in Japan, which would "constitute an irritating and not a stabilizing influence on the Japanese population."[66] Though the need to maintain US forces in Japan would complicate an overall peace treaty, a British official had earlier suggested that US security needs in Japan could be met through "a US-Japanese bilateral pact providing for post-treaty U.S. base facilities in Japan in return for US protection of Japan."[67] However, at this time, tensions between State and Defense hindered the development of an agreed Japan policy.

These disagreements persisted into early 1950, when developments in the US-China relationship changed Washington's calculus. When the United States ceased support of the Chinese Nationalists, some Republican critics lambasted it as "a final betrayal and sellout of an American ally."[68] From the Pentagon's perspective, the decision to abandon Formosa only increased the value of bases in Japan. However, in April 1950, MacArthur felt that 95 percent of Japanese would oppose US bases on Japan's main islands.[69] Fearing that a peace treaty with Japan would lead to the loss of these facilities, Defense officials dismissed diplomatic advice that Japan was eager for the occupation to end. Secretary of Defense Louis Johnson "was convinced that the only propaganda for a peace treaty . . . came out of the Department of State."[70]

Japan's leaders feared that an early US withdrawal could damage the country's security. In August 1949 Sebald cabled Acheson, noting that many Japanese feared that a "withdrawal would open wide the flood-gates of Communism. They point to what happened in China, and reinforce their position by saying that our military withdrawal from [South] Korea has made Soviet control of all Korea inevitable."[71] Although the Japanese prime minister, Shigeru Yoshida, preferred a peace treaty that avoided US bases on Japan's main islands, he felt that some bases were "preferable to an indefinite continuation of the Occupation."[72] Because MacArthur "forbade Yoshida to negotiate directly with Washington on security matters," three Japanese delegates visited Washington to sidestep the supreme commander.[73] The true purpose of their mission was to suggest the conclusion of a peace treaty and an end to the occupation. This delegation met with Joseph Dodge, the financial adviser to SCAP, in Washington on May 2, 1950. Hayato Ikeda, the Japanese finance minister, "conveyed a personal message from Prime Minister Yoshida to Mr. Dodge to the effect that the Government desires the earliest possible [peace] treaty. As such a treaty would require the maintenance of U.S. forces [at bases in Japan] to secure the treaty terms and for other purposes, if the U.S. Government hesitates to make these conditions, the Japanese Government will try to find a way to offer them."[74]

In making this offer, Japan had paid close attention to Royall's February 1949 statement, but Ikeda noted that "emphasis had been given [to] this by later public statements of the United States Government in writing off Formosa . . . [and] the fact that South Korea is not strong and could, perhaps, easily be abandoned." Japan had observed America's behavior toward Korea and Formosa, and worried about suffering the same fate: "The Japanese people are desperately looking for firm ground. . . . They were skeptical on just what and when and where the United States would stand firm, and particularly with respect to Japan."[75]

Unlike South Korea, Japan had been specifically included in Acheson's defensive perimeter speech. Despite this explicit assurance, Japan was sufficiently unnerved by America's treatment of the ROC and ROK that it felt it necessary to seek Washington's recommitment to Japanese security. But unlike Rhee, with his incessant complaints and extortion efforts, Japan brought a significant offer to the table. Yoshida was so disturbed by the prospect of American unreliability that he was willing to make a significant concession in order to improve both that measure of reliability and also Japanese security. His offer of bases in mainland Japan was a decision that would be unpopular in Japan, so Yoshida had no motive to lie or purposefully invoke the issue of American reliability when explaining Japan's willingness to host US forces. This lends credence to Ikeda's presentation of the basing offer: after Royall's statement, and having observed America's treatment of Korea and Nationalist China, Japan feared that American unreliability damaged its own security. In order to improve American reliability and solidify its role as Japan's protector, Yoshida made the critical decision to offer basing rights in mainland Japan.

THE KOREAN WAR DEMONSTRATES AMERICAN RELIABILITY AND CHANGES JAPAN'S CALCULUS

When North Korea invaded South Korea in June 1950, many in Washington believed that the US response would be viewed as a litmus test of America's security reliability. Intelligence analysts thought that Japan would "regard the position taken by the United States as presaging US action should Japan be threatened with invasion." Inaction would "strengthen [an] existing widespread desire for neutrality," but "Rapid and unhesitating US support for the ROK . . . would reassure the Japanese . . . [and] would enhance their willingness to accept US protection and its implications."[76] Following the US intervention, General MacArthur reported that the Japanese were immensely relieved; they believed it meant the United States would "vigorously defend them against Russian invasion."[77] An American official was told that "99 percent of all Japanese supported the Korean operation, despite a widespread antiwar sentiment."[78]

Tokyo had earlier outlined its fears of abandonment and secretly offered to host US forces. Now, the North Korean invasion had reaffirmed both the dangers of Communist aggression and the desirability of a US security guarantee. But US intervention in Korea also changed Japan's calculations: now that Tokyo had a more informed assessment of Washington's reliability—determined by its capabilities and interests in Northeast Asia—it could afford to drive a harder bargain on the issue of military bases. On July 29, 1950, Yoshida told a parliamentary committee that he was "against leasing military bases to any foreign country." When asked about how Japan would ensure its security, a vice minister of foreign affairs intimated that "Japan would rely upon UN protection as in the case of the Republic of Korea." This position puzzled some US officials, who found it "mystifying in view of the Korean war which has pointed out the true character of Communist aggression and the need for firstclass armament and bases to stave off aggression."[79]

But the alliance audience effect theory provides an explanation for Tokyo's reversal. Now that the United States had defended South Korea, Japan could make a more informed judgment of American reliability and adjust policy accordingly. Sebald, in Tokyo, was not as perplexed as his colleagues in Washington. He assessed that Prime Minister Yoshida's comments were "laying the groundwork for future bargaining." Officials in Washington eventually came to a similar conclusion: because the Japanese now knew that "US bases in Japan will prove a critical factor in protecting the whole US position in the Far East . . . it would be logical for the Japanese (who have never hesitated to play power politics on a grand scale) to intimate that the price for these all-important bases in Japan is greater than the US had perhaps reckoned."[80] Embassy officials in Tokyo felt that "notwithstanding official denials and public confusion on the issue, there exists in Japan a large body of opinion which, in light of the Korea conflict, would be in favor of establishing a Japan[ese] defense force." Whereas the United States had once intended to disarm Japan to ensure it would never again threaten its Asian neighbors, the Korean War challenged the feasibility of this policy. The choice was that "either the US assumes the full burden of defending Japan or it must enlist Japan's assistance in helping to provide such defense."[81]

In January 1951, John Foster Dulles was appointed as an ambassador and given responsibility to conclude not only a peace treaty with Japan but also a "mutual assistance arrangement among the Pacific island nations (Australia, New Zealand, the Philippines, Japan, the United States, and perhaps Indonesia)."[82] He arrived in Japan in January 1951 to discuss the peace treaty with Prime Minister Yoshida. By this time, the allied position on the Korean

Peninsula had worsened: after being pushed back to the Pusan beachhead in September 1950, UN forces counterattacked and moved north of the 38th parallel, but Chinese forces had entered the war in October.[83] Dulles, in a memo to Acheson, warned that these developments had harmed the American bargaining position with Japan: items "which in September it seemed that we could obtain unconditionally merely by stipulating them" now had to be the subject of intense negotiation.[84]

In meetings with Japanese officials, Dulles "learned that American military reversals in Korea had, as he feared, stiffened the prime minister's spine."[85] Yoshida now knew the value that Japanese real estate had in the eyes of American strategists, but he also better understood the Communist threat in North Asia. US diplomats had earlier mused on how America must either wholly provide for Japan's defense or convince it to rearm: these circumstances provided an opportunity for Yoshida to press for the former option. He warned Dulles that "it was necessary to go very slowly in connection with any possible rearmament" due to the risks of resurgent militarism and the economic cost of such a decision. Dulles insisted that "Japan should be willing to make at least a token contribution and a commitment to a general cause of collective security," but Yoshida was unwilling to discuss the specifics of rearmament.[86] One Japanese official said, "If we organize 300,000 troops as your Mr. Dulles wanted us to do, your government will insist that we send some of these troops to Korea."[87] Walter LaFeber also notes Yoshida "seemed obsessed by the fear that Americans wanted Japanese troops to be used in Korea."[88]

After a difficult discussion on January 31, Dulles insisted that Japan must create a small army and "until Yoshida accepted his position, Dulles declined to discuss the terms of the peace treaty."[89] Yoshida eventually conceded and "secretly agreed to creating limited ground forces." At 50,000 men it was not the size Dulles had desired, but it was a sufficient sign of good faith.[90] Conveniently for Japan, its small size also meant that it was unlikely to play a role in the defense of South Korea. A draft bilateral agreement, which would be signed following the peace treaty, noted that "Japan desires . . . that the United States . . . should maintain armed forces of its own in and about Japan so as to deter armed attack upon Japan."[91] While this agreement contained only "a vague promise to defend Japan. . . . After Truman's massive response in Korea . . . no sane person doubted how U.S. forces would react if Japan were attacked." Though Dulles wanted more from Japan, he achieved only a "blurred, complicated commitment from Yoshida to rearm."[92]

By February 1951, Dulles had achieved substantial progress toward achieving a settlement with Japan, but he knew this had the potential to complicate relations with other friendly states in Asia. In April 1950 he had commented that any defensive guarantee to Japan "would be regarded as somewhat anomalous by our Allies because Japan, an ex-enemy country, would be obtaining a U.S. commitment which every one of our friendly Allies coveted."[93] Although the February 1951 draft agreement did not explicitly obligate the United States to defend Japan, US officials saw a "danger" if Washington gave "Japan guarantees which we did not give [to] the Philippines, Australia and New Zealand."[94] Such discrimination might mean that these wartime allies would not support a lenient peace treaty with Japan and would instead demand that Japan not be permitted to maintain a postwar defense force. As evidence presented later in this chapter shows, the need to address the risk of allied dissatisfaction was a key determinant of the hub and spoke security architecture.

The Philippines, Australia, and New Zealand

Before the outbreak of the Korean War, Japan and South Korea were not the only countries in Asia worried about Washington's reliability. The primary concern of Australia, New Zealand, and the Philippines was a possible resurgence of Japanese militarism, but there was also a growing awareness about the threat of Communism in Asia. The US embassy in Canberra assessed that Australian "complacency has been somewhat shaken by the withdrawal of United States defenses . . . the collapse of China, and the deteriorating situation in southeastern Asia, and there is evidence of a dawning realization of the dangers of Australia's isolated position."[95] Officials reported that "Australia is anxious to see the US military position in the western Pacific strengthened."[96] Some feared that Australia would tie its acceptance of the Japanese peace treaty to some form of security guarantee. Percy Spender, Australia's foreign minister, felt that Australia did indeed have some bargaining power in this matter due to its role as America's "most important fighting ally in the Pacific war."[97] But America's desire for a peace treaty with lenient terms alarmed Australian officials: it raised the possibility of Australia facing a resurgent Japan without allied support.

The Philippines was also concerned about American reliability and the continued presence of US troops in the Pacific. The development of the North Atlantic Treaty (NAT) raised questions as to why a similar Pacific Pact had not arisen, with President Elpidio Quirino publicly saying that such an arrangement "seems advisable." In March 1949 the American embassy in Manila reported that the idea of a multilateral alliance with the ROC and ROK "reflects the anxious search of the Filipinos for some measure of definite security against possible outside aggression. It does not indicate any change in their basic hope . . . that the United States will come to the defense of the Philippines in the event of an emergency."[98] In a discussion with an American diplomat, Quirino said that the chaos "existing in much of the Far East could not be improved without strong moral and economic leadership . . . the US is the only country that could supply a leadership adequate to remedy existing conditions."[99] Quirino's apprehension was so sincere that he was willing to consider Japanese membership in such a pact. The chargé of the American embassy in Manila cabled Acheson, noting that because "President Quirino holds no love for the Japanese, his idea that Japan should form a part of any Pacific Pact is very significant."[100]

For their part, in late 1949 US officials were reluctant to provide either bilateral security guarantees or support the idea of a Pacific Pact. The assistant secretary of state for Far Eastern affairs, William Butterworth, specifically warned Acheson that Australia might "try to obtain a US security guarantee in return for concurring generally in the substance of our proposals for a Japanese peace settlement." Butterworth was concerned that an "Australian request would attract requests from the Philippines, Korea, and other quarters and revive discussion of a possible Pacific Pact modeled on the Atlantic Pact." Beyond his fear that one bilateral pact might cascade into a series of alliances, Butterworth thought a multilateral Pacific Pact might unintentionally signal that "these are the states we intend to defend and that the rest are being abandoned."[101]

Undeterred by the lack of US enthusiasm, Rhee, Quirino, and Chiang Kai-shek discussed the prospect of a Pacific Pact among themselves. In July, Quirino raised the pact with US embassy officials in Manila: though Washington was "greatly occupied elsewhere, especially Western Europe," Quirino felt that the United States was "making [a] mistake in neglecting [its] real friends in Far East. . . . These friends now feel abandoned, [as a] result (of) US troop withdrawals (from) South Korea . . . and of US abandonment of [its] policy [of] aiding [the] Chinese Government." Though he thought the US should lead, because Washington "was too indifferent or occupied, the Philippines, China and Korea had gone ahead to develop cooperative measures to protect themselves. . . . Should the US wish to participate, it would of course be welcome."[102] Officials from China, Korea, and the Philippines talked up the prospects of a Pacific Pact. A Chinese minister told the US embassy in Manila that the three nations were "determined [to] go ahead with [the] union even if no other states join it. He stated that these three states want US leadership but suggested that leadership might be elsewhere by default."[103]

US officials were more skeptical, noting the divergent interests between the three nations. With the ROK and ROC both desperately in need of US military aid that was not forthcoming, it was assessed that they desired "that Quirino take the lead in 'pulling their chestnuts from the fire,'" with the expectation that the United States would be the "eventual cornerstone" of a Pacific Pact. But to avoid the impression of US interest—which officials feared would give credence to accusations of external interference and colonialism—it was decided that the US would "maintain our present public coolness to the whole idea."[104] For Acheson, the charter membership of the Chinese Nationalists "saddles [the] embryonic union with [a] hopeless mil[itary] problem." Given his suspicions, he instructed diplomats to avoid making statements which could be interpreted as either US support or opposition to the Pacific Pact concept.[105]

The pact's poor prospects became undeniable when the Philippines moved to organize a meeting of Asian nations to discuss the concept. Known as the Baguio Conference, this proposed summit did not receive significant support within the region. New Zealand felt the conference would be "of no value unless it included the United States and the United Kingdom."[106] Australia's response was to seek Washington's view, with the US embassy adding its analysis that the concept of a Pacific Pact would "not prove acceptable [to] Australia, unless there were evidence of strong, immediate or ultimate US backing."[107] The State Department's reply to its embassy in Canberra was that while Australia's attendance should not be discouraged, Washington's final position could not be determined now, though the State Department "considers [the] development of [a] regional coalition [in] SEA [Southeast Asia] more important to its future plans than it has in the past."[108]

Despite America's cautious attitude, on March 10 the Australian foreign minister, Percy Spender, went "all out in support of a Pacific pact." He explained to the Australian Parliament that by this, he meant a "defensive military arrangement" between Australia, the United Kingdom, and other countries. Spender had "in mind, particularly, the US whose participation would give such a pact substance it would otherwise lack. Indeed it would be rather meaningless without her."[109] In this speech, Spender seemed to be signaling that Australia would throw strong support behind a Pacific Pact only if the United States would commit. He was publicly urging Washington to reconsider its position and commit to a larger security role in Asia. Acheson expressed some approval of Spender's speech but the diplomatic stance was unchanged: the US felt it could not provide early help, or promise final support, to any association of states in Asia. Any such organization had to be completely indigenous to the region in order to have the best prospects of success.[110]

The embassy in Canberra, concerned that the importance of Spender's remarks had not been adequately appreciated, again cabled Washington. Ambassador Jarman emphasized that Spender's earlier comments "represent concessions to [the] US position" on a lenient peace treaty with Japan, and that the new government in Australia had "gone out of its way to strengthen [the] US-Australian relationship." Noting that Australia would do "everything possible [to] promote [a] Pacific Pact with military commitments," Jarman reported that Canberra had "not so much turned down [an] invitation" to the Baguio Conference, but thought it of little value without US involvement. Jarman's reporting suggested that Australia was "anxious [to] come to grips soonest with [the] Communist problem in Asia." But doubt about Washington's regional strategy and reliability caused Canberra to hesitate. Jarman wrote that Spender "appears [to] consider that no single Pacific nation, or any combination of such nations, can be expected, unless it has reason to believe it will be backed by the US, to commit itself to a course which might prove futile and even disastrous."[111] As Ambassador Jarman saw it, Australian doubts about the persistence of the US presence in Asia meant that Canberra was unwilling to sign up to any pact which the United States did not also join.

THE US DEFENSE OF KOREA REASSURES FRIENDLY STATES

As discussed earlier, intelligence analysts believed that if US inaction led to the fall of Korea, it would create the impression in Southeast Asia that "the USSR is advancing invincibly, and there would be a greatly increased impulse to 'get on the bandwagon.'"[112] Historians cite concerns about credibility as one of the primary factors in Truman's decision to dramatically reverse American policy on Korea. Gaddis writes that "there was almost immediate agreement in Washington that Korea, hitherto regarded as a peripheral interest, had . . . become vital if American credibility elsewhere was not to be questioned."[113] Kaufman assessed that "the credibility of the administration's foreign policy was at issue . . . both among America's allies and its adversaries."[114]

The decision to defend South Korea did influence the views and policies of US allies in the region. Initially, this was represented in diplomatic exchanges. On June 30, Acheson cabled all US diplomatic missions, noting that "widespread support [of the] SC [Security Council] resolution on Korea and US action in support of res[olution] continue. Pessimism and gloom in Phil[ippines] have been succeeded by vigorous approval US actions which [are] viewed as support of democracy in Asia."[115] On July 28 the Australian prime minister, Robert Menzies, met with President Truman and said that "Australia was wholeheartedly behind American policy and wished to play its full part in the defense of the free world."[116] As Rosemary Foot writes, "the allied response to the U.S. decision to intervene in Korea was all that had been anticipated" by Washington.[117]

Once the full impact of this recommitment to Korea had been realized, states made new assessments of US security reliability and adjusted their policies accordingly. As expected by the alliance audience effect theory, these judgments led them to adopt particular forms of behavior. A US official wrote that while the Australian foreign minister, Percy Spender, had previously focused on obtaining "some assurance that the United States would defend Australia in the event of aggression. . . . This emphasis is no longer important in Spender's or other Australian eyes since our defense of South Korea is more than ample proof to Australia that we would defend them if attacked. . . . [W]hat he really wants is closer participation in all stages of high level Washington planning."[118]

As US intervention in Korea increased Australia's confidence in American reliability, Australia directly supported the military effort in Korea and instead of focusing primarily on a security alliance guarantee, Canberra agitated more strenuously for a closer defense planning relationship.

Dulles had earlier expressed his concern that Australia and New Zealand might seek alliances as their price for endorsing a lenient peace treaty. Now that America had agreed to provide for Japan's security, other countries requested similar arrangements. This issue of consistency was a recurring theme throughout 1950 and 1951. Australia, in particular, freely complained to any US official willing to listen. One wrote that Spender had the "feeling that 'friends don't get the same consideration as weak sisters' and that the Australians 'are not getting a fair go.' Every time we extend the NAT, as to Greece and Turkey, we strengthen that feeling."[119]

In February 1951, at a trilateral meeting in Canberra, the foreign ministers of Australia and New Zealand bluntly told Dulles that due to domestic political concerns, they could not accept a lenient Japanese peace treaty—which permitted Japan to rearm—without some form of security assurance from Washington. Dulles was prepared for this position: his offsider, John Allison, later described Washington's willingness to sign a trilateral alliance as "bait to get Australia and New Zealand to sign the [peace] treaty. They still had great reservations about a treaty which didn't put limitations on Japan's rearmament."[120] Dulles explained that he had authority to discuss security pacts and noted several possible arrangements, such as a series of bilateral alliances, a trilateral Australia–New Zealand–United States pact, or a quadrilateral alliance with the Philippines.[121] By February 17, a draft trilateral treaty had been developed, although it was still possible that the Philippines and Japan might also join the alliance as charter members.[122] However, Dulles concluded that any arrangement which "put the Philippines in the position of being in effect an 'ally' of Japan" was "a step for which their public opinion was not yet prepared."[123] Rather than a multilateral Pacific Pact, it was becoming clearer that the security landscape of Asia would now be dominated by one trilateral and two bilateral alliances.

However, this was not the end of the matter. Once the Philippines discovered that a trilateral alliance had been negotiated, it "strongly deplored the preferred position given to Australia and New Zealand," believing that the absence of such a treaty with the Philippines implied that "the US does not regard the Phil[ippine]s as a sovereign nation." The US ambassador tried to explain to President Quirino that "our public statements regarding the defense and security of the Phil[ippine]s do in fact constitute a closer alliance than is the case with Australia and New Zealand," but this assurance had little impact.[124] Leaders in the Philippines were angered by this apparent inconsistency in alliance commitments, and so the United States agreed to negotiate a bilateral alliance with Manila.

Australia and New Zealand had no objection to the conclusion of such an alliance but they carefully monitored these developments to ensure that Manila did not receive any preferential treatment. In early August 1951, an Australian diplomat "expressed concern as to whether any possible arrangement between the United States and the Philippines might contain provisions which would be harmful to the Australian-New Zealand trilateral."[125] One week later, Australia's ambassador in Washington noted that "if the agreement with the Philippines turned out to be more explicit in its commitments than the treaty with Australia and New Zealand, the reaction in Australia would be very bad."[126] Rusk indicated that the agreement with the Philippines would be no more explicit than that for Australia and New Zealand.

Perhaps unsurprisingly, the Philippines had attempted to secure a more explicit security guarantee: its draft of the treaty stated that "an armed attack against either country shall be considered an attack against both."[127] Despite receiving the US draft—which replicated the language of the draft ANZUS treaty—the Philippines urged Washington to consider a stronger commitment along the lines of the NAT. The US ambassador in the Philippines, Myron Cowan, assessed that President Quirino wanted "to obtain something a little different from [the] Australian New Zealand pact which will give some special recognition to [the] special relationship" between the Philippines and the United States. While Qurino's request could be refused without "serious consequences," Cowan suggested the State "Dep[artmen]t put what frosting it can on his cake."[128]

However, Dulles knew that cake frosting had to be equitably distributed among new allies. The Australians had already indicated that the trilateral ANZUS treaty would be endangered if the provisions of the US-Philippines pact were considered to be more advantageous. When the Philippine foreign minister, Romulo, failed to secure this change, he requested that the agreement be titled a "Mutual Defense Treaty." Dulles noted that although the working title of a "Security Treaty" had been adopted "to keep it consistent with the U.S.-Australia-New Zealand security treaties," he had no objection to this minor change. The difference was not a substantive one, and was thus unlikely to provoke objections from Australia or New Zealand.[129] Having failed to obtain extra frosting on its cake, Manila was able to secure a small, face-saving garnish to differentiate its alliance from ANZUS.

Assessing the Alliance Audience Effect, 1949–1951

KOREA

Throughout 1949 and the first half of 1950, Korean fears of abandonment were inspired, and then bolstered, by a number of events. Several directly concern the US-Korea relationship: the withdrawal of US troops in 1949, the exclusion of Korea from Acheson's defensive perimeter speech, and Washington's unwillingness to provide a security guarantee, all gave Rhee good reason to doubt US reliability. But US policy toward other Asian states also generated South Korean fears of abandonment. Royall's statement, which cast doubt on Washington's obligation to defend Japan, had a significant impact on Rhee. Seoul lamented US vacillation over the issue of Formosa, believing that a similar dynamic could occur if Korea ever needed assistance. The publication of the China White Paper, and the seeming abandonment of the Chinese Nationalists, intensified these fears. Other factors, such as the unwillingness of senior officials to visit Seoul, added insult to injury by suggesting that Japan was valued more than Korea. These facts support H1, which expects that a state will observe its ally's behavior in other alliances and these observations will affect assessments of reliability.

H2 expects that if a state perceives its ally to be unreliable, it will act to mitigate the risk. Rhee tried to reduce the risk of abandonment by first attempting to obtain a security guarantee from Washington. When these pleas fell on deaf ears, he sought to blackmail the United States into providing assistance and also encouraged efforts toward a wider Pacific Pact, which might have provided a regional front against Communist aggression. These efforts persisted until the outbreak of the Korean War.

H3 expects that US actions will be influenced by the possibility that its behavior in one alliance will affect the reliability perceptions of its other allies, and this dynamic was clearly a factor in this period. When US officials became aware that Korea's fears of abandonment were aggravated by their observations of US behavior toward Japan and Formosa, they sought to counteract this by carefully explaining why Korea's security remained important to Washington. Muccio noted that the United States, by modifying its rhetoric about other relationships and ensuring equality of senior official visits, might avoid further aggravation of Korean fears.

JAPAN

As expected by H1, Tokyo closely observed America's treatment of the ROC and ROK, and was unnerved by America's vacillation toward Taipei and seeming abandonment of Seoul. These developments led Tokyo to doubt American reliability even though Japan was still under occupation by US forces, and had been explicitly and deliberately included within the defensive perimeter articulated by Acheson. Despite having good evidence to suggest that Washington would defend Japan against attack, Tokyo still worried about US reliability.

As expected by H2, Japan acted to mitigate this risk: it first tried to solidify America's military presence in the region by offering bases in mainland Japan, as this would reduce the likelihood of abandonment. However, America's involvement in the Korean War—and Japan's reaction to it—provides further support for H1 and H2. After the United States decided to defend South Korea, Japan had new and improved information about US interests. Tokyo believed that if the US would defend South Korea, then it would also defend Japan: this meant that Tokyo could drive a harder bargain on the issue of military bases. As the tide of the Korean War changed, Japan adopted a stronger position on the issue of rearmament. Yoshida feared that the US would pressure Japan to use a newly created army overseas, but was also now confident that the US would defend Japan. This allowed him to bargain hard and create only a token police force despite Dulles's desire for a larger Japanese army. Thus, Yoshida was able to effectively mitigate both the risks of abandonment (through US bases on Japanese soil) and the risk of entrapment (through the creation of only a small Japanese military force).

Finally, as expected by H3, America's behavior toward Japan was influenced by the possibility that it could affect the reliability perceptions of its other allies. US diplomats were aware that US treatment of Japan was being closely watched. Ambassador Muccio, in Seoul, urged Washington to ensure that Japan was not unduly prioritized over other states, like South Korea. Policymakers in Washington believed that if Japan received security assurances, it was likely that wartime allies would demand similar agreements. Throughout 1949 and early 1950, America's preference was to avoid new alliances but it slowly became clear that at a minimum, a new security pact with Japan would be necessary to maintain bases there after the peace treaty was signed. Because wartime allies would be angered if Japan—a former enemy—received a security guarantee and they did not, other pacts were also required as the price of securing regional support for a lenient peace treaty that did not prevent Japanese rearmament.

AUSTRALIAN, NEW ZEALAND, THE PHILIPPINES

Before the outbreak of the Korean War, Australia, the Philippines, and New Zealand were all concerned about the US security presence in Asia. Although it was often not expressed in the same terms as used by Korea or Japan, uncertainty about Washington's commitment to security in Asia alarmed these nations and raised questions about US reliability. Diplomatic reporting tied this feeling to the withdrawal from Korea and the China situation, thus supporting H1.

Uncertainty over Washington's reliability influenced these nations in several ways. First, they were extremely wary of concluding a lenient peace treaty: they felt this would raise the risk of a remilitarized and revisionist Japan. Beyond this, the primary impediment to a multilateral Pacific Pact was US unwillingness to provide early support: Australia in particular was afraid of becoming involved in something that might "prove futile and even disastrous" without US involvement.[130] As H2 expects, pessimistic assessments of Washington's security reliability led these three nations to adopt cautious policies and they were unwilling to countenance a lenient treaty or commit to security agreements unsupported by the United States. This changed when Washington decided to intervene on the Korean Peninsula: now confident of US reliability, these three countries were willing to support the US with military force.

As Dulles negotiated new alliances, he was aware of the need for a level of consistency across the agreements. As H3 predicts, the United States was aware that developments in its relationship with Japan would affect its relationships with Australia, the Philippines and New Zealand, and this possibility influenced US policy. Specifically, this interdependence led to a degree of consistency across the alliance commitments. The US administration knew that to offer Japan an alliance—but refuse such arrangements to wartime allies—would likely result in those allies refusing to support the peace treaty with Japan. But within the development of the Asian alliance system a strange dynamic was also at play: the alliance audience effect was a force for consistency across the alliance texts. Japan, as an occupied and defeated wartime enemy, was the exception: it received an informal security guarantee but ceded many rights to its American occupiers. But Washington believed that it had to treat other allies on a basis of equality, lest one become disgruntled and refuse to sign the peace treaty with Japan. A belief in interdependence led the US to simultaneously manage its alliance negotiations and ensure that no ally felt short-changed due to the more favorable treatment of another US ally.

In August and September 1951, three security agreements were signed in San Francisco. The first was the Mutual Defense Treaty between the United States and the Republic of the Philippines. The second was the ANZUS Security Treaty between Australia, New Zealand, and the United States of America. The third agreement was the US-Japan Security Treaty, which was signed shortly after the overall Japanese Peace Treaty that provided for a multilateral settlement of the Second World War.

On first glance, there may not seem to be a significant degree of interconnectivity between these relationships. However, this chapter has shown that as these security pacts were negotiated and agreed the alliance audience effect was clearly at work. Although other examinations of this period have stressed America's desire for control as the key determinant of the bilateral hub and spoke system, the need to maintain Washington's image as a reliable ally was an immense and pervasive influence on US policy. The road to this eventual outcome looks straightforward in hindsight, but Washington was not always viewed as a reliable security partner in Asia. Until it intervened in Korea, uncertainty over the US security posture in Northeast Asia was very influential: many states feared abandonment and doubted US reliability.

Washington's decision to defend South Korea resulted in several countries assessing the United States to be of greater security reliability. This not only supports H1 and H2 of the alliance audience effect framework but also challenges Mercer's expectation that a demonstration of loyalty does not generate expectations of future loyalty.[131] If allied beliefs about American reliability had not improved as a result of the decision to defend South Korea, Japan would not have bargained hard on basing rights, nor would Australia and New Zealand have placed less emphasis on obtaining a security guarantee than on gaining access to military planning.[132]

By highlighting the role of historical contingency, this chapter also challenges the narrative of Victor Cha's *Powerplay* account. Cha's argument is underpinned by the assumption that the United States *chose* to develop a network of bilateral alliances in Asia, but the reverse chronological order in which he examines his three case studies doesn't adequately recognize the degree to which Washington's policies were shaped by the preferences and actions of regional countries.[133] The bilateral alliance with Japan was an important priority: it was required to place the US military presence on a stable footing. But given fears of a resurgent Japan, lack of common interest between regional countries, a desire to avoid conspicuously excluding nonallies, and the need to secure the agreement of wartime allies to the San Francisco peace treaty, it is hard to conceive of how an alternate alliance structure might have evolved at this time. Contrary to Cha's argument, Washington did not "set out to design a security architecture for Asia that contained the communist threat but also managed the risks associated with these newfound commitments."[134] Instead, historical circumstance—and interdependence between seemingly discrete security relationships—best explain the development of the hub and spoke alliance system.[135]

In September 1951, as alliances with Japan, the Philippines, Australia, and New Zealand were signed, this system was still incomplete. In the next chapter, I examine the formation of alliances with the republics of Korea and China, and also consider how America's alliances coped with the opening stages of a significant security challenge: the First Taiwan Strait Crisis.

Unleashing and Releashing Chiang Kai-shek, 1953–1954

> What preoccupied him, continued Secretary Dulles, was to avoid getting the United States into a war which the whole world would believe we were wrong to be in . . . a major war where world public opinion would be wholly against the United States . . . was the kind of war you lose.

Although hostilities in the Korean War ceased after a mid-1953 armistice, America's alliance posture in Asia continued to evolve.[1] Syngman Rhee, president of the ROK, wanted to restart the war and unify the two Koreas, but the United States worked toward ending the conflict. In order to reassure Rhee, President Dwight Eisenhower publicly promised a mutual security pact if Rhee would agree to a ceasefire and refrain from trying to reunite Korea by force.

The ROC closely observed interactions between the US and the ROK, and Taipei learned—through Washington's treatment of Seoul—that the US would not enter into an alliance if it posed unacceptable entrapment risks. Once the US-ROK alliance was realized, it set the benchmark and precedent for an alliance with the Chinese Nationalists. Although the US was initially concerned about the possibility of being trapped into conflict with Communist China, Taipei demonstrated its willingness to subordinate its interests to those of the US, and this bolstered Taipei's case for a security pact. This alliance, signed in December 1954, completed the hub and spoke system, which persisted in that form until the same alliance ended in 1980.

Throughout 1953 and 1954, tensions also slowly escalated across the Taiwan Strait. Both Communist and Nationalist China were focused on small "offshore islands," like Quemoy and Matsu, not for their strategic value but symbolic significance.[2] For the ROC, which still stationed troops on the islands, they represented a path to reconquering the mainland. For the PRC, they were stepping stones to finally subduing the Chinese Nationalists and

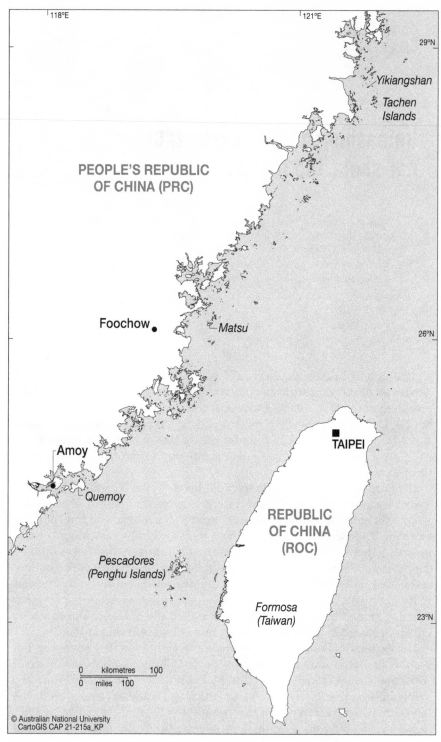

Figure 3. Map of the Taiwan Strait area. Produced by CartoGIS Services, College of Asia and the Pacific, the Australian National University.

unifying China under Communist rule. Occasional military clashes over the islands suited the interest of both the PRC and ROC as they continued the civil war, and also served as an argument against the concept of "two Chinas" existing simultaneously in the international system. Though the United States reversed its earlier policy and decided, in early 1953, that it would no longer restrain the Chinese Nationalists from attacking the mainland, it was unclear whether it would fight alongside the ROC to defend these islands.

In September 1954, tensions across the Taiwan Strait escalated and threatened to erupt in war. Thus, Washington's alliance negotiations with the ROC occurred during a time of security crisis. As expected by the alliance audience effect theory, other allies such as the United Kingdom, Australia, and New Zealand closely observed developments in the US-ROK and US-ROC relationships. These developments influenced their beliefs about American reliability and resulted in changes to their alliance behavior. Most US allies, fearful that a conflict with Communist China could lead to general war with the entire Communist bloc, tried to restrain Washington and encourage a diplomatic settlement. Only President Rhee welcomed the prospect of conflict across the Taiwan Strait, as escalation there aligned with his desire to restart the Korean War. Furthermore, as the historical analysis shows, the need to consider allied preferences was a very strong influence on US policy, and was a key component of the many debates at NSC meetings. Because the superiority of American military capabilities over the PRC was not in doubt, this chapter focuses on how states observed Washington's behavior in order to update their assessments of US interests and reliability.

This chapter contains three sections. The first section covers the period from January 1953 to August 1954 and demonstrates how the ROC was influenced by its observations of the US-ROK relationship. As the US negotiated an end to the Korean War and an alliance with Seoul, the ROC closely watched these developments and was influenced by Washington's approach to South Korea. The second section, covering September to December 1954, examines the first few months of the first Taiwan Strait Crisis and the negotiation of the US-ROC Mutual Defense Treaty. The final section assesses the alliance audience effect framework against the empirical evidence. The remainder of the first Taiwan Strait Crisis (i.e., January to April 1955) is considered in the next chapter. These two chapters provide a complete account of how the alliance audience effect manifested ahead of, and during, the first Taiwan Strait Crisis.

Readers might be surprised by this chapter's analysis of the United Kingdom's alliance fears. While the UK is not part of the Asian alliance system today, in the 1950s the UK still had a substantial military presence in Asia (in Malaya and Hong Kong), and was a founding member of SEATO. Accordingly, the alliance politics of the US-UK relationship is analyzed alongside that of local allies.[3]

January 1953 to August 1954

THE UNLEASHING OF CHIANG KAI-SHEK
CREATES ENTRAPMENT DILEMMAS

In his first State of the Union address on February 2, 1953, President Eisenhower announced that he was rescinding part of President Harry Truman's orders to the US Navy's Seventh Fleet. Denouncing Beijing's unwillingness to agree to a ceasefire in Korea, Eisenhower announced that the US Navy would "no longer be employed to shield Communist China," because Washington had "no obligation to protect a nation fighting us in Korea."[4] The press described this as Eisenhower's "unleashing" of Chiang Kai-shek, the president of the ROC, as he was now free to attack Chinese Communist forces on the mainland.[5]

Eisenhower's announcement was not warmly welcomed by most US allies. "The fact that this [decision] would almost certainly necessitate American intervention produced an international outcry against the policy. U.S. allies, especially in Europe, objected strongly to what they believed to be unwarranted risktaking."[6] The State Department noted that the British were "not prepared to be drawn into a third World War merely to fulfill Chiang Kai-shek's squalid ambitions," while the prime minister of New Zealand "expressed the hope that the decision will not . . . increase the danger of another world war."[7]

In March 1953, the ROC's ambassador to the US, Wellington Koo, met with the new secretary of state, John Foster Dulles. Following Eisenhower's speech, Koo enquired "whether the present would be an opportune time for the Chinese Government to formally propose" a mutual security pact. Koo noted that the United States had recently formed alliances with "Australia, New Zealand and the Philippines as well as with Japan and expressed the opinion that these should be rounded out by the conclusion of a pact with the Government on Formosa."[8] Having seen America formalize its security commitment to these nations, it is unsurprising the ROC worried about its exclusion and sought a similar arrangement.

But Dulles drew a distinction between these pacts and the possibility of similar alliances with both South Korea and Nationalist China. While the United States was "sympathetic to the general proposition of creating security arrangements in the Pacific," ongoing conflict made this difficult. "The Secretary said that the United States would not want to make a treaty which would result in a commitment for the United States to go to war on the mainland of Asia," but treaties with South Korea or Nationalist China would pose such risks. Additionally, Dulles noted that if Washington concluded a treaty with Taipei then this would create pressure for a similar agreement with Seoul, which "had long been urging the conclusion of some form of mutual security pact."[9]

While the Seventh Fleet was no longer tasked with restraining the Chinese Nationalists, it was still defending Formosa against the Communists. Divergent interests between the US and ROC would soon become a dilemma for Washington. Chiang Kai-shek, who desired the defeat of the Communists on the Chinese mainland, would likely be discouraged by the conclusion of an armistice in Korea. The deputy undersecretary of state noted that Chiang "wants to broaden the conflict, not end it," as a general US-China war offered the ROC the best opportunity to restart and win the Chinese civil war. When the United States delivered, as part of its military assistance program, F-84 aircraft to the ROC, the State Department was concerned that Chiang might "undertake some adventures . . . either with or without a deliberate intention of involving the US in a broader war with Communist China."[10] As a result of these fears, modified orders were sent to the commander-in-chief of US forces in the Pacific, Admiral Arthur Radford. His instructions were to defend Formosa and the Pescadore Islands, but he was not permitted to strike targets on the Chinese mainland without prior approval from the JCS. Furthermore, unless the Communists simultaneously attacked Formosa or the Pescadores, Radford was not permitted to defend the offshore islands held by the Chinese Nationalists.[11]

These entrapment risks were considered at an NSC meeting on April 8, 1953, as the council discussed delivery of the F-84 aircraft. Dulles argued that Washington needed "to secure very quickly a commitment from Chiang Kai-shek that he would not use these aircraft recklessly and in a fashion to embarrass United States policy."[12] The Nationalist Chinese, unlike the Koreans, proved quite willing to acknowledge America's concerns and adjust their expectations accordingly. The Chinese foreign minister, George Yeh, emphatically assured the US ambassador to the ROC, Karl Rankin, that Taipei "would under no circumstances initiate operations which it considered might harm US interests whether political or military, national or international." Noting that their opinions might differ on certain actions, Yeh even sought to eliminate whatever wiggle room might have remained and requested "clarification re[garding] practical methods of determining what operations US would consider inimical to its best interests."[13] Through these messages, Nationalist China was trying to showcase its credentials as a reliable ally: though it had its own preferences, it was signaling its willingness to hew closely to US desires regarding operations that might prompt conflict with Communist China. The reply from Washington was that the Nationalists should consult prior to conducting "any operations which would radically alter the pattern or tempo of current operations of the Chinese armed forces, including specifically any offensive use of aircraft."[14]

NATIONALIST CHINA OBSERVES AMERICA'S
TREATMENT OF SOUTH KOREA

As armistice talks in Korea progressed, Eisenhower wrote to President Rhee that he was willing to conclude a mutual security treaty, but only under certain conditions. This letter, which was published in the publicly available *State Department Bulletin*, proclaimed that the United States did "not intend to employ war as an instrument to accomplish . . . political settlements" and implored Rhee to not pursue forceful reunification. It outlined Eisenhower's willingness to negotiate an alliance with Seoul, but noted that it would apply only to "territory now or hereafter brought peacefully under the administration of the ROK."[15]

On October 1, 1953, the Mutual Defense Treaty between the Republic of Korea and the United States was signed. The treaty clearly served as both a security guarantee and a pact of restraint. Rhee tried, on a number of occasions, to secure an agreement that might allow him to restart hostilities with North Korea, but President Eisenhower was clearly skeptical of Rhee's intentions and, in November 1953, sent Vice President Richard Nixon to Seoul. Nixon's ultimatum was that if Rhee did not write to Eisenhower, pledging to refrain from hostile action, then the treaty would not be submitted to Congress for ratification. Through the treaty text and efforts like Nixon's visit, the United States mitigated the entrapment risks posed by President Rhee's desire for reunification.[16]

Throughout this period, the Chinese Nationalists observed Washington's treatment of Seoul and were unnerved by the possibility that the US might not guarantee the ROK's security after an armistice. President Chiang wrote to Eisenhower on June 7, 1953, urging him to give "emphatic assurance to the anti-Communist countries in Asia, more especially those that are under the direct menace of Soviet Russia and Communist China, namely, the Republic of Korea, the Republic of China, Thailand and Indo-China."[17] Later in June Chiang wrote to Eisenhower a second time, again expressing his concern about the consequences of an armistice unaccompanied by a US-ROK alliance. He urged Eisenhower to conclude a mutual security pact with Seoul before the agreement of any armistice, so as to reassure Korea and the other non-Communist nations in Asia.[18]

Dulles interpreted Chiang's letters as an "apparent backing" of Rhee's intransigent approach. He instructed Ambassador Rankin to urgently brief Chiang "that Rhee's attempt to force US troops to fight indefinitely in Korea . . . will not succeed. Plans are being formulated so that if Rhee persists responsibility for Korea will be left wholly to ROK forces. . . . We believe this will be disastrous for Korea but see no alternative to Rhee's absolute refusal to accept [the] armistice."[19] Eisenhower also replied to Chiang's letters. Noting "that there cannot be leadership of those who may be determined to go their separate ways," Eisenhower also drew Chiang's attention to his willingness to conclude a treaty with South Korea.[20] In a meeting with Ambassador Koo, Dulles explained the US position and noted "danger to the whole anti-Communist position in the East if Rhee should force a break with the United States."[21] Dulles also wrote to Chiang, noting that "free world unity is a fundamental necessity in the face of the aggressive Communist threat. . . . Unity and common purpose, however, must inevitably imply certain sacrifices and certain limitations on freedom of action on the part of all partners in a common effort."[22]

Dulles and Eisenhower explained their actions within the US-ROK relationship to the ROC: while they did not want to abandon Rhee, they threatened to do so if he was unwilling to abandon his desire to reunify Korea by force. This message was blunt and unambiguous: American objectives in Asia could not be determined by the preferences of local allies. Dulles had been clear with Rhee, writing him that "the principle of unity cannot work without sacrifice. No one can do precisely what he wants. . . . Because the fighting has not given you all that you had hoped, you seem to be on the verge of wrecking allied unity . . . [this] would mean a horrible disaster."[23] Dulles tasked Ambassador Rankin with conveying a blunt and ominous message to Chiang: if Rhee refused to accept an armistice, the "possible US withdrawal from Korea would doubtless require reconsideration of US-Formosa policy with result not now predictable."[24] Robert Accinelli has noted that "the tenor of Dulles' message, with its dire intimation of a withdrawal of support from the Nationalists . . . [was] an implied threat to remind Chiang that the United States would brook no mischievous interference from him."[25] Rankin, in Taipei, wrote that Chiang correctly interpreted Dulles's message as a "thinly veiled threat."[26]

Dulles wanted to leave no doubt in Chiang's mind: if Korea did not accept America's conditions, it would not receive a security guarantee. Dulles's actions suggest he believed that an alliance audience effect existed and could be used to America's benefit: adopting a strong position with Rhee would deliver a warning shot across Chiang Kai-shek's bow and demonstrate what behavior Washington would not tolerate. In a similar vein, other Americans worried about what conclusions Japan might draw from its observations of the US-ROK relationship. Later in 1953, as Rhee threatened to restart the war in Korea, the US ambassador to Japan warned Dulles that Tokyo was "closely watching US-Korean relations." The ambassador was concerned that if Washington let Rhee go on "writing his own ticket," it would have an undesired effect on Japan. "If Rhee appears to be gaining his ends by continued intransigence, Japanese Government will undoubtedly apply [this] lesson in their own reaction to American desiderata in Japan."[27] US officials were aware that other allies were watching relations between Washington and Seoul, and this influenced their thinking and actions: if Korea got its way through obstinacy and coercion, other allies might attempt to replicate the success. The United States had to be sure that it was managing—rather than being manipulated by—alliance interdependence. Because this interdependence was governed by assessments of reliability, rather than loyalty, Washington was able to carefully manage its relationship with Seoul and set the example for emulation by Taipei.

Although Dulles worried about the possibility of the ROC mischievously interfering with US-ROK relations, it seems his fears were misplaced. In July, Ambassador Rankin reported that President Chiang "evidently was hurt and annoyed by what seemed to him a threat to withdraw support from Formosa because of his supposed backing of Rhee, when actually he had not supported or even been in touch with Rhee" on this issue.[28] In fact, on other occasions, Chiang cautioned Rhee to "seek agreement as soon as possible . . . do everything possible to avoid a break in the negotiations between Korea and the United States." In Rankin's words, the Nationalists assured the United States that "no action which they took had been inspired by Rhee."[29]

Chiang Kai-shek nursed his wounded pride, but it appeared to escape State Department notice until late December 1953. It was only in January 1954 that Dulles reached out to Chiang, writing that he was unaware of Chiang's efforts to encourage restraint and cooperation on Rhee's part. Dulles noted that he "had not known of this and we greatly appreciate what you did. We highly value your friendship and I am personally grateful for the cooperation you have shown in meeting our common problems."[30] Chiang was clearly anxious that neither he nor Nationalist China be associated with Seoul's intransigent approach. This distinction was appreciated by US officials: the assistant secretary of state for East Asian affairs, Walter Robertson, later recalled, "Never . . . did the Chinese ever threaten, at any time, that they would take offensive action against the mainland, except in consultation with us. Now, the exact opposite was true with our friend Syngman Rhee."[31]

Within the US-ROK relationship, the United States had set an example for other allies and the ROC had observed and processed an important lesson: Washington would not enter into an alliance with a state fighting a civil war unless the entrapment risks could be adequately mitigated.

THE UNITED STATES CONSIDERS ITS POLICY
ON THE OFFSHORE ISLANDS

By July 1953, the Central Intelligence Agency (CIA) was warning of a Chinese Communist threat to the offshore islands. Allen Dulles, the Director of Central Intelligence, noted that several smaller islands had been captured by the Chinese Communists and there was an "obvious danger" that the Communists might attack the larger offshore islands, such as the Tachen Island group.[32] The JCS acknowledged that although "there were important political and other considerations involved," they assessed that "from a strictly military standpoint the islands could not be considered essential to the defense of Formosa."[33] For Dulles, Eisenhower, and others, the importance of the islands was not their military value but their psychological value to the Chinese Nationalists. It was believed that if these islands fell, Chiang's dream of returning to the mainland and toppling the Communist government would be destroyed. If this occurred, morale on Formosa would be so damaged as to risk its loss to the PRC through subversion.

Even though the US-ROC security pact would not be signed until December 1954, one US ally was already concerned about America's security commitment to Formosa. As the Chinese Communist threat to the Tachen Islands increased, British diplomats in Washington enquired as to "whether the 7th Fleet was now charged with the protection of the Nationalist-held [offshore] islands."[34] This early inquiry highlights the divergent interests that would influence US alliance relationships over the next two years. NSC 166/1, a classified statement of US policy toward Communist China, assessed "that the Free World will not act as a unit toward Communist China." While some allies, like the ROC and ROK, worried about "any accommodation with Communist China," other allies, like Japan, desired "a *modus vivendi* . . . which will leave internal and external security unimpaired." The document concluded by noting that "U.S. policy toward China must take account of the welter of variant, opposing and emotionally supported views which are held . . . it obviously cannot please everybody. But the United States can avoid the most dangerously divisive potentials of the Chinese Communist issue, by refraining from excessive pressure on its friends to follow American policies with respect to Communist China."[35]

NSC 146/2, concerning US objectives for Nationalist China, endorsed the incorporation of "Formosa and the Pescadores within U.S. Far East defense positions." However, this defensive guarantee did not extend to the offshore islands: the United States would "encourage and assist the Chinese National Government to defend the . . . off-shore islands," but would not defend them unless Formosa itself was attacked.[36] This strategy acknowledged the importance of keeping Formosa and the Pescadores out of Communist hands, and downplayed the importance of the offshore islands. But as Garver writes, "The Nationalist objective, however, was nothing less than the destruction of the Communist regime. . . . Out of this divergence of objectives arose troublesome dilemmas."[37]

America's policy recognized that while many US allies considered Formosa to be important to regional defense, few would welcome the outbreak of hostilities over the offshore islands. If this occurred, it was possible that these allies would not provide the United States with military support. Others were worried about a diversion of US attention: NSC 146/2 noted that "Important Southeast Asian opinion . . . fears that Nationalist operations might develop into general war in the Far East which might envelop Southeast Asia. Japan . . . has been apprehensive lest U.S. support to the Nationalists result in a serious reduction of U.S. strength available to defend Japan."[38]

THE ROC TRIES AGAIN FOR AN ALLIANCE

In mid-November, Ambassador Rankin reported on renewed Chinese Nationalist calls for an alliance "along [the] lines of those signed with Philippines, Japan and Korea." Such a pact would have "considerable political significance" and "grievance that security pact given to ex-enemy Japan and withheld from ally China would be removed."[39] Though Chiang still expressed, at this time, a hope of retaking the Chinese mainland by armed force, he was "careful to point out . . . [that] United States policy will determine whether such an operation is to be made possible."[40] As Townsend Hoopes writes, "With the end of the Korean War and the conclusion of the US security treaty with South Korea . . . Chiang began a sustained effort to obtain comparable treatment."[41] In their meetings and communications with US officials, Nationalist Chinese leaders emphasized their reliability by noting that they would not act in any way that endangered US interests.

Over the course of 1953, Chiang had observed US-Korea interactions and distanced the ROC from Seoul's intransigence. Now, Taipei began a renewed push for its own bilateral alliance. On December 19, 1953, Foreign Minister Yeh handed Ambassador Rankin a draft alliance treaty, noting that it was "based on [the] ANZUS, Philippine and Korean pacts" and that the "Chinese Government would welcome U.S. comments on [the] draft."[42] Yeh wrote to Vice President Nixon, noting that "if the United States could afford to conclude a pact with Korea, she could equally well, if not better, afford to conclude one with Free China along similar lines."[43] In late February 1954, Yeh again pressed the US embassy on the possibility of a mutual security pact. In doing so, he noted the conclusion of security pacts with Australia, New Zealand, the Philippines, and Korea, arguing that it was "difficult for Chinese to understand omission of their country where so much military aid already invested."[44] The State Department supported the proposed pact, provided it contained "safeguards against [the] involuntary extension of . . . commitments as to the defense of Formosa and the Pescadores."[45]

With intelligence assessments continuing to warn of a Communist threat to the offshore islands, Ambassador Rankin was concerned by a policy contradiction: the United States was protecting the Chinese Nationalists on Formosa but the Nationalists were free to conduct attacks against the mainland. The US was effectively creating a privileged sanctuary for Nationalist forces so they could attack the mainland. It had also been decided that the Military Advisory and Assistance Group on Formosa would be responsible for providing logistical support to Nationalist troops on the offshore islands. For Rankin, this policy posed a significant risk of escalation: it was "Uncle Sam tickling the Communist tiger with a feather duster."[46] In April, he pushed for greater clarity: noting that the islands "lie outside our announced defense perimeter," he asked the State Department whether the US was prepared to defend them or would it stand aside and "risk their loss in the near future, with consequent damage to the defenses of Formosa and serious loss of face?" Rankin acknowledged that the offshore islands might seem to have only minor importance, but he emphasized that "we in Formosa regard them as having considerable significance for good or ill."[47]

This theme would pervade American considerations of Formosa throughout 1954 and 1955: the offshore islands, while not particularly important from a purely military perspective, were seen as vital to maintaining Chinese Nationalist morale. For their part, the Nationalists also became more concerned about the possibility of a Communist attack on the offshore islands. Through Rankin, they requested a "public statement to [the] effect 'Seventh Fleet is continuing and strengthening its patrols and surveillance of waters surrounding [the offshore] islands.'"[48]

In May 1954, China's ambassador to the United States, Wellington Koo, again raised the issue of a security pact with Secretary Dulles. Noting that it was "not a simple matter to negotiate a security pact with a country which is actually carrying on military operations," Dulles informed Koo that Washington "is not prepared to assume treaty obligations . . . which might bring about its direct involvement." Dulles explained his reluctance by referring to the US-ROK pact, again noting that it served a dual function: a guarantee of Korean security but also the restraint of President Rhee. While Koo suggested that the defensive purpose of a pact between Nationalist China and the United States could be made clear through careful language, Dulles was "doubtful whether this could readily be done." Dulles said that the US did "not want to commit our military resources or prestige in the vast area of mainland China" but it did want "the Chinese [Nationalist] Government to have the ability to exercise initiative against the Chinese Communists." This "initiative" could not occur if the two sides concluded a mutual defense treaty along the lines of the US-ROK pact.[49]

In an effort to leave open the possibility of a treaty at a later date, Koo asked: "Might an altered situation make the prospect for a mutual security treaty more favorable?" Dulles concurred "that this might be the case" and it was agreed that the issue of a pact remained "under study."[50] Despite Dulles's attempts to downplay and forestall the prospects of a treaty, the matter was not yet settled. Nancy Bernkopf Tucker suggests that Dulles's hesitance can be attributed to the possible "negative effects on Washington's more important relations in Europe," as allies there would be displeased by a US-ROC treaty and the consequent increased risk of conflict.[51]

A few days later, on May 22, the issue of Formosa and the offshore islands was discussed by the president, Dulles, and other senior officials. Intelligence advice suggested that the Chinese Communists might launch an attack against the Tachen Island group, which "could not be held by the Chi-Nat forces without US air power." Eisenhower felt that any public statement committing the United States to the defense of the offshore islands would be "too big a commitment of US prestige and forces. It was agreed that no such public statement should be made." However, Eisenhower decided that the Seventh Fleet would "visit" the Tachen Island group and that such a "show of US strength would make our position clear."[52]

US ALLIES WARY OF RISKS AS CHIANG HINTS AT HIS WILLINGNESS TO BE RELEASED

In May, Chiang Kai-shek lobbied American officials visiting Taipei for a mutual security pact. He expressed "great disappointment and disillusionment over . . . [the] present US position."[53] He was "not asking the U.S. to fight with us in our recovery of the mainland. . . . We shall never take any unwarranted action by ourselves." He closed by emphasizing that Nationalist China had "never once . . . betrayed the United States."[54] During a conversation with Foreign Minister Yeh on June 17, Rankin asked whether the ROC would be willing to give the US a "further commitment . . . not to initiate major military action independently," as opposed to the status quo arrangement of "prior consultation." Yeh said that Chiang "preferred to discuss this point only after the conclusion of a bilateral treaty was substantially assured." Rankin, for his part, was "confident . . . that guarantees could be obtained on this point."[55]

The ROC policy shift was incremental, but significant. Having been rebuffed by Dulles, who explicitly expressed his concerns about a US-ROC pact with reference to the entrapment risks, the ROC modified its position. It was willing to go beyond the status quo of prior consultation before any attack. In order to secure an alliance, Taipei was essentially willing to subordinate its goals and freedom of action to the US strategic interest. On July 8, President Chiang formalized his position in a message to Eisenhower and Dulles. He pledged that if a security pact was concluded, he would "be prepared to expand its consultative commitments. He would seek the prior agreement of the United States before undertaking any important military action."[56] This movement—from prior consultation to prior *agreement*—was a strong signal of how important a security pact was to Taipei. Having observed the US grant the ROK a pact once entrapment risks were mitigated, the ROC moved to demonstrate its reliability to the US. One official in the Far East division wrote that in exchange for an alliance, Chiang seemed "to be offering a secret commitment not to engage in any offensive operations against the advice of the United States."[57]

The British had worried earlier about the offshore islands but new events highlighted Tokyo's concerns. In July 1954 Chinese Communist forces shot down a commercial passenger aircraft, and while US forces were conducting search and rescue operations they were attacked by Communist aircraft: two of the attackers were shot down by American planes. These developments, combined with the activities of the Seventh Fleet, caused consternation in Tokyo. The US ambassador to Japan, John Allison, cabled Dulles, noting that recent US actions had "resulted to date only in alarming our friends . . . and obscuring what I believe is your firm long-term policy for the Far East." Addressing the issue of the Seventh Fleet visiting the offshore islands, Allison wondered "if full implications of this action have been weighed by all competent US authorities. Repercussions if anything goes wrong could be most serious. Japanese Government and people could be thrown into panic which only advance preparation could mitigate."[58]

Allison complained that he had "no authority to explain purpose and to warn appropriate high Japanese officials so they can take necessary steps to reassure public should it be necessary." For Allison, this was a vital issue given the "almost unanimous Japanese belief that our shooting down Chinese Communist planes off Hainan was deliberate act of provocation."[59] Seen from Tokyo, US military actions near the offshore islands damaged Washington's security reliability. According to Allison's cables, Japanese policymakers and the public at large were very concerned about the possibility of these actions precipitating a general war with Communist China. Allison was not alone in his concern: the previous month, an official in the Far East division had assessed that Washington's allies worried "that the US, in an excess of anti-communist zeal, may launch a military crusade against communism and bring on World War III."[60]

This issue of allied concern featured prominently in an August NSC meeting, where Dulles explained that his main preoccupation was "to avoid getting the United States into a war which the whole world would believe we were wrong to be in." While this did not mean "that we should run away from anything or everything that might involve us in war with Communist China," he concluded that a "major war where world public opinion would be wholly against the United States . . . was the kind of war you lose." The conversation then turned to the issue of Formosa's offshore islands. Eisenhower "commented that he had imagined that these islands were vital outposts for the defense of Formosa, and that we should go as far as possible to defend them without inflaming world opinion against us."[61] Dulles also expressed concern that because a defense of the offshore islands would risk war with Communist China, it would require congressional approval. The NSC meeting concluded without a firm decision on policy toward the islands, but Eisenhower's own words highlight that he regarded allied opinion as an important influence on US policy.

However, for State Department officials in Washington, it seems that the need to consider Japan's opinion was paramount only in the event of actual conflict. Allison's concerns were dismissed by the assistant secretary for Far Eastern affairs, Walter Robertson. In a memo to Dulles, Robertson noted that planning for the Seventh Fleet's movements was "highly classified, and it would be a breach of security, as well as unnecessary, to notify the Japanese Government in advance."[62] Dulles wrote to Allison, "I do not think that the Japanese need be alarmed because I do not believe that the Chinese

Communists are in fact now prepared to challenge us in any major or sustained way."[63] The reaction of Dulles and Robertson was typical of Washington decision makers at this time: Allison later lamented that "there was little to show that Washington read our messages very carefully," and that many officials there were intent on making "Japan into a forward bastion of American strategic strength with the Americans calling the tune and the Japanese meekly accepting their secondary role."[64] Allison's concerns were dismissed by Dulles and Robertson, but events would soon prove that Tokyo's apprehensions were well founded.

In late August the Far East division recommended to Dulles that he authorize the negotiation of a US-ROC alliance, with several factors influencing the timing of this decision. First, Robertson noted that the Chinese Communists had recently "launched a violent propaganda campaign promising to 'liberate' Formosa." Second, Chiang had signaled his willingness to seek US permission before he conducted any offensive action, and this would "provide us with greater control than we now enjoy over the circumstances under which our armed forces might become involved in a major conflict." Third, it was noted that because the Manila Pact—which underpinned SEATO—would not include the ROC, this "heightened its desire for treaty ties with the U.S. and its sense of being discriminated against."[65]

Robertson's memo noted the "desirability of keeping the Communists guessing as to our intention respecting defense of the off-shore islands" but suggested this could be preserved by announcing that "a number of these islands may be so intimately connected with the defense of Formosa that the military would be justified in concluding that the defense of Formosa comprehended the defense of those Islands."[66] Before Dulles departed on a visit to the Philippines and Formosa, he recognized "the probability that it will be necessary for us ultimately to negotiate a Mutual Defense Treaty with the GRC [government of the Republic of China] but would prefer to delay decision as to timing because of the complexities of the offshore island problem."[67]

September to December 1954

COMMUNIST CHINA ATTACKS QUEMOY, PROMPTING A RETHINK OF AMERICAN POLICY

On September 3, 1954, the PRC commenced a heavy artillery attack against the island of Quemoy. US leaders immediately considered their response to an attempted invasion of the island. In a message to the president, the acting secretary of defense noted that the JCS were split as to whether Quemoy was of significant importance to the defense of Formosa. The "majority opinion" was that the islands "are important but not essential to the defense of Formosa from a military standpoint." But there was concern about the "psychological effects on the Chinese Nationalist troops and other Asiatic countries inclined to support U.S. policy" if Quemoy was lost.[68]

Though Quemoy was not strategically vital, Gaddis writes that the "psychological effects could not be disregarded."[69] Dulles thought the "loss of Quemoy would have grave psychological repercussions and lead to mounting Communist action . . . which could gravely jeopardize [our] entire offshore position." He thought that the United States should help "hold Quemoy if it is judged defensible with our aid," even though this "committal of US force and prestige might lead to constantly expanding US operations against [the] mainland."[70] Despite his earlier reluctance to pursue a security pact with the ROC due to the fear of entrapment, Dulles's initial response was to stand firm. The Far East division in the State Department argued that if the Chinese Communists attempted to capture one of the offshore islands, the attack "should be met with a positive though limited U.S. military response" that avoided "a U.S. commitment to hold or retake any island."[71] Thus, Washington tried to balance two conflicting goals: prevent the loss of the islands but limit US involvement.

A Special National Intelligence Estimate was provided to senior decision makers on September 4. Noting that the "Chinese Communists will be increasingly willing to undertake probing actions designed to test US intentions," the assessment warned that a US guarantee of the islands would be perceived in different ways by different allies. It "would be considered ill-advised and provocative by the UK" and would "cause uneasiness in Japan, which would fear that it increased the likelihood of war." However, in contrast, a "US guarantee would encourage the governments of the ROK, the Philippines, and Thailand."

This document challenged the domino theory logic which would soon come to dominate US policymaking. It assessed that if the United States did not guarantee the defense of the islands and if they then fell to the Chinese Communists, the primary effect would be limited to Taiwanese morale. "Korea would express great concern at the turn of events," but other allies such as "Japan, the UK and Western Europe would be generally relieved that no crisis had developed. Southeast Asian governments, including that of the Philippines, would not place great importance on the loss of the islands." However, if the United States did guarantee the defense of the islands but then stood aside if they were attacked, the estimate predicted a far greater impact: "US prestige throughout the Far East would suffer a serious blow. Japan would probably reappraise its US alignment, and non-Communist states in Southeast Asia would question seriously the willingness and ability of the US to back up defense commitments in that area."[72]

As expected by the alliance audience effect, different allies perceived US policy in different ways. When the Korean War broke out, Nationalist China viewed it as an opportunity to further its own security: if hostilities widened, then the resulting "third world war could be the salvation" of Nationalist

China.[73] Dulles even went so far as to say that Chiang had a "vested interest in World War III."[74] The same logic could be now applied to a possible conflict across the Taiwan Strait. If Washington went to the defense of Taipei, then escalating hostilities could be an opportunity to restart the Korean War (with or without Washington's approval). It is thus unsurprising that Seoul lamented US caution and encouraged Washington to regard Quemoy as having wider importance. In a meeting with the US ambassador in Seoul, the Korean prime minister urged President Eisenhower to remember that "in this part of [the] world Quemoy can be [a] symbol, [the] loss of which . . . would have serious repercussions in Asia." The ambassador assessed that the "foregoing views are undoubtedly those of President Rhee *also*."[75]

President Eisenhower intuitively grasped that other countries would closely observe America's conduct: "If we go in, our prestige is at stake. We should not go in unless we can defend it." Eisenhower's "hunch" was "that once we get tied up in any one of these things our prestige is so completely involved."[76] He was particularly concerned about the possibility of military action causing a split with the United Kingdom and he considered cabling Prime Minister Winston Churchill to ask him for his views. However, it was decided that the United States should first decide its own position on the matter.[77]

While returning from the Philippines, Dulles stopped over in Taipei for discussions with President Chiang Kai-shek. Chiang lamented America's lack of a "firm policy for Asia and reluctance to give free China [a] treaty similar to those extended [to] other countries." Though he affirmed his belief that Nationalist forces could eventually recapture mainland China, he again repeated his intent to not engage in aggressive actions without prior US approval.[78] Even in the face of Communist aggression against Quemoy, Chiang continued to signal that the ROC would be a reliable and compliant ally.

When the NSC met again on September 9, the JCS remained divided on the importance of the offshore islands: most members now regarded "retention of the off-shore islands as of very great importance" and recommended US forces be committed to their defense, but without any public announcement. But the NSC also agreed that a defense of the islands would involve striking targets on the Chinese mainland. Opinion was also split as to what policy Washington should adopt. The State Department argued that if the islands were defensible, the US should defend them. The secretary of defense, Charles Wilson, argued that there was "a great deal of difference between Formosa and the Pescadores, on the one hand, and these close-in islands, on the other." Wilson believed that it "would be extremely difficult to explain, either to the people of the United States or to our allies, why, after refusing to go to war with Communist China over Korea and Indochina, we were perfectly willing to fight over these small islands." Vice President Nixon wondered whether the United States could commit not to the defense of the islands but instead to their evacuation. Would the country suffer a significant loss of prestige? Allen Dulles said that US prestige "would suffer much less if we completely evacuated the islands . . . as opposed to a simple abandonment" of the islands. But there was disagreement as to what effect this would have on Chinese Nationalist morale—Allen Dulles thought it would have little impact, but Admiral Radford thought it could precipitate a collapse of Nationalist morale and result in the defection of Formosa to the Communists.[79]

Policy confusion persisted for the next few days. There were three options: guarantee and defend the islands, maintain an ambiguous policy, or encourage a Nationalist withdrawal. On September 12, Dulles bluntly wrote that "Quemoy cannot be held *indefinitely* without a general war with Red China." He noted that a commitment to defend Quemoy "would alienate world opinion and gravely strain our alliances, both in Europe and with ANZUS. This is the more true because it would probably lead to our initiating the use of atomic weapons."[80] When the NSC met that day, Dulles briefed the meeting on his recent talks with Chiang Kai-shek, noting that Chiang had again emphasized his willingness to use military force only after US approval. This remarkable restraint was well proven by the fact that "before retaliating for the artillery shelling of Quemoy," Nationalist forces had waited four days "in order to get U.S. approval."[81]

Eisenhower believed that the "Quemoy was not really important except psychologically" and he was "personally against making too many promises to hold areas around the world and then having to stay there to defend them. In each crisis we should be able to consider what was in the best interests of the U.S. at that time. . . . If we get our prestige involved anywhere then we can't get out." He clearly felt the gravity of the situation and of his decision: he remarked that "the Council must get one thing clear in their heads, and that is that they are talking about war." After affirming that the defense of Quemoy would require congressional approval, Eisenhower "reiterated that the islands were only important psychologically."[82]

Dulles equivocated: "An overwhelming case can be made on either side." He felt that "a powerful case can be made that . . . a Chinese Nationalist retreat from the islands would have disastrous consequences in Korea, Japan, Formosa and the Philippines." However, the "other side was that to go to the defense of the offshore islands . . . would involve us in war with Communist China. Outside of Rhee and Chiang, the rest of the world would condemn us." It was against this backdrop that Dulles suggested an approach to the United Nations Security Council (UNSC), with the aim of achieving a ceasefire. If such a measure was vetoed by the Soviet Union, he believed this would increase allied support for the defense of Quemoy, and thus the plan "offered the possibility of avoiding going to war alone." The NSC acknowledged that this approach would entail certain risks and disadvantages, but the meeting concluded with broad support for Dulles's plan.[83]

US ALLIES MITIGATE THE RISKS OF AMERICA'S AMBIGUOUS
OFFSHORE ISLANDS POLICY

In mid-September the British again quizzed Dulles about America's stance on the offshore islands. Dulles explained the United States had "made no decision," but acknowledged that one factor weighing against such a defense was that it might require the use of nuclear weapons. The British were heartened by Dulles's efforts to avoid a defense of the islands, and suggested a withdrawal of Nationalist forces. Citing the effect that such an action would have on Nationalist morale, Dulles thought this was desirable "eventually but not practical now." Dulles candidly acknowledged the indecision wracking senior levels of the US government. Referring to the Chinese Communists, he said: "We're keeping them guessing partly because we're guessing ourselves."[84]

The Nationalists were annoyed that, in response to the attack, the United States had not increased military assistance to Formosa. An "obviously disappointed" President Chiang structured his complaints with reference to other US security partners: "when Korea or Indochina were attacked US aid was immediately stepped up. Now GRC was fighting only hot war anywhere and U.S. seemed 'indifferent.'"[85] But America's indecision, at this point, can be partially explained by the different pressures on its policy. As explained in chapter 2, in 1950 US abandonment of Korea would have weakened security relationships and may have resulted in several countries adopting neutralist positions or shifting toward friendly relations with the Communist bloc. But in 1954 most allies feared that a defense of Quemoy could lead to general war. Thus, as expected by the alliance audience effect framework, allied fears of entrapment were influencing US decision makers to adopt a more restrained policy.

On September 27, Dulles and the UK's foreign secretary, Anthony Eden, developed a plan to place the matter before the UNSC. New Zealand, which was a nonpermanent member of the council, was asked to raise the issue in New York. At a trilateral meeting on October 4, Dulles opined that the United States had to either commit to the defense of Quemoy or risk its loss, which "would constitute a serious blow to the prestige of the United States." Despite these concerns, neither the UK nor New Zealand encouraged a guarantee of the islands: instead, they hoped the US might be able to restrain the Nationalists. When the New Zealand ambassador "expressed the hope of his government that we would be able to 'deal effectively' with the Chinese Nationalists," Secretary Dulles noted that "while we are not able to give orders either to Rhee or Chiang Kai-shek, the latter nevertheless has been cooperative in most matters."[86]

On October 5 Eisenhower approved Dulles's idea to put the issue before the UNSC and this plan became known as "Operation Oracle." A few days later and "in the strictest confidence," Dulles also informed the UK that the

US had, when it delivered F-84 aircraft to the Nationalists, extracted a commitment that these would not be used against the mainland "unless there were what we [recognized] to be unusual and compelling reasons for such action." Dulles also noted that the Nationalists had not responded immediately to the Communist shelling of Quemoy but had waited to obtain US concurrence.[87] Aware that the UK was monitoring America's behavior toward Nationalist China, Dulles revealed that the United States was seeking to restrain Chiang and prevent escalation.

THE UNITED STATES MOVES TOWARD A FORMAL SECURITY COMMITMENT

At an NSC meeting on October 6, Dulles noted that because the Seventh Fleet's orders had their inception in America's Korean War policies, "any U.S. action based on Formosa is becoming more and more tenuous as time goes on and the Korean armistice continues." This was one reason to give "increasing consideration to the conclusion of a security treaty between the United States and Formosa." The conversation soon echoed the NSC meeting held on September 12, when Eisenhower "made it clear that he was not ready to use the armed forces of the United States for the defense of these islands." Dulles chided one participant, noting that "you can talk all you want of the bad effect on Asia if the United States does not fight to defend these offshore islands, but you say nothing about the bad effect on Europe if we do undertake to fight and hold these islands . . . we would be in this fight in Asia completely alone."[88]

The next day, Robertson wrote a memo for Dulles, urging that the US immediately conclude a mutual defense treaty with the ROC. Arguing that the Nationalists would be spooked by any attempt to put the offshore islands in front of the UNSC, Robertson noted Ambassador Rankin's belief that "the disastrous effect on the morale of the GRC . . . could only be offset effectively by an immediate U.S. undertaking to sign a mutual defense treaty."[89] After discussing it with Eisenhower, Dulles authorized Robertson to negotiate a defensive alliance. A draft text, attached to Robertson's memo, restricted the treaty's scope to "Formosa and the Pescadores, together with such other islands as are mutually agreed to be intimately connected with the defense of Formosa and the Pescadores."[90] These suggested words show the United States was wary of how any decision made might be perceived by other powers: it had to keep Communist China guessing but also reassure its other allies that it was not committed to the defense of the offshore islands.

Robertson met with President Chiang Kai-shek several times in mid-October. He explained that the United States "had learned of a proposal to be brought before the UN by New Zealand." While Washington had "been careful to keep the Communists in uncertainty as to the probable U.S. course of action . . . it is highly doubtful that the President could now, without

Congressional authorization . . . enlarge the mission of the Seventh Fleet" to include the defense of the islands. Robertson told Chiang of Eisenhower's belief that "the fate of these off-shore islands, while very important, would not justify him in calling on the American nation to engage in what might become a war of indeterminate scope, intensity, and duration." Because of this judgment, Robertson encouraged Chiang to view New Zealand's action as an opportunity to isolate Communist China in the international community and informed him that the United States was planning to "reaffirm, perhaps more formally, its firm intention to associate itself with the security of Formosa and the Pescadores." Chiang spoke strongly against the ceasefire plan, believing it would aid Beijing's efforts to gain UN membership and secure possession of Formosa. He thought Taipei's acceptance of New Zealand's effort would "be considered as a betrayal . . . by all Chinese who seek the overthrow of the Communist regime." Complaining of US vacillation, Chiang "said with some bitterness that he had believed for some time and still believes that the U.S. policy as to China may change at any time." Regardless, he vowed that Nationalist forces on the offshore islands would "fight to the last man, with or without the . . . Seventh Fleet."[91]

Robertson, again noting that Eisenhower's power was curtailed without congressional authorization, suggested that Free China's security would be enhanced by the conclusion of a mutual defense treaty and a UN-backed ceasefire. But the alliance "could not include a commitment to defend the off-shore islands . . . a pact would have to be purely defensive in character." Chiang argued that pact negotiations should be announced before New Zealand's effort in the UN became public, so that its "harmful effects . . . might be offset or at least greatly mitigated." Robertson agreed that pact negotiations might be announced on the same day as New Zealand acted in the UN, but reaffirmed the pact would "use language which would keep the Chinese Communists guessing as to our intentions respecting the off-shore islands." He noted that the administration was "very anxious to prevent the Communists from learning that the U.S. is not in a position to participate in the defense of the off-shore islands. This would in effect give them a green light to invade the islands." Chiang made one final effort to secure a US commitment to the defense of the offshore islands but Robertson once more swiftly dismissed the idea.[92]

US officials briefed their UK and New Zealand counterparts on Chiang's reaction and informed them of Washington's intent to conclude a mutual defense treaty with the ROC, regardless of what happened to New Zealand's resolution in the UNSC. In response to British questions, the United States confirmed that it would omit the offshore islands from the defense pact and emphasized the defensive nature of the proposed alliance: it would restrain Chiang's ability to attack the mainland.[93] At a later meeting, Secretary Dulles emphasized to New Zealand's ambassador that Chiang had given a solemn undertaking to "abide by any agreement which the U.S. might wish, to ensure that it would not become involved in hostilities initiated by the Chinese Nationalists."[94] On October 23, Eden further quizzed Dulles on America's disposition toward the islands: if New Zealand's ceasefire resolution was vetoed in the UN, would the US then commit to their defense? Dulles's response was unequivocal: "no."[95] Despite this assurance, "the British decided to postpone a decision on Oracle until after they had seen the terms of the U.S. announcement of the impending treaty negotiations." In the words of one historian, allies were using Operation Oracle as "a useful instrument to monitor and moderate U.S. policymaking."[96]

THE PRC ATTACKS THE TACHENS, AND THE US-ROC ALLIANCE IS NEGOTIATED

Chinese Communist forces attacked the Tachen Island group on November 1, and the United States was concerned that "this might be the development of a new pattern foreshadowing an all-out attack by the Communists." As this information was communicated to the UK, Dulles again emphasized that "the U.S. has been exercising a restraining influence on the Chinese Nationalists to keep retaliatory action to a minimum."[97]

As State Department officials considered the best language for an alliance treaty, two issues weighed heavily on their minds: the need to maintain ambiguity over the offshore islands and the strategic preferences of allied countries. At an NSC meeting on November 2, Dulles thought it "desirable, in the text of the proposed mutual defense treaty with Formosa, to 'fuzz up' to some extent the U.S. reaction with regard to a Chinese Communist attack on Formosa as such an attack would affect the Nationalist-held offshore islands." Such fuzzy language "would leave open to U.S. determination whether or not to construe an attack on the offshore islands as an attack on Formosa itself." This would "maintain doubt in the minds of the Communists as to how the U.S. would react to an attack on the offshore islands."[98]

The JCS suggested that the offshore islands be included in the pact but Dulles argued that President Eisenhower had decided in September against defending the islands. In restating this decision, Dulles commented that the views of allies were of critical importance: he noted that "public opinion throughout the free world would be against the United States if we went to war with Communist China over these offshore islands. The effect in Japan would be extremely bad. . . . The Chinese communists would win the sympathy of all our allies, and there would be devastating repercussions both in Europe and Japan. . . . Our enemies would have the backing of world opinion." Eisenhower's position was unchanged: he believed "it was better to accept some loss of face in the world than to go to general war in the defense of these small islands."[99]

Historian John Garver neatly sums up the dilemma facing US leaders: "Eisenhower and Dulles were especially concerned that a general Sino-U.S.

war triggered by the offshores would lack American and international support." But, on the other hand, they believed "the credibility of the United States as an ally was also at stake. . . . Although the United States had no legal obligations to defend the offshores . . . this fine point might be lost on the international audiences that would witness American passivity. . . . If the United States failed the test . . . friends of the United States around the world would be filled with doubt about American resolve."[100] While it seems obvious that any ally was unlikely to hold both concerns simultaneously, Dulles considered these two scenarios to be the horns of the offshore islands dilemma.

For now, the United States decided to straddle this dilemma and pursue an ambiguous policy toward the offshore islands while providing a clear guarantee for the defense of Formosa and the Pescadores. Foreign Minister Yeh, Ambassador Koo, and Dulles began treaty negotiations in November. The United States took particular care to minimize the differences between this new pact and other alliance commitments in Asia. In the Chinese draft, Article V was modeled on the NAT, whereas the US draft contained language identical to its other regional treaties. US officials stated plainly that NAT-like language would prevent the Senate from ratifying the treaty: the Senate "had declared that the formula and language of all mutual security treaties must be consistent."[101]

US officials prioritized consistency of language between this treaty and other defense pacts. Yeh and Koo wanted to delete certain language referring to the UN but Robertson argued against this, saying that "if you omit language in one treaty which appears in other treaties in the area, someone will attach unwarranted significance to the omission and ask about it." Robertson also noted that "it would not be reasonable to ask the U.S. to sign a treaty which was out of the pattern established by other treaties in the area," while another official said that "we could not expect the Philippine Government to assume an obligation from which the Chinese Government was exempt." On several occasions, the United States argued for the greatest level of consistency across different treaty texts. The Chinese requested that a two-year notice period be required to abrogate the treaty, but Robertson said that "we had a one-year termination provision in the Korean, Philippine, ANZUS and Southeast Asian Treaties . . . an exception for the ROC would simply draw criticism and raise questions . . . the treaty could not be made more favorable in any respect than the Philippine Treaty."[102]

American entrapment concerns were to be addressed in a protocol to the treaty, which was intended to "formalize the understanding that without mutual consent, the Chinese Government would not take any offensive action which might provoke . . . invocation of the Treaty." Yeh noted that the ROC had pledged to refrain from offensive action, but this undertaking needed to be kept secret, because "The Chinese people are not prepared for a public renunciation of the nominal right . . . to liberate the Mainland." Yeh argued that this understanding should be formalized in an exchange of notes; not a treaty protocol subject to approval from Nationalist China's legislature. If Washington insisted on a treaty protocol, then "the world [would] see a U.S. leash around the neck of Free China." Yeh "was prepared to go to any lengths to comply with U.S. wishes, provided it was done by note" and not by a public protocol. Dulles ultimately approved the Chinese request for a secret exchange of notes but the Chinese were informed that the United States reserved the right to make these notes public (if Washington decided it was necessary to do so in connection with the planned UNSC resolution).[103]

With Taipei voluntarily—but secretly—restrained, Dulles's desire to keep the Communists guessing was accomplished through a slight modification of Article V. In other alliances, this article referred to an attack "*on* the territories" of the parties. In the US-ROC treaty this article would specify that an attack "*directed against* the territories" of the parties would activate the treaty. This would allow Washington, if it so desired, to interpret an attack against the offshore islands as the opening move in a campaign "directed against" Formosa. Robertson noted that "this language represents an attempt to give some coverage to the off-shore islands and to keep the Communists guessing as to what U.S. intentions are."[104] Following further negotiations concerning the exchange of notes, the treaty texts were agreed and initialed on November 23, 1954.[105]

US ALLIES REACT TO THE TREATY NEGOTIATIONS

While these negotiations progressed, allies continued to raise their concerns about the offshore islands. The British were particularly concerned about the possibility of the islands leading to a general war: they feared that the United States and Communist China "might find themselves eventually in a position where their prestige would be so deeply involved that war would be almost unavoidable."[106] New Zealand was "anxious to know the terms of the proposed U.S. announcement concerning its treaty negotiations with the Nationalist Chinese," and thought this "should emphasize as much as possible the defensive nature of the proposed treaty." Dulles acknowledged the interdependence between this treaty and the prospects of the New Zealand resolution. He specifically noted that the "UK was reluctant to proceed further with the New Zealand resolution until it knew more about the proposed treaty and the form of its presentation . . . their Government could not finally commit to the exercise in question unless and until it felt that our treaty undertaking would be compatible therewith."[107]

In November 1954 the PRC sentenced several American airmen, captured during the Korean War, to prison terms for espionage. One response considered by the United States was to conduct a blockade of Communist China and a Special National Intelligence Estimate assessed the likely worldwide reaction. This assessment is useful because it notes the general strategic preferences of US allies and their willingness (or reluctance) to adopt confrontational stances toward Communist China. The paper assessed that "the ROK, Nationalist China, probably the SEATO nations of Southeast Asia, and elements in other countries would approve . . . [of a naval blockade] against the Communists," but noted that "in those nations which have been hoping for a general relaxation of tensions . . . it would be asserted that the US had seized upon the Chinese Communist action as a pretext to bring about full-scale war with Peiping."[108]

The estimate gave special consideration to Japan and the United Kingdom, as their reactions "would probably be of the greatest importance to the US interests . . . [they] would probably bring considerable pressure on the US to abandon the blockade." Specifically, the paper noted that "Japanese public opinion, at this time strongly influenced by hope of trade with mainland China, and highly fearful of any steps which in the Japanese view involve a risk of general war, would probably be comparable to that of the neutralist countries. The Japanese Government probably would seek to avoid direct use of its ports and facilities by US blockading forces." Support for a blockade would be strongest in the ROK and Free China, as there it would be seen as "an opportunity to involve the US in war with Communist China. The US would have increasing difficulty in restraining both the ROK and the Chinese Nationalists."[109] The possibility of Tokyo seeking to restrict the use of its territory is especially noteworthy, given that at this time the United States had the legal right, under the 1951 Security Treaty, to use bases in Japan without Tokyo's permission.

These conclusions are consistent with other intelligence assessments throughout this period. With the clear exception of Nationalist China and the ROK, and the possible exception of some Southeast Asian nations, most American allies feared entrapment: they were concerned that a confrontation with Communist China could escalate into general war. New Zealand's ambassador raised the prospect that President Chiang might "indulge in bellicose talk for domestic political and psychological reasons," and thus make statements contrary to the defensive intent of the treaty.[110] The UK went even further and suggested that the plan for a ceasefire resolution in the UNSC should be deferred. If introduced in these conditions, it might "do more harm than good."[111]

Dulles concurred, saying that if New Zealand moved its resolution "simultaneously with the treaty, it might well be regarded as part of a double-barreled offensive against the Communists." Given that the signing of the treaty would come so soon after the sentencing of the American prisoners, the American people "might erroneously interpret it as a form of reprisal." Dulles took particular care to emphasize that "he and the President were trying to exert a moderating influence," but caveated this remark by noting that "they would not do so to the extent of abdicating our rights." Acknowledging that recent events had changed the strategic calculus, Dulles said that if an attack were launched against the islands now, "given the present state of public indignation . . . we might even be drawn into the hostilities."[112]

The Mutual Defense Treaty between the United States and the Republic of China was signed on December 2, 1954. Asked about the status of the offshore islands, Dulles answered that "their status is neither promoted by the treaty nor is it demoted by the treaty . . . the injunction to our armed forces is to defend Formosa and the Pescadores."[113] But he also noted that the United States could decide the islands were relevant to the defense of Formosa. Thus, Dulles continued efforts to "keep the Communists guessing" as to Washington's true intent. But as he succeeded in obtaining a Nationalist commitment that no attacks against the Chinese mainland would occur without Washington's approval, it was considered that "Dulles explicitly (albeit secretly) released Chiang."[114]

Assessing the Alliance Audience Effect

THE CLOSING STAGES OF THE KOREAN WAR: JANUARY 1953 TO AUGUST 1954

As the Korean War drew to an ambiguous and unsatisfying stalemate, the alliance audience effect was plainly at work in Asia. The ROC monitored the conclusion of the Korean War and was unsettled by the prospect of an armistice unaccompanied by a US-ROK alliance. The UK and Japan observed US policy and worried that America's ambiguous commitment to the offshore islands could escalate tensions and precipitate either a localized conflict across the Taiwan Strait or a general world war. These dynamics support H1 of the alliance audience effect: US allies monitored Washington's policies within other alliance relationships and these affected perceptions of US reliability in Tokyo, London, and Taipei.

As expected by H2, when allies doubted US reliability they acted to mitigate the risks this posed. When the ROC learned—through observing the US-ROK relationship and direct communication with Eisenhower and Dulles—that Washington feared the possibility of entrapment on the Korean Peninsula, Taipei moved to demonstrate its reliability in the hope securing an alliance. Chiang even made explicit his willingness to be "released" if doing so assured a mutual defense pact. Separately, the United Kingdom and Japan grew more concerned about the likelihood of undesired conflict over the offshore islands and began to pay closer attention to the US-ROC relationship. If, as Mercer claims, present loyalty does not create expectations of future loyalty, then these entrapment concerns would not have been aggravated.

Finally, H3 expects that America's actions will be influenced by the possibility that its behavior in one alliance will affect the reliability perceptions of its other allies. As the United States negotiated with Rhee, it knew that these interactions were being observed by other allies. When Dulles believed that Chiang was encouraging Rhee's obstinacy, he didn't hesitate to threaten negative repercussions in the US-ROC relationship. When Rhee continued to play hardball and resist America's efforts to restrain South Korea, the American ambassador to Japan was concerned that if the US allowed itself to be manipulated, then Japan might emulate these tactics. US officials knew that firm but fair handling of the South Korean issue was needed: Washington needed to reassure Rhee and other leaders who would have been worried by an abandonment of Korea but also needed to ensure that Rhee's intransigence was not emulated by other countries. Washington successfully set the example, and was rewarded when Nationalist China reordered its preferences and made new promises of restraint.

However, one piece of disconfirming evidence from this period needs to be considered. When Ambassador Allison cabled Dulles in July 1954 about Japanese fears of conflict between the United States and Communist China, Dulles seemed utterly unconcerned. Dulles dismissed Japan's alarm because he did "not believe that the Chinese Communists are in fact now prepared to challenge us in any major or sustained way."[115] Prima facie, Dulles's disregard for Japan's view might suggest that Tokyo's concerns did not influence his decision making, and thus would falsify H3.

There is significant evidence demonstrating that at this time, Dulles did not consider Japan to have the same status as that enjoyed by other allies. Until 1951, Japan had been under US postwar occupation and the lingering occupation-era thinking can be regularly observed in the words and actions of US officials in the mid to late 1950s. Allison later complained of American officials who "seemed to think it would be possible to make Japan into a forward bastion of American strategic strength with the Americans calling the tune and the Japanese meekly accepting their secondary role."[116] Up until the late 1950s, Dulles was the most influential US official who thought in such terms. However, as I explain in chapter 5, Japanese perceptions of US reliability were significantly influenced by their observations of the First Taiwan Strait Crisis, and Tokyo's entrapment concerns were an important influence on their desire to revise the terms of the US-Japan alliance. Though dismissive now, Dulles eventually would come to appreciate Tokyo's fears and respond as expected by the alliance audience effect theory.

THE FIRST STAGE OF THE FIRST TAIWAN STRAIT CRISIS: SEPTEMBER TO DECEMBER 1954

As expected by H1, US allies monitored its conduct in other alliances in order to evaluate its reliability. For most allies, Washington's ambiguous commitment to Nationalist China was a point of concern: it increased the risks of escalation and general war, posed dangers of entrapment, and thus damaged US reliability. As expected by H2, allies moved to mitigate this risk: New Zealand and the United Kingdom did so by influencing America's negotiations with the Chinese Nationalists. American decision makers, from Eisenhower down, knew that it was vital to maintain allied support. Allies influenced both the text of the treaty and the mechanisms which underpinned it: though the Nationalists' pledge of restraint was incorporated in a secret note instead of being in the treaty itself, the United States reserved the right to release this document if it became necessary. These findings demonstrate the explanatory power provided by the idea of reliability: allies were not pleased and reassured by US loyalty to the ROC (as expected by deterrence theory). And contrary to Mercer's expectations, this loyalty did create allied expectations of—and thus concerns about—future loyalty.

Finally, H3 expects that Washington would be influenced by the possibility that its behavior in one alliance relationship could affect other allies. This dynamic was clearly visible in this period: Eisenhower and Dulles were quite concerned with how other allies would perceive and react to Washington's policies. Eisenhower knew that some allies would disapprove of America's commitments to Formosa, and Dulles tried to ameliorate these concerns by reassuring allies that the United States was working to restrain the Nationalists. As the text of the treaty was negotiated, the need to maintain consistency was also an influence on US policy. This is another example of the interdependence identified in chapter 2: no bilateral treaty could offer more favorable terms than the others, lest this create problems in another alliance.

The negotiation of the US-ROK alliance was influenced by alliance interdependence in several ways: signing the armistice without an alliance would disturb the ROC, but succumbing to Rhee's intransigent approach would also set a dangerous precedent that might be adopted by other allies. Accordingly, the United States set the example, bargained hard with Rhee, and finally pulled Seoul into line. Because Chiang had closely observed these negotiations, he knew that a US-ROC alliance was impossible unless he was willing to subordinate his goal of national reunification to US preferences. Although the form of the US-ROC treaty would also be influenced by the views of other allies like New Zealand and the United Kingdom, Chiang's willingness to be "released" ensured that he would obtain his own alliance with Washington. With this entrapment possibility addressed, Washington was able to form the US-ROC alliance, and this completed the hub and spoke system of alliances in Asia.

Importantly, pure loyalty to Nationalist China was not the kind of desired behavior expected by other alliance theories. Observing allies desired US loyalty to Taipei on core issues such as the security of Formosa and the Pescadores but lobbied Washington to ensure that it was not excessively loyal, to the point of recklessly risking war for the sake of Quemoy, Matsu, and the other offshore islands. The need to consider allied opinion was a pervasive influence on US policy throughout this period, even though the First Taiwan Strait Crisis had not yet reached its zenith. In the following chapter, I demonstrate that as the crisis continued and tensions escalated, allied opinion substantially influenced—perhaps even determined—Washington's policy toward the Republic of China.

Allies Encourage Limits on US Loyalty to Formosa, 1954–1955

> War was being risked over what appeared to be, physically, worth-less, very small pieces of island real estate. But [Dulles] believed that actually the issue there was whether we honored our commitments, or whether we were going to back down when the pressure got on us; and if we ever started that, it would undermine all our treaties.
>
> —William Macomber (special assistant of intelligence, Department of State)

As demonstrated in chapter 3, in 1954 US allies carefully observed how Washington treated the ROC.[1] These allies were concerned that America's association with the ROC's security could provoke a general war that would be contrary to their own interests. Even as the United States formally committed itself to the ROC through an alliance, the views of other allies were influential: the United Kingdom and New Zealand wanted the US-ROC alliance to restrain, not embolden, the ROC's president Chiang Kai-shek. As the First Taiwan Strait Crisis continued and eventually reached its zenith in April 1955, Secretary of State John Foster Dulles and President Dwight Eisenhower believed that their policy toward the ROC had to consider the disposition of other allies.

While most US allies agreed that the defense of Formosa itself was important, only Washington's most belligerent ally—the ROK—welcomed the prospect of conflict over the offshore islands. Other allies used diplomatic efforts to persuade the United States to adopt a more conciliatory posture and decrease the risk of a general war. Throughout the crisis, US policy toward Nationalist China was strongly influenced—perhaps even decided— by the preferences of its allies. While Washington feared the negative consequences of being perceived as disloyal to the ROC, the greater fear was losing the support of allies such as the UK, Japan, Canada, Australia, and New Zealand. Because the events of the First Taiwan Strait Crisis offer an opportunity to decisively assess the alliance audience effect theory's careful delineation between the concepts of loyalty and reliability, it is a crucial case for examining the alliance audience effect framework.[2]

This chapter contains four sections. The first focuses on the events of December 1954 to February 1955: this includes the PRC's reaction to the US-ROC alliance and the passage of a congressional resolution which gave Eisenhower the ability to interpret attacks against the offshore islands as a prelude to an invasion of Formosa itself. However, as expected by the alliance audience effect framework, the views of US allies influenced Washington's approach. When the small Tachen Island group was attacked by the PRC, US allies advocated a Nationalist withdrawal from the islands. Washington encouraged and eventually assisted this evacuation in early February.

The chapter's second section considers the Eisenhower administration's attempts to convince the ROC to withdraw from the remaining offshore islands of Quemoy and Matsu. When these efforts failed, the United States adopted a belligerent posture and publicly threatened the use of nuclear weapons against mainland China. Allied governments took the final step of strongly distancing their states from the US strategy, and announced that they would not help to defend the offshore islands. This lack of allied support was a key influence on President Eisenhower deciding again, in April 1955, that the United States would likewise not defend the offshore islands.

Because the first two sections of this chapter focus on those allies with the most significant influence on US policy, the third section considers the reactions of two less influential allies: Korea and the Philippines. The fourth section concludes the chapter with an assessment of whether the events examined support or rebut the alliance audience effect framework.[3]

December 1954 to February 1955

UNITED KINGDOM AND NEW ZEALAND LIMIT COOPERATION WITH WASHINGTON DUE TO ENTRAPMENT FEARS

Representatives from the United States, United Kingdom, and New Zealand met shortly after the US-ROC alliance was publicly announced in December 1954. At this meeting, the British ambassador conveyed the concerns of the UK's foreign secretary, Anthony Eden, to Dulles. Because the US-ROC treaty had angered Beijing, Eden felt that Operation Oracle—the cooperative, trilateral effort to place a ceasefire resolution for the Taiwan Strait before the UNSC—should be paused. To improve the situation, Eden recommended that the secret notes attached to the US-ROC treaty be publicly released before proceeding. These notes codified an "understanding that without mutual consent, the Chinese Government would not take any offensive action which might provoke retaliation by the Communists leading to invocation of the Treaty."[4] Although these notes had not been publicly released, Washington had reserved its right to do so.

Dulles was unenthusiastic about this idea and said it was not intended to release these notes publicly "unless it should prove to be necessary in connection with the New Zealand initiative" (Operation Oracle).[5] According to historian Robert Accinelli the UK and New Zealand were "still anxious to restrain Washington," so they suggested that Oracle be postponed.[6] When Dulles discussed the matter with Eden in mid-December, he noted that there was no intelligence to indicate an imminent attack against any of the offshore islands. Because of the "heated atmosphere," further aggravated by the PRC's imprisonment of several American airmen captured in the Korean War, Dulles suggested that the three allies should "adopt a policy of watchful waiting."[7]

Nevertheless, Washington's dilemma continued to grow sharper. A few days after the US-ROC treaty was signed, a memo from the Office of Intelligence Research questioned the wisdom of the administration's policy, designed to "keep the Communists guessing." The memo suggested that "the Communists are unlikely to be deterred by our present policy from progressively expanding their pressure on the offshore islands . . . they will not only continue probing operations but also eventually attempt to conquer the islands, one by one." It also noted that if such attacks occurred "some US Congressional and press opinion . . . would probably call for vigorous action." But if the United States did decide, in this context, to defend the offshore islands, it would "find itself completely isolated from its major allies."[8]

AN ATTACK ON THE TACHENS LEADS THE UNITED STATES TO ENCOURAGE EVACUATION

Chinese Communist actions soon placed further pressure on US policy. On January 10, 1955, the Communists launched an air attack against the Tachen Islands. This was, according to the Nationalists, "larger than any Communist air action in the Korean War" and the most significant attack since September 1954.[9] The ROC's foreign minister, George Yeh, complained to Dulles that "for the last few days all units of the 7th Fleet have given the Tachen Islands a wide berth. They have stayed farther away than usual. This creates an impression of abandonment." When Yeh requested the Seventh Fleet make a show of force, Dulles replied that "the U.S. Government could not afford to bluff in this situation. We cannot indicate that we may intervene unless we are in fact prepared to do so."[10]

At a lunch with Eisenhower, Dulles expressed his concern that "doubt as to our intentions was having a bad effect on our prestige in the area, since it was in many quarters assumed that we would defend the islands, and our failure to do so indicated that we were running away."[11] This comment reveals that Dulles worried about US policy being judged against allied expectations of it, rather than what the United States had actually pledged to do.[12] Dulles suggested that Washington encourage the Nationalists to evacuate the Tachen Islands, with the US Navy providing logistical support. Concurrently, the US could make clear its intent to defend Quemoy, and possibly also Matsu, through a public announcement. The situation in the Strait might then be stabilized by bringing the matter before the UNSC.

Eisenhower approved this plan, and Dulles briefed the British ambassador about the proposed withdrawal from the Tachens. Because this action would damage morale on Formosa, "it was contemplated to state that under present conditions the United States would assist the Nationals in the defense of Quemoy," as it remained "important to the defense of Formosa." The British ambassador asked whether the US intended to incorporate Quemoy into the US-ROC treaty. Dulles "replied negatively, saying that our action would be provisional pending UN action or, alternatively, the Communists using Amoy as a clear staging base for the invasion of Formosa." Dulles suggested that it was now time to commence Operation Oracle and move for a ceasefire in the UNSC.[13]

Without waiting for a formal response from the UK and New Zealand, Dulles then presented his three-pronged plan to the ROC's foreign minister and ambassador. The United States would assist with the evacuation of the Tachen Islands, proclaim its willingness—"under present conditions and pending appropriate action by the UN"—to defend Quemoy, and finally a UNSC ceasefire resolution would be moved. Dulles explained that the president would have to seek congressional approval of this policy, "since we would have to be prepared if necessary to engage in hostilities with Communist China." Regarding Matsu, Dulles said that it "was not believed to be defensible" and suggested that the Nationalists withdraw from it "under cover of the Tachen operation." Dulles drew a clear line between Quemoy and other Nationalist-held positions, arguing that while Quemoy had genuine defensive value, this could not be said for other positions: "It did not make sense to tie up major forces to hold a bunch of rocks."[14]

Dulles made it clear that "If the Chinese Government rejected the proposal, it would lose the whole business," as it would be unable to defend the Tachen Islands alone. Dulles said the United States "could not play a fuzzy game any longer," as the "Communists had already begun to probe and were exposing the indecision. The U.S. must now make clear its position and be prepared to carry out the obligations it was now prepared to assume. Otherwise the U.S. reputation would become tarnished. The U.S. could not afford to back down from any position which it assumed, or to be exposed in a bluff."[15]

When Dulles briefed congressional leadership on this plan, he again emphasized how other countries would be impacted by US behavior toward the Nationalists. If they did not withdraw from the Tachens, the result would be a "falling of the islands one by one, including Quemoy" and the United

States "would be charged with turning and running and making excuses, and the whole effect on the non-communist countries in Asia would be extremely bad." Dulles noted that "sentiment in the Philippines is extremely sensitive to the Formosan situation," and Radford "pointed out that the psychological effect of the loss of Formosa, in Japan and [in] other countries in the Far East would be terrific."[16] At an NSC meeting that day, Dulles thought the US faced "a series of Communist military operations which are ultimately directed toward the capture of Formosa . . . it would have a very grave effect throughout all the nations of free Asia if we were to clarify a U.S. position which in effect amounted to abandonment of all the Nationalist-held offshore islands."[17]

Eisenhower saw several points of merit in Dulles's plan. The evacuation of the Tachen Island group would "have the merit of showing the world that the United States was trying to maintain a decent posture. At the same time, the proposed policy would make clear that this US concession with respect to the Tachens would not mean that the United States was prepared to make any concessions with respect to Formosa." Eisenhower saw Dulles's plan as having the right mix of conciliatory and confrontational measures. Other members of the NSC argued that the United States should use this opportunity to persuade the Nationalists to withdraw from all the offshore islands, but Eisenhower ruled this out on the rationale that "we probably couldn't hold Formosa if Chiang Kai-shek gives up in despair before Formosa is attacked." Dulles also noted that there might be a "revolt . . . in the Congress if the Administration proposed to abandon all the offshore islands." Eisenhower agreed: "there was hardly a word which the people of this country feared more than the term 'Munich.'"[18]

But US allies did not share Eisenhower's enthusiasm for Dulles's plan. The British cabinet "did not like the idea of a 'provisional guarantee' of Quemoy believing that its lack of clarity would confuse all parties and . . . encourage the Nationalists to hang on to the coastal islands."[19] On behalf of Secretary Eden, the British ambassador also noted that Dulles had previously said that "Quemoy could not be defended except with the use of atomic weapons. Eden's question was whether Quemoy was sufficiently vital to risk such wide-reaching developments." Dulles's response was to justify the defense of Quemoy in terms of allied morale, because if "the Tachens are evacuated and no other move made or explanation given, the impression will be that of a collapse in position. The consequences he foresaw in Japan, Korea, the Philippines and very possibly throughout all of Southeast Asia would be extremely serious." Dulles tried to walk back from his earlier comment, professing that "his reference . . . related only to the most extreme hypothesis of the Communists attacking Quemoy in so heavy a human wave as to make it impossible to stop them with ordinary firing power . . . this was a remote possibility." This issue was evidently important to the British officials, who "exchanged a glance and . . . made what was obviously a verbatim note."[20]

FOLLOWING BRITISH LOBBYING, DULLES DECIDES AGAINST A PUBLIC GUARANTEE OF QUEMOY

The next day, Dulles briefed the NSC that the British were unwilling to support Washington's plan to guarantee Quemoy because a public commitment would jeopardize action in the UNSC and if Quemoy was attacked the US "might be obliged to use atomic weapons." Dulles suggested that if Washington committed to aiding Formosa "without publicly identifying those off-shore islands which the United States would help to defend," then the British might support the plan. After some debate, the meeting agreed that Eisenhower would request congressional authority to protect "Formosa and the Pescadores against armed attack" and that this would "include the securing and protection of such related positions now in friendly hands."[21] Allied lobbying achieved a significant change of US policy: instead of Washington publicly committing to the defense of Quemoy, the pledge would remain private as "a concession to the British."[22]

Speaking to Foreign Minister Yeh, Dulles retracted his earlier offer of a public guarantee of Quemoy in exchange for evacuation of the Tachens. As a sweetener, Dulles told Yeh that the United States had decided it was "prepared to assist in the defense of Matsu as well as Quemoy. However, no public declaration would be made at present in this respect." Yeh queried this reversal several times, and Dulles finally answered that "this was a matter of U.S. policy and not of agreement with the Chinese Government, and, therefore, could be changed by the U.S. just as any other policy."[23] The following day, Yeh reported that while the ROC was willing to evacuate the Tachen Islands, President Chiang was insisting that Washington must publicly announce, concurrently with the evacuation, its intent to defend Quemoy. Walter Robertson, the assistant secretary of state for Far Eastern affairs, swiftly refused this request, noting that the congressional resolution would refer to the Formosa area but would not name specific offshore islands.[24] ROC representatives raised this issue again later in January, but Dulles cautioned that Taipei "should not through its public statements get the U.S. in the position of apparently having made a formal commitment" to Quemoy, as "the U.S. Government might have to deny such an implication."[25] Dulles was making it clear that Washington—despite reneging on its earlier promise to publicly guarantee Quemoy—could not be manipulated and that any attempt to do so would prompt a sharp response.

President Eisenhower sent a message to Congress on January 24, 1955, and on January 28 it passed the "Formosa Resolution." This granted Eisenhower the authority to use US forces "for the specific purpose of securing and protecting Formosa and the Pescadores against armed attack, this authority to include the securing and protection of such related positions and territories of that area now in friendly hands."[26] In response, the premier of the PRC, Chou En-lai, released a statement which reaffirmed Communist China's intent to liberate Taiwan, and called on the United States to cease interference in China's internal affairs.[27]

Despite Washington's restraint, the British were still concerned.[28] In reply to a letter from Prime Minister Winston Churchill, Eisenhower emphasized that while he was exercising a "sober approach to critical problems" and had been "working hard in the exploration of every avenue that seems to lead toward the preservation and strengthening of the peace," the United States was concerned about the "solidarity of the Island Barrier in the Western Pacific." In this context, he feared that "the psychological effect in the Far East of deserting our friends on Formosa would risk a collapse of Asiatic resistance to the Communists."[29] But Washington could not evade the actual concerns of allied states, which mainly feared entrapment. Dulles again emphasized this issue in an NSC meeting on January 27: "the big danger resulting from a war . . . was the possibility that it would alienate the allies of the United States."[30]

The Formosa Resolution, with its expansive remit, did not ameliorate allied concerns. Canberra instructed its diplomats in Washington "to watch how [the] Americans intend [to] use these powers. We must continue to press [the] importance of not getting involved in large-scale hostilities over [the] off-shore islands . . . we hope this will not lead to [a] U.S. commitment defined or undefined to defend others of these islands." Of particular concern was an impression that the Americans were now "drifting toward widening obligations."[31] New Zealand's high commissioner to Canada observed similar concerns among his hosts, cabling Wellington that "parts of Eisenhower's Message to Congress have disturbed the Canadians and the [Canadian] Ambassador in Washington has been instructed to express the hope that the power given by Congress will be used with great caution."[32]

Following the passage of the Formosa Resolution, President Chiang dug in his heels. Clinging to Dulles's initial offer, Chiang refused to withdraw from the Tachens unless Washington publicly announced its intent to defend Quemoy and Matsu.[33] A meeting of US officials reconsidered the issue and affirmed that while the Washington was prepared to help defend Quemoy and Matsu, this was "a unilateral decision on our part . . . subject to change" and the United States was "not willing to make a public statement to this effect."[34] The acting secretary of state cleared a response with Eisenhower and cabled it to the US ambassador in Taipei, Karl Rankin, who was to immediately deliver it to President Chiang. It made it clear that the American undertaking to defend Quemoy and Matsu was unilateral, private, and could not be publicly announced by the ROC.[35] Washington's reversal and its new position—that the undertaking must remain secret—were the direct result of allied lobbying.

At this time, Eisenhower reflected on the difficulties of the situation. While the US administration could "state flatly that we would defend . . . Quemoy and the Matsus . . . the world in general, including some of our friends, would believe us unreasonable and practically goading the Chinese Communists into a fight." He lamented the difficulty of finding a policy which could "retain the greatest possible confidence of our friends and at the same time put our enemies on notice that we are not going to stand idly by to see our vital interests jeopardized. . . . Whatever is now to happen, I know that nothing could be worse than global war."[36]

OPERATION ORACLE MOVES AHEAD, BUT US ALLIES REMAIN CONCERNED

In late January, New Zealand placed its ceasefire resolution on the UNSC agenda. The PRC was invited to participate in the council's consideration of the resolution, but Beijing refused because the resolution was intended "to intervene in China's internal affairs."[37] Washington convinced the ROC to withdraw from the Tachens, and evacuation preparations began, but US allies remained concerned that a military clash over the offshore islands could escalate into general war. When several Commonwealth prime ministers met in early February, they were united in their apprehension. The prime minister of Australia, Robert Menzies, noted that "Australian and other British [Commonwealth] opinion would be much opposed to accepting a risk of war over the 'off-shore' islands." To further emphasize the Commonwealth's desire to avoid escalation, he lauded President Eisenhower, saying it was his "coolness, judgment and character . . . which gives me encouragement and hope."[38] American reporting confirmed that Menzies was expressing a common position: "The view of all the Prime Ministers was that no precipitate decisions should be taken, nor positions publicly announced, which might make the situation more difficult."[39] For these allies, "Quemoy and Matsu, like the Tachens, were strategic and political liabilities, indefensible except at the risk of general war."[40] Though the United States worried about its reputation and the possibility of falling dominoes, some of these domino states were themselves dismissing the importance of the offshore islands and thus rejecting the domino theory.[41]

Bilateral representations to the United States reflected this sentiment. The Canadian and British ambassadors both took "great pains to emphasize . . . the importance that is attached to making a distinction between the off-shore islands on the one hand and Formosa and the Pescadores on the other." The assistant secretary of state for European affairs thought the Commonwealth nations "are trying to tell us without putting it into words . . . that they can swing all of the Commonwealth . . . behind our policy if we will indicate that we are prepared to have the Chinese Nationals withdraw from all the offshore islands and make our stand on Formosa and [the] Pescadores."[42]

On February 5, the Chinese Nationalists announced their intent to withdraw from the Tachens with US assistance. When the NSC met on February 10, Admiral Radford briefed that the evacuation was "proceeding very successfully" and "would be completed at the end of the week."[43] But unsurprisingly, this did not allay allied concerns. The director of the Policy Planning Staff, Robert Bowie, wrote that "the free nations in Europe and Asia distinguish sharply between Formosa and the offshore islands." These nations

> consider [that] the off-shore islands do not involve our security interests . . . they look on them as a futile hostage to fortune and the symbol of a rash and quixotic policy . . . they feel that our protection of those islands greatly enhances the risk of war and thereby endangers their own security. This fear will tend to strain the coalition and generate pressures to restrain us. . . . This attitude would put us in a difficult position if the Chi-Coms should attack Quemoy or the Matsus. A war arising over Quemoy would alienate our allies in Europe and much of Asia. The lack of allied support would handicap our conduct of even a limited war and might seriously impair our capabilities if hostilities spread. . . . The U.S. must adopt some other course of action which will keep the free world with us . . . our policy should be directed to disengaging from the offshore islands in a way which will not damage our prestige or leave any doubts as to our will and ability to defend Formosa and the Pescadores.

Bowie's suggestion was that the United States pressure the Chinese Nationalists to withdraw from all of the offshore islands, thus removing a major point of disagreement between America and many of its important allies. By responding "severely" to any Communist attack during the evacuation, the US could demonstrate "both our contempt for the Chinese Communist military power and our desire not to provoke 'useless' conflict."[44]

COULD THE UNITED STATES COERCE CHIANG TO WITHDRAW FROM THE OTHER OFFSHORE ISLANDS?

Until this point, many of Dulles's comments suggest that he believed the loss of the offshore islands would so frighten Asian allies as to lead to their defection or loss to Communist subversion. In a conversation with the Australian ambassador in Washington, Percy Spender, Dulles now suggested that "in the technical sense" the loss of the offshore islands "would not mean the loss of the Philippines and Japan."[45] But morale on Formosa had to be considered: loss of the offshore islands could so affect Nationalist morale as to cause the "loss of Formosa from within." This causal process meant that in Dulles's eyes, "the battle for Formosa is now 'on.'"[46] Aware of Canberra's fears, Dulles "said he hoped that Australia understood that the U.S. was not being reckless and that we did not want war . . . we had been calm and careful."[47]

Eisenhower made a similar argument in a private letter to Winston Churchill: the offshore islands were important for reasons of Nationalist morale—and the consequences on Formosa—and not because their loss would instantly jeopardize the US defensive position in Asia. It would be the subsequent loss of Formosa that would destroy the defensive perimeter, and it was for this reason that the Nationalists "must have certain assurances with respect to the offshore islands." Eisenhower emphasized US restraint: "history's inflexible yardstick will show that we have done everything in our power . . . to prevent the awful catastrophe of another major war."[48] In his reply, Churchill maintained the Commonwealth position: he could not "see any decisive relationship between the offshore islands and an invasion of Formosa . . . nobody here considers [the offshore islands] a just cause of war." Though pleased to see the Tachen Islands evacuation occur peacefully, Churchill was "very anxious about what may happen at the Matsus and Quemoy." He recommended that the United States evacuate all the offshore islands: this strategy would "command a firm majority of support" in the UK and put "an end to a state of affairs where unforeseeable or unpreventable incidents and growing exasperation may bring about very grave consequences."[49]

This seemingly coordinated attempt to influence US policy annoyed Dulles, who felt that Chiang Kai-shek's sacrifices were not adequately appreciated. Speaking with Eisenhower about Chiang, Dulles assessed that "we cannot at this time squeeze any more out of him."[50] In a speech on February 16, Dulles rebutted the idea of further withdrawal, claiming that it was "doubtful that this would serve either the cause of peace or the cause of freedom."[51] However, Dulles had shared his speaking notes with London prior to the speech and had changed some phrases in order to "reassure the British that he did not intend to go beyond the commitments" in President Eisenhower's January message to Congress. Referring to the Commonwealth's preference that the US influence the Nationalists to withdraw from all the offshore islands, Dulles complained to the NSC that "there was apparently no realization among the Commonwealth Prime Ministers of the difficulty of doing this." Eisenhower understood the international perspective, but still believed that "the surrender of the offshore islands would result in the collapse of Chiang's government."[52]

In another letter to Churchill, Eisenhower argued that the current US policy was the best available. Eisenhower admitted that the United States "does not have decisive power in respect of the offshore islands. . . . Chiang would even choose to stand alone and die if we should attempt now to coerce him into the abandonment of those islands." On the allied reaction, Eisenhower argued that "all of the non-Communist nations of the Western Pacific—particularly Korea, Japan, the Philippines, and, of course, Formosa itself, are watching nervously to see what we do next. I fear that, if we appear strong and coercive only toward our friends, and should attempt to compel Chiang to make further retreats, the conclusion of these Asian peoples will be that they had better plan to make the best terms they can with the Communists." Emphasizing Washington's efforts to lower tensions,

Eisenhower described five policy actions taken by the US to "make an express or tacit cease-fire likely." He also referred to US alliance politics with South Korea, arguing that "all that we have done not only here, but in Korea with Rhee, amply demonstrates that we are not careless in letting others get us into a major war."[53]

February to April 1955

A build-up of Communist military forces in February dashed this hope for a tacit ceasefire. Dulles was concerned that this build-up would make "the Matsus and the Quemoy islands . . . indefensible in the absence of massive US intervention, perhaps with atomic weapons."[54] Dulles and Eisenhower hoped that the "Nationalist government may finally conclude that their situation would be improved by withdrawing from the coastal islands," but they agreed that "any approach to Chiang along this line would have to be so skillfully conducted as to make him ostensibly the originator of the idea."[55] While this was Eisenhower's preferred solution, he was not yet willing to try to coerce Chiang: he instructed Dulles to inform Eden that "we do not intend to blackmail Chiang to compel his evacuation of Quemoy and the Matsus as long as he deems their possession vital."[56]

In late February, at a SEATO meeting in Bangkok, Dulles again discussed the offshore island issue with Eden. As Thomas Stolper notes, throughout the crisis US defense planners assessed that "there was never any solid evidence of PRC preparation for an invasion of Quemoy and Matsu, let alone Taiwan." This was "a fact that Washington recognized, but one to which it sometimes seemed not to give due weight."[57] This meeting with Eden was one of those moments. Dulles said that his assessment of the Chinese Communists had changed: "we are in a battle for Taiwan . . . [the] Communists still give every evidence [of an] intention [to] take Taiwan by force." For Dulles, "Further retreat would have [a] grave effect on Taiwan and in Asia. . . . Further retreat could swing Asia. . . . Further retreat or [the] loss of Formosa would convince Japan [that] communism [is the] wave of [the] future. Consequent effect on Okinawa and other parts of Asia obvious."[58]

Despite Dulles's alarmist views, other allies supported the UK's position. O. Edmund Clubb writes that "the British Commonwealth countries . . . backed away from the thesis expounded by Dulles at the February SEATO meeting . . . that war in one sector of East Asia would automatically involve the entire front (that is, all of America's allies)."[59] Eden was unmoved: while Formosa must be defended, "public opinion in the Commonwealth and elsewhere does not see [the] necessity of stirring up a row over these [offshore] islands and would not support our fighting for them."[60] Eden believed that an "abandonment of Quemoy and Matsu would be justified by increased support of [the] resultant position by Commonwealth and Western European public opinion." Dulles was unconvinced, feeling that Eden failed to "appraise adequately [the] dangers to non-Communist morale in Far East, notably in Taiwan, Korea, Japan and the Philippines."[61]

On his return to Washington, Dulles told Eisenhower that while he hoped "Chiang might reorient his policies so that less importance would [be] attach[ed] to these islands," he "did not think that as things now stood we could sit by and watch the Nationalist forces there be crushed by the Communists."[62] Because defensive action would require the use of nuclear weapons, Dulles suggested (and Eisenhower concurred) that the US public should be forewarned. In a public speech just two days later, Dulles said "that the administration considered atomic weapons 'interchangeable with the conventional weapons' in the American arsenal."[63] According to H. W. Brands, after this nuclear threat "European on-lookers, especially the British, reacted strongly, feeling that the U.S. was treading far too close to war."[64] British diplomats approached Beijing and sought a renunciation of the use of force, but this effort was rebuffed.[65] Dulles grew more pessimistic about the situation: he thought US-PRC conflict over Formosa was "a question of time rather than a question of fact."[66] However, he did begin to consider the issue of Nationalist morale with greater rigor: he said the United States "must know how much pressure we can safely put on Chiang. What inroads is subversion making? . . . we need more and better information."[67] The CIA pledged to report again on the issue of morale.

Meanwhile, Washington's allies were growing even more concerned about the United States using nuclear weapons against mainland China and thus running the risk of a general war. A Canadian diplomat described this possibility as "very disturbing to our friends and allies in the free world."[68] Accordingly, allies continued to suggest methods of reducing tensions with Communist China. Australia's prime minister Menzies met with Dulles and asked whether Chiang might withdraw from the offshore islands if "a group of nations joined with the United States in guaranteeing the defense of Formosa." While Dulles expressed some interest in the proposal, he again returned to the familiar theme of fragile morale: "constant retreat was likely to have a disastrous effect."[69] In a memo to Dulles, the British ambassador also emphasized the advantages of restraint, noting that if the West did not "exercise moderation in our statements and attitudes," it might "frighten the Asians into China's arms."[70]

With Washington rattling the nuclear saber, and unwilling to coerce Chiang into a withdrawal, allies publicly distanced themselves from US policy. Speaking in parliament on March 8, "Eden for the first time openly advocated a Nationalist withdrawal from Quemoy and Matsu on the condition that the Chinese abstain from an assault against either these islands or Taiwan."[71] As he confided to a US military officer, "not one percent of British people" would support a fight over the offshore islands, and he could not "increase that percentage no matter how hard I tried."[72] In early March Canada's secretary of external affairs, Lester Pearson, warned Dulles that if the United States used nuclear weapons against the Chinese mainland then the US "would be on their own so far as Canada was concerned."[73] Though Dulles told the Canadian cabinet, on March 18, that "the loyalty and morale of the forces on Formosa became a vital link of the whole Western position,"[74] on March 24 Pearson publicly announced that Canadian forces would not fight for the offshore islands.[75] Australia privately accepted the inevitability of being pulled into a "great war" if one were to break out, but insisted that Australian public opinion would "not support a war over the Offshore Islands."[76] In August 1954, Dulles had worried that a "major war where world public opinion would be wholly against the United States . . . was the kind of war you lose."[77] Washington was now on the precipice of such a conflict.

NEW THINKING ON NATIONALIST MORALE

In March, another National Intelligence Estimate considered how US policy toward the ROC would affect other countries and allies: "most non-Communist governments" would have an "unfavorable" reaction to an American defense of the offshore islands. If U.S. forces attacked the Chinese mainland, "non-Communist reactions would be considerably more unfavorable, reflecting a fear of the immediacy of general war." Although there would be "increased strains between the US and its allies," the estimate assessed that "existing US alliances would remain intact." However, if the United States used nuclear weapons, "the predominant world reaction would be one of shock." This "would be particularly adverse if these weapons were used to defend the offshore islands. . . . The general reaction of non-Communist Asians would be emotional and . . . extremely critical of the US. In the case of Japan, the Government would probably attempt to steer a more neutral course."[78] In late March the Japanese prime minister told a news columnist that "the Japanese people don't want a war and particularly they don't want a war started over those islands."[79]

According to the estimate, if the Nationalists evacuated the offshore islands, "with or without US assistance or pressure," it would cause

a deterioration of morale on Taiwan and great disappointment in the ROK. In the Philippines such an evacuation would stimulate concern that the US was not prepared to commit its forces in forward areas. To a lesser extent this reaction would occur in Thailand, Laos, Cambodia and South Vietnam. However, the dominant reaction among other interested non-Communist states would probably be one of relief followed at least for some time by increased support for US policies with respect to the defense of Taiwan.[80]

Despite such assessments, and their own discussions with foreign diplomats, Eisenhower and Dulles continued to view the situation in terms of falling dominoes. Eisenhower asked a friend: "If you became convinced that the capture of [Quemoy and Matsu] . . . would inevitably result in the later loss of Formosa to the free world, what would you do . . . [T]he opinion in Southeast Asia is that the loss of Formosa would be catastrophic; the Philippines and Indonesia would rapidly be lost to us."[81] At this time, Eisenhower regarded the object of this dispute as not simply the offshore islands, but the fate of free Asia. Overlooking the fact that the evacuation of the Tachen Island group—which could be considered as the first domino—had not resulted in the fall of Quemoy or Matsu, Dulles complained that "our allies really had comparatively little knowledge of the intricacies of the situation which we face with respect to Quemoy and the Matsus. . . . They fail to consider the tremendous morale effect that the loss of these islands might well have."[82]

As the preceding analysis has shown, this was clearly not the case. Allies acknowledged US concerns about Nationalist morale as valid, but still did not regard the islands as worthy causes of war. They felt that Nationalist morale would be better supported by making more secure the ROC's position on Formosa, even if this involved a withdrawal from the offshore islands. American allies felt the islands were expendable and that the better course was to reinforce Formosa itself.

Other US officials were also less concerned about Nationalist morale. In late March, Ambassador Rankin cabled the results of an informal survey to the State Department. This showed that American officials and military officers in Taipei "do not think that morale in Taiwan has changed significantly over the past year. . . . Subversion is well under control in Taiwan. . . . Chinese-American cooperation continues to be satisfactory despite some recriminations over our attempts to get a cease-fire in the Taiwan Strait and our failure to commit ourselves on the defense of Matsu and Quemoy."[83]

As new information about Chinese morale opened up the possibility of a different approach, "the distance between the United States and the Commonwealth trio of Britain, Canada, and Australia . . . was also greater than ever."[84] The essential dilemma had not changed throughout the crisis: Washington could defend the offshore islands, with the risk that allies would not support this policy, or abandon the islands, with the risk that it might damage not only regional beliefs about US security reliability, but also morale on Formosa. As Accinelli eloquently explains, "events had not forced a choice between these grim options; yet the horns of the dilemma were sharper than ever."[85] Eisenhower's friends continued to write him, warning that a defense of the offshores would isolate the U.S. in world opinion. One worried that "our allies definitely would be opposed. . . . In this troubled world we need allies badly, and to lose them would be a disaster much more serious than any consequences proceeding from the loss of these islands."[86] As pressure built, Eisenhower felt the United States could not "remain inert awaiting the inevitable moment of decision between two unacceptable choices."[87]

Resolving that one of these choices was, in fact, acceptable, Eisenhower finally aligned US preferences with those of its allies. He decided that the "desirable solution" was to convince the Chinese Nationalists to "voluntarily evacuate Quemoy and Matsu" and prepare for a defense of Formosa, thus providing "a constant military and psychological threat to the Chicom régime." In exchange, Eisenhower thought the United States should station a Marine division on Formosa, improve air defense and air force assets there, and "extend the U.S. Mutual Defense Treaty with the Nationalists to include other powers, such as Australia." While "no decision was reached in this discussion . . . time for action by the U.S. was becoming acute. . . . It was entirely possible that the U.S. could be drawn into a fight to protect the off-shore islands, whether it liked it or not."[88]

Eisenhower formalized his instructions in a letter to Dulles on April 5. Simply titled "Formosa," this document prominently notes that were the United States to defend the offshore islands, "our active participation would forfeit the good opinion of much of the Western world, with consequent damage to our interests in Europe and elsewhere." This letter contains a subtle—but significant—shift of language. Whereas Eisenhower had previously argued that the fall of the offshore islands would *inevitably* lead to the fall of Formosa, he now took a more skeptical tone, noting that a "refusal to participate in the defense of the offshore areas *might* have equally disadvantageous results" and that "further retreat in front of the Chinese Communists *could* result, *it is alleged*, in the disintegration of all Asian opposition" to Communism.[89] He also wrote that because the defense of the offshore islands would require the use of nuclear weapons, this would result in the United States becoming "isolated in world opinion, and this could affect very disadvantageously our treaties with Japan and in the SEATO region."[90]

Eisenhower decided that the preferable policy choice was to convince Chiang to withdraw. A defense of Quemoy and Matsu, even if it was "temporarily successful . . . would in no way remove the existence of the permanent threat . . . because our prestige would have become involved." Eisenhower acknowledged that a "retreat from the Matsus and Quemoy—if occasioned by any influence of ours—might create consternation among our friends in Asia, particularly in Thailand, the Philippines, Laos and Cambodia." But he explicitly noted that this in "no wise refutes the clear conviction that militarily and politically we and the ChiNats would be much better off if our national prestige were not even remotely committed to the defense of these islands." If Chiang could show that a decision to withdraw from Quemoy and Matsu was a "shrewd move to *improve* his strategic position, his prestige should be increased rather than diminished."[91]

Eisenhower's memo cast doubt on "the sincerity of Chiang's contention that the retention or loss of the offshore islands would spell the difference between a strong and a destroyed Nationalist government. If this is so, his own headquarters *should* be on the offshore islands." Eisenhower suggested that if the islands were attacked, the Nationalist forces should inflict serious losses on the Communist attackers and then withdraw from the offshore islands, thus removing a serious thorn in the US-ROC relationship. This plan would ensure that the loss of the offshore islands would "occur only after the defending forces had exacted a fearful toll from the attackers, and Chiang's prestige and standing in Southeast Asia would be increased rather than decreased."[92]

Many of these phrases and sentences were incorporated into a draft policy statement on Formosa, which was later reviewed by the State Department's Policy Planning Staff, headed by Bowie.[93] Bowie wrote that for Chiang, the offshore islands were "the most likely means for involving the U.S. in hostilities with the Chinese Communists which could expand to create his opportunity for invasion." Because of this, "Chiang can hardly be persuaded . . . [to withdraw from Quemoy and Matsu] unless he is completely convinced that the U.S. has no intention of participating in their defense." Bowie also argued that "in order not to impair its own prestige and the confidence of its allies . . . the U.S. would have to make publicly clear in advance its intentions regarding the coastal islands."[94] Bowie thought Eisenhower's new plan was a step in the right direction, but likely to fail if Washington did not coerce Chiang into a withdrawal by publicly stating that the United States would not defend the islands.

Another National Intelligence Estimate, received by the president on April 16, provided the most detailed consideration yet of how US allies would react to different American policies. The evacuation of the islands before a Communist attack:

> would stimulate concern [in the Philippines] that the US was not prepared to commit its forces in forward areas, and might cause the Government to request a clearer definition of the US commitment to defend Philippine security. There would be a lesser concern in Thailand, Laos, Cambodia, and South Vietnam. ROK leaders would be greatly disappointed. However, the dominant reaction in Japan would be one of general relief. Moreover, none of the governments under discussion would be unduly concerned by an evacuation if the US reaffirmed its intent to defend Taiwan at all costs, and none of them would materially change their policies as a result of the evacuation.

If the islands fell to a Communist attack to which the United States did not respond:

> there would be severe criticism of the US in the ROK, and to a lesser degree in the Philippines. Most other governments under discussion, especially the Japanese, would be relieved that hostilities between the US and Communist China had not developed. However, the adverse effects on morale arising from loss of the islands, as described . . . above, would be more sharply evident . . . US prestige would suffer. Laos, South Vietnam, Cambodia, and

Thailand, in which the US does not maintain forces or bases, would probably feel increased doubts as to whether the US would defend them in case of need. These countries would probably be disposed to increasing caution in their policies toward the Communists.[95]

The following day, Dulles met with Eisenhower and suggested a method of persuading the Chinese Nationalists to withdraw all of their forces from the offshore islands. If Taipei agreed to withdraw, the United States would conduct a maritime blockade for over 500 miles of the Chinese mainland's coastline, preventing Chinese Communist forces from receiving weapons and logistical support via sea. It would also provide more anti-aircraft weapons to Formosa and station additional US troops there.[96] The prospect of expanding the US-ROC alliance to include Commonwealth countries could also be used to encourage a Nationalist policy shift. Eisenhower approved this new strategy and dispatched Robertson and Radford—the two Americans closest to Chiang Kai-shek—to Taipei. At the conclusion of their meeting, Dulles and Eisenhower agreed that this new plan "would immeasurably serve to consolidate world opinion" behind the United States.[97] As Accinelli writes, if Chiang accepted this proposal "the U.S. would appease its concerned allies and define a policy . . . much more acceptable to . . . world opinion."[98]

DE-ESCALATION

The United States soon "found a means of escape not through the ill-conceived evacuation-blockade scheme but an unexpected offer from the Chinese Communists."[99] On April 24, 1955, Chou En-lai stated that he was willing to discuss security tensions with the US administration. Concurrently, in Taipei, Robertson and Radford failed to convince President Chiang to withdraw from the offshore islands. When he was informed that the US was rescinding its private pledge to assist in the defense of Quemoy and Matsu, Chiang vowed to stand firm regardless, insisting that "soldiers must choose proper places to die. Chinese soldiers consider Quemoy–Matsu are proper places for them."[100]

Washington's initial response to Chou En-lai's statement was "discouragingly tepid." Dulles thought it a ruse, and a senior Republican, Senator William Knowland, described it as an "invitation to another Munich."[101] In stark contrast, US allies seized on Chou En-lai's offer. Australia's prime minister cabled Dulles, encouraging him to follow it up with the idea of achieving a "settlement wider than off-shore islands and Taiwan."[102] The UK moved to "sound out Chou on this subject" and was "anxious to do anything it could to help."[103] Gradually, Dulles and Eisenhower realized "friendly governments would expect a receptive reaction from Washington" and so modified their position accordingly.[104] On July 25, the US and PRC announced that they would meet in Geneva, for "further discussions and settlement of certain other practical matters now at issue between both sides."[105] Chinese Communist attacks subsided as negotiations replaced confrontation, at least for a time.

The Philippines and South Korea

So far, this chapter has focused on the disposition of those allies which had the most direct influence on Washington. But two other allies—the Philippines and the ROK—were also closely monitoring US actions. In his memoirs, Eisenhower noted that US decision makers "were receiving, almost daily, throughout diplomatic and private channels, questions from other Asiatic nations concerning the firmness of our intentions."[106] Though such a claim might suggest that allies in Asia were desperate for the United States to take a strong stand against Communist China, the preferences of most allies aligned with the Operation Oracle countries: they wanted to prevent the conquest of Formosa but feared a general war. The ROK was the only clear exception to this trend, as conflict offered the prospect of reunifying the Korean Peninsula.

Japan's reaction to the First Taiwan Strait Crisis was less immediate, but its fear of entrapment was very influential in subsequent negotiations for the revision of the US-Japan Security Treaty. I cover these matters, in great detail, in the next chapter.

THE PHILIPPINES

Manila's reaction was affected by misunderstanding and excessive confidence in American military capabilities. Initially, the Philippines was quite alarmed about the prospect of retreat in the face of a Communist threat. Foreign Secretary Carlos Garcia, reacting to the PRC's January attack against the Tachen Islands, "expressed alarm for [the] safety [of the] Philippines as [a] result [of the] Tachen incidents." He briefed the press that Manila was "'closely watching' Tachen development[s]" and that the "entire democratic free world's faith in America will hinge on your ability to cope with [the] situation." A senior foreign affairs adviser in Manila, Felino Neri, warned that "from [the] psychological point of view, loss of islands around Formosa would have [a] telling effect on other countries in Asia which have joined in common resistance of [the] Red advance."[107]

In this context the president of the Philippines, Ramon Magsaysay, warmly welcomed Eisenhower's policy as expressed in the Formosa Resolution. But reporting from the US embassy shows that Magsaysay's position was contingent on the "erroneous assumption [that the] US resolution constituted [a] firm commitment [to] defend Quemoy [and] Matsu." Manila was worried by the prospect of American retreat in the face of a Communist advance. The US embassy believed "Neri honestly stating what he considers widespread conviction US must defend offshore islands [to] maintain its prestige and power in Far East." Thus, the Philippines was more unnerved than other allies by the prospect of the United States abandoning the offshore islands.[108]

Despite Neri's apprehension that a retreat from the offshores would severely damage US prestige in the Philippines, there were no "serious reactions" to the withdrawal from the Tachens. Asked about Manila's likely reaction to five offshore islands scenarios, the US embassy assessed that any seeming retreat would have negative consequences. The Nationalists evacuating the offshore islands due to US pressure would require careful public explanation. If it was depicted as a decision to "withdraw to [a] militarily stronger position which [the] US [was] committed and fully capable [to] defend, adverse effect on morale could be kept under control." But if this public explanation did not take hold, then although Manila's "will to resist communism would remain strong," the withdrawal would be interpreted as a "convincing demonstration of US unwillingness or inability [to] support friends with force [of] arms." In response, Manila would "insist [on] material evidence in Philippines of American will to fight, in terms [of] more material, planes and all forms [of] military equipment on [the] ground."[109]

If the offshore islands fell due to American nonintervention, then "failing prompt vigorous US actions helping [to] restore confidence [in] our intention and capabilities, present negligible support for neutralist, appeasement policies would increase somewhat." But the most alarmist forecast was reserved for the scenario in which the offshore islands fell despite limited US intervention: it "would be accepted by all here as . . . evidence that US [is] not capable [of] furnishing support necessary against Communists in Far East. Philippine Government would probably remain determined [to] resist [the] Communists, but in utter hopelessness, and would demand utmost from US in terms [of] military support."[110]

President Magsaysay, who had voiced his support of Eisenhower's position on the mistaken belief that the United States had pledged to defend Quemoy and Matsu, was criticized for not adequately understanding US policy. The "keep them guessing" nature of this policy was unhelpful and in early April Neri implored US diplomats to provide a clearer explanation of Washington's policy. Neri encouraged them to "understand [the] Asian mind. To us a retreat on Quemoy and Matsu means a retreat in all of Asia."[111] Days later, a State Department memo noted that "sentiment in the Philippines is very strongly against anything smacking of abandonment of Quemoy and Matsu. The islands are generally thought to be important to the defense of Taiwan. Loss of the islands . . . would cause serious concern . . . that the United States was unwilling, unable, or both, to fulfill its Pacific commitments."[112] Later in April, Neri complained that "many Filipinos fear

U.S. determination is wavering, especially under pressure [from] British, Canadian allies, and that failure [to] defend Quemoy, Matsu would lead inevitably to withdrawal from Formosa and Phil[ippine]s." But the US embassy believed that Neri's position rested on an incorrect assumption: American diplomats thought that "most Filipinos . . . do not include serious considerations of world war possibilities, but rather take for granted that U.S. strength sufficiently great so that Formosan issue can be limited to local action."[113] Given this mistaken belief, it is unsurprising that Manila supported a firmer US stance in defense of the offshore islands. Other allies—with different understandings of the military situation—were more fearful of escalation.

Despite fears that an abandonment of the offshore islands would precipitate a collapse in America's defensive line, when Chou En-lai's comments raised the possibility of an informal ceasefire, Neri was "highly elated at [the] news" and phoned a diplomat at the embassy. This "reaction [was] striking in view [of the] previous Philippine insistence [that the] U.S. should not retreat from Quemoy, Matsu."[114] Aware that there was still some nervousness in the Philippines, US diplomats tried to arrange for Assistant Secretary Robertson to return from Taipei via Manila, so that he might reassure Filipino leaders of America's security commitment. But Robertson and Radford had already departed Taipei for Washington and the crisis drew to a close shortly afterward.[115]

SOUTH KOREA

Among US allies in this period, South Korea was the real outlier. As described in chapter 3, America had earlier encountered difficulties in trying to restrain Syngman Rhee. Given his desire to restart the Korean War, it is unsurprising that Seoul was the regional capital most critical of Eisenhower's determination to avoid war. One American diplomat wrote that South Korea's foreign minister, Pyun Yong Tae, held the "basic premise that World War III is inevitable and believes sooner the better." Pyun also worried that Washington's willingness to risk general war might be tempered by "possible opposition of its allies."[116] Korean officials hoped that a Chinese Communist attack on Formosa would lead to general war against the PRC and thus offer an opportunity to reunify the Korean Peninsula. At a press conference, the Korean ambassador to the ROC said he was "sure" that in the event of an attack against Formosa, the United States would "allow Korea to start its 'long withheld military drive into North [Korea].'"[117]

By invoking reputational concerns about prestige, Korea might have been trying to manipulate the United States into a defense of the offshore islands. In September 1954 Foreign Minister Pyun sent a message to Dulles: "In this part of [the] world Quemoy can be [a] symbol, [the] loss of which especially at [this] particular juncture would have serious repercussions in Asia."[118] While this case study does suggest that South Korea viewed the Taiwan

Strait Crisis as a test of US reliability, Washington was unmoved by South Korea's pleas. Unsurprisingly, the Eisenhower administration's acceptance of Chou En-lai's offer of negotiations was denounced by the South Korean press, which claimed that the "president's judgement is in error" and that he was "risking alienation of America's only real friends in [the] Far East."[119]

Assessing the Alliance Audience Effect

Following the structure of the historical narrative above, I first assess the reactions of those allies most involved in the crisis deliberations and then turn to the reactions of the Philippines and South Korea.

CRISIS ESCALATION: DECEMBER 1954 TO FEBRUARY 1955

H1 expects that a state will monitor its ally's behavior in other alliances and these observations will affect perceptions of reliability. The evidence presented above shows that the United Kingdom, Canada, Australia, and New Zealand were all concerned that America's policy toward the ROC— because it raised the risk of an undesired war—made Washington a less reliable ally. As expected by H2, these states acted to mitigate the risk of American unreliability. The UK and New Zealand successfully convinced the US to refrain from publicly guaranteeing the security of Quemoy. Working through Operation Oracle, these countries exercised a strong influence on Washington and, once the Tachens had been successfully evacuated, they encouraged the United States to coerce Chiang Kai-shek into a withdrawal from all the offshore islands.

H3 expects the United States to be influenced by the prospect of alliance interdependence, and the evidence examined shows that leaders knew that they had to simultaneously manage several different alliance relationships. The State Department's Policy Planning Staff recognized the alliance risks posed by excessive belligerence and urged senior decision makers to "adopt some other course of action which will keep the free world with us."[120] To this end, Dulles's decision to not publicly announce Washington's intent to defend Quemoy and Matsu was a reversal of his earlier promise to the ROC and this decision was clearly influenced by allied lobbying. If, as deterrence theory and Mercer expect, a demonstration of disloyalty only generates expectations of future disloyalty, then US allies never would have encouraged such a policy shift. As Brands writes, "The State Department contended that the disadvantages of losing the offshore islands did not overbalance the turmoil that another war with the PRC would create in the American alliance system."[121]

In the face of these pressures, Eisenhower and Dulles invested significant time and energy into preserving allied unity. They thought the withdrawal from the Tachens would be a sign of good faith to allied capitals and regularly explained US-ROC developments to other allies such as the UK, New Zealand, Canada, and Australia. On several occasions, Eisenhower wrote Churchill at some length, consistently emphasizing that Washington was doing its best to maintain the defensive line without unnecessarily risking war. In response to allied concerns, the United States modified its initial policy of providing a public guarantee of Quemoy and Matsu, and kept this as a private commitment that could be changed, at any time, without embarrassment or damage to US prestige.

THE CRISIS REACHES ITS ZENITH: FEBRUARY TO APRIL 1955

As the crisis escalated and risks of war grew, the alliance audience effect intensified. As expected by H1, US policy toward the ROC influenced how other allies judged American reliability. By February most allies were already concerned about the possibilities of escalation across the Taiwan Strait and Dulles's comments about nuclear weapons added fuel to this fire. American diplomats reported that Dulles's remarks were "very disturbing to our friends and allies in the free world."[122]

These friends and allies did not sit still, but tried to mitigate the risks posed by American unreliability. Specifically, these allies strongly encouraged Washington to pressure the Nationalist regime into withdrawing from the offshore islands. As an inducement toward this end, Australia even suggested that a group of countries might join with the United States in guaranteeing the security of the ROC on Formosa itself, provided that Taipei withdrew its forces from the offshore islands. When these efforts did not succeed, US allies took the final step of distancing themselves from Washington's policy: several publicly announced that they would not assist in a defense of the offshore islands. These events clearly support H2's prediction of allies attempting to mitigate the risk of unreliability.

H3, which predicts that a state's policy in one alliance will be influenced by the possibility this will affect the reliability perceptions of its other allies, was also supported by the evidence considered in this period. Allied concerns were a significant influence on US policy: when Eisenhower decided to not defend Quemoy and Matsu, but instead to strongly encourage a Nationalist withdrawal, he justified his decision with reference to allied support.

THE PHILIPPINES AND SOUTH KOREA

The Philippines carefully monitored the US-ROC alliance during the First Taiwan Strait Crisis and these observations caused Manila to doubt American reliability. Perhaps due to an excessive faith in US military power, and the belief that hostilities would be localized and not risk a general war, Filipino diplomats and leaders urged Washington to defend Quemoy and Matsu. These dynamics support H1 and H2 of the alliance audience effect framework. As the above evidence has shown, the United States did consider Manila's reaction during its crisis deliberations. When, in late April, it became clear that the US would not intervene if the offshore islands were attacked again, the embassy tried to organize a visit of Assistant Secretary Robertson. However, the crisis soon deescalated and further reassurance of Manila was not needed. Though Manila was not given the same attention as other allies, the available evidence still supports H3—the United States considered, and was influenced by, the possibility that its behavior in the US-ROC alliance would affect Manila's beliefs about Washington's reliability.

It does not appear that the possibility of South Korea observing US-ROC interactions, and these observations influencing the US-ROK alliance, had much of an effect on American policy. Given the fractious nature of US-Korean relations in the mid-1950s, this is not particularly surprising. Washington knew that Korea's preference was to restart the Korean War but this could not be done without significant US support. South Korea's dependence meant that Washington could ignore Seoul's complaints without consequence.

While unsurprising, this is a definite challenge to H3, which expects that a state's actions will be influenced by the possibility that its behavior in one alliance will affect the reliability perceptions of its other allies. This instance and the example of Japan discussed in chapter 3 suggest that a simple caveat is needed for H3: when a state is highly dependent on its alliance for security and does not have feasible alternatives to the alliance, and/or is mitigating the risk of unreliability in a way unlikely to adversely impact the ally, then the ally does not need to worry about the possibility of an alliance audience effect.

The zenith of the First Taiwan Strait Crisis is a critical case for how my theory delineates between the concepts of loyalty and reliability. This chapter demonstrates that US allies constantly monitored America's interactions with the Chinese Nationalists throughout the 1954–1955 period. Most thought that America's commitment to the Chinese Nationalists posed significant risks of entrapment in a war with Communist China and perhaps the Soviet Union. In response, American allies pursued a variety of diplomatic initiatives intended to reduce the likelihood of conflict. By March 1955, when it appeared that these efforts had been in vain, some allies publicly announced that they would not participate in a conflict over the offshore islands. Despite Eisenhower's and Dulles's concern for reputation, they gradually shifted US policy closer to the more conciliatory position favored by the UK, Canada, New Zealand, and Australia.

In hindsight, Dulles and Eisenhower made two significant mistakes in their handling of the crisis. First, they placed far too much emphasis on the importance of Nationalist morale. According to Accinelli, the British consul in Taipei observed that the Chinese Nationalists used hints of collapsing morale as a "'highly effective counter' to any objectionable American suggestion."[123] As noted earlier in this chapter, Dulles and Eisenhower quickly concluded that the loss of the offshore islands would inevitably lead to the loss of Formosa to subversion or defection, but for several months this logic was not tested against the available intelligence or diplomatic reporting.

The second mistake was to assume that allies were judging America's loyalty to the ROC. This is a key expectation of other theories, and the evidence examined here demonstrates the folly of such beliefs. There were many good reasons to doubt this logic even at the time: Dulles often complained that a conciliatory approach toward the PRC would cause allies to lose faith in America's alliance commitments, but he also worried that an aggressive posture would alienate allied governments. Intelligence assessments consistently and prominently noted that most US allies desired a more conciliatory approach, but official views often contradicted this advice. Dulles's State Department and ambassadors were telling him that the policies he viewed as disloyal to the ROC would be welcomed by many allies. Despite this advice, Dulles continued to see his choices in moral terms: he feared that the US "would be charged with turning and running and making excuses."[124] Had Dulles realized that US allies were worried about America's reliability—not its loyalty—he may have been more willing to deescalate the crisis at an earlier time. In the end it was Eisenhower himself, not Dulles, who broke the stalemate and decided that the United States would not defend the offshore islands if the price of doing so was breaking faith with so many allies.

Revision of the US-Japan Alliance, 1955–1960

> When a treaty which is in force becomes considered by one of the
> parties to that treaty as not only not its own interest, but inimical to
> its own self-interest, the treaty isn't really worth very much. Because
> if you ever had to apply it and get cooperation from the other side,
> you wouldn't get it.
> —Douglas MacArthur II (US ambassador to Japan)

Efforts to revise the US-Japan Security Treaty, which produced the new Treaty of Mutual Cooperation and Security in 1960, are often described as being motivated by the demands of an increasingly resentful Japanese population, which desired a greater degree of "equality" with the United States.[1] Authors such as John Swenson-Wright, Michael Schaller, Walter LaFeber, Roger Buckley, and George Packard argue that a variety of factors prompted the emergence of this sentiment in Japan. The conduct of American troops in Japan is identified by all as a contributing factor. Packard suggests that even if "each U.S. soldier [had] been a model of good behavior, there would still have been misunderstandings and friction . . . [but] a number of unfortunate incidents stirred deep resentment among the Japanese people."[2] Many historical accounts of the treaty revision—even if they acknowledge Japan's "first serious effort to alter the security treaty" in 1955—commence in 1957, when the infamous "Girard incident" occurred.[3] This event, in which an American soldier murdered a Japanese woman, did indeed generate resentment in Japan and intensified Japan's desire for a more "equal" relationship. Though the occupation had ended in 1951, the United States still retained control over Okinawa and the right to quash protests on Japanese soil. Because of Japan's semisovereign status, desires for the treaty revision are often explained with primary focus on this domestic politics lens.

While unarguably important, this was not the only reason Japan desired a new treaty. I show that while other accounts are not incorrect, they do not

115

adequately recognize the influence of the First Taiwan Strait Crisis on Japan's fears of entrapment. These fears generated doubts about US reliability and were an important cause of Japan's desire to revise its alliance. Because the 1951 Security Treaty gave the US the right to "dispose . . . land, air and sea forces in and about Japan" without Japanese approval, decisions made in Washington could easily and quickly entrap Japan in a US-instigated conflict.[4]

There is strong evidence to suggest that Tokyo's desire to revise the treaty was prompted by fears of entrapment. First, Japan was extremely worried about entrapment risks during the First Taiwan Strait Crisis, and the US embassy reported extensively on these concerns. The American ambassador in Tokyo warned Washington that Japan might not permit US forces to use bases in Japan in the event of a US-PRC conflict, even though the United States had the legal right to do so. Japan's wariness over its potential role in such a conflict predates other events, such as the Girard incident, which are often cited as precipitating movement toward a new treaty. Within months of the First Taiwan Strait Crisis receding, Japan launched its first efforts to revise the treaty and mitigate these entrapment risks.

Second, when Japanese officials discussed their entrapment concerns they referred—sometimes directly and publicly but more often privately and obliquely—to Nationalist China's offshore islands and the risk of US-China conflict in the Taiwan Strait. Terms like "equality" and "mutuality" were regularly used in the alliance revision negotiations, and US officials identified these as representing Tokyo's desire to exercise a veto over military action launched from bases in Japan. Though Japanese officials often couched their position in vague language, US negotiators knew that these terms represented concrete fears about Japan's involvement, against its will, in a US-PRC war. In the 1955–1960 period, the offshore islands were the most likely cause of such a conflict.

Finally, if Japan did fear entrapment and sought to mitigate these risks through alliance revision, then my theory would expect this to be a priority item in any treaty negotiations. The new treaty, signed in 1960, effectively mitigated Japan's most severe entrapment risks. Once this was signed, Tokyo could veto US military action from bases on mainland Japan, with one secret exception: Tokyo preemptively gave its approval for use of these bases to defend South Korea against a North Korean attack. The form of the new alliance agreement suggests that Tokyo's entrapment fears were stoked by the possibility of being dragged not into a war to defend Korea but into an unnecessary conflict over the offshore islands. Thus, the primary outcome of the revised treaty was to restrict America's ability to respond to contingencies around the Taiwan Strait without Japanese concurrence. That the treaty took this form further supports the argument that Japanese desires for treaty revision were not driven solely by domestic political factors, but also by clear efforts to minimize entrapment risks in a Taiwan Strait conflict of questionable relevance to Japanese security.

Unlike the earlier case studies, this chapter explores more the possible degradation of military capabilities. As explained below, the treaty area covered by the new alliance was of interest to the ROC and ROK: had the treaty covered Okinawa, this might have limited the military usefulness of US bases on this island and thus reduced Washington's ability to respond to any Communist attack against Seoul or Taipei.

This chapter contains four sections. The first, covering August 1954 to December 1956, describes Japan's reaction to the escalating Taiwan Strait Crisis and Tokyo's initial effort to revise the 1951 Security Treaty. The second covers January 1957 to September 1958 and assesses Japan's second, and more considered, push for alliance revision. This prompted a period of internal deliberation in Washington, as the Defense and State Departments quarreled over whether treaty revision was prudent. The third section, covering the events of October 1958 to January 1960, explores the content of the treaty negotiations and the signing of the new treaty in 1960. The fourth section concludes the chapter by examining how events in these periods support or challenge the alliance audience effect framework.

August 1954 to December 1956

By August 1954, Japan had begun to distance itself from Washington's position in Asia. Finance Minister Hayato Ikeda told the US ambassador to Japan, John Allison, that "many Japanese were beginning to feel that US had no real benevolence toward Japan."[5] Allison assessed that "Japan does not consider itself an ally or partner of the United States but rather a nation which for the time being is forced by circumstances to cooperate . . . [it intends] to wring out of this relationship every possible advantage at the minimum cost."[6]

Because Japan wanted to trade with Communist China, US-sponsored trade restrictions with the Communist bloc were of particular concern. In August 1953, an embassy officer wrote that with the "exception of the problems arising from the presence in Japan of United States Armed Forces . . . no other single issue affects Japanese-United States relations so adversely."[7] Japan resented the fact that, due to US pressure, its trade options with Communist China were limited, whereas Washington's European allies were able to trade more freely with the Communist bloc.

Tokyo was also unsettled by Washington's policies toward Nationalist China. In his memoirs, Allison wrote that the Japanese foreign minister, Mamoru Shigemitsu, would raise the issue of Formosa with him in "almost every monthly meeting." Though Tokyo believed that "Formosa should not be allowed to be taken over by the government in Peking by force . . . from that point the Japanese people are not sure what should be done." Japanese views toward Formosa were complicated by their desire to boost trade links with the Chinese Communists. Shigemitsu "stressed the cultural, historical, religious and even economic ties to the mainland of China which were felt by the Japanese . . . eventually these ties would have to be recognized in some manner." Allison would report these exchanges to the State Department in Washington, but "would get no reply."[8] It would take several years for the State Department to recognize the significance of such diplomatic reporting from the embassy in Tokyo. As Roger Buckley notes, officials in Washington were often dismissive of Tokyo's views: "The belief that Japan was still an American vassal that could be granted the occasional concession if and when the United States government judged the moment opportune, had yet to be corrected."[9]

JAPAN REACTS TO OFFSHORE ISLAND RISKS AND STARTS A NEW PHASE IN US-JAPAN RELATIONS

The First Taiwan Strait Crisis, covered in chapters 3 and 4, put significant pressure on Tokyo. Japan did not desire a war with Communist China, as it would upset its economic aspirations and—due to the presence of US forces throughout the Japanese archipelago—unavoidably embroil it in a regional conflict. As historian Walter LaFeber puts it, "As Americans vigorously dueled with China to protect Taiwan, the Japanese worked to increase trade with both China and Taiwan."[10]

In February 1955, before the First Taiwan Strait Crisis reached its peak, Allison reported that Japan "believes that the U.S. maintains military bases in Japan not wholly or even primarily for the purpose of defending Japan, but for the safe-guarding of the U.S.'s own strategic interests. . . . As such, she considers that U.S. bases, while providing protection for Japan, are also a great source of danger."[11] In March 1955, as the crisis escalated, there were clear indications that Japan feared entrapment in a war with mainland China. Ambassador Allison cabled the secretary of state, John Foster Dulles, with the warning that Japan regarded Formosa and the Pescadores "as being in an entirely different category than Quemoy and Matsu, which they have always regarded as being part of China proper." Allison assessed that "despite their morbid national fear of involvement the Japanese would in general approve of the use of force by the US to defend" Formosa and the Pescadores. However, "in [the] majority of Japanese eyes the U.S., rather than Communist China, would be the principal 'war monger' if it sought to deny by force the capture of these islands by . . . [Communist] China."[12]

Allison warned that these sentiments would affect Japan's cooperation in any conflict. He thought that "even if hostilities began under the most favorable psychological circumstances—if the US appeared to be wholly 'in the right,' and the Communists obviously guilty of aggression—we could expect little 'positive' assistance from Japan." The passive assistance that Japan might provide was also uncertain. Under favorable circumstances, Allison thought Japan would provide roughly the same level of support as it did during the Korean War, but warned that

> if it appeared that as a result of attempting to defend [the] offshore islands hostilities were spreading to attacks on . . . targets on the China mainland and/or if nuclear weapons were used, a decisive swing in Japan's public opinion against the US would be likely. . . . The government could, therefore, be expected to take more positive steps to assure Japanese non-involvement. These steps might be limited to a failure to act officially against left wing stimulated strikes at US bases or they could be carried to a request not to use Japanese bases for the staging of attacks on the China mainland or even for assistance to the US forces involved in the offshore island hostilities. It is entirely within the realm of possibility that continued hostilities involving nuclear weapons would lead to a request for the withdrawal of US forces from Japan and a sharp swing of Japan into the ranks of the neutral nations. The present government, even more than its predecessor, is reluctant to become involved in what it would consider "American adventurism."[13]

Allison understood that his diplomatic cables would not be warmly welcomed in Washington. Noting that although his "estimate of Japanese reactions may appear to be alarmist," he doubled down: the "Japanese do not consider holding of offshore islands essential . . . and our involvement in their defense would alienate Japanese opinion and might well jeopardize our whole position in this country."[14] The ambassador supported his analysis by noting that both the Japanese prime minister, Ichiro Hatoyama, and the foreign minister, Shigemitsu, had privately voiced their concerns to a visiting American journalist: "war must . . . not be permitted to develop over the off-shore islands." Allison assessed that if the offshore islands fell because the United States stood aside, the outcome was "likely to be greeted with relief, even praised," in Tokyo.[15] While Dulles and others had consistently and repeatedly claimed that such a disloyal act would lead to Japan doubting American reliability, Tokyo actively desired America's disloyalty to Taipei.

These views were not confined to the American embassy in Tokyo. An April 1955 NSC report noted that while Japan was reliant on the United States for external security, Tokyo feared entrapment: US bases were thought to guarantee American support but were also "dangerously exposing Japan to nuclear attack in the event of war."[16] A draft of this NSC paper recommended that the US negotiate a new treaty that would maintain basing rights in Japan, but Dulles had little patience for this idea. Expressing his "profound disagreement," he argued that a new treaty would involve "a grave loss of advantage to the United States," as the Japanese "will certainly want to model such a treaty on the existing mutual defense treaties between the U.S.

and South Korea and the U.S. and the Philippines. This would mean that the United States would have to forgo its *right* to maintain forces and bases in Japan, and the privilege of doing so would be dependent on the agreement of the Japanese Government." Despite the suggestion for a new treaty arising from his own State Department, Dulles was "firmly opposed" to this "unless pressure in Japan . . . became a great deal stronger."[17]

Dulles was correct that Japan would seek alliance equality: Allison soon reported that Tokyo was interested in "adjusting base and other arrangements to assure completely parallel treatment with the NATO powers."[18] But Dulles was, at this stage, insistent that the United States could maintain its rights under the 1951 treaty. Allison later attributed Dulles's obstinacy to "pride of authorship of the original [1951] security treaty," but diplomatic reporting from Tokyo made it clear that America's legal rights would quickly become irrelevant if US policy threatened to entrap Japan.[19] Allison argued that it was "most unrealistic to assume that the Japanese will docilely agree to our retention of 'idle bases' for a rainy day . . . in general the trend is definitely in the direction of restricting, rather than broadening, U.S. rights and bases in Japan . . . any effort we make to fight this trend head on by insisting on our 'rights' is not likely to be successful and can only result in further aggravating our current relations with Japan to the detriment of our long-term base position here."[20]

On July 25, 1955, only three months after tensions had subsided across the Taiwan Strait, Shigemitsu requested that negotiations begin on a new mutual defense treaty: he thought "Japan could not be considered as truly an independent and sovereign nation as long as [the] security treaty in its present form remained." Allison warned Dulles "that time is rapidly running out when we can continue to maintain our forces and bases here as at present. . . . If present trends should increase over [the] next two years . . . we might well find ourselves with only paper rights and no effective means of utilizing them."[21]

Shigemitsu's proposal made provision for the full, but phased, withdrawal of US troops from Japan, with the caveat that "until completion of withdrawal US forces will be utilized for mutual defense purposes only and that position of US forces will be similar to that given them by NATO countries." Although Allison's record of this conversation does not note any explicit reference to Taiwan, he emphasizes that the "days are numbered during which we can continue to have military rights in Japan on present basis—if [we] insist on them and on continuing to get our pound [of] flesh we run [the] real risk of losing all—either by outright repudiation or by passive resistance to fulfilling obligation under present treaty."[22] Though this first effort to revise the treaty would prove unsuccessful, the timing is significant: within three months of the First Taiwan Strait Crisis concluding, Tokyo attempted to obtain a greater influence over the use of US forces in Japan. This effort long predates domestic factors—such as the Girard incident—which are cited as precipitating movement toward a revised alliance. The assistant secretary of state for Far Eastern affairs, Walter Robertson, believed that a new treaty was "clearly undesirable," as the 1951 treaty gave the United States very broad rights for the use of military bases in Japan. However, while these rights were "wider than any we can possibly get" under a new treaty, Robertson's analysis notes that "to some extent these rights are illusory."[23] Allison's assessment from Tokyo—that America's entitlements under the 1951 treaty were fast becoming "paper rights"—was slowly gaining traction in Foggy Bottom.

In early August, an embassy official met with the head of the Japanese Foreign Office's Treaty Bureau to discuss what a new alliance might involve. When asked about what assistance Japan would provide if conflict broke out in Korea or the Taiwan Strait, the Japanese response was revealing. "Assuming [the] resumption [of] Korean hostilities . . . United States forces could utilize Japanese bases as before," but for "operations in Formosa . . . if United States action [was] pursuant [to] international agreement, UN or otherwise, then possibly . . . Japan could agree to United States use [of] bases."[24] Only a few months after the Taiwan crisis, Japanese officials were expressing their view that a new treaty was necessary. Further, they were already making a clear distinction between Korea and Formosa: while an arrangement could be made for the security of the ROK, there was obviously greater reluctance when it came to the ROC.

Allison felt that this approach "reflects wide Japanese sentiment and perhaps [the] indication [of the] beginning of [a] new phase [in] our relations."[25] In analyzing the draft text of Shigemitsu's new treaty, one State Department official noted that "Japan would thus not be committed to help the United States if we were attacked in the Formosa area, or in Korea, or in the Philippines." Though Shigemitsu's draft treaty contained a "Japanese promise to act to meet an armed attack against areas under our jurisdiction in the West Pacific," the United States was "better off with the present arrangements." This promise was "worth less . . . than the unlimited right to dispose our forces in and about Japan," but this of course applied only "so long as we can effectively exercise that right . . . so long as there is real Japanese consent. If the antagonism to the presence of our forces, which is already considerable, should grow, the present arrangement will become of doubtful value."[26]

Some in the State Department could see the writing on the wall: the United States could not sustain its military presence in Japan without popular support, which was quickly evaporating. In an August meeting, one official noted that "the Japanese had made it clear . . . that in event of a new outbreak of hostilities in Korea or fighting on Formosa the Japanese would not consider themselves bound to afford us the use of our bases." This suggestion seemed to anger the legally minded Dulles, who insisted that "the Japanese had no jurisdictional basis for questioning our use of the bases, regardless of what political interpretation they might choose to put on the agreement."[27] Dulles continued to insist that the US could claim and rely upon what the embassy in Tokyo, and others at the State Department, now considered to be only paper rights.

In his August 1955 visit to Washington, Shigemitsu discussed treaty revision with Dulles. Shigemitsu noted that the "situation in Japan differs from that in Formosa and the Philippines, since the Japanese people do not believe that they are being treated as equals under the present arrangements." When Dulles noted that the United States had a basing agreement with the Philippines, Shigemitsu "replied that Japan would like to be in the same position." But Dulles was in no hurry and insisted that it was "premature to talk of changing the present treaty at this time" because Japan had not built up adequate defense forces.[28] One Japanese participant later described Dulles as believing it was "ridiculous for Japan even to consider the revising of the Security Treaty. He spoke over one hour in a very stern manner on this subject, and I thought to myself, what a hard-headed, difficult old man he was."[29]

Though there was no direct reference to Taiwan in this meeting, Shigemitsu's approach suggests that he wanted what other allies had: the ability to veto US military action from bases on their nations' soil. Undeterred by Dulles's lack of enthusiasm, Shigemitsu returned again to the subject of a new treaty: he "emphasized that Japan wanted to be an equal partner like other countries . . . and said that Japan is determined to move ahead with its defense." With this, Dulles demurred slightly and "thought appropriate language could be worked out in the joint communiqué."[30] In this document, it was agreed that when Japan could "assume primary responsibility for the defense of its homeland and be able to contribute to the preservation of international peace and security in the Western Pacific . . . it would be appropriate to replace the present Security Treaty with one of greater mutuality."[31]

TOKYO'S ENTRAPMENT CONCERNS PERSIST AS STATE CONSIDERS POSSIBLE REGIONAL EFFECTS

Though Dulles had rejected this attempt to revise the treaty, US intelligence assessments continued to cast doubt on America's ability to exercise its paper rights for unrestricted base use in Japan. In October 1955 a National Intelligence Estimate assessed that "Japan will . . . seek an equal voice in arrangements for the defense of Japan and is unlikely over the long term to agree to . . . bases under exclusive US control." It also noted that if Tokyo were faced with an outbreak of hostilities which risked escalation into a general war, "Japan might attempt to assume a neutral position in an effort to avoid nuclear destruction."[32]

In the absence of movement toward a new treaty, Japanese fears of entrapment did not abate. A paper prepared in the US embassy described a real fear in Japan that her ties with America will involve Japan in America's war—and that Japan will be destroyed in the process. The Japanese . . . are thinking of this in quite specific terms: if war came in the Far East the United States would use Japan as a base for atomic attack, and Japan would consequently undergo atomic bombing in retaliation. This feeling has subsided considerably since last spring, *when the danger of war in the Formosa Straits seemed imminent* . . . but among ordinary reasonably well-informed Japanese there appears to be little feeling that the deterrent power of American striking forces on her territory constitutes a source of security for Japan.[33]

This reference to the Formosa Straits strongly suggests that the First Taiwan Straits Crisis was an important driver of Japan's entrapment concerns.

In September 1956, Ambassador Allison warned Washington that Japan "is aligned with us superficially and temporarily, but there are strong undercurrents . . . deriving partly from her fears of nuclear war in the future . . . drawing her toward neutralism." Arguing that the relationship needed "mutuality," Allison noted that on issues such as nuclear tests or troop redeployments, "we seldom provide more than the casual courtesy of a few hours advance notice, and sometimes not that."[34] Another cable bluntly warned that "in the event of limited or localized hostilities, it is uncertain that Japan . . . would permit the United States to use Japanese soil as a staging area and base of operations." Allison wrote that "fear of involvement might cause Japan to deny the use of its facilities to the United States. In its present temper, it would almost certainly be a reluctant ally whose lack of cooperation, already demonstrated in time of peace, would greatly reduce its effectiveness."[35]

These issues were also becoming prominent in the public sphere, with Japanese Diet debates focusing on how the alliance was "'one-sided,' 'unilaterally favorable to the United States' and forced upon Japan due to its military weakness." The embassy in Tokyo warned that "complacency is by no means warranted by the fact that the United States position in Japan is not in imminent danger. . . . When the United States is no longer welcomed or required in Japanese eyes, the Japanese are fully capable of making the United States position here sufficiently uncomfortable irrespective of legal rights." The embassy noted that desire for a new treaty was not a passing fad but had "indeed [been] expressed confidentially much earlier than the recent public debates."[36]

In November 1956, embassy officers met with staff from Japan's foreign office to discuss US-Japan relations. After complaining about US policy toward Communist China, which the Japanese officials characterized as one of "hostility," discussion turned to Japan's "vague but nevertheless deep-seated feeling that the US-Japan relationship is 'unequal.'" "On the theme of 'inequality,' the most concrete comments . . . [were] that it would help if there were greater 'mutuality' and consultation in defense planning . . . the US more often than not makes her military decisions in this part of the world, and carries them out, unilaterally, without bothering to inform the Japanese until after the event . . . advance consultations on a basis of equality would improve the situation considerably."[37] As noted earlier, several authors have traced Japanese desires for treaty revision to ideas such as "mutuality" or "equality," but reports such as this one suggest that these terms were coded ways of referring to Japan's entrapment fears. When Japanese officials were pressed for greater detail on exactly what was meant by "equality" or "mutuality," they referred to unilateral American action and the need for consultation in advance of military activity.

Throughout 1956, the State Department began to associate terms such as equality and mutuality with concerns about entrapment and their warnings about base issues became more explicit. In December Marshall Green, a senior official in the Far East division, warned that "without adequate modification of policy, the U.S. can expect to retain its bases in Japan for 2 to 4 years, though at the possible cost of future close relations with Japan. . . . Even during this period, U.S. capabilities to utilize its bases in Japan for military actions outside the Japanese area and for the deployment of nuclear weapons may be seriously restricted."[38] Like American diplomats in Tokyo, Green interpreted Japan's vague references to independence, equality, and mutuality as representing Tokyo's specific concerns about entrapment in a regional and/or global war.

As American officials began to contemplate revision of the US-Japan alliance, they knew that such a change would be of great concern to other regional allies, such as Korea. At this stage, it was anticipated that a new treaty would involve the withdrawal of significant numbers of US forces from Japan, so Green cautioned that "for the Republic of Korea, any withdrawal of our forces in Japan would have decidedly adverse [effects]. It would remove the present logistic and support base for U.S. forces in Korea and might imply prospective withdrawal or reduction of our troops in Korea. It would raise the spectre of disastrous delays . . . in the event of renewed hostilities."[39]

Green assessed that "for Taiwan . . . [a] sudden troop withdrawal from Japan would have some of the same results noted in the case of Korea . . . we must be careful regarding any decision to withdraw suddenly from any country." Green's comments demonstrate that Washington was approaching the US-Japan alliance not as a discrete bilateral arrangement but rather as one part of an interdependent system. Green knew that developments in one alliance would be observed by other allies and could affect their beliefs about American reliability. He cautioned that "a great deal might be read into such decisions about basic shifts in U.S. policy . . . our actions must be neither convulsive nor without full consultation and consideration of worldwide consequences."[40]

January 1957 to September 1958

A NEW PRIME MINISTER AND A NEW AMBASSADOR
WORK TOWARD A NEW TREATY

At the start of 1957, Dulles was the primary obstacle to alliance revision, and his State Department began to bluntly warn him that the time for a new treaty had come. Robertson argued that "if we do not take the initiative in moving in this direction, we run the gravest risk of a deterioration of relations." As he recommended a review of America's security relationship with Japan, Robertson acknowledged that a new treaty "would involve some concessions by us," but he argued that these "would be well worthwhile if the result were to create a durable association" with Japan.[41]

The January 1957 election of Prime Minister Nobusuke Kishi in Japan was followed just one month later by the appointment of a new US ambassador, Douglas MacArthur II. Kishi's first formal meetings with MacArthur focused on security treaty revision: he delivered a paper which noted that the Japanese people were very critical of US foreign policy, as they believed it to be implacably aggressive toward the Communist bloc. The paper specified that Tokyo's concerns were "caused by following factors: (A) Japanese aversion to war as against global policy of US, particularly its military policy towards Japan. (B) Resentment against Japan's subordinate position to US under Japan-US Security Treaty arrangements."[42]

Kishi's primary argument did not focus on vague complaints about the need for greater mutuality or equality. Instead, he bluntly noted that "many Japanese people . . . believe that [the] foreign policy of US is ultimately a policy of war aiming at overthrow by force of Communist bloc, and that Japanese-American cooperation under [the] existing formula amounts to subjugation [of] their country to US policies that may lead Japan to war."[43] Another note given to MacArthur specified that the "point subject to severest criticism is that [the] Security Treaty grants [the] US [the] right to use such forces [based in Japan] regardless of intention of Japan and in certain cases for purposes irrelevant to [the] direct defense of Japan, thereby involving Japan in such hostilities as might occur somewhere else in Far East."[44] Kishi was casting his arguments in terms that provide clear support to H1 and H2. Having observed American behavior, and concluded that Washington's policy was one aimed at the violent defeat of Communism, Japan now desired to revise the 1951 Security Treaty to reduce the risk of entrapment.

In another meeting only a few days later, Kishi made specific policy proposals to MacArthur. Arguing that it was "essential to dispell [sic] such apprehensions" about a US policy of aggression toward the Communist bloc, Kishi suggested that the two governments reaffirm the defensive nature of the US-Japan alliance. Kishi thought the United States should emphasize that it "has no intention whatsoever to utilize its armed forces stationed in Japan and other Far Eastern areas unless overt aggression [occurs] in these areas."[45] He believed that such a statement would reassure the Japanese public and help Tokyo consolidate support for the alliance.

But the real change would go beyond words: when Kishi listed his desired changes to the treaty, the first aspect nominated was that the "disposition and use of US forces under [the] treaty will in principle be effected through mutual agreement."[46] Kishi was placing Washington on notice: no longer would Japan tolerate a situation where US military action, launched from bases in Japan without Tokyo's approval, could commit Japan to war. As Roger Buckley has noted, Kishi's paper represented "a more defiant approach towards . . . relations . . . with the United States. It reads at times as more of a declaration of independence . . . than an aide memoire to one's closest ally."[47] In a 1964 interview, Kishi described his own efforts at treaty revision as a continuation of Tokyo's earlier efforts: "when Mr Shigemitsu met Dulles, he proposed the Security Treaty be revised for a more equal footing between Japan and the United States. But Mr Dulles at that time said it was too early. . . . Then, when I went to Washington in 1957, I again told Mr. Dulles about the revision—on equal footing."[48] These remarks support the idea that analyses of Japan's treaty revision efforts should commence with Shigemitsu's efforts in 1955.

MacArthur cabled the State Department with his bluntest assessment yet: "We have reached the turning point in our relations with Japan." While Kishi's exact proposals were unsurprising, MacArthur was taken aback by "the sudden authority and completeness with which they have now emerged at the highest level. . . . They call for the most searching analysis and considered response on our side." MacArthur argued that the United States needed to "put our relations with Japan as rapidly as possible on the same basis of equal partnership that we have with other allies." Otherwise, he feared that Japan would "drift progressively into neutralism."[49] Dulles's reply was anything other than the "considered response" requested by MacArthur. The secretary of state was concerned that Kishi would try to commence negotiations during his June 1957 visit to Washington. Believing that Japan was, at that moment, better prepared than the United States to discuss issues of security treaty revision, Dulles told MacArthur that he should simply meet Kishi less frequently.[50]

When Kishi visited the United States in June, he didn't hesitate to press for alliance revision. In his meeting with President Dwight Eisenhower, Kishi emphasized that while he himself did not feel that "Japan was in a 'subjugated' position under the Treaty," there were "some matters which we would like to see reconsidered." The very first aspect Kishi mentioned was that "the employment of your forces in Japan is subject to the unilateral determination of the United States; we would like to have this subject to consultation with the Japanese side."[51] Like Shigemitsu's efforts in 1955, Kishi's discussion of possible treaty revision in 1957 focused on measures that would reduce Japan's risk of entrapment.

In a later meeting with Dulles, Kishi again noted that "Japan . . . should have the right of consultation concerning the disposition of United States forces in Japan." While Dulles "thought he could agree in principle . . . this would not apply in an emergency situation where there was not time for consultation." Dulles chastised Kishi for Japan's low level of defense spending and told him petulantly: if "it is the desire of the Japanese Government that we divorce ourselves from Japan, we will accommodate ourselves to that wish." Kishi deftly rebutted this suggestion, arguing that he sought a relationship of greater mutuality in order to preserve and strengthen the US-Japan alliance. If this could not be achieved, the Socialist Party might gain power in Japan, and this would likely result in the divorce Dulles feared.[52]

When Dulles and Kishi met the following day to negotiate their communiqué, further differences emerged. Kishi wanted it to mention that an "intergovernmental committee" would "study basic problems concerning the implementation of the Security Treaty and . . . consult, wherever practicable, regarding the disposition and employment of United States forces in Japan." Dulles demurred, thinking that "the sentence would not be very good in that form." In response, Kishi gave a detailed explanation of why he desired a revised treaty. He "said that the most troublesome thing in Japan in connection with the Security Treaty was the fear that Japan could be gotten into a state of war involuntarily or without its knowledge." It must be noted that given Japan's willingness to allow US forces access to bases for the defense of Korea—a subject discussed later in this chapter—the process of elimination leaves only one major flashpoint in Northeast Asia to which Japan's concerns could apply: the Taiwan Strait. Dulles reassured Kishi that the United States would "maintain very close relations" with Japan if there was "any critical development in the Japan area," and that Washington "would not want in any way to act, unless it was imperative, in any way that was abrupt or lacking in the normal courtesy between friendly governments."[53] Kishi later obtained Dulles's agreement to make this last statement publicly available.[54]

The joint communiqué noted that an "intergovernmental committee," known as the Japan-America Security Committee, would "study problems arising in relation to the Security Treaty including consultation, whenever practicable, regarding the disposition and employment in Japan by the United States of its forces." It also hinted at the possibility of a new or revised treaty, with Eisenhower and Kishi affirming "their understanding that the Security Treaty of 1951 was designed to be transitional in character and not in that form to remain in perpetuity."[55] With these pledges secured, Kishi's visit was "little short of a diplomatic triumph."[56]

Though Dulles was the primary stumbling block in the State Department, certain elements of the US military were also concerned about alliance revision. The military's Far Eastern Command warned that a Japanese veto of US freedoms in mainland Japan would be "unacceptable." If Tokyo declined to allow the use of bases in Japan for the defense of other Asian nations, it "would have an almost catastrophic effect on our defense position in the Pacific. It would be difficult to overestimate the danger implicit in announcing to the communists that Japanese bases would not be available for use against them if they attack Korea, Taiwan, or the Philippines, for example."[57]

THE STATE AND DEFENSE DEPARTMENTS ARGUE ABOUT AMERICA'S RIGHTS IN JAPAN

By early 1958, Dulles had been convinced of the need for treaty revision. According to Walter Robertson, Dulles now believed that "if we continue to base our presence solely on our treaty rights we may end up by being forced out." MacArthur was instructed to consider these issues and make recommendations.[58] He replied that it was a "matter of greatest urgency . . . as time passes without necessary adjustment . . . [the] risk may increase that Japan would come to believe its interests [are] best served by termination of [the] treaty without any replacement."[59]

MacArthur's sentiments were strongly endorsed by the Far East division's North Asia branch, which prepared a lengthy report arguing for a new policy toward Japan. This assessed that it was "impossible for Japan to support our policies toward Peiping and Taipei," because "Japan desires strongly to separate itself from the hostile aspects of United States policy toward China." Tokyo believed that "Peiping has abandoned its aggressive phase," and thus the US alliance system in Asia now seemed "offensive rather than defensive." The report elaborates:

> Taken in conjunction with this implacable confrontation of the two power centers across the Formosan strait the system of alliances seems to many Japanese to invite the threat of war rather than to dispel it. . . . Japan is no longer the sturdy link in our Pacific defense chain that it once was. As already demonstrated the China policy of the United States is to a large extent responsible for this development. If we do not change our China policy, and there are no indications that we will, it will be a continuing major irritant in our relations with Japan; there will be increasing disengagement of Japan's alignment with the United States and growing neutralism in Japan, possibly with an orientation towards Communist China.[60]

On February 18, 1958, MacArthur drafted a new mutual security treaty and sent it to Dulles and Robertson. He noted that "the crux of the matter will probably be the definition of the treaty area." While some US officials had argued that a truly mutual alliance should commit Japan to defend the continental United States, MacArthur argued that this was not feasible given Japan's restrictive constitution: he believed it was "*not* essential for Japan to be committed to come to our aid except within a fairly limited area." While the new treaty "would not be as advantageous to us" as the 1951 arrangement, MacArthur emphasized that reluctance to negotiate a new treaty would "run the risk that Japan will come to believe that its best interests are served by terminating the existing Treaty with no replacement."[61]

Robertson supported MacArthur's analysis, vividly advising Dulles that "we are not in a position today in Japan to exercise fully those treaty rights which we theoretically hold. Even in a critical situation it is highly doubtful that we could utilize our forces in Japan—except perhaps for a one-shot air strike—without Japanese approval."[62] The position of US forces in Japan had become so precarious that Robertson hinted Tokyo would actively and deliberately prevent the United States from exercising its legal base rights. If American planes undertook a combat mission from bases in Japan without Tokyo's approval, they would not be permitted to take off a second time.

Perhaps anticipating some of the objections that would be later raised by the Department of Defense, MacArthur wrote Robertson and further explained his views about a new treaty. Noting that there was not "'alleged' inequality" in the 1951 treaty but "actual inequality," MacArthur couched his position with reference to America's other alliance agreements:

> Our bases in Japan must in practice be linked with our base structure elsewhere in Asia. This Japan recognizes, but it is unwilling to grant us in advance the unilateral right to use them as we please in hostilities in which we may be engaged but in which Japan is not. The Japanese are no different in this respect from our other allies. They cannot and will not accept . . . a treaty arrangement which manifestly deprives them in advance of any say as to how their territory is to be used by another power.

MacArthur also noted that the Japanese had observed Dulles's public comment that US bases in the United Kingdom and Italy could be used only "with the consent and participation" of the respective governments.

MacArthur's next comment reveals the extent to which Japan's desire for treaty revision was motivated by fears of entrapment. While some US officials would fret that a new treaty would damage America's ability to provide security in the Far East, MacArthur argued that Japan's desire for a new treaty was not unreasonable: "Japan . . . seeks to exercise control over the use of our bases here, particularly during an emergency, not necessarily because it desires to restrict such use rigidly, but because it wishes to assure that any U.S. actions from these bases involving major consequences for Japan will be taken in consultation and agreement with the Japanese Government and for objectives which the Japanese see as being in *their* national interest as well as ours."[63]

In a separate letter, MacArthur warned Dulles and Robertson that "Japan will not grant to us 'rights' which go far beyond those we have obtained from other sovereign allies, many of whom are considerably less important in this world than Japan." MacArthur noted that the Japanese Socialist Party had "intensified parliamentary and popular pressures on the government by pinpointing the absence of treaty safeguards against independent U.S. actions from bases in Japan which might involve Japan in a war not of its choosing. *In particular, the Japanese have been apprehensive about the situation in the Taiwan Straits.*"[64] Though the need to be seen as equal to other allies was no doubt important from a domestic political standpoint, Ambassador MacArthur identified a strategic incentive for treaty revision along these lines: the fear of entrapment in a conflict against Japan's interests. Furthermore, he linked this fear to a specific locale: the Taiwan Strait.

Japan's enthusiasm for a new treaty worried the Department of Defense. The political adviser to Admiral Harry Felt, commander-in-chief of the Pacific, wrote that within the Defense Department "there is considerable unjustified suspicion of Kishi's basic motives." But he also noted some legitimate security concerns: "any restriction against use of Japanese bases for [the] 'hot' defense of Korea, Formosa and other areas beyond Japanese territory would change our entire strategic defensive position in Asia. . . . We might well lose a war in Asia before it would reach Japanese territory." Trying to strike a middle ground between the Defense and State positions, the adviser concluded by noting that "we need to remind ourselves rather frequently that a treaty is not worth much more than the actual mutuality to which the agreement only gives expression."[65]

But Defense continued to object to the prospect of a new treaty. In a telegram to the JCS, Admiral Felt wrote that although the United States could accept the idea of consultation with Japan, the "U.S. cannot accept any Japanese veto over U.S. operations which U.S. considers essential to its security commitments." For Admiral Felt, Washington could not agree to any new treaty which required "Japanese consent to the use of U.S. Forces or bases in Japan to support operations elsewhere in the Far East which . . . are consonant with the security interests of Japan (as determined by the U.S.)."[66] This was a remarkable position, which confirms how some US officials conceived of Japan as a second-class ally. In Felt's view, it was America's prerogative to determine Japan's national interests.

MacArthur continued to argue that such arrangements were no longer possible and that any attempt to maintain America's privileges in Japan would be catastrophic. If the United States tried "to exercise the so-called 'right' to use our military forces in Japan . . . without first seeking Japanese consent . . . not only would our whole security relationship with Japan collapse but [the] Japanese Govt would undoubtedly take effective steps to inhibit any further use of our bases in Japan. Whether we like it or not, this is the reality of Japanese-US relations today."[67] When MacArthur met with Dulles and Robertson in September, he told them that if the United States "did not act quickly the situation would deteriorate. We would be faced with a formal request to refrain from introducing nuclears and to refrain from operating out of our bases prior to Japanese approval."[68]

As Schaller notes, this internal US debate "resembled the civilian-military conflict that preceded the 1951 treaty."[69] At a joint State-Defense meeting, Defense officials outlined their concern that a new treaty would weaken regional defense arrangements. Though they acknowledged that a new treaty would merely place Japan on an equal footing with allies such as the United Kingdom, they felt that on the issue of base access, "if we were to ask Japan we would be refused, while we would not be refused if we were to ask England." Admiral Burke, the Chief of Naval Operations, specifically noted that the "idea of consultation . . . would stymie us in the Taiwan Straits." MacArthur's reply was that the United States "could not treat Japan differently from our other allies. If we did so, we would go out of business," as Tokyo could simply "close off the Japanese labor force and the utilities used by our bases." He then went on to draw a critical distinction: if there was "an attack on Taiwan, we would, no doubt, get the consent of the Japanese to use our bases there, but not if the attack were only against the off-shore islands."[70] In this meeting, MacArthur went further than in his previous assessments: earlier, he had linked Japan's entrapment concerns to the Taiwan Strait, but in this meeting he specified that Tokyo's fears centered on a conflict over the offshore islands. According to MacArthur—the American best placed to assess Japan's fears—Tokyo believed Taiwan itself was worth fighting for, but the same could not be said for the offshore islands.

This delineation angered Burke, who "thought that we had better pull out of Japan if we could not count on her." MacArthur again argued that the Japanese made a distinction between the offshore islands and other territories. "MacArthur said we could count on Japan for Korea, Taiwan and the Pescadores, but not for the off-shore islands. However, this was academic," as if the United States did not negotiate a new treaty, and if Japan went neutral as a result, then "our military men could scratch South Asia. These other Asians would run foot races to Peiping."[71] Despite MacArthur's advocacy, the JCS prepared another report which concluded that "there must be no obligation, implied or explicit, to grant Japan a veto power over the employment of U.S. forces."[72] Although it was Defense that was most vociferous in its comments, the importance of Japan to other security alliances in the Far East was not lost on the State Department. In an August 1958 cable to MacArthur, Dulles noted that "moving ahead in security area in Japan will of course require very careful consideration including evaluation effects any action taken on other allies particularly in FE [Far East]. This aspect of problem presently under consideration here."[73]

Japan's new foreign minister, Aiichiro Fujiyama, visited Washington in September 1958 to further discuss the possibility of alliance revision. In talks with Dulles, Fujiyama clarified Japan's position: "when Japan was used as an operational base, it was desired that the Japanese Government be consulted, but when it was used for logistics or supplies the present basis was satisfactory."[74] Dulles, by this point convinced that a new treaty was necessary, agreed that discussions could commence in Tokyo, with MacArthur representing the United States.

The following day, Walter Robertson wrote Dulles with another draft treaty. Using a US-UK agreement as a template, Robertson suggested that the issue of consultation be covered in a statement that "The deployment of United States forces and their equipment into bases in Japan and the operational use of these bases in an emergency would be a matter for joint consultation by the Japanese Government and the United States Government in light of the circumstances prevailing at the time."[75] Dulles authorized MacArthur to commence treaty negotiations with Tokyo, instructing him to pay close attention to the issue of consultation: "Defense desires you raise with Kishi personally the importance we attach to the use of the facilities in Japan in the event of Communist aggression directed against another free Asian nation wherein Japan's safety is threatened."[76] Such approaches demonstrate Washington's awareness that although the US-Japan alliance required revision, changes could impact nearby US allies such as the republics of Korea and China.

October 1958 to January 1960

THE TREATY NEGOTIATIONS

As discussions commenced in Tokyo, the treaty area was a critical point of negotiation. It was agreed that it would not include the Ryukyu or Bonin Islands (known as the "Article III islands") and that Japan would not be required to defend these areas if they came under attack.[77] This arrangement meant that while the United States was not obliged to consult with Japan about how it used forces and bases on Okinawa, neither was Japan obligated to support an American defense of these islands. The exclusion of the Article III islands from the treaty area created an important geographic loophole to the idea of a Japanese veto over American military action. It meant that if American military action were launched from Okinawa, and if this resulted in Okinawa being attacked, then Japan would be able to avoid being dragged into Okinawa's defense (and thus into a wider conflict).[78]

MacArthur thought the exclusion of Okinawa and the other Ryukyu Islands was of "very substantial advantage to us. . . . (Incidentally the ChiNats and ROK will also be much happier if Ryukyus are not included)."[79] In short, this exclusion maintained Washington's ability to launch military action from Okinawa without Tokyo's approval.[80] This allowed the US to reassure the ROC and ROK that a revised alliance with Japan would not dramatically reduce the quality or quantity of military forces available to fulfill other US alliance commitments. For Japan, it allowed the effective quarantining of entrapment risks on to the island of Okinawa.[81]

During the Second Taiwan Strait Crisis, further evidence emerged to support the proposition that Japan's entrapment fears focused on the offshore islands. At the sixth meeting of the Japan-America Security Committee, Fujiyama privately affirmed Japan's interest in Korean security, saying that Korea was a "vital strategic position with respect to Japanese security." In contrast, and although Japan viewed the current tensions in the Taiwan Strait with "great concern," Fujiyama said that Japan trusted that the "US which bears great responsibility for maintaining peace in [the] area will act in [the] best interests of free nations."[82] In a September meeting with foreign correspondents in Tokyo, Fujiyama publicly connected Japan's desire for treaty revision with the situation over Quemoy and Matsu, noting that Tokyo desired "that adjustments include provision for consultation between US and Japan in event US desires use bases here in connection with hostilities elsewhere, such as [the] current situation on the offshore islands."[83] Japanese leaders continued to refer—often obliquely, but sometimes specifically and publicly—to the entrapment risks posed by Quemoy and Matsu. Schaller notes this accurately reflected Japanese public opinion, which feared that the United States would attempt to revise the treaty "to obligate Japan to intervene in the Taiwan Strait."[84]

The conduct of the treaty negotiations further supports my argument that Japan's entrapment fears were primarily motivated by America's commitments to Taiwan. In September 1951, a bilateral agreement (known in the US government as the "Acheson-Yoshida notes") had committed Japan to "permit and facilitate the support in and about Japan" of "members of the United Nations . . . engaged in any United Nations action in the Far East."[85] In practice, these notes committed Japan—logistically, at least—to supporting the American effort in the Korean War. But in 1958, the Japanese Foreign Office wanted to know if these notes would apply to any future UN action in the Far East. Tokyo's preferred interpretation was that these notes applied only to the Korean conflict. MacArthur assessed that Japanese officials "appeared troubled not by obligation to support UN forces in event of resumption of Korean hostilities but by what they thought might be our notion of advance Japanese commitment to give support automatically to any and all future UN actions in Far East."[86] It seems that Tokyo was trying to create further room to maneuver, by asserting that it would not be compelled to support a UN-endorsed defense of the offshore islands (if this ever came about).

This effort, as well as MacArthur's earlier assessment that Japan would allow the operational use of bases for a defense of Korea or Formosa—but not the offshore islands—provide further evidence as to the exact nature of Japan's entrapment concerns. Firstly, Tokyo was willing to contribute, through the operational use of bases on Japanese soil, to the defense of South

Korea. Japan considered that preventing Communist domination of the Korean Peninsula—sometimes described as a "dagger pointing at the heart of Japan"—was a key national interest. Likewise, the preservation of Taiwan as an anti-Communist bastion was considered to be important to Japanese security. What was not important, however, was the fate of Taiwan's offshore islands. In November 1958, Fujiyama made this clear to MacArthur. In a discussion of the treaty area, which Fujiyama described as the "most critical point of the treaty revision," he noted that the Japanese government could not support the inclusion of the Ryukyu or Bonin Islands in the treaty. He listed several reasons as to why this was a political impossibility, including the fact that if these islands were included in the treaty, and "if [the] US and Nationalist China became engaged in hostilities with Communist China over Quemoy and Matsu the US would probably be obliged to use Okinawa as a base to attack Communist forces. This might lead to an attack on Okinawa by Communist China which, by the terms of the new treaty, would bring Japan into the conflict if [the] Article III islands are included in [the] treaty area." Because America's free use of bases in Okinawa was essential to fulfilling its security obligations to other allies in Asia, if the treaty included the Article III islands it would have practically, if not legally, brought "Japan into [a] multilateral security treaty with Republic of China, ROK and the Philippines."[87]

A SECRET MINUTE CONFIRMS JAPAN WAS MAINLY CONCERNED ABOUT THE TAIWAN STRAIT

In May 1959 the Acheson-Yoshida notes were discussed again, but this time Japan seemed to be placing further limits on the support it would provide US forces in the event of a conflict on the Korean Peninsula. Japan's view was that because the Acheson-Yoshida notes accompanied the 1951 Security Treaty, they would need to be reaffirmed, or new notes exchanged, when a new security treaty was signed. MacArthur thought this should be done through another exchange of diplomatic notes and Fujiyama agreed. However, Fujiyama also told MacArthur that Japan's interpretation of the 1951 agreement was that Japan would provide logistical support but that bases in Japan would not be available for combat operations without prior consultation.[88] This was the first time in the treaty negotiations that Japan had signaled that such a restriction would apply to operations in the defense of Korea. In attempting to get US concurrence with this interpretation, Japan was trying to exercise full authority over US bases in Japan (with the exception of those on the Article III islands).

Japan's suggestion alarmed the State and Defense departments: a joint cable to MacArthur noted that it was "highly desirable to preserve notes particularly with respect [to the] renewal [of] Korean hostilities. . . . We are thus not prepared [to] accept or acknowledge in any way unilateral GOJ [government of Japan] interpretation."[89] In his reply, MacArthur wrote that "both Kishi and Fujiyama have made it forcefully and unequivocally clear that if hostilities were to break out in Korea whether or not security treaty and related agreements are revised, their interpretation of their commitment under Acheson-Yoshida notes would be as set forth [earlier]. . . . Their interpretation has nothing to do with entry into force of new security treaty since they have made clear that it applies to the situation now."[90]

MacArthur believed that Washington had little choice but to accept Japan's position. He wrote that if the United States refused to accept this interpretation of the Acheson-Yoshida notes and "reserved [our] right to launch direct combat operations from Japanese bases without consultation," then "we would shortly be told that our position flatly contradicted spirit of new era of equal partnership . . . and that we could either agree to consult or get out." For MacArthur, acceptance of Japan's interpretation would actually only be an acknowledgment of the status quo. He argued that if hostilities broke out in Korea, and if the US response "deliberately committed Japan to an act of belligerency without even consultation, we would be out of business here within a matter of hours."[91]

The JCS argued Japan's position, if accepted, would risk Washington's ability to defend South Korea. It

> would result in further reduction in military effectiveness of US forces in Japan, which has already been drastically reduced by those provisions of new Security Treaty, which require consultation prior to launching of combat operations . . . Joint Chiefs of Staff strongly recommend that every effort be made to obtain private assurances from GOJ which would provide that, in event hostilities recur in Far East, Japanese would facilitate and support any United Nations action in same manner and under same condition as obtained during last period of hostilities. . . . [I]f above-mentioned assurances cannot be obtained, Joint Chiefs of Staff believe that decrease of military effectiveness of US forces in Japan would require serious consideration of their withdrawal.[92]

This threat—coming so late in the treaty negotiations—was upsetting even to State officials in Washington, who cabled MacArthur that they were "embarrassed to transmit to you the message from Defense." The acting secretary of state cabled MacArthur, "I personally am averse to treaties saying one thing and private assurances saying another. Of course it would be helpful if the Japanese would agree to put action in Korea in a different category than action in the Far East in general."[93]

MacArthur replied that the JCS had misunderstood his point. Regardless of the legal status of the Acheson-Yoshida notes, Japan had already decided that they would not allow US forces to launch attacks from bases in Japan without prior consultation. He savaged the JCS proposal "that we go to the

Japanese and say that we expect them [to] facilitate and support, without any consultation, any military combat actions the UN may take at any future time. . . . [A]ny such proposal will . . . be categorically rejected by Kishi."[94] MacArthur had convinced the State Department to abandon the paper rights of the 1951 Security Treaty, but some in the Defense Department were determined to preserve as much freedom of action as possible.

Dulles—perhaps still nursing his grudge about the slow pace of Japan's rearmament and its unwillingness to play a greater role in Far Eastern defense—had some sympathy for the Defense perspective. He cabled MacArthur, stating that the JCS were

> convinced that our security position in Northeast Asia would be jeopardized if [the] UN is not able to respond to renewal of Communist aggression in Korea by any military actions deemed appropriate and necessary without first consulting with Government of Japan. Requirement to consult first . . . would, in military judgement, seriously risk our ability to contain [a] Communist attack in Korea and could, in fact, lead to the loss not only of [the] Korean peninsula but also place Japan in [a] precarious situation. . . . [You are to] take up Acheson-Yoshida [notes] matter with Kishi personally and stress to him in [the] strongest possible terms [the] vital security considerations involved including Japan's own security.[95]

Dulles also noted that the United States was "prepared [to] seek [an] exception to [the] consultation requirement . . . only with respect to renewal UN action in Korea."[96] Perhaps Dulles suspected that Japan would refuse any such agreement if it covered Taiwan or the offshore islands. His instructions to MacArthur were clear: the US needed a promise that if the Korean War resumed, Japan would "continue to facilitate and support, without need for prior consultation, UN action in Korea."[97]

MacArthur conveyed Dulles's position to Kishi and Fujiyama, arguing that if Washington was unable to respond instantly because of the need to consult with Tokyo, then this could result in the "loss of the entire Korea peninsula, thus placing Japan in a most precarious position." However, he also emphasized that the United States "is entirely willing to subject other military combat operations of US armed forces initiated from Japanese bases to consultation under the agreed formula."[98] Kishi replied that although this "raised very serious problems," Japanese leaders "would do their utmost to try to find solution with which both the US and GOJ could live."[99] While Kishi shared America's concern about South Korean security, it was "not feasible to have explicit public exception to application of new consultation formula." Instead, he suggested that immediately after the treaty was signed, both nations could publicly exchange notes on the issue of support during a Korean contingency, with the Japanese note stating that the "Government of Japan will, in the prior consultation, favorably consider consenting to the use of facilities and areas in

Japan as bases for military combat operations . . . in case of a resumption of the attack against the United Nations forces in Korea."[100]

However, a secret agreement would go far beyond this public commitment. It was agreed that at the first meeting of a new US-Japan Security Consultative Committee, the allies would consult about Washington's ability to respond instantly, from Japanese bases, to any Communist attack against South Korea. Such a response would comply with US obligations "by virtue of consultation that had already technically taken place under [the] agreed formula." MacArthur's advice to Washington was that he did "not believe we are going to be able to get anything better than something along lines he proposes. . . . Kishi believes . . . to remain in power, [he] must insist that principle of consultation should apply across the board."[101]

The exact wording of the secret agreement, which would become known as the "Korea Minute," was negotiated in detail. Eventually, it was agreed that at the first meeting of the Security Consultative Committee—on the day that the new treaty was signed—MacArthur would discuss the importance of South Korea's security and request "the views of the Japanese Government regarding the operational use of bases in Japan in the event of an exceptional emergency." Fujiyama would reply that "in the event of an emergency resulting from an attack against the United Nations forces in Korea, facilities and areas in Japan may be used for such military combat operations as need be undertaken immediately."[102] With this sly arrangement, America's ability to defend Korea from bases in mainland Japan was affirmed and the integrity of the public consultation formula maintained.

The arrangement codified in the secret Korea Minute is further evidence that Japan's entrapment concerns were specific to the situation in the Taiwan Strait. If Tokyo's entrapment fears concerned both the Korean Peninsula and the Taiwan Strait, it would not have agreed to the conditions of the secret Korea Minute. That Japan was willing to make this vital exception for Korea supports the argument—also evidenced by Japanese support for the Korean War effort, covered in chapter 2—that Tokyo believed it had a vital interest in South Korea's security. However, the same could not be said for the ROC's offshore islands. Rattled by America's willingness to threaten the use of nuclear weapons over the offshore islands in 1955, Tokyo slowly but steadily worked to minimize its involvement in future Taiwan Strait emergencies.

Assessing the Alliance Audience Effect Framework

FIRST ATTEMPTS TO REVISE THE ALLIANCE: AUGUST 1954 TO DECEMBER 1956

As Schaller describes it, in 1955 Shigemitsu made Japan's "first serious effort to alter the security treaty."[103] Though it was ultimately unsuccessful, this attempt provides direct support for H1 and H2 of the alliance audience effect framework. Based on their observations during the First Taiwan Strait Crisis, Japanese officials were concerned that Washington's determination to support Nationalist China, and America's legal right to use bases in Japan without Tokyo's consent, posed significant of entrapment risks which in turn made America an unreliable ally.

Within three months of the First Taiwan Strait Crisis subsiding, Shigemitsu made a serious attempt to revise the unequal 1951 treaty. Had this effort been successful, it would have sharply curtailed entrapment dilemmas and thus mitigated the risk of American unreliability. Japanese officials expressed their desire for greater "equality" or "mutuality," but US officials correctly identified that these vague terms referred to concrete concerns about Japanese sovereignty and security. Individual officers in the State Department then realized that Japanese concerns about entrapment were intensifying rather than abating and that the 1951 Security Treaty should be revised. As expected by H2, Japanese officials did not happily tolerate the risks posed by American unreliability but attempted to revise the treaty to reduce the risk of entrapment. If, as Mercer expects, past loyalty does not generate expectations of future loyalty, then Tokyo would have had no need to secure any treaty revision, because US behavior in 1954–1955 would not have suggested future US loyalty to the ROC.

Finally, the events examined support H3, which expects that America's actions will be influenced by the possibility that its behavior in one alliance will affect the reliability perceptions of its other allies. As US officials came to accept the necessity of alliance revision, they considered how it might affect other regional allies. Marshall Green appreciated the possible consequences for Seoul and Taipei, as Washington's ability to fulfil these alliance commitments could be constrained by changes to the US-Japan alliance. US policy had to be "neither convulsive nor without full consultation and consideration of world-wide consequences."[104]

THE UNITED STATES ACCEPTS THE PROSPECT OF TREATY REVISION: JANUARY 1957 TO SEPTEMBER 1958

Kishi's frank discussions with US officials demonstrate that Japan was very concerned by the perilous entrapment risks the 1951 Security Treaty could pose for Japan. The State Department's North Asia branch assessed that "Japan desires strongly to separate itself from the hostile aspects of United States policy toward China."[105] When these aspects were discussed within the US government, Ambassador MacArthur specifically noted Japan's entrapment concerns centered on the offshore islands. He argued that if there were "an attack on Taiwan, we would, no doubt, get the consent of the Japanese to use our bases there, but not if the attack were only against the off-shore islands."[106] This evidence strongly supports H1, which expects that a state will monitor its ally's behavior in other alliances and these observations will affect perceptions of reliability.

H2 expects that a state will mitigate the risk posed by an unreliable ally, and significant evidence supports this hypothesis. Despite Dulles rebuffing Japan's first attempt to negotiate a new treaty, Japanese policymakers were undeterred. When Kishi visited Washington in 1957, he was able to secure an American acknowledgment that the 1951 treaty "was designed to be transitional in character and not in that form to remain in perpetuity."[107] Japan's efforts toward a new treaty—though not yet successful—support H2.

Finally, H3 expects that America's actions will be influenced by the possibility that its behavior in one alliance will affect the reliability perceptions of its other allies. This was clearly on the mind of US officials, who were concerned that if Japan could veto American military action launched from bases in Japan, it would undermine US alliances with Korea and Nationalist China.

TREATY NEGOTIATIONS: OCTOBER 1958 TO JANUARY 1960

As the United States and Japan negotiated the 1960 treaty, a new formula on consultation ensured that Japan had the right to veto American military action launched from bases in mainland Japan. But the fact that Japan was willing to allow a secret exception—for military action to defend South Korea—supports my argument that Tokyo was especially concerned about the risks of entrapment in a conflict across the Taiwan Strait. The evidence presented suggests that Japan's entrapment fears prompted efforts to negotiate a revision of the 1951 US-Japan Security Treaty, and this is a strong data point of support for H1 and H2.

H3 expects that America's actions will be influenced by the possibility that its behavior in one alliance will affect the reliability perceptions of its other allies. Thus, in this case, H3 would expect America's negotiations behavior to be influenced by the possibility of adverse effects on the ROC and ROK. But the early exclusion of Okinawa from the treaty area reduced this likelihood. Excluding Okinawa meant that the United States would maintain full use of its bases there: no Japanese approval was necessary for it to launch military missions—perhaps for the defense of Formosa or the offshore islands—from Okinawa. Accordingly, Ambassador MacArthur noted that the exclusion of Okinawa from the treaty area would be of "very substantial advantage" to the United States and that "the ChiNats and ROK will also be much happier if Ryukyus are not included."[108] The preservation of America's military autonomy in Okinawa would be useful in reassuring these allies that America's military capabilities remained sufficient to defend then, that the US determination to maintain these capabilities reflected its intent to defend its allies, and thus that Washington continued to be reliable. As I show in chapter 6, when the United States and Japan did negotiate for the reversion of Okinawa, the ROC and ROK paid very close attention to developments which could affect the use of US military capabilities and did not hesitate to act when their fears of abandonment were stoked.

When Prime Minister Kishi visited Washington in January 1960, he signed a treaty that dramatically reduced the risk of Japan's entrapment in a war over the offshore islands. Japan did not, at this time, regain complete control over all its territories: the United States maintained full rights in Article III islands like Okinawa and could use other Japanese bases to respond immediately to North Korean aggression on the peninsula. But the content of the final agreement supports the argument that Japanese perceptions of American reliability were influenced by America's behavior toward the Republic of China and that Tokyo's fears of entrapment were focused on the offshore islands. In the new alliance agreement, Japan's new veto rights effectively ensured that its main islands would not be dragged into hostilities over Quemoy and Matsu.

US decision makers were also mindful of how changes to the US-Japan alliance might influence alliances with the ROC and ROK, but Japan's willingness to exclude the Ryukyu Islands from the treaty area swiftly resolved this dilemma—at least for now. Because the United States maintained full rights on Okinawa and had secured the Korea Minute exception, and because Japan was willing to allow the use of other bases for logistics support, the new treaty did not jeopardize America's capability to defend the ROC or ROK. One result of the new alliance, however, was to place far greater importance on Okinawa. As I show in the next chapter, the ROC and ROK would now pay close attention to any suggestion that America's rights in Okinawa might be diminished.

Negotiating the Reversion of Okinawa, 1967–1969

> The task of the American negotiators . . . was to assure the continued
> effectiveness of American military capabilities. It would not be
> desirable to signal to friend or foe an impairment of American power
> to cope with or deter threats against those to whom America had
> given a commitment. Credibility was at stake.
>
> —Armin Meyer (US ambassador to Japan)

The negotiations for the reversion of Okinawa to Japanese administration were, in many respects, similar to those for the revision of the US-Japan Security Treaty in 1960.[1] The persistence of the US-Japan alliance depended on Washington's willingness to grant Japan a vital concession and Tokyo's willingness to assume a more active role in supporting security in Asia. Reversion was completed in 1972, but the critical negotiations occurred between 1967 and 1969. As described in chapter 5, under the 1960 US-Japan Security Treaty the United States could use bases in Okinawa to conduct whatever operations it liked, for any purpose, without first seeking Tokyo's permission.

Because the 1960 treaty did not significantly degrade the US military capabilities available for the defense of South Korea or Taiwan itself, these allies did not object to the new alliance terms. However, because the reversion of Okinawa to Japanese administration could restrict America's ability to use bases on the island, this had the potential to significantly impede America's ability to defend the ROC and the ROK. This chapter explores an important instance of how two allies, prompted by a possible degradation of US military capability, monitored the US-Japan alliance and responded to developments within it.

As H1 of the alliance audience effect framework expects, Seoul and Taipei closely observed the US-Japan negotiations between 1967 and 1969. When they felt their interests were not receiving sufficient consideration, and that

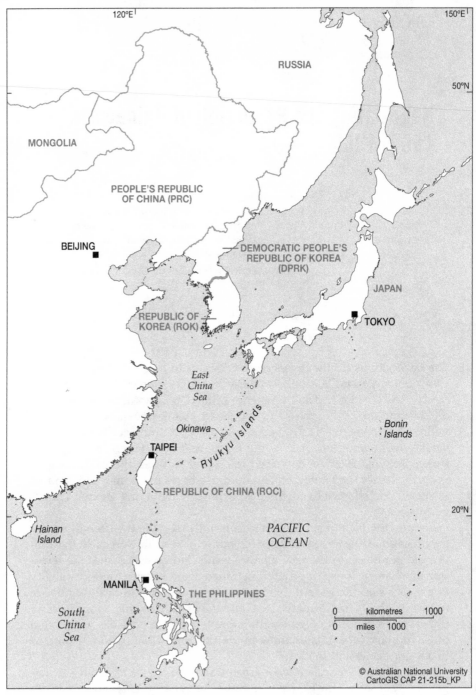

Figure 4. Map of Northeast Asia. Produced by CartoGIS Services, College of Asia and the Pacific, the Australian National University.

this was suggestive of US unreliability, they didn't hesitate to lobby both Washington and Tokyo to remind them of Okinawa's vital role in Asian security. This activity supports H2, which expects states to try to mitigate the risk of allied unreliability. In turn, as expected by H3, this alliance interdependence had a significant impact on US policy: it influenced the negotiation process, determined Washington's basic bargaining posture, and prompted Washington to reach out to Seoul and Taipei with a "hand-holding operation" to reassure them that the US remained reliable.[2]

This chapter contains five sections. The first, covering the period from January to November 1967, describes the initial tensions over Okinawa within the US-Japan relationship. These were observed by the ROC and, to a lesser degree, the ROK and they both expressed concern that their security interests could be jeopardized by reversion. The second section, examining the period from December 1967 to December 1968, describes efforts by the Japanese government to prepare domestic political sentiment for a reversion deal that permitted the United States to maintain militarily useful bases in Okinawa. The third section covers January to August 1969, during which preliminary reversion negotiations took place. Concerned that the ROK's security had already been damaged by Washington's unreliability, Seoul was extremely worried that Okinawan reversion could further weaken their strategic situation. Accordingly, the ROK attempted to mitigate the risk of a reversion deal that would restrict US rights on Okinawa. The fourth section, covering August to November 1969, examines how the final agreement—encapsulated in a joint communiqué and a speech from the Japanese prime minister—took into account America's other alliance commitments. The fifth and final section examines whether these events challenge or support the alliance audience effect framework.

There are several excellent histories of the reversion negotiations, but they focus on the issues as they affected US-Japan relations.[3] This chapter does not present a full history of the negotiations but instead looks closely at those aspects that generated concern in other US alliances.

January to November 1967

THE OKINAWA ISSUE GROWS CLAWS
AND CONCERNS OTHER US ALLIES

When Ural Alexis Johnson became the ambassador to Japan in late 1966, he assessed that "Okinawa was the single biggest job." The Japanese prime minister, Eisaku Sato, was scheduled to visit Washington in November 1967 for talks with President Lyndon B. Johnson and this summit "imposed a welcome pressure on negotiations" regarding Okinawa.[4] Japanese agitation for the return of administrative rights over the Ryukyu Islands—the Okinawa and Bonin Island chains—had intensified shortly after the 1960 revision of the Security Treaty. Once Japan had gained the right to prior consultation for bases in "homeland" Japan, the next logical step was for this right to be obtained for the Ryukyus as well.[5] In the 1960s, US administration and control of Okinawa were the last vestiges of the 1951 Security Treaty. Okinawa connected two elements of US foreign policy—its relationship with Japan and the escalation of the war in Vietnam—in a way that demanded political action in Tokyo. Bases on Okinawa were regularly used to launch air attacks against North Vietnam, despite the Japanese public's opposition. The Vietnam War would soon begin to "cast a dark shadow over all Japanese-American relations."[6]

US officials knew that pressure for the return of administrative rights over Okinawa would increase in the lead-up to 1970, when the ten-year term of the US-Japan Security Treaty would expire. Japanese opposed to the treaty were preparing for this date and according to the embassy in Tokyo, 1970 "assumed the proportions of a mythic calendar beast": only effective action on Okinawa would deprive it of its "claws."[7] In 1967, the State and Defense departments agreed that the Okinawa issue required resolution, but only once security tensions in Asia had subsided. Morton Halperin, a Defense official, described how a task force was established in 1966 with the "explicit premise" that "reversion would not occur until the 'sky was blue,' that is, until there were no clouds in the sky, no threats to peace and security in Asia."[8] In practice, this meant that the United States wanted Okinawa's reversion to occur after the end of the Vietnam War.

But the mythically beastly nature of 1970 and the possibility that popular sentiment in Japan might complicate a renewal of the alliance treaty meant that demands for Okinawa's reversion could not be easily dismissed. Some State officials worried that "the ultimate risk was setting off a series of events in Japan which would jeopardize the very existence of the security treaty."[9] But in 1967, the task force secretly concluded that if US bases on Okinawa were subjected to the same "prior consultation" principle as bases on homeland Japan, then the reversion of Okinawa—even if it involved "giving up the right to store nuclear weapons" on the island—"would not adversely affect our security interests."[10] Washington had decided that it could afford a generous arrangement with Japan, but this position was kept carefully concealed in order to maximize US bargaining power.

However, the ROC was not so sanguine about the implications of a possible reversion to Japanese sovereignty. Taipei closely observed the America-Japan relationship for movement on the Okinawa issue. In the late 1950s and early 1960s, Taipei had voiced concern to US embassy officials that the status of Okinawa should not be determined solely by the United States and Japan but rather by those allied powers that had participated in the Potsdam and Cairo declarations.[11] The ROC was so closely observing the US-Japan relationship that in March 1967, Taipei even complained about seemingly unimportant events, such as Prime Minister Sato referring to the future reversion of Okinawa.[12]

For the ROC, these minor issues created concern that US policy on Okinawa was shifting. Because the status of the Ryukyus had been agreed at the San Francisco peace conference, in March 1967 the ROC insisted that any change in Okinawa's status required the agreement of the peace treaty's signatories.[13] In May 1967, the ROC's foreign minister, Wei Tao-ming, told a visiting US official that "any US withdrawal accompanied by reversion to Japan would cause strategic and military problems." Despite the official promising that "we firmly intend to maintain US rights in Okinawa so long as East Asian security required," the ROC wasn't reassured. The US official felt that the ROC's "major motivation" on this matter was "a desire to exercise some diplomatic leverage. . . . They feel they have in this matter one of the very few opportunities to take the initiative in their relations with the US, and also with Japan."[14] Though the ROC's historical ties to the Ryukyu Islands could explain their interest in Okinawa, subsequent events suggest that the ROC's actions were motivated by concerns about US reliability.

With US officials seemingly unconcerned, a Ministry of Foreign Affairs vice minister called on the US ambassador in Taipei, Walter McConaughy, to "remind us of previous [1953] US commitment to keep GRC informed of steps toward future disposition [of Okinawa] and to protest recent failures to consult."[15] The vice minister did not suggest that Taipei had any claim of ownership but rather emphasized that "the Ryukyu Islands are closely related to the security of the East Asia and Pacific region." Despite Nationalist Chinese officials explicitly noting their security concerns, US embassy officers believed these "periodic GRC expressions of opinion" on Okinawa "constitute chiefly an effort to maintain remnants of GRC status as full partner of U.S." The ambassador recommended that the United States keep Taipei informed but also cautioned that the ROC's president, Chiang Kai-shek, displayed "sensitivity to any sign of US inattention to GRC . . . orders for present demarche came from Gimo [the Generalissimo, Chiang Kai-shek] himself."[16]

The secretary of state, Dean Rusk, instructed the embassy to reply to the verbal demarche in writing. This response noted the ROC's interest in "the security of East Asia and the Pacific region" and explained that because of this, Washington would "keep the [GRC] . . . informed of developments regarding the status of the islands." Noting that the issue of Okinawa might assume greater prominence in November, when Japanese prime minister Sato was scheduled to meet with President Johnson, Rusk instructed the embassy to brief Taipei "on developments concerning the future status of the Ryukyus at such time."[17]

While some State officials thought the ROC's efforts a desperate attempt to cling to great power status, the Bureau of Intelligence and Research argued that although "face . . . plays a part," realpolitik was of greater relevance. They judged that the ROC's "primary concern appears to be the possibility of a weakening of Taiwan's security if the Ryukyus are returned to Japan and the US military bases there are dismantled. . . . [GRC actions] probably indicate a desire at least to delay as long as possible any transfer of authority from the US to Japan."[18]

THE JOHNSON-SATO COMMUNIQUÉ

In the lead-up to Prime Minister Sato's visit to Washington in November 1967, the United States decided that pressures for the reversion of Okinawa might be sated if the Bonin Islands—which had far less military significance—could be returned to Japan.[19] But Washington was unwilling to move quickly on Okinawa, for fear of damaging US military capabilities. Ambassador Johnson told the Japanese foreign minister, Takeo Miki, that bases there were a key "deterrent to aggression," and that if US "freedom of action on Okinawa was reduced, this deterrent would be also."[20]

In discussions throughout 1967, US officials emphasized the importance of Okinawa's regional defense role: the island was relevant to US alliances with Taiwan and Korea, and also to the ongoing war in Vietnam.[21] In August, Ambassador Johnson encouraged US officials to emphasize the "significance in regional sense of various Okinawa defense functions per se, on degradation overall graduated deterrent and war-fighting position if these functions could not be carried out from Okinawa, on importance of flexibility and availability full range of options in event needed, and in consequence on intelligent future management by both our countries of this unique security asset."[22]

In September 1967, Foreign Minister Miki visited Washington in preparation for Sato's November visit. In a meeting with Rusk, Miki promised that he "did not under-estimate the important role of Okinawa in maintaining security in the Far East." Rusk said that before any decision could be made the US government would "wish to explore fully the significance of the base if the United States is to carry its responsibilities for the security of Japan and Korea." Rusk explained that the United States was

> thinking seriously of the effect on third countries of any decisions on Okinawa while Communist China continues its present attitude. For example, how would it affect the Republic of Korea, the Republic of China and the Philippines. Would such a step appear to be a drawing away of the U.S. presence and a reduction of United States commitments. He said the issue should be studied comprehensively and both nations should make a judgement as to what would be wise to do under the present circumstances.[23]

This situation had eerie parallels with that of the late 1950s: Japanese officials were keen to amend the security relationship to better align with both their strategic and their domestic political interests, but US officials were concerned about Washington's ability to fulfill other alliance commitments. With Japan reluctant to publicly acknowledge its regional security role, the United States was unwilling to surrender administrative control of Okinawa if doing so impaired Washington's ability to defend Seoul or Taipei.

As Miki returned to Japan, reports of his talks with Rusk brought "attention to security considerations bound up with [Okinawa] reversion and must have beenebisappointing [recte been disappointing] to any Japanese who were genuinely optimistic about early reversion." However, conservative Japanese politicians saw America's firm stance on reversion as an opportunity to "heighten Japanese awareness of security considerations. GOJ [Government of Japan] spokesmen . . . [explained] that security of Far East is as important to U.S. as 'national sentiment' is to Japan." The embassy reported that "government spokesmen . . . are now telling people that U.S. position is tough because of U.S. security responsibilities in area and that reversion is something for future." The embassy correctly predicted that the GOJ would try to increase the Japanese public's "appreciation [for the] U.S. role in defense of [the] area." The GOJ would also "hope for and expect U.S. willingness to cooperate in creating [the] impression of mo[d]est but satisfactory progress toward reversion."[24] According to the *Yomiuri* newspaper, Rusk told Miki that the United States doubted "Japan could support politically and psychologically [the] role of US bases in a reverted Okinawa in assuring the security of [the] ROK and GRC."[25]

After Miki's visit, Tokyo began to talk more frankly and publicly about Okinawa's role in regional defense. The director-general of the Japanese Defense Agency noted that it would be a "subject for concern" if Okinawa's reversion "were to mean that the ability of US bases there to defend Japan and [the] Far East was to be diminished."[26] By November, the State Department had noted an "encouraging recognition by the GOJ of its regional responsibilities and recognition of [the] relationship between Ryukyus settlement and its own and broader regional security. . . . GOJ public efforts to place [the] Ryukyu issue on [a] realistic security basis have been in right direction." As officials worked out the details of the joint communiqué that would be issued at the Johnson-Sato summit, it was clear that while Washington was willing to return the Bonin Islands in short order, Okinawa itself was a longer-term project.[27]

As the summit approached, the ROC began to agitate over the possibility that their security interests might be harmed by a US-Japan deal. In September, when Prime Minister Sato visited Taipei, Chiang Kai-shek discussed the ROC's interest in Okinawa, "underscoring [the] security importance of Okinawa and advising Japan to be patient in dealing with reversion issue."[28] In response, Sato emphasized Tokyo's "appreciation of the security importance of [the] U.S. bases" on Okinawa.[29] Before the Johnson-Sato summit, the ROC ambassador to the United States, Chow Shu-kai, told the assistant secretary of state for East Asia and the Pacific, William Bundy, that he was under instructions to "reaffirm GRC concern for this problem and to convey hope that GOJ would not press too far and that present status of Okinawa would not be affected." Bundy reassured Chow that the summit might produce "some new verbal formula relating to question of Okinawa but that this would not involve any change in status. He added that we would keep GRC informed of developments."[30]

The Johnson-Sato communiqué, which was released on November 15, 1967, affirmed that the Bonin Islands would revert to Japanese control and that negotiations would arrange for "the early restoration of these islands without detriment to the security of the area." On Okinawa, the communiqué anticipated an agreement for reversion "within a few years," but Sato also publicly "recognized that the United States military bases on these islands continue to play a vital role in assuring the security of Japan and other free nations in the Far East."[31]

The reaction to the communiqué in Japan was not particularly positive: the idea that the reversion of Okinawa was contingent upon preserving its usefulness to the American military rankled domestic opinion. The return of the Bonins was welcomed, but the Japanese press worried about Tokyo's "recognition [of the] role of Okinawa bases in Far East security" and feared that "broader commitments might lie behind [the] public document."[32] One newspaper alleged that Sato "sacrificed Okinawa for the 'so-called security of the Far East.'"[33] Despite the GOJ's initial efforts to educate the Japanese population on Washington's security requirements for Okinawa, the island's regional security role was not yet commonly accepted.

December 1967 to December 1968

TOKYO MOVES TO INCULCATE DEFENSE-MINDEDNESS IN JAPAN

On Sato's return to Japan, the opposition Democratic Socialist Party questioned the prime minister on his intentions for Okinawa, insisting that he should commit to a "homeland level" reversion, whereby the prior consultation clause of the 1960 treaty would also apply to Okinawa. By Sato's refusing to give such guarantees, the US embassy thought he "threw into clear relief the idea that Japanese decisions on post-reversion bases in Okinawa should be made on basis of national interest, not of ideological preconceptions." In his remarks, Sato suggested that two options were feasible: an early reversion with American bases "accorded freedom of use" for conventional operations and the storage of nuclear weapons, or a postponed reversion at the "homeland level."[34]

The possibility that Okinawa hosted nuclear weapons was a contentious issue, given Japan's three nonnuclear principles (that it would not manufacture nuclear weapons, possess them, or permit their entry into Japanese territory). Although the United States maintained a policy of neither confirming nor denying the presence of nuclear weapons in any area or on any vessel, nuclear capable bombers and missiles were known to be stationed on Okinawa. One concern with reversion was that if Japan's three nonnuclear principles were applied to Okinawa, general and graduated nuclear deterrence in Asia might be weakened. Japanese leaders were aware that the bases on Okinawa served a role in nuclear deterrence and hoped that the advent of Polaris—a submarine-launched nuclear missile—would obviate the need to store nuclear weapons on Okinawa, but American officers insisted this was not the case. Admiral Ulysses Sharp, commander-in-chief of the Pacific, told Sato in May 1967 that "Okinawa remained very important even though Polaris has entered the picture, because Polaris represents the ultimate offensive while it is necessary to have a dual purpose capability in the Western Pacific to react to lower level situations and to provide for a graduated [nuclear] response." In reply, Sato emphasized he "realized the importance of Okinawa as an 'unsinkable battleship.'"[35] The Japanese government also continued its efforts to reassure the ROC that Taipei's interests would not be damaged by Okinawa reversion. In late 1967 the ROC's defense minister, Chiang Ching-kuo, was given "more specific reassurances on the Sato Government's intentions vis-à-vis . . . Okinawan reversion."[36]

After the Johnson-Sato summit, the prime minister "initiated a year of debate on 'defense-mindedness' in Japan" and "indicated that the Japanese people would have to consider the possibility . . . of a special status for the Okinawan bases allowing the continued presence of nuclear weapons."[37] The US embassy reported these efforts approvingly, noting that they "clearly conveyed [the] impression of Sato['s] intention to lead public opinion to [the] point where it would accept US bases in Okinawa with present freedoms."[38] Secretary Rusk trusted Sato, and in a letter to the secretary of defense, Robert McNamara, wrote that "Sato understands . . . he must . . . permit us continued use of the Ryukyuan bases with our present rights largely unimpaired."[39]

Convincing the Japanese public was not an easy process and it was made more difficult by events in the region. In January 1968, a North Korean commando attack on South Korea's presidential palace, known as the Blue House, was followed several days later by the capture of the USS *Pueblo*, a US Navy intelligence vessel. Japan's response to these events was tepid and US officials attributed this sentiment to a fear of entrapment. The State Department's country director for Japan, Richard (Dick) Sneider, wrote that the Japanese feared these events "could lead to broader hostilities . . . and greater risk of Japanese involvement. . . . The emphasis, therefore, is . . . on endorsing U.S. restraint, [and] efforts to negotiate."[40] While Japan provided some private support to Seoul after the Blue House raid, its public response left the impression "that Japan, despite its large and acknowledged stake in Korea, has its head in the sand, fearful of military involvement."[41]

Ambassador Johnson explained that Tokyo's reticence was because "Sato's political position has been somewhat destabilized as [a] result [of] his efforts to develop a 'defense consciousness' among the Japanese . . . he has not felt able to take a more forthright position on Korea."[42] But Tokyo's hesitance infuriated Secretary Rusk, and in a cable he castigated Japan for "whining about Okinawa while we are losing several hundred killed each month [in Vietnam] on behalf of our common security in the Pacific." Rusk suggested that "surely the time has come for us to begin to resist attempts by the Japanese to erode our base in Okinawa on the grounds of Japanese 'sensibilities.'"[43]

President Johnson wrote to Sato in January 1968, encouraging him to "consider approaching the Soviet Union . . . [and] the North Koreans . . . to impress on them the seriousness of the situation."[44] In Tokyo, Ambassador Johnson approved of this stronger approach toward Japan. He wrote to Sneider: "the stakes for us in Vietnam and Korea are so high and so urgent that we should no longer hold back our punches with the GOJ." Johnson thought the risks of this approach were manageable, because Japan's security dependence on the US was a source of leverage: "we are not forcing Japan into the arms of anyone else because they well know that they have no one else to whom to turn."[45] But this logic overlooked the possibility that Japan might seek to escape Washington's embrace even in the immediate absence of another willing lover.

Soon, events would lead Japan to simultaneously fear both abandonment and entrapment. In May 1968 Kei Wakaizumi, a Japanese academic who served as an unofficial envoy of Prime Minister Sato, described to Sneider and Bundy Japanese fears of abandonment. The apparent success of the Vietcong's Tet offensive alarmed some in Japan, but this was intensified when President Johnson announced that he would not run for reelection and also signaled his intent to open negotiations with Communist North Vietnam. Wakaizumi said this speech became "commonly known as the 'Johnson shock.'" Many Japanese believed the United States was "withdrawing from Asia," was "no longer trustworthy," and could "no longer be considered a dependable ally. . . . [S]ome are recommending that Japan keep its distance from the U.S. and make the necessary accommodation with Communist China." Though these beliefs were "oversimplified and not yet commonly held," Wakaizumi thought they "could lead to a crisis in 1970 involving in the first instance the Security Treaty and Okinawa, but more fundamentally, the total US-Japanese relationship."[46]

Japan observed as the United States redefined its strategic interests in Indochina and feared that a similar process could occur with Washington's China policies. In February 1968 US reliability had been doubted because after the Blue House raid and the capture of the USS *Pueblo*, Tokyo feared entrapment in a new Korean conflict. Now, American reliability was questioned because its overall Asia policy seemed to be in a dangerous period of flux, and this posed risks of abandonment. Ambassador Johnson later recalled that President Johnson's speech was "universally interpreted by the Japanese press as being a prelude to a complete withdrawal and a reversal of policy on Vietnam. I spent some five hours alone with the Prime Minister . . . trying to convince him this wasn't the case."[47] By June 1968, the embassy in Tokyo was reporting that events in Vietnam had "thrown doubt on US firmness and invincibility." One effect of Japan's diminished confidence was that the "possibility of GOJ accepting reversion of Okinawa with substantially greater freedom of use than enjoyed by bases in Japan proper has receded considerably."[48]

This sentiment might seem counterintuitive but as Japan was questioning American staying power in Asia it was also fearful that Communist China's possession of nuclear weapons—combined with the presence of American forces in Japan—posed a serious risk to Japanese security. In February 1966, Communist China had warned Japan that if US forces in Japan attacked the mainland, Japan could be targeted for retaliation.[49] The possibility of nuclear coercion—but with Korea, not Vietnam, as the precipitating cause—was discussed at a meeting between Bundy, Ambassador Johnson, and the Japanese ambassador to the United States, Takeso Shimoda, in June 1968.[50]

These circumstances created an unusual situation, in which Tokyo simultaneously feared both entrapment and abandonment. There was fear that the "Johnson Shock" signaled a US withdrawal from Asia and this precipitated a fear of abandonment. However, the presence of US forces in Okinawa, and the possible use of bases in Japan for conflicts in Asia, continued to worry Japanese decision makers. These events resulted in seemingly contradictory signals and created a situation where Japan complained about the presence of the US military, and the possible entrapment risks it created, but also feared a wholesale change of Washington's Asia policy, and the risks of abandonment it could create. Given the unpredictable nature of US foreign policy at this time, it is not particularly surprising that Japan simultaneously feared both entrapment and abandonment.[51]

These mixed sentiments vexed Secretary Rusk, who reprimanded Ambassador Shimoda by noting that "400 or 500 Americans are dying weekly in Viet-Nam to prove our commitment to our Asian allies." But Rusk also suggested that America's role in Asia was changing: "no longer will the American people accept the role of unilateral policeman and the key question for them is who else will share these responsibilities." Japan's deputy vice minister of foreign affairs insisted that he understood America's position, but noted that "regrettably many Japanese are out of touch with reality and this cannot be disregarded by the Japanese Government."[52]

During the second half of 1968 the Sato government continued its campaign to educate the Japanese people on "defense-mindedness." Sato argued that the United States needed greater support from its allies in Asia, including Japan. In July, he publicly described the idea of a homeland-level reversion of Okinawa as "unrealistic," because it didn't address "the basic problem of the defense of free Asia as a whole."[53] In August, he affirmed that he had no intention of modifying the security treaty's clauses on the Far East, since "Asian stability [is] related to Japan's peace and stability."[54] Also in August, in the communiqué issued after a ministerial meeting between Japan and the ROK, Japan recognized "that the security and prosperity of Korea greatly affect[s] the security and prosperity of Japan." As one Korean official pointed out, this was the "first time GOJ has expressed in writing such connection between Korea and Japan."[55] Ambassador Johnson continued to remind Tokyo about Okinawa's regional importance: in October he spoke of a defensive chain of American bases in Asia, and warned that "if one link is pulled out the chain is weakened and loses a portion of its total capability."[56]

Sato's efforts were not immediately successful. A September report from the US embassy noted that

> the Japanese public continues to regard . . . Contributions to Far East regional security . . . as of interest only to the United States. Base utilization for these purposes tends to be begrudged as a dangerous Japanese concession to the United States. . . . Those who willingly accept the concept of bases in Japan (and Okinawa) as in Japan's interest because they are needed for [the] defense of the Republic of Korea or other neighboring areas . . . are a minority over all. Nor do these backers of a regional role for our bases care to espouse this publicly for fear of popular reaction.[57]

In an interview with an American journalist, Sato connected the issue of bases in Japan to America's broader defense posture in Asia, saying that "the question cannot be settled unless we give thought to what should be done about the security of Japan, including Okinawa, and the Far East. . . . [T]he form of bases in the homeland is determined in conjunction with the bases in Okinawa, the Republic of Korea and Taiwan, and the form of bases in Okinawa alone cannot be decided separately."[58]

By late 1968, Japan's government had a plan for 1969. Kiichi Aichi, who would soon become the country's foreign minister, suggested to the embassy that in early 1969, Tokyo could agree a timeline for Okinawa negotiations with the incoming administration of President Richard Nixon. In Japan, a midyear decision on allowing the automatic extension of the 1960 Security Treaty could precede a prime ministerial visit to the United States in the second half of the year. A Nixon-Sato summit could involve a public "agreement on the manner and timing of Okinawan reversion," and would be followed by the dissolution of the Diet and fresh elections in Japan. This could "defuse . . . an Okinawan time bomb that increasingly threatens . . . the Japan-U.S. relationship."[59]

ALLIED REACTIONS TO US-JAPAN DEVELOPMENTS IN 1968

While allied activity in 1968 was limited compared to 1967 and 1969, this is easily explained by the substantive agreements reached in these bracketing years. That said, the ROC did observe and react to some events in the US-Japan relationship. In February 1968, Foreign Minister Wei publicly affirmed his interest in Okinawa developments and said that "the GRC is following U.S.-Japanese talks on the Ryukyus closely." The US embassy thought that this statement might have been prompted by "a need to reaffirm its position in view of the new U.S.-Japanese consultative machinery provided in the Johnson-Sato communique being set up to associate Japan more closely with the Ryukyus."[60] These concerns were expressed not only in private diplomatic representations but also in the public sphere. In June 1968, a newspaper editorial described Okinawa as having "incomparable importance to the collective security of free nations in this area. . . . China is afraid that, if the Ryukyus should come to belong to Japan, the bases of our all[y] might be menaced, and that the joint security of all nations concerned might be endangered."[61]

Washington, for its part, continued to keep the ROC informed of Okinawa developments. In October 1968, when it was agreed that representatives from Okinawa could participate in the Japanese Diet, the United States informed the ROC before a public announcement was made. The State Department cabled the embassy in Taipei, noting that "in view [of] GRC sensitivity to changes in situation surrounding Okinawa," it was "preferable that we inform [the] GRC in advance of this major step being taken in cooperation with GOJ."[62] While the ROC was appreciative of the effort to keep it informed, it also expressed "concern" at the decision and asked if this "move 'implied any effect on determination of future status' of [the] islands."[63]

However, Taipei's efforts were low-key and did not reflect widespread alarm or panic at the thought of Okinawan reversion: instead, they suggest that the ROC was keeping a watchful eye on developments. At first glance, and when contrasted with the ROC, the lack of ROK activity during this time period might seem puzzling. However, 1968 was an incredibly eventful year for the US-ROK alliance, and Korean decision makers did not need to look beyond their own interactions with the United States in order to make reliability assessments. As Victor Cha notes, "Washington's ambivalent response to the three North Korean provocations in 1968 and 1969 seriously undermined South Korean confidence in American defense commitments."[64] Following a January 1968 North Korean commando raid on the South Korean president's residence, "Washington responded with decided restraint," and the American ambassador warned "that any South Korean attempts at retribution would meet with strong U.S. opposition." When North Korean forces seized the USS *Pueblo* only two days later, "the U.S. response was again passive. Washington declined all requests from [South Korean president]

Park [Chung-hee] for retaliatory air strikes against Pyongyang."[65] With such clear signals present within the bilateral relationship, Korean officials did not need to observe external relationships in order to form judgments about US reliability. However, as negotiations over Okinawa progressed and became publicly prominent in 1969—and as tensions on the Peninsula abated somewhat—the ROK would take greater notice and play a more active role.

I did not discover any evidence that Japan was concerned by America's tepid reaction to these provocations on the Korean Peninsula. America's apparent lack of loyalty to Korea did not worry Japan because this actually aligned with Tokyo's interests. Sneider thought Japan feared these incidents "could lead to broader hostilities . . . and greater risk of Japanese involvement. . . . The [Japanese] emphasis, therefore, is . . . on endorsing U.S. restraint."[66] Had the United States supported Seoul in a stronger fashion, this might have increased the risk of war on the peninsula and the involvement of Communist China. Just as in the First Taiwan Strait Crisis, Japan was primarily concerned about its own interests and not America's loyalty to another ally.

January to August 1969

ROK AND ROC CONCERN ABOUT OKINAWA PROMPTS THE UNITED STATES TO HOLD THEIR HANDS

On January 1, 1969, Sato held a press conference on foreign policy. While he "considered the feelings of the Okinawa people to be [the] most important component of [the] reversion equation . . . [he] urged sufficient consideration be given to [the] role of [the] bases in protecting [the] people of Okinawa as well as Japan and East Asia."[67] This emphasis on the regional role of Okinawa was a major theme for the Japanese government throughout 1969. When Ambassador Shimoda publicly suggested that Okinawa might revert at something less than homeland-level terms, the Japanese opposition was critical. But the US embassy in Tokyo thought Shimoda's move was a "calculated risk to begin [the] process of measuring what 'extra freedoms' for US bases on Okinawa Japanese public opinion will accept."[68] In late January, Japan moved to establish a timetable for the Okinawa negotiations. Shimoda met with Bundy, outlining Sato's desire to visit Washington in November in order to resolve the issue. Shimoda also noted that "there should be 'special treatment' regarding US use of Okinawa bases in view of [the] situations in Korea and Viet-Nam and uncertain communist intentions."[69]

As momentum toward negotiations accelerated, the ROK's concerns intensified. US embassy reporting suggested that Seoul was intent on creating the Pacific-Asian Treaty Organization (PATO), a multilateral alliance that could contribute to security in Asia as the United States withdrew from Vietnam.[70] The proposed members included the Asian countries contributing troops in Vietnam: the four core members would be South Korea, Nationalist China, South Vietnam, and Thailand.[71] While the ROK was the primary instigator of the concept, the ROC also appeared to be interested. The ROK's prime minister told the US embassy that PATO "had been discussed by President Park with General Chiang on a highly secret basis," and that Chiang was "interested in learning more about [the] Korean proposal."[72]

Concurrent with this heightened interest in PATO, diplomatic reporting emphasized Seoul's "sudden and keen interest in Okinawa reversion problem. . . . [C]ommentators have described Okinawa as key to Korean security and have expressed great concern over its probable return to Japanese." South Korean observers feared that a "US pullback from Okinawa could signal [the] beginning of [a] US withdrawal from Asia."[73] When the deputy secretary of state sought guidance on Seoul's PATO thinking, an official from the department's Korea section advised that "what the ROKG [ROK government]—and probably also the ROC—have in the back of their minds is some type of reassurance of US military support and a long term reinsurance of our present security commitments."[74]

The available evidence suggests, but does not establish, that PATO may have been an effort by the ROK and ROC to sabotage the reversion negotiations. In late February, a secret meeting was held between Chiang Ching-kuo and South Korean president Park. US intelligence reported that at this meeting, Park "proposed that . . . a collective effort be made immediately . . . to call for a halt to the withdrawal of U.S. military forces from Okinawa." The ROK was to seek out the views of other countries in Asia, with the hope that they might support the effort.[75] When Chiang Ching-kuo discussed this meeting with the US embassy in Taipei, he reported that South Korean leaders had "expressed strong opposition to any reversion of Okinawa to Japan in present circumstances," and "voiced [the] strong feeling that [the] USG [United States government] should not transfer administrative control to Japan."[76]

The State Department thought that if any public movement toward PATO became associated with Okinawan bases, this could threaten the US-Japan negotiations. Secretary of State Rusk worried

> that any GRC-ROK efforts to realize [a] security alliance with SVN [South Vietnam] and Thailand would undoubtedly become public knowledge in the near future. Linking of role of US bases in Okinawa to this nascent security alliance would gravely complicate current USG efforts to achieve agreement with GOJ on maximum flexible use of Okinawan bases . . . If USG allows impression to be created that USG seeking "flexibility" in future use of Okinawan bases . . . at behest of and in order to assist PATO members, reaction on part of Japanese people would be definitely negative, and the possibility of obtaining this flexibility thereby reduced.[77]

The available declassified documents do not conclusively establish that there was an intent to sabotage reversion negotiations by linking them to a prospective PATO, but the US ambassador in Seoul, William Porter, also saw a potential connection, and speculated about a secondary motive in Seoul's PATO efforts. In his view, President Park called for the United States "to put pressure on Japan to recognize necessity for regional collective defense" despite the ROK's "reservations about desirability of Japanese membership" in the prospective PATO. Porter thought that Korean concerns about Okinawa likely prompted Park's statement: "Since they are unable to bring much pressure to bear on GOJ, [the] ROKs are attempting [to] influence GOJ indirectly through U.S. while at same time attempting to persuade us of necessity of keeping free use of Okinawa bases."[78] Cables such as these suggest that due to concerns about American reliability—which were influenced by the possible loss of rights on Okinawa—Seoul was exploring methods of pressuring Japan to allow a regional defense role for Okinawa, and also investigating the possibility of a new collective alliance in Asia.

The ROK also went further, and in a press interview on March 15, 1969, the prime minister emphasized South Korea's willingness to host American forces and "said his country welcomed more US troops and bases should US be forced to withdraw facilities from Okinawa."[79] In a late March meeting with Bundy, the Korean ambassador also suggested that the forces on Okinawa could be relocated to South Korea.[80] Bundy declined this offer, explaining that Washington intended to come to a satisfactory agreement with Tokyo, but also noted "the ROK should be assured that we have no intention of giving up our base rights in Okinawa."[81]

The United States, aware of the concern felt by the ROK and ROC, moved to manage these alliances simultaneously alongside the US-Japan relationship. In a cable titled "Okinawa: What to tell ROKG and ROC," the embassy in Tokyo noted that it was in America's interest to discourage "attempts by our Asian allies to pre-determine [the] means by which US support for Asian security is expressed. This important observation has particular relevance to attitudes toward Okinawa reversion. . . . Seoul and Taipei . . . appear to think that [the] US is in [an] adversarial bargaining situation . . . with [the] effectiveness of our bases at stake. Both seem anxious to 'help' us by asserting their own claims to a share of interest in the special base rights."[82]

To allay allied concerns, the embassy suggested that the ROK and ROC be briefed on the US-Japan negotiations, with emphasis on the fact that Washington's "security commitments to ROK and ROC . . . [are] not in jeopardy in Okinawa reversion negotiations" and that both "USG and GOJ will be cooperating to arrange reversion in manner that will take due account of Asian security role of Ryukyu bases." A shot across the bow was suggested: the allies should be warned that "anything which calls attention unnecessarily to aspects of problem that are controversial in Japan . . . is likely to render cooperatcke [*recte* cooperative] USG-GOJ approach to problem more difficult."[83]

The State Department cabled Seoul, Taipei, and Tokyo, suggesting that "ROKG concern that US might scant their interests in Okinawa issue could be reduced by [the] early initiation of [a] hand-holding operation." The embassy in Seoul was instructed to reassure the ROK that "USG is of course fully aware of [the] high importance of US bases in Okinawa and Japan to security of Korea. . . . This is [a] difficult issue but we believe [a] satisfactory solution will be reached. . . . As [the] situation develops we will provide ROKG with more information."[84] When these points were presented to Korea's vice foreign minister, he "expressed appreciation for information on subject but as might be expected, attempted [to] characterize present and future exchanges as 'consultations.'" This was a common South Korean tactic: by describing discussions with US diplomats as "consultations," it sought to create the impression that Okinawa reversion could occur only with Seoul's consent. The US embassy reminded the vice foreign minister "of [the] political problems faced by [the] GOJ and cautioned that while [the] U.S. appreciates security concerns of allies, [the] implication of U.S. consulting would create [a] problem for GOJ."[85]

These exchanges highlight the intricate interdependencies between these alliances. Korea was watching the US-Japan relationship and worried that progress toward the reversion of Okinawa was affecting America's security reliability. Even as the United States moved to reassure South Korea, it had to do so knowing that Seoul would attempt to mischaracterize these discussions as consultations. This, in turn, would be observed by Japan and would affect Japanese beliefs about US conduct. Thus, the actors in one alliance interaction were simultaneously the audience of another. This example neatly illustrates the complex interdependencies expected and explained by the alliance audience effect framework.

In April, the Korean prime minister met with Nixon and "expressed great concern" on reversion, for "Okinawa is very important to Korean security."[86] Separately, the deputy assistant secretary of state for East Asian and Pacific affairs, Winthrop Brown, assured the prime minister that the United States "fully understood the Koreans' concern about Okinawa." Brown explained that it was not a matter of fighting for base rights, but ensuring that basing arrangements were feasible over the longer term.[87] U. Alexis Johnson, newly promoted to the position of undersecretary of state for political affairs, offered more explicit reassurance to a visiting Korean politician, saying "there was no real question of our bases in Okinawa being withdrawn, but only of a readjustment in the conditions under which we occupy them."[88] Despite such efforts, in April Korean politicians "expressed concern that Japan [was] seeking prior consultation rights on US use of bases after reversion."[89] Seoul sent an aide memoire, "expressing ROKG concern over [the] reversion of Okinawa," to the Japanese embassy in Seoul.[90] An aide memoire was also presented to the US embassy in Seoul, requesting that Washington "consult fully with ROKG in settling question of Ryukyus."[91] Believing that its previous communications had been sufficient, and wary of creating the impression that it had an obligation to defer to Korean preferences, the United States decided to not formally reply.[92]

Interestingly, it appears that at this time the ROK was more concerned than the ROC. When Marshall Green visited Korea and Taiwan in April, it seems that the role of Okinawa was discussed only with Korean leaders, not the Nationalist Chinese.[93] Contemporary press reporting also noted this discrepancy: a *Washington Post* article about the reversion negotiations said that "South Korea is watching nervously," but the ROC was described as "less insistent."[94] The heightened concern of the ROK is best explained by its more precarious defense position at this time: developments in the US-Japan negotiations over Okinawa were happening against the backdrop of events in 1968, when American timidity had disappointed the ROK. This alliance dynamic had already demonstrated to Seoul that America's preference ordering affected its reliability as an ally, and the possibility that US power might be impeded by the reversion of Okinawa was thus further fuel for reliability concerns. Secondly, as described earlier in this chapter, Japan had made efforts to reassure the ROC, through Sato's visit to Taipei and Chiang Ching-kuo's visit to Japan.[95] Though the ROC was still concerned about Okinawan reversion, it is unsurprising that it was not as concerned as the ROK.

AMERICA PREPARES FOR FURTHER NEGOTIATIONS WITH JAPAN

Against this backdrop of allied agitation, internal differences in Washington were resolved. Henry Kissinger, President Nixon's national security adviser, wrote that America's position on Okinawa was decided on April 30, 1969: "if we could not obtain Japanese agreement to unrestricted use of the bases for combat operations throughout Asia we could settle for unrestricted rights for the defense of Korea, Taiwan, and Vietnam." Beyond this, if Japan would commit to allowing the reintroduction of nuclear weapons in times of regional crisis, then President Nixon would "take into account Japanese sensitivities on the nuclear issue" and agree that after reversion, no nuclear weapons would be stationed on Okinawa.[96]

In Tokyo, Japanese officials were continuing to acknowledge that Okinawa's regional defense role would persist. In late April, Foreign Minister Aichi explained to the US embassy that while the GOJ had often considered the prior consultation arrangement merely as a mechanism to veto American action, it was now moving to emphasize the possibility of approving American action under the prior consultation formula.[97] Efforts to raise public awareness also continued: a Foreign Ministry official briefed the press that Washington could not endorse "a settlement which would tie its hands in carrying out security requirements. . . . Japan should think more of [the] effect on [the] ROK and GRC of [any] weakening of [the] base structure."[98] Slowly but surely, the Japanese government was becoming more explicit in confirming and explaining Okinawa's ongoing regional security role.

For their part, American diplomats were thinking ahead to the November 1969 Nixon-Sato summit and becoming increasingly confident that a satisfactory deal could be struck. Richard Finn, the State Department's new country director for Japan, thought that for the conventional (nonnuclear) use of bases in Okinawa "we can work out some kind of understanding. . . . This could reinforce a strong statement in the Nixon-Sato communique to the effect that both governments attach special importance to security in the area of Northeast Asia. Such a statement would prepare public opinion in Japan and *give the right signal to other interested EA* [East Asian] *nations.*"[99]

The embassy in Tokyo shared this confidence, noting that press articles "reflect [a] clear effort by GOJ briefers to get across [the] point that [the] GOJ recognizes the importance of the role played by US bases . . . in [the] defense of Far East: thus, while [the] view of GOJ as a sovereign state must be reflected in [the] prior consultation process, that process will be operated flexibly and Japan will be willing to say 'yes' to [the] use of bases for combat operations in areas 'around Japan.'"[100]

Aichi, in a midyear trip to the United States, met with President Nixon. Rather than focusing on the terminology of homeland-level reversion, Aichi stated that the "GOJ wished to put to rest any question on defense matters by the flexible application of the Security Treaty." This concept of "flexible application" became a subtle signal that Japan was ready to assume greater regional defense responsibilities. "Aichi said that the effective presence of the United States was essential . . . to the security of the area as a whole, and Japan felt that it was essential to create an environment which would make possible effective cooperation to that purpose."[101]

In Aichi's meeting with U. Alexis Johnson, the communiqué for the upcoming Nixon-Sato summit was discussed. Johnson was explicit in noting that "US capabilities for carrying out commitments with respect to Korea and other areas in the Far East must be manifest in whatever language is developed."[102] Johnson clearly believed the contents of the Nixon-Sato communiqué would be closely scrutinized by other allies, as they looked for any sign that the reversion of Okinawa could damage US reliability. Once Aichi returned to Tokyo, the new US ambassador, Armin Meyer, emphasized the regional importance of Okinawa. In July, he told Aichi that the final reversion agreement would have to "signal to both friend and foe that USG military capability remains basically unimpaired."[103]

ROC AND ROK REACTIONS

Despite having been cautioned by the US against public discussion of Okinawa, South Korea continued its efforts to pressure both Japan and the United States. At a Tokyo meeting of the Asia-Pacific Council, the foreign ministers of the ROK and ROC gave "pre-conference press interviews . . . while their governments had no objection to reversion itself, settlement should not adversely affect the military value of the Okinawa bases."[104] On the sidelines of this regional summit, Korean foreign minister Choi Kyu-hah also met with Aichi. When Choi complained that the aide memoire sent to the Japanese embassy in April had not generated a reply, Aichi said that in a statement to the Diet he would "acknowledge Japanese awareness of Okinawa's role as backup for ROK and ChiNat security, and Aichi proposed that [the] ROKG consider such a statement as substitute for [a] reply."[105] Aware of ROC and ROK interest in Okinawan reversion, Tokyo sought to affirm its understanding of the island's importance to Korean and Nationalist Chinese security. In early July, the US embassy in Tokyo reported that since Aichi's visit to Washington, "Sato and other Government spokesmen have stated that an emergency on Taiwan or on [the] Korean Peninsula could very well affect [the] security of Japan's interest and conceivably, therefore, result in affirmative GOJ response to a U.S. reque[s]t to use its bases in Japan for military action in these cases."[106]

But these statements had little effect on Korea's concerns about the reversion of Okinawa. On July 31, Foreign Minister Choi sent Secretary Rusk two memos, which the embassy in Seoul described as "noteworthy for their unrestrained tone." The embassy reported that the "ROKG is watching with concern the development of negotiations between US and Japan on Okinawa. [The ROK believes that the] Okinawa question should be dealt with in broader context of peace and security of free Asian nations and not merely in bilateral context. [The] United States should retain unrestricted use of military base[s] on Okinawa and should there be major changes in the status of Okinawa, the US should consult in advance with ROK."[107]

In contrast to the intensification of Korea's concerns, the ROC seemed quite confident in US reliability. In an exchange with Japan's foreign minister Aichi, ROC foreign minister Wei believed "there was no need for concern, because [the] GRC would be pleased to have nukes moved to Taiwan if Japan did not want them in Okinawa. Aichi said [the] GRC Fo[reig]n Min[ister] seemed to have absolute faith that U.S. would not abandon Taiwan."[108] While this contrast might seem to pose a challenge to my theory, the discrepancy can be explained by both the different circumstances facing the ROC and ROK and Japan's earlier efforts to reassure Taipei. Even without the issues posed by the reversion of Okinawa, South Korea had been unimpressed by the US response to three important events in 1968–1969: the Blue House raid, the capture of the USS *Pueblo,* and the North Korean shooting down of an

American reconnaissance aircraft. These events had all demonstrated that America had only a very limited appetite for actions that could increase the chance of conflict on the Korean Peninsula. In this context, as Cha writes, the reversion of Okinawa was "unnerving to Seoul as it might ultimately make U.S. defense of Korea contingent on Japanese approval."[109]

On the Japan-ROC front, in September 1967 Sato had visited Taiwan and assured Chiang Kai-shek that Tokyo appreciated the defensive role that Okinawa played, and this assurance was repeated when defense minister Chiang Ching-kuo visited Tokyo later in 1967.[110] Given that Japanese leaders had reassured the ROC on several occasions that Okinawa's defensive role would not be impeded, it is unsurprising that at this time the ROC was more relaxed about the possible impact of Okinawa's reversion. In 1967, US intelligence reporting noted that Sato's visit to Taiwan, which prompted the PRC to denounce Sato for "'conspiring with the US imperialists' two China plot . . . underlined the existence of a special relationship" between Japan and the ROC.[111]

August to November 1969

NEGOTIATIONS CULMINATE IN THE NOVEMBER 1969 NIXON-SATO SUMMIT

A roving Japanese ambassador, Hiroto Tanaka, called on Undersecretary of State Johnson in August and discussed the importance of bases on Okinawa. Johnson emphasized that "problems of availability of nuclear weapons and free use of Japanese and Okinawan bases are of great concern to the U.S. If U.S. troops are to be kept in Korea, for example, U.S. must be able to support and protect them."[112] In a meeting between Tanaka and the new assistant secretary for East Asia and the Pacific, Marshall Green, "Green stressed the U.S. determination to carry out its commitments and to avoid [any] impairment of our ability to use our bases. . . . It is important that U.S. be able to assure its friends and deter foes in the area . . . both Korea and the Republic of China have shown concern over Okinawa reversion."[113]

Tokyo had received the message, and it became clear that base access would not be a major sticking point in the Nixon-Sato communiqué. The first draft of Sato's unilateral statement—which would eventually take the form of a speech to the National Press Club—met almost all of Washington's needs. While it was agreed that Okinawa would revert to Japanese administration on a homeland level, with the prior consultation clause applying to bases on Okinawa, Japan would publicly affirm the importance of ROC and ROK security to Japan's own situation. This draft of Sato's speech noted that Japan would decide its "response to prior consultation in the light of the need to maintain the security of the Far East," and noted that "if an armed attack against the Republic of Korea were to occur, the security of Japan would be seriously affected." This draft promised that in such circumstances Tokyo would "decide promptly its position on the basis of the foregoing recognition," but in Sato's actual speech this was upgraded to a pledge that Japan would "decide its position positively and promptly."[114] On Taiwan, the initial draft proclaimed that Japan's "policy is to keep a close watch on the situation and deal with it as our national interest requires."[115] This language was significantly strengthened in Sato's speech, but it was still a lesser commitment than that given to Korea: Sato noted that if the US-ROC alliance was ever "invoked against an armed attack from the outside, it would be a threat to the peace and security of the Far East, including Japan. . . . [W]e would deal with the situation on the basis of the foregoing recognition, in connection with the fulfilment by the United States of its defense obligations."[116]

Although not all of the relevant records have been declassified, it is likely that these modifications—all of which were a strengthening of Japan's initial position—were American suggestions, intended to reassure the ROC and ROK.[117]

THE UNITED STATES MOVES TO MANAGE
THE REACTIONS OF THE ROC AND ROK

In the lead-up to the Nixon-Sato summit, Seoul continued its efforts to influence reversion negotiations. In an August interview, President Park expressed his concern that a "downgrading of U.S. bases" in Okinawa could be one of several factors that "may create [a] power vacuum in this part of world."[118] The State Department assessed that the ROK maintained the objective of securing new American bases in Korea, "particularly if U.S. bases in Japan and especially Okinawa are lost or their use is excessively circumscribed."[119] At a joint ministerial conference between South Korea and Japan, South Korea's foreign minister "stressed . . . Japan's and ROK security closely connected. . . . ROK seriously concerned about Okinawa reversion." Choi also pressed Aichi in private and was told that "GOJ advocates firm maintenance Japan-US Security Treaty."[120] Though less publicly vocal, the ROC presented an aide memoire to the United States, and in response Green "assured Ambassador Chow that we have fully in mind the security interests of the GRC and other countries directly concerned."[121]

The State Department was aware that allied concerns were likely to intensify as the Nixon-Sato summit approached. On September 23, the department cabled its embassies in Seoul, Taipei, and Tokyo, suggesting that Dick Sneider, who was now playing a lead role in the reversion negotiations, visit the three countries to "present general summary of negotiations . . . to selected host government officials."[122] The embassy in Seoul cautiously welcomed this idea, but suggested that any briefing be done in a low-key manner. Diplomats also noted that South Korea "has been relatively silent on this issue of late mainly because of indications that Japanese Government has taken into consideration ROK views."[123] The embassy in Taipei reported that a visit by Sneider would be "most valuable," even if it was used by the ROC to "reiterate their own views."[124]

Sneider visited Taipei in late October, and the embassy reported that his visit "appears to have been quite useful in bringing subject of Okinawa reversion into more realistic discussion—despite lack of any stated agreement on issues involved." Sneider tried to reassure the ROC by describing Japan's "apparent recognition that [the] U.S. capability to fulfil its defense obligations to other countries in East Asia like GRC and Korea was important not only for those countries, but also for Japan." He also "emphasized firmness of U.S. defense commitments as expressed by President Nixon."[125]

Despite the best efforts of the United States and Japan, the ROC and ROK still feared that the reversion of Okinawa would risk their interests. Only a few days before Prime Minister Sato arrived in Washington, the ROC foreign minister, Wei Tao-ming met with Secretary Rusk, "apparently on instructions from President Chiang." Rusk told him that the United States had "worked hard in negotiations to provide for GRC security interests," and intimated that "there will be language in joint communique which in effect will indicate that Japan will look affirmatively on our use of Okinawan bases to honor our treaty commitment to [the] GRC." Prior to Sato's speech and the release of the Nixon-Sato communiqué, this appears to be the most explicit statement of reassurance given to either the ROK or ROC. Wei seemed content and said "If you find security arrangements satisfactory, I think we will go along with you on that."[126]

The ROK's concern persisted, and on November 17 it presented yet another aide memoire to the United States. It noted the ROK was "strongly opposed to any form of change which would impair value of the military bases and their speedy and effective utilization . . . any such change will inevitably entail adverse effect on security of ROK."[127] Seoul also planned to summon the Japanese ambassador and, "on direct instruction [from] President Park," issue him a similar document. The US embassy in Seoul reported that despite assurances from the United States and Japan, the ROK "continues to be concerned [with] issues [of] nuclear weapons and unrestricted use of bases in emergency."[128]

THE COMMUNIQUÉ AND PRESS CLUB SPEECH

With Sato's press club speech and the release of the Nixon-Sato communiqué scheduled for November 21, the Japanese and US governments prepared to brief the ROC and ROK.[129] The communiqué itself made provision for the full reversion of Okinawa to Japanese administration. U. Alexis Johnson later described this as meaning "no nuclear weapons, and no direct operations against targets outside of Japan, without prior consultation." But this was accompanied by Sato's press club speech, in which he implied that "the Japanese government would in practice respond favorably to American requests to use bases in both Japan and Okinawa in the event of communist aggression against Korea or Taiwan."[130]

In order to shape media reporting on the communiqué and Sato's speech, U. Alexis Johnson gave an off-the-record press briefing in which he drew special attention to Sato's comments on Korea and Taiwan. Johnson noted that "the whole background of the communique is based around the Japanese Government taking certain positions . . . consultation does not necessarily mean that its attitude is going to be negative in these particular situations . . . this represents a somewhat considerable change in Japanese public position."[131] The State Department also instructed its embassies in a variety of Asian countries to explain the communiqué and press club speech to their hosts. US missions were to note that despite American bases in Okinawa now being subject to the prior consultation clause, "forthright statements by Prime Minister [Sato] . . . provide [the] basis for [a] common understanding in the event of [any] contingency requiring prior consultation. Statements . . . regarding Korea, Taiwan and Vietnam merit special emphasis."[132]

The ROK and ROC reactions were, all things considered, mild. The ROC issued a statement in which it described the "joint communique's attention to relationship between Ryukyu problem and Asian regional security as 'appropriate.'"[133] Privately, Chiang "expressed his appreciation for the Japanese position."[134] As might be expected given its higher level of concern, Korea was unwilling to signal even such a tacit acceptance. In an oral statement, the foreign minister simply noted that the ROK "continually requested that both the United States and Japanese Governments take necessary measures not to reduce the value of United States military bases in Okinawa and not to impair their speedy and effective utilization." The embassy in Seoul considered the statement "relatively restrained in view of [intense] concern of President Park over future U.S. bases Okinawa. ROKG has cloaked its dissatisfaction because it cannot admit communique represents evidence its attempts influence U.S. and Japanese Government to accept its 'no change whatever' position have failed."[135]

THE NUCLEAR ISSUE

One particularly sensitive issue was that of nuclear weapons and the possibility that they might be reintroduced into Okinawa during an emergency. Paragraph 8 of the Nixon-Sato communiqué was a masterpiece of diplomatic obfuscation: "The President . . . assured the Prime Minister that, without prejudice to the position of the United States Government with respect to the prior consultation system under the Treaty of Mutual Cooperation and Security, the reversion of Okinawa would be carried out in a manner consistent with the policy of the Japanese Government as described by the Prime Minister."[136]

The official explanation of this paragraph was that while Okinawa would revert to Japanese administration without any nuclear weapons present, the United States could request the reintroduction of nuclear weapons under the prior consultation arrangements. However, in a secret minute, Sato and Nixon agreed that Japan would permit the reintroduction of nuclear weapons to Okinawa in times of crisis. This was not dissimilar to the preapproval arranged in the secret Korea Minute of 1960, except that Sato promised to respond favorably during the prior consultation process, which would take place at the time of "great emergency."[137]

Given the maritime nature of Taiwan's security situation, and the more precarious continental threat faced by the ROK, it would be unsurprising if the United States made a special effort brief to Seoul on paragraph eight of the communiqué. The embassy in Seoul made some effort to brief the ROK but reported that Korean leaders "professed [an] inability [to] understand [the] implications of para 8 of communique on nuclear weapons. Would appreciate any additional interpretation you may wish to provide, but please keep in mind ROK propensity . . . to view with alarm [the] details of any explanation we may offer."[138] The available records do not reveal the extent of any further explanation given to the ROK. It seems unlikely that the State Department would explicitly confirm to Seoul the existence of the highly secret nuclear agreement between Nixon and Sato. But this oblique reference raises the possibility that some further effort was made to reassure South Korea about American intent and capability to defend it with nuclear weapons, if required.

Assessing the Alliance Audience Effect

THE OKINAWA ISSUE GROWS CLAWS: JANUARY TO DECEMBER 1967

H1 expects that a state will monitor its ally's behavior in other alliances and these observations will affect perceptions of reliability. The ROC carefully observed developments within the US-Japan alliance and was concerned that this deal could jeopardize America's use of bases on Okinawa and thus reduce its capability to defend the ROC in a conflict with Communist China.

To mitigate this risk of unreliability, Taipei initiated discussions with Washington on Okinawa's importance. Taipei's efforts to glean more information from Washington, and its encouragement that the United States not neglect its security interests in Okinawa, are clear evidence in support of H2, which expects that if a state perceives its ally to be unreliable, it will act to mitigate this risk. US loyalty to Japan involved, in this case, a willingness to follow through on its earlier recognition that Tokyo had residual sovereignty over Okinawa and the other Article III islands, but the ROC was not pleased by this loyalty. Beyond interactions with American officials, the ROC also moved to raise its concerns directly with the Japanese government.

Finally, H3 expects that America's actions will be influenced by the possibility that its behavior in one alliance will affect the reliability perceptions of its other allies. This was a clear influence on US behavior in this period: American officials repeatedly emphasized—both privately, to the Japanese, and in public, for the benefit of other observers—that any deal for the reversion of Okinawa would have to preserve the island's regional security role. Washington made clear that it could not return administration to Tokyo if doing so would jeopardize US security commitments to the ROC and ROK.

SATO ATTEMPTS TO BUILD DEFENSE-MINDEDNESS: DECEMBER 1967 TO DECEMBER 1968

As Sato endeavored to build "defense-mindedness" in Japan, the ROC continued to display sensitivity to Okinawa developments. Concerned that Okinawan reversion might jeopardize the ROC's security, Taipei reminded Washington—both privately and publicly—that it was watching the US-Japan alliance closely. These developments support H1.

The fact that the ROC continued to register its concern with the United States also supports H2. While this might seem like a low standard of proof, it must be remembered that there wasn't significant and overt progress toward Okinawa revision in 1968. In such an environment—and with Sato publicly striving to inculcate "defense-mindedness" in the Japanese people—it was enough for Taipei to maintain its position of carefully monitoring developments while occasionally reminding Washington of its interest.

While there were no significant US actions in this period, H3 is supported by the fact that US officials were pleased to see Sato's real and sustained attempts to educate the Japanese public about the regional security role of Okinawa and improve "defense-mindedness." They knew that when the serious negotiations over Okinawa began in 1969, Tokyo would need convince the Japanese people that Okinawa's regional security role was in Japan's national interest. This, in turn, would be critical for reassuring the ROC and ROK.

ALLIED CONCERN BUILDS, PROMPTING A US RESPONSE: JANUARY TO AUGUST 1969

The first eight months of 1969 were an eventful period: though Japan continued to recognize the regional security role of Okinawa and pledged that this would not be jeopardized by reversion, the ROK was alarmed—

and the ROC cautious—about Okinawa's future. The events of this period support H1: Seoul and Taipei were both concerned that the reversion of Okinawa would jeopardize American use of bases there and thus damage US reliability.

As expected by H2, the ROK tried to exercise influence over the reversion of Okinawa. Seoul's efforts to create PATO probably served two purposes: The first was to solidify American policy in the wake of force reductions in Vietnam. The second—hinted at in intelligence and diplomatic reporting, but not conclusively established—was that publicly linking PATO to concerns over Okinawa might inflame public opinion in Japan and thus sabotage the reversion negotiations. Further, Seoul's offer to host additional US forces was also an effort to secure additional commitments to South Korean security. The ROC's inactivity in this time period is best explained by the pledges Japan had offered in 1967: having been assured by Sato and other Japanese leaders that the reversion of Okinawa would not harm Taipei's security, Chiang Kai-shek did not emulate the ROK's extensive lobbying efforts.

H3 is supported by America's efforts at simultaneous alliance management in this period. Aware that allied capitals were growing more concerned as the Nixon-Sato summit approached, Washington advised them to keep their diplomatic representations low-key, so that they would not hinder the bilateral reversion negotiations. To reassure Seoul and Taipei, the State Department launched a "hand-holding operation" to promise that the United States would keep their security interests in mind.[139] These efforts worked for the ROC but—given the events of 1968 and early 1969—it is unsurprising that Washington was unable to adequately reassure Seoul.

THE NIXON-SATO COMMUNIQUÉ: AUGUST TO DECEMBER 1969

Despite America's best efforts to reassure the ROC and ROK, they remained concerned that Okinawan reversion would damage their own security. With few other options to pursue, they continued to publicly and privately encourage—and occasionally demand—that the United States not permit reversion to occur if it resulted in unacceptable restrictions to the use of military bases on Okinawa. The ROC and ROK presented several demarches to Washington and publicly implored both Washington and Tokyo to consider Okinawa's regional role. These events support H1 and H2 of the alliance audience effect framework.

H3 is strongly supported not only by the Nixon-Sato communiqué itself but also by the way it was explained by the United States. Amid communiqué negotiations, the State Department continued its hand-holding operation by arranging for Dick Sneider to visit and brief both Taipei and Seoul.[140] In Washington, Secretary Rusk reassured the ROC's foreign minister that Taipei's security would not be damaged by the reversion of Okinawa. Several drafts of the joint communiqué and Sato's speech show that over time, the sections on Korea and Taiwan were made more explicit. Although the available documents do not establish it irrefutably, it is very likely that this reflected Washington's determination to, in the words of Ambassador Meyer, "signal to both friend and foe that USG military capability remains basically unimpaired."[141] This argument is supported by the fact that the United States made a special effort to emphasize these carefully negotiated sentences: Johnson highlighted their significance to the press, and American embassies in Asia were instructed to highlight them to host nations. These extensive measures show that as Washington finalized the reversion negotiations, it paid close attention to how the joint communiqué and Sato's speech would be perceived by other allies.

The alliance audience effect framework is clearly supported by the events examined in this chapter. As Marshall Green later reflected, "The bases in Japan and especially the Ryukyus were also very important to carry out our treaty commitments in other parts of East Asia. To some extent it might appear to our other allies in East Asia that the Japanese had some kind of controlling hand over the use of our facilities in support of missions for the defense of those other countries. That could wreak havoc with the fabric of our relationships with those countries."[142]

While the administrative details of Okinawa's reversion were negotiated after the Nixon-Sato summit—and actual reversion did not occur until 1972—the main negotiations took place from 1967 to 1969. During this period, the ROK and ROC closely observed the US-Japan relationship and sought information about the conduct of negotiations. Concerned that the reversion of Okinawa might reduce the usefulness of US military capabilities in the region, and thus adversely affect their security, the ROK and ROC pursued several courses of action to mitigate the risk that Okinawan reversion could threaten their interests. Both countries repeatedly and consistently reminded Washington and Tokyo of their own dependence on Okinawa and encouraged an outcome which would not impair the value of US bases there. They explored the possibility of a new collective defense organization, PATO, but this idea—like the "Pacific Pact" two decades earlier—was not feasible without active American support.

The knowledge that the ROC and ROK were closely watching the Okinawa negotiations prompted Washington to proactively manage these relationships simultaneously alongside the negotiations with Japan. The complex interdependencies at play in this situation provide strong support for the alliance audience effect framework. The ROK was watching the US-Japan negotiations and, concerned that its interests were at stake, privately and publicly proclaimed the defensive value of Okinawa. These US-ROK interactions were in turn observed by Japan, and led the United States to discourage the ROK's lobbying efforts, lest they spark entrapment fears in Japan and hinder the reversion negotiations.

The final content of the Nixon-Sato communiqué and Sato's press club speech shows that in the reversion negotiations, Washington was aware that it needed to produce a result that would reassure Seoul and Taipei. Over time, the communiqué and speech were revised to very strongly hint that Okinawan bases could be used for the defense of Taiwan and South Korea. Johnson, in his background briefing to the press, went beyond strong hints and made it clear that these statements represented a Japanese commitment to respond favorably if the ROC or ROK were attacked. US officials knew that these legally discrete alliances were—in practice—interdependent.

Conclusion

In this book, I examine, critique, and challenge one of the oldest and most commonly believed maxims of foreign policy: that disloyalty to one ally will undermine other alliances. This is a central tenet of deterrence theory and while it has swayed the judgment of leaders throughout history, it was especially influential on US decision makers during the Cold War.

This concluding chapter contains four sections. The first summarizes the alliance audience effect theory and evaluates its validity in the case studies examined. The second section considers the contributions made by the theory and discusses its limitations. In the third section, I briefly explore how the theory can explain behavior within multilateral alliances through an examination of the Southeast Asian Treaty Organization (SEATO). In the fourth section I consider the theory's relevance for other alliance concepts, and explore its practical and contemporary relevance.

Assessing the Alliance Audience Effect Theory

WHAT DID THE CASE STUDIES REVEAL?

The alliance audience effect theory expects that a state will observe its ally's behavior in other alliances and that these observations will affect that state's beliefs about the ally's reliability. If a state doubts its ally's reliability, it will act to mitigate the risks caused by this unreliability. If the ally is unreliable because it poses risks of entrapment, the state will attempt to distance itself from the ally's policies, reduce tensions, conciliate adversaries or restrain the ally. If the ally poses risks of abandonment, the state will seek to improve its security by confirming common interests with the ally, by improving its own defense capabilities, by seeking new allies, or by settling disputes with adversaries. If these two hypotheses are supported, then the framework expects this causal dynamic to influence the behavior of the common ally. The common ally might acknowledge the possibility of flow-on effects on other alliances but seek to reduce these through a policy of simultaneous alliance management. Alternatively, the common ally might seek to manipulate this alliance interdependence for its own ends: in an effort to set the example, the common ally might deliberately adopt—or eschew—a policy within one alliance precisely because this decision will influence the attitudes of other allies.

> H1: A state will observe its ally's behavior in other alliances. If this behavior reveals that the ally's interests diverge from the observer state's, and thus raises entrapment or abandonment fears, the state will assess the ally as unreliable.

The case studies I examined provide strong support for H1. In the uncertain environment of Asia after the Second World War, those states aligned with the United States carefully observed Washington's policies toward other friendly nations. Given Washington's vacillation and the obvious Communist threat to the republics of China and Korea, policy choices such as the China White Paper, the withdrawal of US forces from the Korean Peninsula, and Acheson's "defensive perimeter" speech all affected confidence in US reliability. Later, in the mid-1950s, Washington's commitment to Nationalist China security caused consternation for several of its allies with security interests in Asia. While Formosa itself was of significant strategic value, most allies could not say the same for the offshore islands of Quemoy and Matsu. The primary interest for these allies was avoiding a general war between the Communist and Western blocs, so these allies restrained Washington through diplomatic means and, ultimately, a refusal to fight alongside the United States in any battle for the offshore islands.

The First Taiwan Strait Crisis strongly influenced Tokyo's concerns about US reliability. The Japanese people already chafed under the vestiges of the postwar occupation, but the one-sided security treaty did more than generate domestic discontent. Washington's legal right to use bases in Japan for any purpose related to the security of the Far East gave the United States the ability to commit Japan to a war against Tokyo's will. Whereas, in 1950, Japan had feared a US withdrawal from Asia, in the mid-1950s Tokyo feared that Washington's bellicose attitude toward the Communist bloc posed perilous risks of entrapment. Finally, nearby allies like the ROC and ROK paid careful attention to the evolution of the US-Japan alliance relationship. While the 1960 treaty revision did not imperil their security interests, the reversion of Okinawa certainly had the potential to do so. As US-Japan negotiations progressed in the late 1960s, Taipei and Seoul deliberately and carefully monitored these for any sign that Japanese administration of Okinawa would reduce its military usefulness.

> H2: If a state assesses its ally to be unreliable, it will act to mitigate the specific risk posed.

The case studies examined clearly demonstrated the risk mitigation activity expected by H2. In 1949 and early 1950, fearing that the United States would withdraw from Asia, states adopted a variety of measures intended to solidify the US presence. Japan offered basing rights, while the ROC, ROK, Australia, New Zealand, and the Philippines attempted to negotiate bilateral or regional security pacts. Countries supported the defense of South Korea by providing combat troops, base usage, and logistical support. During the First Taiwan Strait Crisis, countries fearful of entrapment worked to restrain Washington: they used diplomatic means, like "Operation Oracle," to monitor and influence US policy toward deescalation. Japan, due to the 1951 Security Treaty, was unable to quickly mitigate the risk of entrapment, but did so over the longer term by revising its alliance to enable prior consultation for military operations launched from mainland Japan. Finally, from 1967 to 1969 the ROC and ROK lobbied Washington and Tokyo in an effort to ensure that their security interests were not jeopardized by negotiations for the reversion of Okinawa.

> H3: A state's actions will be influenced by the possibility that its behavior in one alliance will affect the reliability perceptions of its other allies.

The final hypothesis of the alliance audience effect theory expects that US policies will be influenced by the prospect of alliance interdependence: that is, the prospect that its behavior in one alliance will affect the reliability perceptions of its other allies. The case studies I examine demonstrate qualified support for this causal relationship. There were several cases where the likely reaction of US allies was an unambiguous influence on policymaking: the decision to defend South Korea, Eisenhower's policy toward the offshore islands in 1955, and the conduct of Okinawa reversion negotiations were the most prominent instances. However, there were also a number of cases where the views of allies were disregarded by US decision makers: South Korea's insistence that Quemoy held symbolic value did not sway Eisenhower, and Dulles was unworried about Japan's fears during the First Taiwan Strait Crisis. As discussed earlier, the common theme is that in these instances, the United States held significant leverage and influence because of the ally's limited realignment options. South Korea had no choice but to continue to rely upon the United States for security, and in the mid-1950s Tokyo was unable to quickly modify its security relationship with Washington. Such exceptions show that H3 applies most strongly in cases where the risk-mitigation actions taken by the observer ally are significant and could adversely affect US interests. In such circumstances, Washington will consider, and be influenced by, the ally's views. But when the ally's risk-mitigation behavior is unlikely to adversely affect the United States, then Washington does not need to carefully manage alliance interdependence.

The Theory's Contributions and Limitations

Most importantly, this book demonstrates the need to carefully delineate between ideas of loyalty and reliability within alliance politics. These terms have often been regarded as synonymous but the evidence examined shows that states will not inevitably suffer a crisis of confidence if their ally is disloyal to one of its other allies. That is, a state's disloyal treatment of one ally might be welcomed by the state's other allies as proof of reliability. More important than any moral judgment about an ally's loyalty is whether its actions demonstrate its reliability. During the First Taiwan Strait Crisis, most US allies were utterly unconcerned about the idea of limited disloyalty to Taipei—indeed, most of them actively desired and advocated it.

My theory's second contribution is to show that a state's allies do not share a universal or common belief about that state's alliance reputation. Because states have different interests, they will interpret allied behavior in different ways. This was most clearly demonstrated during the First Taiwan Strait Crisis: Tokyo, London, Ottawa, Canberra, and Wellington were all fearful that the offshore islands could spark a general war, and these capitals were relieved when the crisis subsided. For these allies, US reliability increased as security tensions decreased. But for the ROK—driven by Rhee's desire to restart the Korean War—Washington's unwillingness to defend the offshore islands was further proof that US interests were not convergent with those of Seoul, and thus US policy toward the offshore islands was evidence of unreliability.

Third, my analysis shows that it can be very useful for the United States to be perceived as a reliable ally as this can prevent allies from adopting policies contrary to Washington's interests. States doubting the reliability of their ally will pursue policies designed to improve their own security, but these may not be—from Washington's perspective—desired changes. Had there been more serious US-PRC military clashes during the early years of the Cold War, it is entirely feasible that Japan would have concluded that the best security policy available was a form of lightly armed neutrality. Such a decision would have severely curtailed Washington's military power projection capabilities in Asia. In order to demonstrate US reliability to Japan, Washington needed to adopt less confrontational postures toward the PRC and reduce the entrapment risk faced by Tokyo. Once the United States did so, Japan was able to adopt a closer security association with Washington and also publicly accept its own role in regional security.

Another contribution of the book is to show that because alliance interdependence is underpinned by reliability, not loyalty, Washington can use this interdependence for its own purposes. It is often assumed that any form of alliance interdependence must work against US interests, entrapping or entangling Washington into unnecessary wars due to concerns for "credibility" or "prestige." President Johnson thought that if the United States were "driven from the field in Viet-Nam, then no nation [could] ever again have the same confidence in American promise or in American protection."[1] But because alliance interdependence is determined by assessments of reliability, rather than reputations for loyalty, we now know that the interdependence of alliance commitments is not so strict. It is true that alliance interdependence has regularly required Washington to adopt a policy of simultaneous alliance management: it has needed to reassure observing allies that their alliance remains solid, despite events in another alliance. The reversion of Okinawa is a classic example of this dynamic: Marshall Green's "hand-holding operation" was designed to reassure the ROC and ROK that their interests would not be sacrificed in efforts to revise the US-Japan alliance.[2] However, there were also instances where the United States successfully used alliance interdependence for its own purposes: to set the example of what behavior is acceptable from allied states. Based on his observations of Washington's firm negotiations with the ROK in 1953, Nationalist China's president, Chiang Kai-shek, knew that in order to obtain his own alliance with the United States, he would have to sacrifice his dream of reuniting China by force. Alliance interdependence may sometimes be an irritating and complicating influence on US decision makers, but it is not a reputational straitjacket requiring the United States to always support its allies. To the contrary, alliance interdependence—if managed cleverly—can sometimes be used to pursue US interests.

LIMITATIONS

The alliance audience effect framework does have limitations. Most importantly, it does not predict *how* states will attempt to mitigate the unreliability of their ally: it offers no view on whether states will balance or bandwagon in response to allied unreliability. However, the case studies do provide insights to guide further research.

In the period examined, the first instinct of US allies fearing abandonment was to seek information in an effort to more accurately assess and encourage US reliability. Once allies had done so—and they were confident that their interests converged with Washington's—they then adopted policies intended to cement the US presence and security responsibilities in Asia. Allies did this in a variety of ways: Japan sought to solidify Washington's Asian presence through an offer of bases in 1950, Nationalist China encouraged the United States to guarantee Korea's security, and Korea advocated an aggressive approach in the First Taiwan Strait Crisis. Washington was often, but not always, responsive to the concerns of its allies: it understood their apprehensions and, where it could, offered detailed explanations of its policies in an effort to reassure allied capitals. Though, during the 1949–1969 period, the first instinct of allies fearing abandonment was to reassure themselves of US reliability, this does not preclude the possibility that allies

might, under different circumstances, increase their own defensive arma-
ments, build nuclear weapons, or seek new security partners.[3]

When allies feared entrapment, they shared these concerns with Washington and attempted to influence US policy—their first instinct was to raise
their different perspective with US decision makers in constructive attempts
to resolve differences between friends. As expected by H3, Washington was
often responsive to these concerns. US actions were influenced by allied
opinion throughout the First Taiwan Strait Crisis, although its overall policy of supporting the Nationalists was not quickly reversed by a lack of allied support. However, Eisenhower's decision to not defend the offshore islands was very significantly influenced—perhaps even determined—by
the concerns of US allies. The evolution of US policies during this crisis demonstrates the crucial influence that allies can have on Washington's outlook
and actions.

However, there were several instances where the concerns of allies were
known to Washington but did not appear to have a noticeable or immediate impact on US policy. Examples include Korea's pleas for an alliance in
1949, Japan's fears of entrapment during the mid-1950s, and Seoul's encouragement of an aggressive policy in the First Taiwan Strait Crisis. In these
instances, policymakers appear to have concluded that allied concerns did
not require action. Korea would not align with the Communist Bloc simply
because Washington was unwilling to sign an alliance. Japan could not
quickly detach itself from the United States because of the unequal nature
of the 1951 Mutual Security Treaty. In 1955, Seoul's security was still completely dependent on the US military presence: it was not going to adversely
change its defense policies due to dissatisfaction with Washington's approach to cross-Strait conflict. Accordingly, the preferences of these allies
did not need to influence US policymaking at those times. As noted in chapter 4, examples like these show that the case studies examined provide only
qualified support for H3. It is clear that when a state is highly dependent on
its alliance for security and does not have feasible alternatives to the alliance, and/or is mitigating the risk of unreliability in a way unlikely to adversely impact the ally, then the ally does not need to worry much about
the possibility of an alliance audience effect.[4]

GENERALIZABILITY

In this book, I advance and consider a narrow application of the alliance
audience effect framework. I do so because, as explained in chapter 1, there
is a need to first demonstrate alliance interdependence before attempting
the more advanced task of identifying the exact conditions under which it
might be more or less prevalent.

Chapter 2 considers the formation of the first three Asian alliances, and
the interdependence dynamics observed did not change significantly after

the signing of the treaty texts. Given that these patterns of interdependence do not appear to have significantly changed even though an alliance was formalized, this constancy suggests that the alliance audience effect framework could be applied in situations where formal alliances do not exist. One advantage of the audience effect theory, therefore, is that it may not be limited only to alliance relationships. For example, "security partners" who cooperate militarily with the United States but are not treaty allies might observe Washington's other relationships for indications of US reliability, and formal allies might watch Washington's treatment of nonallied security partners.

Further research is required to see whether the framework is applicable beyond the Asian alliance system. Promising avenues of inquiry include the Chinese reaction to Soviet policy during the Cuban Missile Crisis, the reactions of Middle Eastern security partners to the US abandonment of the Mubarak government in Egypt, and the examples provided in the book's Introduction. The framework might yield insights for understanding allied reactions, and alliance interdependence, beyond the Asian hub and spoke alliance system.

OTHER CASE STUDIES FROM COLD WAR ASIA

During the second half of the Cold War, US allies again had concerns about the direction, intent, and constancy of Washington's Asia policy, and perceptions of reliability appear to have declined in response. The Guam Doctrine and Okinawa reversion negotiations were followed by Nixon's decision to reduce troop numbers in Asia (from "727,300 in January 1969 to 284,000 by December 1971"), an increasingly dissatisfied US Congress endeavoring to limit the president's authority in conflict, the initiation of the Paris Peace Accords in January 1973, the withdrawal of all combat troops from Vietnam in March 1973, Nixon's resignation in August 1974, and the fall of Saigon in April 1975.[5]

The defense policies of US allies in this period deserve a book of their own, but perhaps the most important developments were the efforts of Korea and Taiwan to develop their own nuclear weapons. Several events are cited by different authors as being the catalysts for these efforts: most note the impact of the Guam Doctrine, but other authors note the troop reductions in Korea, rumors of a complete withdrawal from Korea, and the eventual withdrawal from Vietnam.[6] The ROC's nuclear program is thought to have begun in response to the PRC's successful nuclear test in 1964.[7] But events in the following years gave Taipei further cause for concern: in 1969 the United States cautiously approached a rapprochement with Communist China and in November 1969 President Nixon ordered the Seventh Fleet to no longer patrol the Taiwan Strait.[8] Changes to the US-PRC relationship throughout the 1970s gave the ROC even more cause to doubt US reliability. In 1977, the US embassy in Taipei warned that "the underlying security fears of the ROC . . . will continue to exist as our own role and policies in Asia develop and change, and our 'protection' becomes increasingly less credible. These fears will continue to provide some elements of the ROC with an argument for nuclear weapons development."[9]

In this period, the alliance audience effect was probably also at work in Japanese observations of US behavior. Although the United States did reduce its forces in Japan, Victor Cha writes that Tokyo was also apprehensive about the US posture on the Korean Peninsula: "Japan clearly linked the American troop cuts in Korea with its own security. Sato expressed his apprehension over the decision with uncharacteristic fervor in meetings with Secretary of State William P. Rogers."[10] Later, Cha claims that the withdrawal from "Vietnam and the Carter plan [for troop withdrawals from Korea] shook confidence in the United States as a reliable ally in Tokyo."[11] Exchanges such as this suggest that Japan—just like in 1950—was concerned by the withdrawals from the Korean Peninsula and worried about US reliability.

Washington's Vietnam War policies also provide support for H3. Johannes Kadura argues that although Nixon and Kissinger desired a situation in which South Vietnam might be propped up indefinitely by the limited intervention of US air power, a secondary "insurance policy" was employed. This "two-track approach" involved "further maneuvers to uphold South Vietnam and simultaneous disassociation from the ally," so that if South Vietnam fell Washington could attribute this to Saigon's incompetence, not a lack of U.S. resolve or loyalty.[12] In 1969, President Nixon's national security adviser (and later secretary of state), Henry Kissinger, said, "However fashionable it is to ridicule the terms 'credibility' or 'prestige,' they are not empty phrases; other nations can gear their actions to ours only if they can count on our steadiness."[13] In language reminiscent of John Foster Dulles's alarmist predictions during the First Taiwan Strait Crisis, in February 1975, Kissinger told secretary of defense Robert McNamara, "if we lose Vietnam, Korea may go; Japan will shift and we will have bitter divisiveness here for years."[14] Such evidence suggests that beliefs about alliance interdependence were also very influential in the 1970s. However, it again appears that fears about the regional effects of disloyalty were not realized. As Kadura notes, "Korea, the Philippines, and to some degree Thailand were continuing to rely on Washington—they simply had no other option. . . . Malaysia, Australia and Singapore were even turning more to the United States after the fall of Indochina."[15] Despite what some might have described as US disloyalty to South Vietnam, Washington's allies maintained some degree of confidence in US reliability. This again reinforces the usefulness of delineating between loyalty and reliability, and the need to worry most about the reaction of allies who have viable options other than their alliance with the United States.

The rupture of ANZUS was perhaps the most dramatic alliance interaction of the 1980s and it too appears to support the alliance audience effect framework. The New Zealand Labour Party, in its 1984 election platform, adopted a nuclear-free policy. After its election, New Zealand's new government was warned by Washington that "it was incumbent on an ally to accept the visits of American vessels," and this included those capable of carrying nuclear weapons.[16] When Washington requested that a vessel, the USS *Buchanan*, receive approval to visit New Zealand, Wellington decided that it would not permit a port visit unless Washington confirmed that the *Buchanan* was not carrying nuclear weapons. This, of course, would have broken long-standing US policy, which was to "neither confirm nor deny" (NCND) the presence or position of nuclear weapons. Wellington's refusal to back down and Washington's refusal to break the NCND policy resulted in the United States suspending its alliance commitment to New Zealand. In August 1986, the US secretary of state George Shultz announced that "we part company as friends, but we part company as far as the alliance is concerned."[17]

Why did the United States react so harshly to one of the original Asia-Pacific allies? It was afraid of an alliance audience effect prompting other allies to adopt similar positions. As Gerald Hensley, a former New Zealand official writes, Wellington's decision "opened up the possibility of similar movements in Australia and Japan."[18] Had the United States caved in and broken the NCND policy, Washington feared that this would precipitate identical demands from other allies. As Hensley notes, "NCND was vital and the US could not have different policies among its alliances."[19] This is a clear illustration of H3 at work: Washington believed that other allies would observe interactions within ANZUS and that if a special deal were brokered with Wellington, other allies would demand similar concessions. Accordingly, Washington dealt harshly with Wellington to set the example for other observing allies.

As expected by H1 and H2 of the alliance audience effect framework, it does seem that developments within ANZUS were being observed by other allies and affecting their beliefs about US reliability. Press reports at the time noted the obvious implications for the US-Japan alliance. One author, writing about New Zealand's efforts to receive explicit confirmation that US Navy vessels were not carrying nuclear weapons, assessed that "if New Zealand persists—and succeeds—it will be very difficult for the ruling party in Tokyo to deflect antinuclear forces in Japan."[20] The implications for the US-Philippines alliance were also considered in media reporting during 1986.[21]

Reliability in Multilateral Alliances: The Case of SEATO, 1960–1962

In this book, I test my theory against the US Asian alliance system, comprising four bilateral alliances and one trilateral alliance. But is the alliance audience effect framework applicable to larger multilateral alliances? In this section, I conduct a short plausibility probe by examining how SEATO responded to the Laotian civil war and how its inaction affected Thailand's assessments of alliance reliability. Other works explore the Laotian civil war in detail, and some examine SEATO itself, but for reasons of brevity many of these events are not explored below.[22] For my purposes it is the reaction of Thailand that is most significant: because the country shares a land border with Laos, the Thai government was concerned about the possibility of a neighboring Communist government threatening Thailand itself.

SEATO was formed in 1954 after John Foster Dulles could not secure allied support for a "United Action" strategy to prevent the loss of French Indochina. Though its initialization may evoke comparisons to NATO, SEATO was not intended to have static military forces and a formalized command structure. Instead, SEATO members pledged to "act to meet the common danger" in the event that any member suffered "aggression by means of armed attack." If the member was threatened "in any way other than by armed attack," then the members pledged to "consult immediately in order to agree on the measures which should be taken."[23] Though Laos was prohibited, by the 1954 Geneva Agreement, from joining any military alliance, the signatories of the Manila Pact signed a separate protocol affirming that Laos, Cambodia, and South Vietnam would receive SEATO protection. They thus became known as "protocol states."

In Laos, the Eisenhower administration had supported the pro-US government led by Phoumi Nosavan, but by late 1960 there was a significant risk of this government being overthrown by a Communist insurgent group called the Pathet Lao (PL). As Eisenhower met with President-elect Kennedy, he warned against the possibility of a negotiated settlement with Communist groups. Kennedy "came away from that meeting feeling that the Eisenhower administration would support intervention . . . it was preferable to a communist success in Laos."[24] Eisenhower specifically warned against the idea of "neutralizing" Laos by allowing the formation of a coalition government containing Communist forces.[25]

Washington's basic dilemma was a choice between two courses of action, epitomized by two different Laotian leaders. The first option was to intervene in Laos with military force to support Phoumi Nosavan: this could be a unified SEATO effort, a coalition of some (but not all) SEATO members, a bilateral initiative with Thailand, or unilateral. The second option was to support a neutralist, coalition government: this would be led by Phoumi's rival, Souvanna Phouma. The first option was supported by Thailand, South Vietnam, and—for a time—Australia and New Zealand, but opposed by France and the United Kingdom. Throughout 1960–1962, Paris and London thought that any SEATO action in Laos would guarantee the failure of diplomatic efforts for a negotiated outcome. The latter strategy was supported by France and the United Kingdom but bitterly opposed by Thailand. US policy was complicated by the fact that Phoumi Nosavan was the nephew of Thailand's prime minister, Sarit Thanarat, and Washington eventually learned that Bangkok often encouraged him to sabotage any progress toward a coalition neutralist government. Bangkok regarded Souvanna Phouma as, at a minimum, having Communist sympathies that would inevitably result in a Communist Laos.

From late 1960, the divergent interests of SEATO members jeopardized an effective and united response by the alliance. In December the Thai foreign minister, Thanat Khoman, discussed whether SEATO could take action in Laos "without [the] unanimous agreement [of the] parties" to the treaty.[26] Thailand's concerns were well founded, as France thought military intervention "would not be acceptable . . . [France] does not consider SEATO proper vehicle for solution in Laos."[27] It is vital to note just how severely the interests of SEATO member-states diverged at this time: there was even evidence to suggest that the French were keeping Souvanna Phouma informed on the content of confidential SEATO discussions.[28] In early 1961, the US ambassador to Thailand, U. Alexis Johnson, reported that "SEATO morale [is] at [a] low ebb and I fear the organization may be fatally discredited if some early action [is] not taken which will persuade members from area that it can play [a] useful role in [the] present Laos situation."[29]

In January 1961, the Royal Laotian government asked SEATO to investigate reports that the Soviet Union was supplying the PL with weapons. At a meeting of the SEATO Council representatives—a regular, working-level meeting in Bangkok, usually attended by member-state ambassadors—the Thai representative "accused SEATO members of unwillingness to act" on the request.[30] The US ambassador described another meeting which was "desultory and unproductive" because the "UK and French representatives [were] obviously under instructions [to] discuss nothing substantive."[31] Bangkok's dissatisfaction intensified and Thanat expressed his desire that SEATO "find some formula whereby views of majority c[ou]ld not indefinitely be blocked by minority," and also for the United States and Thailand to sign a bilateral defense alliance.[32] Disturbed by SEATO's disunity, Bangkok had grown to regard the alliance as unreliable but still hoped for intensified bilateral cooperation with the United States. In response, Secretary of State Dean Rusk provided Prime Minister Sarit with a confidential aide memoire, which noted that the US commitment to Thailand under the Manila Pact "is not conditioned on the prior unanimous agreement of all SEATO Members."[33]

Contemptuous of SEATO, Thanat considered canceling the SEATO Council meeting—usually held at the secretary of state or foreign minister level—scheduled for March 1961, as it would "only exacerbate and publicly higtlight [*recte* highlight] differences which could not be concealed beneath [the] veneer of traditional communiques."[34] Thailand again pressed the United States for a bilateral defense guarantee, but Washington thought that if such a public commitment was made then it might "have the effect of downgrading SEATO at [the] very time and place we [are] supposed to be upholding it."[35] The March SEATO Council meeting produced a communiqué on Laos that warned that "members of SEATO are prepared, within the terms of the treaty, to take whatever action may be appropriate," and Rusk thought that this "had the effect of breathing new life into this alliance."[36] However, subsequent events show that this resolution was only a temporary fix that could not reconcile the divergent interests of the SEATO members.

In May 1961, after a Laotian ceasefire had been established in April, a second Geneva conference was convened. As Logevall notes, "The thirteen months of negotiations that followed brought forth a consensus that the only compromise with any chance of success was one wherein the procommunist Pathet Lao and the neutralist faction were given positions reasonably commensurate with their actual power."[37] Thailand's despair grew, as Thanat became convinced that the British and French were "prepared [to] give Laos up to [the] commies . . . through [a] face-saving interim step in which Souvanna Phouma [is] Pri[me] Min[ister]."[38] If this occurred, then Thailand would "be forced [to] make [a] fundamental review [of] its policies and orientation."[39]

The US government was sensitive to Thailand's concerns. A paper prepared ahead of a May 1961 visit to the region by Vice President Lyndon B. Johnson assessed that "still lacking confidence in SEATO, the Thai believe that the United States holds the key to the problem . . . they have watched U.S. moves closely and will judge U.S. strength and determination in Southeast Asia on the outcome in Laos. To date, the Thai have felt that U.S. actions in Laos have not been sufficiently vigorous and firm. This feeling undoubtedly has led to questioning of Thai confidence in the United States."[40]

Seeking to reassure, Johnson asked Sarit whether he thought it necessary to station US forces in Thailand. Sarit did not desire such a deployment "at this moment," but told Johnson that "nations in [the] region look to [the] US directly much more than they look to SEATO." When Sarit asked about the likely US response if the Geneva conference collapsed, Johnson warned "that because of [the] present state of American public opinion it is not possible to speak with finality at this time. [The] US Congress believes [the] public is in no frame of mind to send American boys to fight in Laos."[41]

Attributing SEATO's unreliability to the principle of unanimity, which was repeatedly stymied by the British and French, Thailand renewed its efforts to create a bilateral defense alliance with Washington. A US briefing paper assessed that "Thai leaders have expressed mounting dissatisfaction and anxiety over SEATO. . . . Their interest in . . . a bilateral defense agreement . . . has correspondingly increased."[42] As the drawn-out negotiations in Geneva progressed, Bangkok grew more and more disillusioned. In June, the new US ambassador in Bangkok, Kenneth Young, warned that "Thai officials and all ranks of Thai opinion seems to be in various stages of trauma over Laos." The present situation meant that "SEATO [is] all but lost." The

Thai secretary-general of SEATO, Pote Sarasin, also warned Young about the "tendency of top Thais [to] write SEATO off."[43] This pessimism was no passing fad: in late August, Young reported that in Thailand "there appears to be growing agreement [in Bangkok] that SEATO no longer represents anything useful."[44] Pote believed that "SEATO has reached 'rock bottom and can fall no further.' Unless something is done quickly, it will 'crumble' to pieces."[45] Thailand began to concertedly agitate for a change to voting procedures, so a lack of unanimity could not prevent other members from taking action under the SEATO banner.[46]

SEATO was straining under the stresses of British and French determination to avoid intervention in Laos, Thai dissatisfaction with this policy, and US efforts to somehow preserve the alliance. A memo prepared for deputy national security adviser Walt Rostow described the United States as trying "to hold the organization together with chewing gum and baling wire until it comes completely apart," and warned that if the US initiated military action in Laos to satisfy Thai concerns then SEATO's "breakup would be hastened."[47] Fearful that these intra-alliance disagreements could become public and amplify the perception of SEATO disunity, Washington continued to privately reassure Bangkok of its willingness to act on a bilateral basis if necessary. Though Thailand seemed to have given up on SEATO, it still considered that the United States might yet prove to be a reliable ally. A paper, prepared ahead of an October meeting between Thanat and President Kennedy, assessed that the "intensification of the Lao crisis, together with Thai dissatisfaction with SEATO, have led Thailand to desire more specific, bilateral assurances from the U.S." The US administration decided that although "a limited bilateral character has already been given to our SEATO commitment to Thailand," SEATO provided the "advantage, not readily replaced, for legal, Senate-supported commitments . . . in the collective defense of the area."[48]

When Thanat visited Washington, DC, he was discouraged from pursuing any voting reform in SEATO.[49] Kennedy told him that SEATO's "unanimity rule does not limit US actions or obligations. Other SEATO members could act despite [the] opposition of one or two."[50] Kennedy also emphasized that any changes to SEATO's voting procedures "would amount to a different treaty arrangement, which would have to be submitted to the Senate."[51] Thanat seemed to accept this outcome, but was upset that the United States was unwilling to negotiate and conclude a separate bilateral alliance.[52] When he returned to Bangkok, he proceeded to agitate for SEATO voting reform on the dubious premise that "he had reached [a] 'gentleman's agreement' in Washington" to do so.[53]

US-Thai relations had reached a critical inflection point. Frustrated with Washington's unwillingness to intervene in Laos, Bangkok grew increasingly dissatisfied with SEATO and encouraged Phoumi Nosavan's obstinance in the negotiations at Geneva. When the United States discovered this duplicity, the State Department warned Ambassador Young that "we cannot countenance overt or covert steps . . . deliberately to sabotage our efforts at peaceful and acceptable settlement," and asked for his "frank views" on the "possibility that the RTG [Royal Thai government] might now be giving Phoumi covert backing."[54] To reassure Sarit, Washington decided that if Thailand would cooperate "in achieving [a] Souvanna [Phouma] solution . . . [the] US [would] give full effect to its obligations under . . . Manila Pact . . . not conditioned on prior unanimous consent all SEATO members. This is fullest commitment US can give . . . and will be confirmed in writing if desired." Though Thailand could not obtain its own bilateral defense treaty, the United States could offer the next best thing: a written, public confirmation that the Manila Pact created a bilateral defense obligation. Young was instructed to tell Prime Minister Sarit that "no commitment under [a] bilateral [treaty] with Thailand could be stronger. . . . [I]n effect Thailand has legally all protection under this article that it could reasonably expect from bilateral . . . if treaty were to be negotiated under present conditions."[55] This was the best Thailand could hope for, and perhaps the only measure that would prompt Bangkok to end its covert support of Phoumi.

Young warned that "we need [to] continue convincing and reassuring them without letup," he found "nothing . . . that convinces me that they are now encouraging Phoumi to defy us."[56] Though Bangkok was now cooperating on this issue, Thai leaders grew more and more exasperated with SEATO. Sarit stated that "we don't want your commitments under SEATO. We want them just from US . . . SEATO is no good." Pote Sarasin warned Young that a "serious crisis over SEATO is brewing and [the] US must do something."[57] With Thailand continuing to threaten departure from SEATO unless voting procedures were amended, it appeared to Washington that Bangkok was trying once more to extract a bilateral alliance. Young was instructed to explain that if Bangkok "destroys SEATO by irresponsible and unwarranted actions . . . it thereby destroys the legal basis of our bilateral obligations."[58] This warning did not immediately resolve the crisis, and Thailand's determination to reform SEATO's voting procedure persisted: Sarit wanted "SEATO with no veto or no SEATO."[59] If voting procedures were not changed, Sarit promised "we will leave SEATO or at least not attend meetings." He remarked that "America is not SEATO and SEATO is not America. I think it would be better to be out of SEATO like Vietnam and just get assistance from [the] US."[60] Thanat also delineated between the reliability of SEATO as a whole, and of individual member-states: he "insisted on difference between U.S. (and Australia) whose help Thais believe in and depend on, and SEATO organization which offers no security."[61]

To solve the impasse, Thanat was invited to Washington once more. In a previsit letter, Secretary of State Rusk stressed that the United States was determined to preserve SEATO. But he reaffirmed the existence, thanks to the Manila Pact, of a bilateral security obligation with Thailand: this obligation "is not subject to the prior consent of any other signatory." Though Washington was unable to offer Bangkok a bilateral defense pact, Rusk was willing to discuss these assurances with Thanat to determine "a suitable form by which they could be best publicly expressed."[62] To minimize the possibility of further aggravation and any public display of SEATO disunity, the SEATO Council meeting scheduled for April 1962 would also be postponed.

When Thanat visited Washington in March 1962, he reiterated the Thai preference for a new bilateral treaty but promised that Thailand was "willing to let the SEATO treaty continue." He delivered a letter from Sarit to Kennedy, requesting a "US security assurance from the highest level . . . [which] could be published in Thailand."[63] A joint statement, which became known as the Thanat-Rusk communiqué, was agreed upon and released on March 6, 1962. This document affirmed that US obligations to Thailand under the Manila Pact did "not depend upon the prior agreement of all other parties to the Treaty, since this Treaty obligation is individual as well as collective." In effect, this communiqué publicly bilateralized the US Manila Pact commitment to Thailand. In return, Thailand pledged to support US policy in Laos: "full agreement was reached on the necessity for . . . a free, independent and truly neutral Laos."[64]

This communiqué was by no means the end of Thai-US disagreements over Laos, SEATO, and Southeast Asian security: Bangkok continued to agitate for voting reform in SEATO and to lament a degradation of the military situation in Laos. Thailand was angered by an International Court of Justice decision in June, and this only strengthened Thai antipathy toward France and Bangkok's determination to avoid any SEATO gathering. But despite Thailand's ongoing frustration with the SEATO organization, voting procedures, and membership, Thai leaders seemed to still regard the United States as a fundamentally reliable ally. In May, when a PL attack in northern Laos raised the prospect of incursions into Thailand, Bangkok accepted the deployment of allied troops from the US, the UK, Australia, and New Zealand. But what really mattered was the promise of US support: when responding to the attack, Thai leaders were "far from welcoming . . . other [non-US] contributions enthusiastically . . . Sarit and Thanat [are] by no means inclined [to] acknowledge SEATO context of deployments or request other SEATO nations to participate."[65]

Based on this plausibility probe, it seems that the alliance audience effect theory can usefully explain interdependence dynamics within multilateral alliances. The fact that Britain and France lobbied against US intervention in Laos shows that London and Paris were utterly unconcerned about the prospect of disloyalty to Vientiane or Bangkok, and this supports my theory's delineation between the concepts of loyalty and reliability. Second, the United States was clearly conscious of alliance interdependence in this period and worked to ensure that bilateral animosities did not destroy the broader SEATO alliance. Finally, Thailand's reactions suggest that allies do not assess the reliability of an *alliance*, but rather the reliability of individual *allies*. Even though SEATO was unreliable because of French and British membership, specific allies within the alliance proved to be reliable at least on the core issue of Thailand's physical security. Though further research is needed, this case suggests not only that the alliance audience effect theory can be usefully applied to multilateral alliances but also that conceiving of such alliances as webs of bilateral commitments—rather than as monolithic alliance blocs—may enable more accurate assessments of alliance cohesion and interdependence. In some cases, multilateral alliances might not be more than the sum of their bilateral parts.

Contributions to the Alliance Literature

The alliance audience effect framework intersects with, and has relevance for, other components of alliance theory.

ALLIANCE RESTRAINT

Research on alliance restraint—particularly restraining the nuclear ambitions of allies—intersects neatly with the alliance audience effect framework.[66] Though an alliance might be formed in order to restrain a state, this alliance can then be observed by other allies. More alliances mean more data for observer allies, and thus the more alliances a state has, the greater its need to carefully manage the interdependence of these alliances. As demonstrated in chapter 3, a strong stance within one alliance relationship can set the example for other allies and encourage them to adopt or eschew particular policies. In such scenarios, the alliance audience effect can manifest in two seemingly opposed forms. For example, in 1953, Eisenhower felt that allies would react poorly to any perceived abandonment of Korea but Washington could not allow Seoul to drag it into a war so obviously contrary to US interests. To allow this would be to set a dangerous example for other allies: it would show that Washington, out of concern for its reliability or loyalty images, could be manipulated by devious allies. By adopting a firm but fair policy toward Seoul, and by explaining this policy to Taipei, Washington influenced Chiang Kai-shek's expectations. In turn, Chiang calibrated his own alliance requests to minimize Washington's entrapment risks and thus maximize his prospects of attaining an alliance.

Chapter 1 argues that at its extreme, the alliance audience effect could prompt a state—after having observed its ally's behavior in a separate alliance—to conclude that the ally was totally unreliable, and that the risk of abandonment should be mitigated by the development or acquisition of nuclear weapons. While this did not occur in the period examined in this book, the attempted proliferation of nuclear weapons by US allies in the

1970s shows that such scenarios remain plausible. Studies of attempted proliferation suggest that declining faith in the reliability of an ally can indeed
prompt efforts to develop nuclear weapons, and the case studies in this book
show that events external to an alliance relationship can still influence member beliefs about the ally's reliability.[67] The possibility of allied nuclear ambitions will likely be a key focus for US policy over the next few decades.
Unlike the 1970s, today some allies in Asia may be able to develop nuclear
weapons before coercive restraint attempts can stop them. As Washington
considers this issue, the interdependent nature of the alliance system will
also influence policy: the United States would find it difficult to accept the
nuclear status of one ally but deny the same option to other allies.

CLIENT STATES AND POWERPLAYS

My findings also directly challenge Victor Cha's "powerplay" thesis.[68]
Cha argues that a bilateral alliance system was formed so that the United
States could exercise control over client state allies, but the empirical material examined in this book shows that the security commitments (and eventual alliances) granted to the ROC and ROK regularly limited Washington's
policy options. The formation of these alliances did enable Washington to
influence Seoul and Taipei but at no point did this influence approach "near-
total control over [the] foreign and domestic affairs of its allies."[69] It is also
unclear whether Washington's influence was actually increased by the signing of an alliance or whether this influence was simply a function of a
state's security dependence upon the United States.

By signing alliances with Seoul and Taipei, Washington may have actually decreased its freedom of action—and perhaps its ability to restrain the
ROC and ROK—because it was formally committing its "prestige" to their
defense. The desire to ensure that other allies retained favorable views of
US reliability meant that Washington had to devote considerable time and
attention to the ROK and ROC. In 1950, South Korea—even before it was a
formal ally—had to be defended, lest Japan and other nations lose confidence
in the United States and drift toward neutralism. In 1953, Washington could
not simply walk away from an intransigent Syngman Rhee—because this
might be interpreted as another abandonment of South Korea—but nor
could he be allowed to restart the Korean War. In 1955, Washington lobbied
the ROC to withdraw from Quemoy and Matsu, but US leaders could not
coerce Chiang Kai-shek into doing so. Indeed, Dulles complained to the New
Zealand ambassador, Leslie Munro, "on more than one occasion" that many
people viewed Chiang Kai-shek as "purely a satellite—that he would do
what he was told to do by the Americans. . . . [Dulles] said that was far from
being the case."[70]

While the United States was able to simultaneously manage its alliances,
set appropriate examples, and avoid the worst outcome in each instance, the

security commitments given to the ROC and ROK might have actually decreased Washington's ability to coerce them into actions that aligned with US interests. These countries were able to maintain confrontational postures toward more powerful adversaries only because their alliances with the United States created the possibility of allied support. Though, as Cha argues, the bilateral structure of the Asian alliance system may seem to maximize Washington's power over smaller states, signing alliances created interdependence, and this meant that Washington felt the need to protect beliefs about US reliability. Thus, it is possible that by signing alliances with the ROC and ROK, Washington actually decreased its leverage over Taipei and Seoul.

The powerful influence of this interdependence stems from the alliance audience effect. Significant interactions, when they occur in front of the alliance audience, can have system-level effects. This, in turn, raises questions about the importance of the "why was there no Pacific NATO?" debate. The focus on this issue has meant that a possibly more important question—Do the Asian alliances interact in a system-like fashion?—has, until now, been overlooked. Given the interdependence between the legally discrete Asian alliance treaties, there is a greater need to examine the entire alliance system superstructure and the interdependencies within it.

Because this book focuses on the fears, assessments, and actions of US allies, the case studies demonstrate why Washington sometimes found it difficult to manage these alliance commitments. The United States often regarded its alliances in Asia as existing mainly to serve its own purposes, and Cha has argued that the Washington was able to exercise "near-total control over foreign and domestic affairs of its allies."[71] But this book demonstrates that this was clearly not the case: Washington grew frustrated with its allies when they declined to either actively support US policy or fulfill their (US-designated) role as anti-Communist bastions on the periphery of the Sino-Soviet bloc. Given the obvious Communist threat, it might seem odd that these allies were so regularly willing to disagree and bicker with the United States. But they had their own interests, preferences, and agency, and—in retrospect—it seems inarguable that alliance bargaining often influenced Washington toward more sensible, restrained, and sustainable positions. This also raises the question as to whether states should want their ally to be loyal to the extreme of participating in some foolish endeavor (the British and Australian reaction to the Iraq War in 2003 comes to mind) or should they want it to exercise good judgment and abstain despite the possibility of straining the alliance (the French reaction).

FREE-RIDING THROUGH MANIPULATION

In recent years, US allies in Asia have again complained about the uncertain direction of Washington's strategic policy in Asia. Stephen Walt has expressed concern that by appealing to Washington's "credibility obsession," allies might try to manipulate the United States into subsidizing their own security. Walt writes that "the credibility obsession also made it easier for U.S. allies to free-ride . . . because they could always get Uncle Sucker to take on more burdens by complaining that they had doubts about American resolve."[72] Walt is especially suspicious about such dynamics in modern Asia. Against the backdrop of aggressive Chinese actions, he argues that the credibility concept creates a situation in which allies don't make adequate provision for their own defense: it is "easier to complain about U.S. credibility than to dig deep and buy some genuine military capacity."[73]

The case studies I examined suggest that US alliances do not raise significant risks of manipulation, because Washington has strong incentives to detect and reject such efforts. In the First Taiwan Strait Crisis, self-interested appeals to US credibility—such as Seoul's claim that "in this part of [the] world Quemoy can be [a] symbol, [the] loss of which . . . would have serious repercussions in Asia"—did not achieve the desired result.[74] Furthermore, on those occasions when Washington did suspect that allies were attempting policies of manipulation—such as Rhee's efforts to obtain an alliance that did not restrict his desire for reunification—the United States responded strongly in order to demonstrate that it could not be duped. The idea of manipulating allies by appealing to their credibility or reliability images warrants further research, but the case studies I examine suggest that this risk is not especially prevalent.

ALLIANCE ENTANGLEMENT

The alliance audience effect framework also has relevance for what Michael Beckley calls "entanglement theory": the idea that "alliances drag states into wars by placing their reputations at risk, socializing their leaders into adopting allied interests and norms, and provoking adversaries and emboldening allies."[75] Entanglement occurs when "loyalty trumps self-interest: a state is driven by moral, legal, or reputational concerns to uphold an alliance commitment without regard to, and often at the expense of, its national interests."[76] Concluding that US concerns about entanglement are often exaggerated, Beckley notes that on a number of occasions the views of allies have influenced Washington toward policies of restraint.

My analysis of the First Taiwan Strait Crisis provides much greater detail on one of Beckley's cases and supports his conclusion that allied concerns about US reliability are not always demands for a more aggressive policy from Washington. Though it is sometimes argued that Washington's alliances regularly entrap or entangle it into unnecessary and costly conflicts, my case studies demonstrate the exact opposite dynamic at work. As Beckley notes, "allies often help . . . by . . . encouraging the United States to stay out of wars altogether."[77]

It is often assumed that because any interdependence between discrete alliance commitments must hinge on loyalty, alliance interdependence only creates entrapment risks for the United States. By delineating between loyalty and reliability, I show that alliance interdependence can actually help to mitigate entrapment risks for the United States. If Washington's general loyalty mattered most to other allies, then the United States would never be able to effectively restrain an ally or abandon it in response to its reckless and aggressive behavior. But there is a risk that excessive US loyalty could lead other allies to believe that Washington can be manipulated—to conclude that by appealing to Washington's reputation for credibility or its reliability image, they could entrap the United States into a war against its interests. Because Washington will never want its allies to believe that it can be easily manipulated, the alliance audience effect can actually convince the United States to not get too preoccupied with its own sense of loyalty. In short, Washington needs to be seen as reliable, but never gullible.

Ideas about loyalty, disloyalty, reputation, and alliance interdependence have been powerful and pervasive influences on US policy. The belief that disloyalty to one ally would lead other allies to lose confidence in the United States almost resulted in war between the US and Communist China in 1955. Absent psychological factors, the objectives would have been strategically worthless real estate: Quemoy and Matsu. But the real issue at stake was Washington's image as a reliable ally: Dulles was convinced that to abandon the offshore islands would cause other allies to distrust the United States. As the preceding analysis has shown, this belief—based on the idea of a loyalty reputation—was wrong. Other allies like the United Kingdom, Canada, New Zealand, Japan, and Australia were concerned about a surfeit— not a deficit—of loyalty to Nationalist China. These allies wanted US policy to demonstrate that Washington's interests were convergent with their own. They wanted an ally that was *reliable*: this was far more important than whether the ally was completely *loyal* to Taipei.

Washington's decision to intervene in the Korean War—and the positive reaction of regional allies—might seem to challenge this skeptical treatment of loyalty. But these allies were not reacting to an affirmation of moral and upright national character, epitomized in US loyalty to Seoul. Rather, they were relieved that Washington's interests were convergent with their own and that common action could be concerted to achieve shared goals.

Jonathan Mercer concludes his book by arguing that the United States should not fight for its reputation because commitments are not interdependent.[78] The alliance audience effect theory, and the case studies examined in this book, suggest that this is not the case. Collective reputations do not exist—because each US ally will have its own view on US policy—but there will undoubtedly be situations in which the likely reactions of allies should be a significant influence on US policy. Though it is usually assumed that alliance interdependence only ever manifests in a way inimical to US interests—that the need to protect a loyalty reputation will inevitably drag Washington in to unnecessary conflicts—this is not the case. US allies do not inevitably encourage aggressive responses but they definitely observe, and are influenced by, US policy toward other allies.

Though alliance interdependence might create the risk that concern for Washington's reliability image could be manipulated by allies, the case studies examined do not suggest that this possibility is particularly problematic. Allies were usually honest and forthright in explaining their fears to the United States, and Washington—to its credit—usually listened carefully. Notably, alliance interdependence did not result in the entrapment or manipulation of the United States. Rather, the need to demonstrate that Washington could not be duped by its allies was more influential than self-interested appeals to reputation. Furthermore, the case studies show that the United States can sometimes exploit alliance interdependence to further its own goals.

In the 1949–1969 period, the first instinct of allies doubting US reliability was to cling closer to Washington: to seek reassurance, to gain access and insight, to influence policy, and to reconfirm that Washington's interests remained convergent with their own. But different reactions are possible: doubts about US reliability in the 1970s prompted some allies to start nuclear weapons programs, and these were brought to an end only by a combination of US coercion and reassurance. US policies should not be solely determined by the likely reactions of allies but it is unwise to suggest that these reactions should not be considered at all. By carefully managing alliance interdependence—either through simultaneous alliance management or the skillful setting of examples—US decision makers adroitly managed their Asian alliances through the first twenty years of the Cold War. Given China's rise, divergent allied views and preferences, and recurring doubts about Washington's reliability in Asia, similar finesse will be required in the years ahead.

Notes

Abbreviations Used in Notes

AWF	Ann Whitman File
CDF	Central Decimal Files
DDEPL	Dwight D. Eisenhower Presidential Library
D-HS	Dulles-Herter Series
FRUS	United States Department of State, *Foreign Relations of the United States* series
HCARI	History of the Civil Administration of the Ryukyu Islands
JFD OHP	John Foster Dulles Oral History Project
JFKPL	John F. Kennedy Presidential Library
NAA	National Archives of Australia
NARA	National Archives and Records Administration
NPM	Nixon Presidential Materials
NSCF	National Security Council Files
NSF	National Security Files
PPK	Papers of President Kennedy
RG	Record Group
RMNPL	Richard M. Nixon Presidential Library
SNF	Subject-Numeric File
TaC	Trips and Conferences

Introduction

1. Thomas C. Schelling, *Arms and Influence* (New Haven, CT: Yale University Press, 1966), 124–125.

2. President Harry Truman, as quoted in Daryl G. Press, *Calculating Credibility: How Leaders Assess Military Threats* (Ithaca, NY: Cornell University Press, 2005), 2.

3. See Thom Shanker and Lauren D'Avolio, "Former Defense Secretaries Criticize Obama on Syria," *New York Times*, September 18, 2013; and Dan De Luce, "Hagel: The White House Tried to 'Destroy' Me," Foreign Policy, December 18, 2015, http://foreignpolicy.com/2015/12/18/hagel-the-white-house-tried-to-destroy-me/.

4. Office of the Secretary of Defense Vietnam Task Force, *United States–Vietnam Relations, 1945–1967* (a.k.a. Pentagon Papers), Part V. A, vol. 2, *Justification of the War—Public Statements: D. The Johnson Administration* (Washington, DC: National Archives and Records Administration, 2011), http://www.documentcloud.org/documents/205536-pentagon-papers-part-v-a-volume-ii-d.html.

5. See, for example, Aaron Friedberg, "Will We Abandon Taiwan?" *Commentary*, May 1, 2000, https://www.commentarymagazine.com/articles/will-we-abandon-taiwan/.

6. John Mearsheimer, "Say Goodbye to Taiwan," *National Interest*, February 25, 2014, http://nationalinterest.org/print/article/say-goodbye-taiwan-9931.

7. Nancy Bernkopf Tucker and Bonnie Glaser, "Should the United States Abandon Taiwan?" *Washington Quarterly* 34, no. 4 (2011): 32.

8. The United Nations Security Council Budapest Memorandum for Ukraine (joint declaration issued on December 5, 1994 at Budapest by the leaders of the Russian Federation, Ukraine, the United Kingdom of Great Britain and Northern Ireland, and the United States of America) is formally entitled the Memorandum on Security Assurances in Connection with Ukraine's Accession to the Treaty on the Non-Proliferation of Nuclear Weapons. It may be found in United Nations documentation as A/49/765 and S/1994/1399, December 19, 1994, http://www.securitycouncilreport.org/atf/cf/%7B65BFCF9B-6D27-4E9C-8CD3-CF6E4FF96FF9%7D/s_1994_1399.pdf.

9. Helene Cooper and Martin Fackler, "U.S. Response to Crimea Worries Japan's Leaders," *New York Times*, April 5, 2014. See also Natan Sachs, "Whose Side Are You on? Alliance Credibility in the Middle East and Japan," *Order from Chaos* (blog of the Brookings Institution), May 31, 2016, https://www.brookings.edu/blog/order-from-chaos/2016/05/31/whose-side-are-you-on-alliance-credibility-in-the-middle-east-and-japan/.

10. Helene Cooper and Jane Perlez, "White House Moves to Reassure Allies with South China Sea Patrol, but Quietly," *New York Times*, October 27, 2015.

11. See Gene Gerzhoy and Nick Miller, "Donald Trump Thinks More Countries Should Have Nuclear Weapons: Here's What the Research Says," *Washington Post*, April 6, 2016.

12. Michael Mandelbaum noted the connection between extended nuclear deterrence and fears of abandonment. See Michael Mandelbaum, *The Nuclear Revolution: International Politics before and after Hiroshima* (Cambridge: Cambridge University Press, 1981), 152–153.

13. For analysis of how these different events contributed to regional beliefs about Washington's alliance reliability, see Johannes Kadura, *The War after the War: The Struggle for Credibility during America's Exit from Vietnam* (Ithaca, NY: Cornell University Press, 2016); Sung Gul Hong, "The Search for Deterrence: Park's Nuclear Option," in *The Park Chung Hee Era: The Transformation of South Korea*, ed. Byung Kook-Kim and Ezra Vogel (Cambridge, MA: Harvard University Press, 2011), 483–510; Philipp Bleek and Eric Lorber, "Security Guarantees and Allied Nuclear Proliferation," *Journal of Conflict Resolution* 58, no. 3 (2014): 429–454; Lyong Choi, "The First Nuclear Crisis in the Korean Peninsula, 1975–1976," *Cold War History* 14, no. 1 (2014): 71–90; and Eugene Kogan, "Proliferation among Friends: Taiwan's Lessons from 1970s–1980s," paper prepared for the Nuclear Studies Research Initiative Conference, Austin, TX, October 2013.

14. The term "hub and spoke" was coined by John Foster Dulles, the architect of the alliance system. The hub of the wheel was the United States, while its alliances with Japan and the Philippines, as well as Australia and New Zealand, were the spokes. See Percy Spender, *Exercises in Diplomacy: The ANZUS Treaty and the Colombo Plan* (Sydney: Sydney University Press, 1969), 66.

15. See Victor D. Cha, *Alignment despite Antagonism: The US-Korea-Japan Security Triangle* (Stanford, CA: Stanford University Press, 1999).

16. See Andrew Moravcsik, "Active Citation and Qualitative Political Science," *Qualitative and Multi-Method Research* 10, no. 1 (2012): 33–37; and Andrew Moravcsik, "Active Citation: A Precondition for Replicable Qualitative Research," *PS: Political Science and Politics* 43, no. 1 (2010):

29–35. Though I do not adopt Moravcsik's "active citation" approach, in order to assist replication I provide, where possible, the most readily accessible primary document reference. This is usually the *Foreign Relations of the United States* (*FRUS*) series, which is freely available online. Full details are included in the bibliography.

17. See, for example, Junghyun Park, "Frustrated Alignment: The Pacific Pact Proposals from 1949 to 1954 and South Korea-Taiwan Relations," *International Journal of Asian Studies* 12, no. 2 (2015): 217–237, for detail on the South Korean and Taiwanese archives.

18. Stephen M. Walt, "The Credibility Addiction," Foreign Policy, January 6, 2015, http://foreignpolicy.com/2015/01/06/the-credibility-addiction-us-iraq-afghanistan-unwinnable-war/.

19. See Cha, *Alignment despite Antagonism*; Victor D. Cha, *Powerplay: The Origins of the American Alliance System in Asia* (Princeton, NJ: Princeton University Press, 2016); and Thomas Christensen, *Worse Than a Monolith: Alliance Politics and Problems of Coercive Diplomacy in Asia* (Princeton, NJ: Princeton University Press, 2011).

20. Alexander George and Andrew Bennett, *Case Studies and Theory Development in the Social Sciences* (Cambridge, MA: MIT Press, 2005), 153.

21. Some of the theory and empirical material in this book is also in Iain D. Henry, "What Allies Want: Reconsidering Loyalty, Reliability, and Alliance Interdependence," *International Security* 44, no. 4 (2020): 45–83.

22. See Cha, *Powerplay*; and Yasuhiro Izumikawa, "Network Connections and the Emergence of the Hub-and-Spokes Alliance System in East Asia," *International Security* 45, no. 2 (2020): 7–50.

1. Alliances, Reliability, and Interdependence

1. Stephen M. Walt, *The Origins of Alliances* (Ithaca, NY: Cornell University Press, 1987), 12.

2. Glenn H. Snyder, *Alliance Politics* (Ithaca, NY: Cornell University Press, 1997), 4, 6.

3. Snyder, *Alliance Politics*, 8.

4. Brett Ashley Leeds et al., "Alliance Treaty Obligations and Provisions, 1815–1944," *International Interactions: Empirical and Theoretical Research in International Relations* 28, no. 3 (2002): 238.

5. Kenneth Waltz, *Theory of International Politics* (Long Grove, IL: Waveland, 1979), 118. For a review of the literature on internal versus external balancing, see James Morrow, "Alliances: Why Write Them Down?" *Annual Review of Political Science* 3 (2000): 76–77. On a related subject, concerning whether a state should provide a security partner with arms, a formal alliance, or both, see Keren Yarhi-Milo, Alexander Lanoszka and Zack Cooper, "To Arm or to Ally? The Patron's Dilemma and the Strategic Logic of Arms Transfers and Alliances," *International Security* 41, no. 2 (2016): 90–139. On the concept of damaging opposing alliances—known as wedging—see Yasuhiro Izumikawa, "To Coerce or Reward? Theorizing Wedge Strategies in Alliance Politics," *Security Studies* 22, no. 3 (2013): 498–531; and Timothy Crawford, "Preventing Enemy Coalitions: How Wedge Strategies Shape Power Politics," *International Security* 35, no. 4 (2011): 155–189.

6. Glenn H. Snyder, "The Security Dilemma in Alliance Politics," *World Politics* 36, no. 4 (1984): 462–463.

7. The term is taken from James Morrow, "Alliances and Asymmetry: An Alternative to the Capability Aggregation Model of Alliances," *American Journal of Political Science* 35, no. 4 (1991): 907. The idea of a tradeoff between autonomy and security is an important contribution of Morrow's work. See also James Morrow, "Alliances, Credibility, and Peacetime Costs," *Journal of Conflict Resolution* 38, no. 2 (1994): 270–297.

8. Morrow, "Alliances and Asymmetry," 928.

9. Michael Altfield, "The Decision to Ally: A Theory and Test," *Western Political Quarterly* 37, no. 4 (1984): 529.

10. Snyder, *Alliance Politics*, 181–182. Abandonment fears exist despite research demonstrating that approximately 75 percent of alliance commitments are fulfilled. See Brett Ashley Leeds, Andrew Long, and Sara Mitchell, "Reevaluating Alliance Reliability: Specific Threats, Specific Promises," *Journal of Conflict Resolution* 44, no. 5 (2000): 686–699.

11. Snyder, "Security Dilemma in Alliance Politics," 467.

12. Snyder, *Alliance Politics*, 181. Recent research suggests that entrapment fears are exaggerated. See Michael Beckley, "The Myth of Entangling Alliances: Reassessing the Security Risks of U.S. Defense Pacts," *International Security* 39, no. 4 (2015): 7–48.

13. Snyder, *Alliance Politics*, 182.

14. Snyder, "Security Dilemma in Alliance Politics," 467.

15. For an excellent examination of the problems with strict definitions of entrapment, including some analysis of broadening the concept to nonconflict scenarios, see Tongfi Kim, "Why Alliances Entangle but Seldom Entrap States," *Security Studies* 20, no. 3 (2011): 350–377.

16. Another way of conceiving this dynamic is that entrapment occurs when a state's desire to protect its alliance from risk is stronger than its desire to avoid costs, though the state would have preferred the situation had never arisen. Uncertainty is generated by two factors: the costs of supporting the ally might be higher than expected and the costs of abandoning the ally might be lower than expected. For example, a state might decide to fight alongside its ally out of a belief that if it does not, the ally will abrogate the alliance. But this is not certain: an alliance may persist despite such a blatant instance of abandonment.

17. However, as chapter 6 shows, in some circumstances the two fears can be held simultaneously.

18. See, for example, Schelling's explanation of the American "tripwire" forces in Europe during the Cold War. Schelling, *Arms and Influence*, 47. On the deterrence value of stationing nuclear weapons on allied territory, see Matthew Fuhrmann and Todd Sechser, "Signaling Alliance Commitments: Hand-Tying and Sunk Costs in Extended Nuclear Deterrence," *American Journal of Political Science* 58, no. 4 (2014): 919–935.

19. For more on avoiding abandonment and entrapment, see Snyder, *Alliance Politics*, 183–186.

20. Cha, *Alignment despite Antagonism*, 41.

21. Snyder, *Alliance Politics*, 9.

22. Schelling, *Arms and Influence*, 55.

23. For an examination of the domino theory from an Asian perspective, see Cheng Guan Ang, "The Domino Theory Revisited: The Southeast Asia Perspective," *War and Society* 19, no. 1 (2001): 109–130.

24. Robert Jervis, "Deterrence Theory Revisited," *World Politics* 31, no. 2 (1979): 289.

25. Alex Weisiger and Keren Yarhi-Milo, "Revisiting Reputation: How Past Actions Matter in International Politics," *International Organization* 69, no. 2 (2015): 475.

26. See Ernest R. May, *"Lessons" of the Past: The Use and Misuse of History in American Foreign Policy* (New York: Oxford University Press, 1973); and Yuen Foong Khong, *Analogies at War: Korea, Munich, Dien Bien Phu and the Vietnam Decisions of 1965* (Princeton, NJ: Princeton University Press, 1992).

27. Glenn Herald Snyder and Paul Diesing, *Conflict among Nations: Bargaining, Decision Making, and System Structure in International Crises* (Princeton, NJ: Princeton University Press, 1977), 432.

28. Snyder, *Alliance Politics*, 53.

29. Snyder and Diesing, *Conflict among Nations*, 432.

30. Ted Hopf, *Peripheral Visions: Deterrence Theory and American Foreign Policy in the Third World, 1965–1990* (Ann Arbor: University of Michigan Press, 1994).

31. Robert Jervis, "Domino Beliefs and Strategic Behavior," in *Dominoes and Bandwagons: Strategic Beliefs and Great Power Competition in the Eurasian Rimland*, ed. Robert Jervis and Jack Snyder (Oxford: Oxford University Press, 1991), 37.

32. See Jonathan Mercer, *Reputation and International Politics* (Ithaca, NY: Cornell University Press, 1996), chap. 2.

33. Mercer, *Reputation and International Politics*, 15, 227.

34. Mercer, *Reputation and International Politics*, 228.

35. Press, *Calculating Credibility*, 32.

36. Weisiger and Yarhi-Milo, "Revisiting Reputation," 492.

37. Frank P. Harvey and John Mitton, *Fighting for Credibility: US Reputation and International Politics* (Toronto: University of Toronto Press, 2016), 47. For an excellent discussion of the research agenda for the reputation/credibility debate, see Robert Jervis, Keren Yarhi-Milo, and

Don Casler, "Redefining the Debate over Reputation and Credibility in International Security," *World Politics* 73, no. 1 (2021): 167–203.

38. Harvey and Mitton, *Fighting for Credibility*, 245.

39. Gregory D. Miller, *The Shadow of the Past: Reputation and Military Alliances before the First World War* (Ithaca, NY: Cornell University Press, 2012), 44.

40. Miller, *Shadow of the Past*, 51. Miller's hypothesis—that "An unreliable state will be more constrained by the design of its alliances"—was supported in 95.2 percent of observations. See also 186–187.

41. Miller, *Shadow of the Past*, 49.

42. Miller, *Shadow of the Past*, 207.

43. Stephen M. Walt, "Why Alliances Endure or Collapse," *Survival* 39, no. 1 (1997): 170.

44. Other authors also assume that observer states are monitoring allied behavior in order to make dispositional judgments. See Douglas Gibler, "The Costs of Reneging: Reputation and Alliance Formation," *Journal of Conflict Resolution* 52, no. 3 (2008): 434, for an interesting example that prioritizes interests for adversarial threats but character-based explanations for alliance promises.

45. Mercer, *Reputation and International Politics*, 228.

46. The analysis in this book focuses mainly on how states obtain better information about the interests and intent of their ally but the alliance audience effect framework does expect that this desire for better information would also apply in circumstances when an ally's capabilities are in doubt. See, for example, Paul Huth, "Reputations and Deterrence: A Theoretical and Empirical Assessment," *Security Studies* 7, no. 1 (2007): 76–79. Also, critiques of Mercer's work note that even within Mercer's theory—which allows for the prospect of allies doubting US resolve—it might be worth fighting some conflicts in order to "maintain alliance cohesion." See Dale Copeland, "Do Reputations Matter?" *Security Studies* 7, no. 1 (2007): 33–71.

47. Snyder, *Alliance Politics*, 317.

48. Brett Ashley Leeds, "Alliance Reliability in Times of War: Explaining State Decisions to Violate Treaties," *International Organization* 57, no. 4 (2003): 824.

49. Mercer, *Reputation and International Politics*, 228.

50. Miller, *Shadow of the Past*, 49.

51. It might be more accurate to say that the costs of the alliance become accepted and normalized to the extent that they do not register as being at all onerous or burdensome. The persistence of NATO and various alliances in Asia after the end of the Cold War challenges the argument that the decline of a threat will result in the dissolution of an alliance. See Stephen M. Walt, "Alliances in a Unipolar World," *World Politics* 61, no. 1 (2009): 86–120; and Walt, "Why Alliances Endure or Collapse."

52. This focus on reputations for resolve, and adversarial perceptions thereof, can be seen in recent (and excellent) scholarship such as Keren Yarhi-Milo, *Who Fights for Reputation: The Psychology of Leaders in International Conflict* (Princeton, NJ: Princeton University Press, 2018); Joshua D. Kertzer, *Resolve in International Politics* (Princeton, NJ: Princeton University Press, 2016); and Danielle Lupton, *Reputation for Resolve: How Leaders Signal Determination in International Politics* (Ithaca, NY: Cornell University Press, 2020).

53. Snyder, *Alliance Politics*, 356–357. I thank Timothy Crawford for reminding me about Snyder's halo concept and for suggesting that I incorporate it into the argument.

54. It is also conceivable that, in some circumstances, a state might actually want its adversary to stand firm and fight: for example, the state might be trying to tie down the adversary's forces in one theater, so that they cannot be used in another. Or it may simply want to completely eliminate the adversary.

55. Weisiger and Yarhi-Milo, "Revisiting Reputation," 478.

56. My concept of reliability is similar—but not identical—to Miller's, and it is explained and justified in a different way. Because my conception allows for a state's disloyalty to one ally to relieve the entrapment fears of another ally, I argue that A's disloyalty to ally B can actually improve C's assessment of A's reliability. See Miller, *Shadow of the Past*, 43–44, and Gregory D. Miller, "Hypotheses on Reputation: Alliance Choices and the Shadow of the Past," *Security Studies* 12, no. 3 (2003): 55.

57. On this idea of intra-alliance bargaining over strategy, see the explanation of "Leader," "Hero," and "Protector" games in Snyder and Diesing, *Conflict among Nations*, chap. 2.

58. As defined earlier, abandonment occurs when "a state decides its interests are best served by not supporting an ally's policy," and entrapment occurs when "a state supports its ally's policy despite being unsure whether the value of the alliance will outweigh the costs of this support."

59. See Armin H. Meyer, *Assignment Tokyo: An Ambassador's Journal* (Indianapolis: Bobbs-Merrill, 1974), 112, and chap. 4.

60. A similar dynamic is explored in Ronald R. Krebs and Jennifer Spindel, "Divided Priorities: Why and When Allies Differ over Military Intervention," *Security Studies* 27, no. 4 (2018): 575–606.

61. Mercer, *Reputation and International Politics*, 6. Miller defines reputation as "a shared perception about one state's prior behavior that is used to predict future behavior." See Miller, *Shadow of the Past*, 37.

62. Of course, this does not preclude two or more states having a similar view about their common ally's reliability. My point is that this shared perception will not be reached through judgments of national character against the standard of loyalty.

63. See Mercer, *Reputation and International Politics*, 47. In table 1, Mercer hypothesizes that an ally standing firm will lead an observer to making situational attributions because standing firm is desired behavior.

64. Mercer, *Reputation and International Politics*, 6, 17.

65. This sentiment is echoed in Miller's assessment of Mercer's book. Miller deduces three hypotheses of how Mercer's theory should apply to reliability in alliances—all three suggest that a state's reliability should not influence its alliance relationships. See Miller, *Shadow of the Past*, 57.

66. Weisiger and Yarhi-Milo, "Revisiting Reputation," 474. See also Shiping Tang, "Reputation, Cult of Reputation, and International Conflict," *Security Studies* 14, no. 1 (2005): 27.

67. Harvey and Mitton, *Fighting for Credibility*, 47.

68. I first used this definition in Henry, "What Allies Want," 53. This use of convergent or divergent interests as a way of assessing the health or reliability of an alliance is also implicit in Walt, "Why Alliances Endure or Collapse," 167.

69. Of course, in some circumstances both allied interests *and* allied capabilities will need to be carefully scrutinized to form accurate assessments of reliability. For example, if several states share the same ally, and if there is a risk that these states might be attacked simultaneously, then demand for allied assistance may exceed the available supply. Alternatively, an adversary may embark on a sustained military build-up, and proof of an equivalent response from an ally may be necessary to prevent perceptions of unreliability, because the lack of such a response would, in itself, suggest a divergence of interests. Because interests will determine a state's decisions on military capability, I believe that interests are the more important influence on reliability. It remains possible, of course, that a deceitful ally's military capability decisions will hint at undisclosed changes to its interests and such situations will raise the importance of monitoring allied military capabilities.

70. Of course, this assumes that the alliance was not a secret one. Also, as noted earlier, this prioritization of interests may not have been simply private information—it may have been previously unknown information. The state may have never entertained the thought of abandoning its ally, but when the moment of truth arrived it found this course to be in its preferred response. As an analogy: few couples get engaged without a genuine desire to get married, but many engagements end not with wedding ceremonies but with heartbreak.

71. See Mercer, *Reputation and International Politics*, 66–67.

72. Mercer, *Reputation and International Politics*, 67.

73. Walt, "Credibility Addiction."

74. Stephen M. Walt, "Pay No Attention to that Panda behind the Curtain," Foreign Policy, April 23, 2014, http://foreignpolicy.com/2014/04/23/pay-no-attention-to-that-panda-behind-the-curtain/.

75. Press, *Calculating Credibility*, 154.

76. Miller, *Shadow of the Past*, 49.

77. See Miller, *Shadow of the Past*, 187.

78. Miller, *Shadow of the Past*, 51.

79. Gerald Hensley, *Friendly Fire: Nuclear Politics and the Collapse of ANZUS* (Auckland: Auckland University Press, 2013), 192–193 (emphasis in the original).

80. Don Oberdorfer, "U.S. Withdraws New Zealand's ANZUS Shield," *Washington Post*, June 28, 1986. See also Jervis, "Domino Beliefs and Strategic Behavior," 33.

81. This dynamic is similar to Snyder's description of the "composite security dilemma," which involves simultaneous interactions with an adversary and an ally, except this involves simultaneous interactions with two allies (and perhaps, also, an adversary). See Snyder, "Security Dilemma in Alliance Politics," 468–471.

2. Forming Alliances in Asia, 1949–1951

1. The ambassador in Australia (Jarman) to the Secretary of State, March 24, 1950, in *FRUS, 1950*, vol. 6, *East Asia and the Pacific*, Document 30. The quote refers to the views of the Australian foreign minister, Percy Spender.

2. See Victor Cha, "Powerplay Origins of the U.S. Alliance System in Asia," *International Security* 34, no. 3 (2009–2010): 158–196, and Cha, *Powerplay*.

3. Christopher Hemmer and Peter Katzenstein, "Why Is There No NATO in Asia? Collective Identity, Regionalism, and the Origins of Multilateralism," *International Organization* 56, no. 3 (2002): 575–607. See also John Duffield, "Why Is There No APTO? Why Is There No OSCAP? Asia-Pacific Security Institutions in Comparative Perspective," *Contemporary Security Policy* 22, no. 2 (2001): 69–95.

4. David W. Mabon, "Elusive Agreements: The Pacific Pact Proposals of 1949–1951," *Pacific Historical Review* 57, no. 2 (1988): 147–177. See also Charles M. Dobbs, "The Pact that Never Was: The Pacific Pact of 1949," *Journal of Northeast Asian Studies* 3, no. 4 (1984): 29–42, and Park, "Frustrated Alignment."

5. John Foster Dulles, "Security in the Pacific," *Foreign Affairs* 30, no. 2 (1952): 175–187.

6. Izumikawa, "Network Connections."

7. This is not to endorse the view that China was ever Washington's to lose. See, for example, Warren Cohen, "Symposium: Rethinking the Lost Chance in China," *Diplomatic History* 21, no. 1 (1997): 71–75.

8. On the US presence in Asia after the Second World War, see Daniel Immerwahr, *How to Hide an Empire: A History of the Greater United States* (London: Vintage, 2019), chap. 14.

9. John Garver, *The Sino-American Alliance: Nationalist China and American Cold War Strategy in Asia* (London: M. E. Sharpe, 1997), 11.

10. Garver, *Sino-American Alliance*, 17–18.

11. Max Hastings, *The Korean War* (New York: Simon and Schuster, 1987), 26.

12. Nancy Bernkopf Tucker, *Taiwan, Hong Kong, and the United States, 1945–1992: Uncertain Friendships* (New York: Twayne, 1994), 24.

13. Nancy Bernkopf Tucker, *Strait Talk: United States–Taiwan Relations and the Crisis with China* (Cambridge, MA: Harvard University Press, 2009), 13.

14. Dean Acheson, "Speech on the Far East," speech delivered to National Press Club, January 12, 1950, https://www.cia.gov/readingroom/docs/1950-01-12.pdf.

15. For an excellent analysis on the internal US government debate about the importance of Taiwan, see Paul Heer, *Mr. X and the Pacific: George F. Kennan and American Policy in East Asia* (Ithaca, NY: Cornell University Press, 2018), chap. 4.

16. John Lewis Gaddis, *The Long Peace: Inquiries into the History of the Cold War* (Oxford: Oxford University Press, 1987), vii.

17. Enclosure 2 to The Secretary of State to the Secretary of Defense (Marshall), January 9, 1951, in *FRUS, 1951*, vol. 6, pt. 1, *Asia and the Pacific*, Document 34.

18. John Lewis Gaddis, *Strategies of Containment: A Critical Appraisal of Postwar American National Security Policy* (Oxford: Oxford University Press, 1982), 109.

19. The Assistant Secretary of State for Occupied Areas (Saltzman) to the Under Secretary of the Army (Draper), January 25, 1949, in *FRUS, 1949*, vol. 7, pt. 2, *The Far East and Australasia*, Document 193.

20. The Special Representative in Korea (Muccio) to the Secretary of State, January 27, 1949, in *FRUS, 1949*, vol. 7, pt. 2, Document 196.

21. The Acting Political Adviser in Japan (Sebald) to the Secretary of State, February 12, 1949, in *FRUS, 1949*, vol. 7, pt. 2, Document 25. Under the occupation, there was no American ambassador in Tokyo: Sebald, as the political adviser, was the highest-ranking diplomat.

22. Memorandum of Conversation, by the Secretary of the Army (Royall), February 8, 1949, in *FRUS, 1949*, vol. 7, pt. 2, Document 199.

23. Memorandum of Conversation, by the Special Representative in Korea (Muccio), February 25, 1949, in *FRUS, 1949*, vol. 7, pt. 2, Annex to Document 199.

24. NSC 8/2, Position of the United States with Respect to Korea, March 22, 1949, in *FRUS, 1949*, vol. 7, pt. 2, Document 209.

25. Gaddis, *Strategies of Containment*, 92.

26. NSC 8/2, Position of the United States with Respect to Korea, March 22, 1949, in *FRUS, 1949*, vol. 7, pt. 2, Document 209.

27. As quoted in NSC 8/2, Position of the United States with Respect to Korea, March 22, 1949, in *FRUS, 1949*, vol. 7, pt. 2, Document 209.

28. Charles M. Dobbs, *The Unwanted Symbol: American Foreign Policy, the Cold War, and Korea, 1945–1950* (Kent, OH: Kent State University Press, 1981), 169.

29. William Stueck, *Rethinking the Korean War: A New Diplomatic and Strategic History* (Princeton, NJ: Princeton University Press, 2002), 78.

30. William Stueck, *The Korean War: An International History* (Princeton, NJ: Princeton University Press, 1995), 28. US leaders regularly feared Japan shifting to a neutralist outlook, or even joining the Communist bloc, but postwar Japanese leaders were usually focused on strengthening Japan's free world alignment and US-Japan relations while simultaneously managing the risks of entrapment. As explored in chapter 5, a reflexive US suspicion of Japanese motives was often an unhelpful impediment to a stronger alliance. See also Walter LaFeber, *The Clash: US-Japanese Relations throughout History* (New York: W. W. Norton, 1997), 304–306.

31. NSC 8/2, Position of the United States with Respect to Korea, March 22, 1949, in *FRUS, 1949*, vol. 7, pt. 2, Document 209.

32. NSC 8, as quoted in NSC 8/2, Position of the United States with Respect to Korea, March 22, 1949, in *FRUS, 1949*, vol. 7, pt. 2, Document 209.

33. John Lewis Gaddis, "Korea in American Politics, Strategy, and Diplomacy: 1945–1950," in *The Origins of the Cold War in Asia*, ed. Yonosuke Nagai and Akira Iriye (New York: Columbia University Press, 1977), 283.

34. NSC 8/2, Position of the United States with Respect to Korea, March 22, 1949, in *FRUS, 1949*, vol. 7, pt. 2, Document 209.

35. The Special Representative in Korea (Muccio) to the Secretary of State, April 14, 1949, in *FRUS, 1949*, vol. 7, pt. 2, Document 219.

36. Draft Letter from the President of the Republic of Korea (Rhee) to the Special Representative in Korea (Muccio), April 14, 1949, in *FRUS, 1949*, vol. 7, pt. 2, Enclosure to Document 220.

37. Memorandum of Conversation, by the Ambassador in Korea (Muccio), May 2, 1949, in *FRUS, 1949*, vol. 7, pt. 2, Document 230.

38. The Ambassador in Korea (Muccio) to the Secretary of State, May 6, 1949, in *FRUS*, vol. 7, pt. 2, Document 235.

39. Bruce Cumings, *The Origins of the Korean War*, vol. 2, *The Roaring of the Cataract, 1947–1950* (Princeton, NJ: Princeton University Press, 1981), 383.

40. The Ambassador in Korea (Muccio) to the Secretary of State, May 9, 1949, in *FRUS, 1949*, vol. 7, pt. 2, Document 238.

41. The Secretary of State to the Embassy in Korea, May 9, 1949, in *FRUS, 1949*, vol. 7, pt. 2, Document 239.

42. Memorandum of Conversation, by the Director of the Office of Far Eastern Affairs (Butterworth), May 11, 1949, in *FRUS, 1949*, vol. 7, pt. 2, Document 244.

43. The Ambassador in Korea (Muccio) to the Secretary of State, May 16, 1949, in *FRUS, 1949*, vol. 7, pt. 2, Document 247. See also Dobbs, *Unwanted Symbol*, 171–175.

44. Cumings, *Origins of the Korean War*, 2:382.

45. Park, "Frustrated Alignment," 221.

46. Memo from the Acting Secretary of State to the Director of the Bureau of the Budget (Pace), May 16, 1949, in *FRUS, 1949*, vol. 7, pt. 2, Document 248.

47. The Ambassador in Korea (Muccio) to the Secretary of State, May 20, 1949, in *FRUS, 1949*, vol. 7, pt. 2, Document 253.

48. United States Department of State, *Department of State Bulletin* 20, no. 517 (May 29, 1949): 696.

49. See Memorandum of Conversation, by the Counselor of the Embassy in Korea (Drumright), May 28, 1949, in *FRUS, 1949*, vol. 7, pt. 2, Document 326. See also The Chargé in the Philippines (Lockett) to the Secretary of State, July 12, 1949, in *FRUS, 1949*, vol. 7, pt. 2, Document 332.

50. The Ambassador in Korea (Muccio) to the Secretary of State, May 31, 1949, in *FRUS, 1949*, vol. 7, pt. 2, Document 255.

51. *Department of State Bulletin* 20, no. 520 (June 19, 1949): 781.

52. Memorandum for the Chief of Staff, U.S. Army, June 23, 1949, in *FRUS, 1949*, vol. 7, pt. 2, Appendix B to Document 266. The Truman Doctrine was to provide financial support to non-Communist states threatened by the Soviet Union.

53. Tucker, *Uncertain Friendships*, 4.

54. Memorandum by the Ambassador at Large, Philip C. Jessup, January 14, 1950, in *FRUS, 1950*, vol. 7, *Korea*, Document 1.

55. Acheson, "Speech on the Far East."

56. Memorandum of Conversation, by Mr. John Z. Williams of the Office of Northeast Asian Affairs, January 20, 1950, in *FRUS, 1950*, vol. 7, Document 3.

57. Interview with Myun Chang, September 27, 1964, Seoul, John Foster Dulles Oral History Project (JFD OHP), Mudd Library, Princeton University.

58. Memorandum of Conversation, by the Officer in Charge of Korean Affairs (Bond), April 3, 1950, in *FRUS, 1950*, vol. 7, Document 20.

59. Christensen, *Worse than a Monolith*, 54.

60. The Ambassador in Korea (Muccio) to the Assistant Secretary of State for Far Eastern Affairs (Rusk), May 25, 1950, in *FRUS, 1950*, vol. 7, Document 42.

61. The Ambassador in Korea (Muccio) to the Assistant Secretary of State for Far Eastern Affairs (Rusk), June 1, 1950, in *FRUS, 1950*, vol. 7, Document 45.

62. Peter Lowe, *The Origins of the Korean War* (Edinburgh Gate: Addison Wesley Longman, 1997), 184.

63. Memorandum of Conversation, by the Director of the Office of Northeast Asian Affairs (Allison), June 19, 1950, in *FRUS, 1950*, vol. 7, Document 56.

64. Interview with Myun Chang, September 27, 1964, Seoul, JFD OHP.

65. The Acting Political Adviser in Japan (Sebald) to the Secretary of State, February 12, 1949, in *FRUS, 1949*, vol. 7, pt. 2, Document 25.

66. Department of State Comments on NSC 49, June 15, 1949, in *FRUS, 1949*, vol. 7, pt. 2, Enclosure to Document 145 (emphasis in the original).

67. Memorandum of Conversation, by Mr Marshall Green of the Division of Northeast Asian Affairs, September 9, 1949, in *FRUS, 1949*, vol. 7, pt. 2, Document 134.

68. Howard Schonberger, *Aftermath of War: Americans and the Remaking of Japan, 1945–1952* (Kent, OH: Kent State University Press, 1989), 240.

69. Cumings, *Origins of the Korean War*, 556.

70. Memorandum of Conversation, by the Special Assistant to the Secretary (Howard), April 24, 1950, in *FRUS, 1950*, vol. 6, Document 708.

71. The Acting Political Adviser in Japan (Sebald) to the Secretary of State, August 20, 1949, in *FRUS, 1949*, vol. 7, pt. 2, Document 127.

72. Schonberger, *Aftermath of War*, 244.

73. Michael Schaller, *Altered States: The United States and Japan since the Occupation* (New York: Oxford University Press, 1997), 27.

74. The Special Assistant to the Under Secretary of the Army (Reid) to the Assistant Secretary of State (Butterworth), May 10, 1950, in *FRUS, 1950*, vol. 6, Document 714.

75. The Special Assistant to the Under Secretary of the Army (Reid) to the Assistant Secretary of State (Butterworth), May 10, 1950, in *FRUS, 1950*, vol. 6, Document 714.

76. Intelligence Estimate Prepared by the Estimates Group, Office of Intelligence Research, Department of State, June 25, 1950, in *FRUS, 1950*, vol. 7, Document 82.

77. As quoted in Rosemary Foot, *The Wrong War: American Policy and the Dimensions of the Korean Conflict, 1950–1953* (Ithaca, NY: Cornell University Press, 1985), 60.

78. William Sebald, *With MacArthur in Japan: A Personal History of the Occupation* (New York: W. W. Norton, 1965), 190.

79. Memorandum by the Officer in Charge of Japanese Affairs (Green) to the Director of the Office of Northeast Asian Affairs (Allison), August 2, 1950, in *FRUS, 1950*, vol. 6, Document 742.

80. As quoted in Memorandum by the Officer in Charge of Japanese Affairs (Green) to the Director of the Office of Northeast Asian Affairs (Allison), August 2, 1950, in *FRUS, 1950*, vol. 6, Document 742.

81. Memorandum by Mr. Douglas W. Overton of the Office of Northeast Asian Affairs to the Deputy Director (Johnson), September 15, 1950, in *FRUS, 1950*, vol. 6, Document 760.

82. Enclosure 2 to The Secretary of State to the Secretary of Defense (Marshall), January 9, 1951, in *FRUS, 1951*, vol. 6, pt. 1, Document 34.

83. Burton L. Kaufman, *The Korean Conflict* (Westport, CO: Greenwood, 1999).

84. The Consultant to the Secretary (Dulles) to the Secretary of State, January 4, 1951, in *FRUS, 1951*, vol. 6, pt. 1, Document 467.

85. Schaller, *Altered States*, 34.

86. Memorandum of Conversation, by the Deputy to the Consultant (Allison), January 29, 1951, in *FRUS, 1951*, vol. 6, pt. 1, Document 487.

87. As quoted in John Dower, *Empire and Aftermath: Yoshida Shigeru and the Japanese Experience, 1878–1964* (Cambridge, MA: Harvard University Asia Center, 1979), 388–389.

88. LaFeber, *The Clash*, 299.

89. Schaller, *Altered States*, 35.

90. LaFeber, *The Clash*, 291. See also Schaller, *Altered States*, 36 and the Editorial Note in *FRUS, 1951*, vol. 6, pt. 1, Document 495.

91. Unsigned Draft of Bilateral Agreement, February 5, 1951, in *FRUS, 1951*, vol. 6, pt. 1, Document 497.

92. LaFeber, *The Clash*, 291.

93. Memorandum of Conversation, by the Special Assistant to the Secretary (Howard), April 7, 1950, in *FRUS, 1950*, vol. 6, Document 702.

94. Memorandum by Mr. Robert A. Fearey of the Office of Northeast Asian Affairs, February 5, 1951, in *FRUS, 1951*, vol. 6, pt. 1, Document 498.

95. The Chargé in Australia (Foster) to the Secretary of State, May 13, 1949, in *FRUS, 1949*, vol. 7, pt. 2, Document 77.

96. Memorandum by Mr. Marshall Green, of the Office of Northeast Asian Affairs, July 29, 1949, in *FRUS, 1949*, vol. 7, pt. 2, Document 124.

97. Spender, *Exercises in Diplomacy*, 47.

98. The Chargé in the Philippines (Lockett) to the Secretary of State, March 21, 1949, in *FRUS, 1949*, vol. 7, pt. 2, Document 312.

99. The Chargé in the Philippines (Lockett) to the Secretary of State, March 22, 1949, in *FRUS, 1949*, vol. 7, pt. 2, Document 313.

100. The Chargé in the Philippines (Lockett) to the Secretary of State, March 24, 1949, in *FRUS, 1949*, vol. 7, pt. 2, Document 315.

101. Memorandum by the Assistant Secretary of State for Far Eastern Affairs (Butterworth) to the Secretary of State, November 18, 1949, in *FRUS, 1949*, vol. 7, pt. 2, Document 164. See also W. David McIntyre, *Background to the ANZUS Pact* (Christchurch: University of Canterbury Press, 1995), 249–253.

102. The Chargé in the Philippines (Lockett) to the Secretary of State, July 14, 1949, in *FRUS, 1949*, vol. 7, pt. 2, Document 335.

103. The Chargé in the Philippines (Lockett) to the Secretary of State, July 15, 1949, in *FRUS, 1949*, vol. 7, pt. 2, Document 336. "Elsewhere" was a reference to the United Kingdom.

104. Memorandum by the Policy Information Officer of the Officer of Far Eastern Affairs (Fisher) to the Director of the Office (Butterworth), July 15, 1949, in *FRUS, 1949*, vol. 7, pt. 2, Document 338.

105. The Secretary of State to Certain Diplomatic and Consular Officers, July 20, 1949, in *FRUS, 1949*, vol. 7, pt. 2, Document 344.

106. Memorandum of Conversation, by the Director of the Office of Philippine and Southeast Asian Affairs (Lacy), February 21, 1950, in *FRUS, 1950*, vol. 6, Document 8.

107. The Ambassador in Australia (Jarman) to the Secretary of State, February 24, 1950, in *FRUS, 1950*, vol. 6, Document 11.

108. The Secretary of State to the Embassy in Australia, February 25, 1950, in *FRUS, 1950*, vol. 6, Document 12.

109. The Ambassador in Australia (Jarman) to the Secretary of State, March 10, 1950, in *FRUS, 1950*, vol. 6, Document 21.

110. See The Secretary of State to the Embassy in Australia, March 21, 1950, in *FRUS, 1950*, vol. 6, Document 28.

111. The Ambassador in Australia (Jarman) to the Secretary of State, March 24, 1950, in *FRUS, 1950*, vol. 6, Document 30.

112. Intelligence Estimate Prepared by the Estimates Group, Office of Intelligence Research, Department of State, June 25, 1950, in *FRUS, 1950*, vol. 7, Document 82.

113. Gaddis, *Strategies of Containment*, 109.

114. Kaufman, *Korean War*, 37.

115. The Secretary of State to All Diplomatic Missions and Certain Consular Offices, June 30, 1950, in *FRUS, 1950*, vol. 7, Document 173.

116. Memorandum of Conversation, by the Secretary of State, July 28, 1950, in *FRUS, 1950*, vol. 7, Document 369.

117. Foot, *Wrong War*, 60.

118. Memorandum by the Assistant Secretary of State for European Affairs (Perkins) to the Secretary of State, October 27, 1950, in *FRUS, 1950*, vol. 7, Document 111.

119. Memorandum of Conversation, by Mr. Ward P. Allen, Adviser, United States Delegation to the United Nations General Assembly, October 12, 1950, in *FRUS, 1950*, vol. 7, Document 77.

120. Interview with John M. Allison, April 20, 1969, New York City, JFD OHP.

121. Memorandum by Mr. Robert A. Fearey, of the Office of Northeast Asian Affairs, February 16, 1951, in *FRUS, 1951*, vol. 6, pt. 1, Document 51.

122. The best and most comprehensive account of these discussions is McIntyre, *Background to the ANZUS Pact*.

123. Draft Memorandum for the President, April 5, 1951, in *FRUS, 1951*, vol. 6, pt. 1, Enclosure to Document 61.

124. The Ambassador in the Philippines (Cowen) to the Secretary of State, July 17, 1951, in *FRUS, 1951*, vol. 6, pt. 1, Document 85.

125. Memorandum of Conversation, by the Deputy Director of the Office of Philippine and Southeast Asian Affairs (Melby), August 2, 1951, in *FRUS, 1951*, vol. 6, pt. 1, Document 94.

126. Memorandum of Conversation, by the Assistant Secretary of State for Far Eastern Affairs (Rusk), August 9, 1951, in *FRUS, 1951*, vol. 6, pt. 1, Document 100.

127. The Ambassador in the Philippines (Cowen) to the Secretary of State, August 6, 1951, in *FRUS, 1951*, vol. 6, pt. 1, Document 97.

128. The Ambassador in the Philippines (Cowen) to the Secretary of State, August 12, 1951, in *FRUS, 1951*, vol. 6, pt. 1, Document 106.

129. Memorandum by Mr. Robert E. Barbour of the Bureau of Far Eastern Affairs, August 27, 1951, in *FRUS, 1951*, vol. 6, pt. 1, Document 109.

130. The Ambassador in Australia (Jarman) to the Secretary of State, March 24, 1950, in *FRUS, 1950*, vol. 6, Document 30.

131. See chapter 1 for a discussion of Mercer's argument on this point.

132. Mercer has examined the American decision to defend South Korea and the response of allied nations, but confined his analysis to the reaction of European allies. See Jonathan Mercer, "Emotion and Strategy in the Korean War," *International Organization* 62, no. 2 (2013): 221–252.

133. See the Preface to Cha, *Powerplay*.

134. Cha, *Powerplay*, 39.

135. See Izumikawa, "Network Connections."

3. Unleashing and Releashing Chiang Kai-shek, 1953–1954

1. The epigraph for this chapter comes from: Memorandum of Discussion at the 211th Meeting of the National Security Council, August 18, 1954, in *FRUS, 1952–1954*, vol. 14, pt. 1, *China and Japan*, Document 256.

2. Quemoy is now called Kinmen, but for the sake of consistency I use Quemoy through-out the book.

3. Some of the argument and empirical material in this chapter is also covered in Henry, "What Allies Want."

4. President Dwight Eisenhower, State of the Union Address, February 2, 1953.

5. Tucker, *Taiwan, Hong Kong, and the United States*, 36.

6. Nancy Bernkopf Tucker, "John Foster Dulles and the Taiwan Roots of the 'Two Chinas' Policy," in *John Foster Dulles and the Diplomacy of the Cold War*, ed. Richard Immerman (Princeton, NJ: Princeton University Press, 1992), 240.

7. Memorandum from Mr Allison to the Secretary of State, February 11, 1953, NARA, Central Decimal Files (CDF), 1950–1954, RG 59, Box 4203, 793.00/2-1153.

8. Memorandum of Conversation, by the Assistant Secretary of State for Far Eastern Affairs (Allison), March 19, 1953, in *FRUS, 1952–1954*, vol. 14, pt. 1, Document 83.

9. Memorandum of Conversation, by the Assistant Secretary of State for Far Eastern Affairs (Allison), March 19, 1953, in *FRUS, 1952–1954*, vol. 14, pt. 1, Document 83.

10. Memorandum by the Deputy Under Secretary of State (Matthews) to the Secretary of State, March 31, 1953, in *FRUS, 1952–1954*, vol. 14, pt. 1, Document 88. See also Yarhi-Milo, Lanoszka, and Cooper, "To Arm or to Ally?"

11. See The Joint Chiefs of Staff to the Command in Chief, Pacific (Radford), April 6, 1953, in *FRUS, 1952–1954*, vol. 14, pt. 1, Document 91.

12. Memorandum of Discussion at the 139th Meeting of the National Security Council, April 8, 1953, in *FRUS, 1952–1954*, vol. 14, pt. 1, Document 93.

13. The Ambassador in the Republic of China (Rankin) to the Department of State, April 16, 1953, in *FRUS, 1952–1954*, vol. 14, pt. 1, Document 98.

14. The Secretary of State to the Embassy in the Republic of China, April 17, 1953, in *FRUS, 1952–1954*, vol. 14, pt. 1, Document 99.

15. "President's Letter to Syngman Rhee on Proposed Korean Armistice," June 6, 1953, *Department of State Bulletin* 28, no. 729 (June 15, 1953): 836.

16. See Cha, "Powerplay," 175–176.

17. The President of the Republic of China (Chiang Kai-Shek) to President Eisenhower, June 7, 1953, in *FRUS, 1952–1954*, vol. 14, pt. 1, Document 108.

18. See The Charge in the Republic of China (Jones) to the Department of State, June 24, 1953, in *FRUS, 1952–1954*, vol. 14, pt. 1, Document 113.

19. The Secretary of State to the Embassy in the Republic of China, June 24, 1953, in *FRUS, 1952–1954*, vol. 14, pt. 1, Document 114.

20. The Secretary of State to the Embassy in the Republic of China, June 25, 1953, in *FRUS, 1952–1954*, vol. 14, pt. 1, Document 115.

21. Memorandum of Conversation, by the Secretary of State, June 29, 1953, in *FRUS, 1952–1954*, vol. 14, pt. 1, Document 116.

22. The Secretary of State to the Embassy in the Republic of China, June 30, 1953, in *FRUS, 1952–1954*, vol. 14, pt. 1, Document 117.

23. Letter from the Secretary of State to President Syngman Rhee, June 22, 1953, NARA, CDF, 1950–1954, RG 59, Box 4287, 795.00/6-2353.

24. The Secretary of State to the Embassy in the Republic of China, June 24, 1953, in *FRUS, 1952–1954*, vol. 14, pt. 1, Document 114.

25. Robert Accinelli, *Crisis and Commitment: United States Policy toward Taiwan, 1950–1955* (Chapel Hill: University of North Carolina Press, 1996), 119.

26. Letter from Ambassador Rankin to Walter Robertson, January 18, 1954, NARA, CDF, 1950–1954, RG 59, Box 4292, 795.00/1-1854.

27. Commander-in-Chief United Nations Command's CX-65208 to Secretary of State, September 26, 1953, NARA, CDF, 1950–1954, RG 59, Box 4289, 795.00/9-2653.

28. Memorandum of Conversation, by the Ambassador in the Republic of China (Rankin), July 1, 1953, in *FRUS, 1952–1954*, vol. 14, pt. 1, Document 119.

29. Letter from Ambassador Rankin to Walter Robertson, January 18, 1954, NARA, CDF, 1950–1954, RG 59, Box 4292, 795.00/1-1854.

30. The Secretary of State to the Embassy in the Republic of China, January 13, 1954, in *FRUS, 1952–1954*, vol. 14, pt. 1, Document 164.

31. Interview with Walter Robertson, July 23 and 24, 1965, Richmond, Virginia, JFD OHP.

32. Memorandum of Discussion at the 153rd Meeting of the National Security Council, July 9, 1953, in *FRUS, 1952–1954*, vol. 14, pt. 1, Document 121. The Tachen Islands are now called the Dachen Islands, but for the sake of consistency I use Tachen throughout the book.

33. Memorandum by the Deputy Assistant Secretary of State for Far Eastern Affairs (Johnson) to the Acting Secretary of State, August 3, 1953, in *FRUS, 1952–1954*, vol. 14, pt. 1, Document 132.

34. Memorandum of Conversation, by the Deputy Director of the Office of Chinese Affairs (Martin), August 19, 1953, in *FRUS, 1952–1954*, vol. 14, pt. 1, Document 136. At this stage, the British were told that "the 7th Fleet's mission remained the same" (i.e., they were not tasked with defending the offshore islands).

35. NSC 166/1, Statement of Policy by the National Security Council, November 6, 1953, in *FRUS, 1952–1954*, vol. 14, pt. 1, Document 149. On US-UK differences, see Thomas K. Robb and David James Gill, *Divided Allies: Strategic Cooperation Against the Communist Threat in the Asia-Pacific during the Early Cold War* (Ithaca, NY: Cornell University Press, 2019).

36. NSC 146/2, Statement of Policy by the National Security Council, November 6, 1953, in *FRUS, 1952–1954*, vol. 14, pt. 1, Document 150.

37. Garver, *Sino-American Alliance*, 54.

38. NSC 146/2, Statement of Policy by the National Security Council, November 6, 1953, in *FRUS, 1952–1954*, vol. 14, pt. 1, Document 150.

39. The Ambassador in China (Rankin) to the Department of State, November 18, 1953, in *FRUS, 1952–1954*, vol. 14, pt. 1, Document 154.

40. The Ambassador in the Republic of China (Rankin) to the Department of State, November 30, 1953, in *FRUS, 1952–1954*, vol. 14, pt. 1, Document 155.

41. Townsend Hoopes, *The Devil and John Foster Dulles* (London: Andre Deutsch, 1974), 263.

42. The Ambassador in the Republic of China (Rankin) to the Department of State, December 19, 1953, in *FRUS, 1952–1954*, vol. 14, pt. 1, Document 161.

43. The Ambassador in the Republic of China (Rankin) to the Department of State, December 19, 1953, in *FRUS, 1952–1954*, vol. 14, pt. 1, Document 162.

44. The Charge in the Republic of China (Jones) to the Department of State, February 24, 1954, in *FRUS, 1952–1954*, vol. 14, pt. 1, Document 172.

45. Memorandum by the Assistant Secretary of State for Far Eastern Affairs (Robertson) to the Secretary of State, February 25, 1954, in *FRUS, 1952–1954*, vol. 14, pt. 1, Document 173.

46. The Ambassador in the Republic of China (Rankin) to the Deputy Assistant Secretary of State for Far Eastern Affairs (Drumright), February 20, 1954, in *FRUS, 1952–1954*, vol. 14, pt. 1, Document 169.

47. The Ambassador in the Republic of China (Rankin) to the Deputy Operations Coordinator (Berry) in the Office of the Under Secretary of State, April 21, 1954, in *FRUS, 1952–1954*, vol. 14, pt. 1, Document 186.

48. The Ambassador in the Republic of China (Rankin) to the Department of State, May 11, 1954, in *FRUS, 1952–1954*, vol. 14, pt. 1, Document 188.

49. Memorandum of Conversation, by the Director of the Office of Chinese Affairs (Mc-Conaughy), May 19, 1954, in *FRUS, 1952–1954*, vol. 14, pt. 1, Document 193.

50. Memorandum of Conversation, by the Director of the Office of Chinese Affairs (Mc-Conaughy), May 19, 1954, in *FRUS, 1952–1954*, vol. 14, pt. 1, Document 193.

51. Tucker, "John Foster Dulles and the Taiwan Roots of the 'Two Chinas' Policy," 241.

52. Memorandum of Conversation, by the Special Assistant to the President for National Security Affairs (Cutler), May 22, 1954, in *FRUS, 1952–1954*, vol. 14, pt. 1, Document 196.

53. The Ambassador in the Republic of China (Rankin) to the Department of State, May 29, 1954, in *FRUS, 1952–1954*, vol. 14, pt. 1, Document 202.

54. Closing Remarks of President Chiang Kai-shek, May 24, 1954, Ann Whitman File (AWF), International Series, Box 10, Dwight D. Eisenhower Presidential Library (DDEPL), Abilene, Kansas.

55. The Ambassador in the Republic of China (Rankin) to the Secretary of State, June 22, 1954, in *FRUS, 1952–1954*, vol. 14, pt. 1, Document 223.

56. Memorandum by the Ambassador in the Republic of China (Rankin) to the Secretary of State, July 8, 1954, in *FRUS, 1952–1954*, vol. 14, pt. 1, Document 228.

57. Letter from Mr Drumright to the Secretary of State, July 24, 1954, NARA, CDF, 1950–1954, RG 59, Box 4297, 795.5/6-2254.

58. The Ambassador in Japan (Allison) to the Department of State, August 16, 1954, in *FRUS, 1952–1954*, vol. 14, pt. 1, Document 253.

59. The Ambassador in Japan (Allison) to the Department of State, August 16, 1954, in *FRUS, 1952–1954*, vol. 14, pt. 1, Document 253.

60. Mr Ogburn to Mr Drumright, S/P Paper on United States Policy in Indochina, July 2, 1954, NARA, Lot Files, RG 59, Records of the Office of Chinese Affairs, Box 46.

61. Memorandum of Discussion at the 211th Meeting of the National Security Council, August 18, 1954, in *FRUS, 1952–1954*, vol. 14, pt. 1, Document 256.

62. Memorandum by the Assistant Secretary of State for Far Eastern Affairs (Robertson) to the Secretary of State, August 19, 1954, in *FRUS, 1952–1954*, vol. 14, pt. 1, Document 258.

63. The Secretary of State to the Embassy in Japan, August 20, 1954, in *FRUS, 1952–1954*, vol. 14, pt. 1, Document 260.

64. As quoted in Dower, *Empire and Aftermath*, 430–434.

65. Memorandum by the Assistant Secretary of State for Far Eastern Affairs (Robertson) to the Secretary of State, August 25, 1954, in *FRUS, 1952–1954*, vol. 14, pt. 1, Document 262.

66. Memorandum by the Assistant Secretary of State for Far Eastern Affairs (Robertson) to the Secretary of State, August 25, 1954, in *FRUS, 1952–1954*, vol. 14, pt. 1, Document 262.

67. Memorandum by the Acting Secretary of State to the Assistant Secretary of State for Far Eastern Affairs (Robertson), September 1, 1954, in *FRUS, 1952–1954*, vol. 14, pt. 1, Document 269.

68. The Acting Secretary of Defense (Anderson) to the President, September 3, 1954, in *FRUS, 1952–1954*, vol. 14, pt. 1, Document 270.

69. Gaddis, *Long Peace*, 134.

70. The Secretary of State to the Department of State, September 4, 1954, in *FRUS, 1952–1954*, vol. 14, pt. 1, Document 273.

71. Memorandum by the Assistant Secretary of State for Far Eastern Affairs (Robertson) to the Acting Secretary of State, September 4, 1954, in *FRUS, 1952–1954*, vol. 14, pt. 1, Document 275.

72. Special National Intelligence Estimate, September 4, 1954, in *FRUS, 1952–1954*, vol. 14, pt. 1, Document 276.

73. Lowe, *Origins of the Korean War*, 130.

74. As quoted in Michael Schaller, *The United States and China: Into the Twenty-First Century* (Oxford: Oxford University Press, 2002), 142.

75. Seoul's 283 to Washington, September 10, 1954, NARA, CDF, 1950–1954, RG 59, Box 4209, 793.00/9-1054 (emphasis in the original).

76. Memorandum of Telephone Conversation Between the President and the Acting Secretary of State, September 6, 1954, in *FRUS, 1952–1954*, vol. 14, pt. 1, Document 280.

77. See The President to the Acting Secretary of State, September 8, 1954, in *FRUS, 1952–1954*, vol. 14, pt. 1, Document 284.

78. The Ambassador in the Republic of China (Rankin) to the Department of State, September 9, 1954, in *FRUS, 1952–1954*, vol. 14, pt. 1, Document 288.

79. Memorandum of Discussion at the 213th Meeting of the National Security Council, September 9, 1954, in *FRUS, 1952–1954*, vol. 14, pt. 1, Document 289. Radford's hawkish position would persist throughout the crisis. He believed that "a showdown with the Mao regime was inevitable," and this led him to put forward recommendations that were "thinly disguised effort[s] to provoke war with China." See Hoopes, *The Devil and John Foster Dulles*, 265.

80. Memorandum Prepared by the Secretary of State, September 12, 1954, in *FRUS, 1952–1954*, vol. 14, pt. 1, Document 292 (emphasis in the original). This memo contained Dulles's talking points for the September 12 NSC meeting.

81. Memorandum of Discussion at the 214th Meeting of the National Security Council, September 12, 1954, in *FRUS, 1952–1954*, vol. 14, pt. 1, Document 293.

82. Memorandum of Discussion at the 214th Meeting of the National Security Council, September 12, 1954, in *FRUS, 1952–1954*, vol. 14, pt. 1, Document 293.

83. Memorandum of Discussion at the 214th Meeting of the National Security Council, September 12, 1954, in *FRUS, 1952–1954*, vol. 14, pt. 1, Document 293.

84. Memorandum by the Assistant Secretary of State for European Affairs (Merchant) to Roderic L. O'Connor, Special Assistant to the Secretary of State, September 19, 1954, in *FRUS, 1952–1954*, vol. 14, pt. 1, Document 298.

85. The Ambassador in the Republic of China (Rankin) to the Department of State, September 21, 1954, in *FRUS, 1952–1954*, vol. 14, pt. 1, Document 299.

86. Memorandum of Conversation, by the Assistant Secretary of State for International Organization Affairs (Key), October 4, 1954, in *FRUS, 1952–1954*, vol. 14, pt. 1, Document 317.

87. Memorandum of Conversation, by the Secretary of State, October 10, 1954, in *FRUS, 1952–1954*, vol. 14, pt. 1, Document 335.

88. Memorandum of Discussion at the 216th Meeting of the National Security Council, October 6, 1954, in *FRUS, 1952–1954*, vol. 14, pt. 1, Document 322.

89. Memorandum by the Assistant Secretary of State for Far Eastern Affairs (Robertson) to the Secretary of State, October 7, 1954, in *FRUS, 1952–1954*, vol. 14, pt. 1, Document 325.

90. Memorandum by the Secretary of State to the Assistant Secretary of State for Far Eastern Affairs (Robertson), October 8, 1954, in *FRUS, 1952–1954*, vol. 14, pt. 1, Document 327, footnote 3.

91. Memorandum of Conversation, by the Director of the Office of Chinese Affairs (McConaughy), October 13, 1954, in *FRUS, 1952–1954*, vol. 14, pt. 1, Document 337.

92. Memorandum of Conversation, by the Director of the Office of Chinese Affairs (McConaughy), October 13, 1954, in *FRUS, 1952–1954*, vol. 14, pt. 1, Document 337.

93. See Memorandum of Conversation, by the Deputy Director of the Office of United Nations Political and Security Affairs (Bond), October 14, 1954, in *FRUS, 1952–1954*, vol. 14, pt. 1, Document 342.

94. Memorandum of Conversation, by the Assistant Secretary of State for International Organization Affairs (Key), October 18, 1954, in *FRUS, 1952–1954*, vol. 14, pt. 1, Document 351.

95. Memorandum of Conversation, by the Assistant Secretary of State for European Affairs (Merchant), October 23, 1954, in *FRUS, 1952–1954*, vol. 14, pt. 1, Document 359.

96. Accinelli, *Crisis and Commitment*, 170–171.

97. Memorandum of Conversation, by the Assistant Secretary of State for European Affairs (Merchant), November 3, 1954, in *FRUS, 1952–1954*, vol. 14, pt. 1, Document 379.

98. Memorandum of Discussion at the 221st Meeting of the National Security Council, November 2, 1954, in *FRUS, 1952–1954*, vol. 14, pt. 1, Document 375.

99. Memorandum of Discussion at the 221st Meeting of the National Security Council, November 2, 1954, in *FRUS, 1952–1954*, vol. 14, pt. 1, Document 375.

100. Garver, *The Sino-American Alliance*, 124, 128.

101. Memorandum of Conversation, by the Director of the Office of Chinese Affairs (McConaughy), November 4, 1954, in *FRUS, 1952–1954*, vol. 14, pt. 1, Document 382.

102. Memorandum of Conversation, by the Director of the Office of Chinese Affairs (Mc-Conaughy), November 4, 1954, in *FRUS, 1952–1954*, vol. 14, pt. 1, Document 382.

103. Memorandum of Conversation, by the Director of the Office of Chinese Affairs (Mc-Conaughy), November 6, 1954, in *FRUS, 1952–1954*, vol. 14, pt. 1, Document 385. See also Memorandum of Conversation, by the Director of the Office of Chinese Affairs (McConaughy), December 7, 1954, and Memorandum of Conversation, by the Director of the Office of Chinese Affairs (McConaughy), December 13, 1954, both in *FRUS, 1952–1954*, vol. 14, pt. 1, Documents 432 and 439.

104. Memorandum of Conversation, by the Director of the Office of Chinese Affairs (Mc-Conaughy), November 12, 1954, in *FRUS, 1952–1954*, vol. 14, pt. 1, Document 392 (emphasis in the original).

105. See Memorandum of Conversation, by the Director of the Office of Chinese Affairs (Mc-Conaughy), November 23, 1954, in *FRUS, 1952–1954*, vol. 14, pt. 1, Document 402.

106. Memorandum of Conversation, by the Director of the Office of Chinese Affairs (Mc-Conaughy), November 6, 1954, in *FRUS, 1952–1954*, vol. 14, pt. 1, Document 386.

107. Memorandum of Conversation, by the Deputy Director of the Office of United Nations Political and Security Affairs (Bond), November 9, 1954, in *FRUS, 1952–1954*, vol. 14, pt. 1, Document 388.

108. Special National Intelligence Assessment, November 28, 1954, in *FRUS, 1952–1954*, vol. 14, pt. 1, Document 411.

109. Special National Intelligence Assessment, November 28, 1954, in *FRUS, 1952–1954*, vol. 14, pt. 1, Document 411.

110. Memorandum of Conversation, by the Deputy Director of the Office of United Nations Political and Security Affairs (Bond), November 30, 1954, in *FRUS, 1952–1954*, vol. 14, pt. 1, Document 416.

111. Memorandum of Conversation, by the Deputy Director of the Office of United Nations Political and Security Affairs (Bond), November 30, 1954, in *FRUS, 1952–1954*, vol. 14, pt. 1, Document 416, footnote 2.

112. Memorandum of Conversation, by the Deputy Director of the Office of United Nations Political and Security Affairs (Bond), November 30, 1954, in *FRUS, 1952–1954*, vol. 14, pt. 1, Document 416.

113. United States Government, *Department of State Bulletin* 31, no. 807 (December 13, 1954): 896.

114. Tucker, "John Foster Dulles and the Taiwan Roots of the 'Two Chinas' Policy," 244.

115. The Secretary of State to the Embassy in Japan, August 20, 1954, in *FRUS, 1952–1954*, vol. 14, pt. 1, Document 260.

116. Dower, *Empire and Aftermath*, 434.

4. Allies Encourage Limits on US Loyalty to Formosa, 1954–1955

1. This chapter's epigraph comes from an interview with William Macomber, January 12 and 19, 1966, Washington DC, JFD OHP.

2. On the idea of crucial cases, see Harry Eckstein, "Case Study and Theory in Political Science," in *Case Study Method: Key Issues, Key Texts*, ed. Roger Gomm, Martyn Hammersley, and Peter Foster (London: Sage, 2009), 118–164.

3. Some of the argument and empirical material in this chapter is also covered in Henry, "What Allies Want."

4. Memorandum of Conversation, by the Director of the Office of Chinese Affairs (Mc-Conaughy), November 6, 1954, in *FRUS, 1952–1954*, vol. 14, pt. 1, Document 385.

5. Memorandum of Conversation, by the Deputy Director of the Office of United Nations Political and Security Affairs (Bond), December 6, 1954, in *FRUS, 1952–1954*, vol. 14, pt. 1, Document 428.

6. Accinelli, *Crisis and Commitment*, 177.

7. The Secretary of State to the Department of State, December 17, 1954, in *FRUS, 1952–1954*, vol. 14, pt. 1, Document 447.

8. Memorandum by Henry Owen of the Office of Intelligence Research to the Director of the Policy Planning Staff (Bowie), December 7, 1954, in *FRUS, 1952–1954*, vol. 14, pt. 1, Document 431.

9. Memorandum of a Conversation, Department of State, Washington, January 12, 1955, in *FRUS, 1955–1957*, vol. 2, *China*, Document 8.

10. Memorandum of a Conversation, Department of State, January 19, 1955, in *FRUS, 1955–1957*, vol. 2, Document 16.

11. Memorandum of a Conversation, The White House, January 19, 1955, in *FRUS, 1955–1957*, vol. 2, Document 17.

12. Dulles's thoughts further support the need to consider expansive ideas of loyalty, like those suggested by Snyder's "halo" concept. See chapter 1.

13. Memorandum of a Conversation, Department of State, January 19, 1955, 3:15 p.m., in *FRUS, 1955–1957*, vol. 2, Document 18.

14. Memorandum of a Conversation, Department of State, January 19, 1955, 3:45 p.m., in *FRUS, 1955–1957*, vol. 2, Document 19.

15. Memorandum of a Conversation, Department of State, January 19, 1955, 3:45 p.m., in *FRUS, 1955–1957*, vol. 2, Document 19.

16. Memorandum of a Conversation, Department of State, January 20, 1955, in *FRUS, 1955–1957*, vol. 2, Document 22.

17. Memorandum of Discussion at the 232d [sic] Meeting of the National Security Council, Washington, January 20, 1955, in *FRUS, 1955–1957*, vol. 2, Document 23.

18. Memorandum of Discussion at the 232d [sic] Meeting of the National Security Council, Washington, January 20, 1955, in *FRUS, 1955–1957*, vol. 2, Document 23.

19. Memorandum of a Conversation, Department of State, January 20, 1955, in *FRUS, 1955–1957*, vol. 2, Document 25. Australia was also against a provisional guarantee. See Memorandum of Conversation, January 21, 1955, NARA, CDF, 1955–1959, RG 59, Box 3938, 793.5/1-2155.

20. Memorandum of a Conversation, Department of State, January 20, 1955, in *FRUS, 1955–1957*, vol. 2, Document 25.

21. Memorandum of Discussion at the 233d [sic] Meeting of the National Security Council, Washington, January 21, 1955, in *FRUS, 1955–1957*, vol. 2, Document 26.

22. Accinelli, *Crisis and Commitment*, 190.

23. Memorandum of a Conversation, Department of State, January 21, 1955, in *FRUS, 1955–1957*, vol. 2, Document 28.

24. See Memorandum of a Conversation, Department of State, January 22, 1955, in *FRUS, 1955–1957*, vol. 2, Document 30.

25. Memorandum of a Conversation, Department of State, January 28, 1955, in *FRUS, 1955–1957*, vol. 2, Document 50.

26. Joint Resolution by the Congress, January 29, 1955, in *FRUS, 1955–1957*, vol. 2, Document 56.

27. Editorial Note, in *FRUS, 1955–1957*, vol. 2, Document 35.

28. See Letter from President Eisenhower to British Prime Minister Churchill, January 25, 1955, in *FRUS, 1955–1957*, vol. 2, Document 41, footnote 2.

29. Letter from President Eisenhower to British Prime Minister Churchill, January 25, 1955, in *FRUS, 1955–1957*, vol. 2, Document 41.

30. Memorandum of Discussion at the 234th Meeting of the National Security Council, January 27, 1955, in *FRUS, 1955–1957*, vol. 2, Document 44.

31. Cable from Department of External Affairs (Canberra) to Australian Embassy (Washington), January 25, 1955, in National Archives of Australia (NAA), A1838, 852/21/2 Part 3, *Formosa*, 28.

32. Cable from New Zealand High Commission (Ottawa) to Minister for External Affairs (Wellington), January 26, 1955, in NAA, A1838, 852/21/2 Part 3, 49.

33. See Telegram from the Ambassador in the Republic of China (Rankin) to the Department of State, January 29, 1955, in *FRUS, 1955–1957*, vol. 2, Document 59.

34. Memorandum of a Conversation, Washington, January 30, 1955, in *FRUS, 1955–1957*, vol. 2, Document 61.

35. See Telegram from the Acting Secretary of State to the Embassy in the Republic of China, January 31, 1955, in *FRUS, 1955–1957*, vol. 2, Document 69.

36. Letter from the President to the Supreme Allied Commander, Europe (Gruenther), February 1, 1955, in *FRUS, 1955–1957*, vol. 2, Document 71.

37. Editorial note, in *FRUS, 1955–1957*, vol. 2, Document 77.

38. Telegram from the Ambassador in the United Kingdom (Aldrich) to the Department of State, February 4, 1955, in *FRUS, 1955–1957*, vol. 2, Document 82.

39. See Telegram from the Ambassador in the United Kingdom (Aldrich) to the Department of State, February 4, 1955, in *FRUS, 1955–1957*, vol. 2, Document 82, footnote 4.

40. Accinelli, *Crisis and Commitment*, 205.

41. I am indebted to Evelyn Goh for suggesting this phrasing.

42. Memorandum from the Assistant Secretary of State for European Affairs (Merchant) to the Secretary of State, February 4, 1955, in *FRUS, 1955–1957*, vol. 2, Document 83.

43. Editorial Note, in *FRUS, 1955–1957*, vol. 2, Document 101.

44. Memorandum from the Director of the Policy Planning Staff (Bowie) to the Secretary of State, February 7, 1955, in *FRUS, 1955–1957*, vol. 2, Document 97.

45. Memorandum of a Conversation, Department of State, February 11, 1955, in *FRUS, 1955–1957*, vol. 2, Document 105.

46. Cable from Australian Embassy (Washington) to Australian High Commission (London), February 11, 1955, in NAA, A1209, 1957/5035.

47. Memorandum of a Conversation, Department of State, February 11, 1955, in *FRUS, 1955–1957*, vol. 2, Document 105.

48. Letter from President Eisenhower to Prime Minister Churchill, February 10, 1955, in *FRUS, 1955–1957*, vol. 2, Document 104.

49. Message from Prime Minister Churchill to President Eisenhower, undated, in *FRUS, 1955–1957*, vol. 2, Document 110.

50. Memorandum of a Telephone Conversation Between the President and the Secretary of State, February 16, 1955, in *FRUS, 1955–1957*, vol. 2, Document 112.

51. US Department of State, *Department of State Bulletin* 32, no. 818 (February 28, 1955): 329.

52. Memorandum of Discussion at the 237th Meeting of the National Security Council, February 17, 1955, in *FRUS, 1955–1957*, vol. 2, Document 115.

53. Telegram from the Secretary of State to the Embassy in the United Kingdom, February 18, 1955, in *FRUS, 1955–1957*, vol. 2, Document 119.

54. Telegram from the Secretary of State to the Department of State, February 21, 1955, in *FRUS, 1955–1957*, vol. 2, Document 123.

55. Telegram from the Acting Secretary of State to the Embassy in Thailand, February 21, 1955, in *FRUS, 1955–1957*, vol. 2, Document 124. Eisenhower asked Roy Howard, an American media executive, to pursue this idea with President Chiang on a visit to Taipei. See Diary Entry by the President's Press Secretary, February 24, 1955, in *FRUS, 1955–1957*, vol. 2, Document 128.

56. Telegram from the Acting Secretary of State to the Embassy in Thailand, February 21, 1955, in *FRUS, 1955–1957*, vol. 2, Document 124.

57. Thomas Stolper, "China, Taiwan, and the Offshore Islands Together with an Implication for Outer Mongolia and Sino-Soviet Relations," *International Journal of Politics* 15, no. 1/2 (1985): 86.

58. Telegram from the Secretary of State to the Department of State, February 25, 1955, in *FRUS, 1955–1957*, vol. 2, Document 129.

59. O. Edmund Clubb, "Formosa and the Offshore Islands in American Policy, 1950–1955," *Political Science Quarterly* 74, no. 4 (1959): 527.

60. Telegram from the Secretary of State to the Department of State, February 25, 1955, in *FRUS, 1955–1957*, vol. 2, Document 129.

61. Telegram from the Secretary of State to the Department of State, February 25, 1955, in *FRUS, 1955–1957*, vol. 2, Document 131.

62. Memorandum of a Conversation between the President and the Secretary of State, March 6, 1955, in *FRUS, 1955–1957*, vol. 2, Document 141.

63. Gordon H. Chang, "To the Nuclear Brink: Eisenhower, Dulles and the Quemoy-Matsu Crisis," *International Security* 12, no. 4 (1988): 106.

64. H. W. Brands Jr., "Testing Massive Retaliation: Credibility and Crisis Management in the Taiwan Strait," *International Security* 12, no. 4 (1988): 142.

65. See Letter from the British Ambassador (Makins) to the Secretary of State, March 7, 1955, in *FRUS, 1955–1957*, vol. 2, Document 143.

66. Memorandum of Discussion at the 240th Meeting of the National Security Council, March 10, 1955, in *FRUS, 1955–1957*, vol. 2, Document 146.

67. Notes Taken During Meeting, March 11, 1955, AWF, International Series, Box 9, DDEPL.

68. Memorandum of a Conversation, March 28, 1955, NARA, CDF, 1955–1959, RG 59, 794a.5/3-2855, Box 3976.

69. Memorandum of a Conversation, March 14, 1955, in *FRUS, 1955–1957*, vol. 2, Document 154.

70. Memorandum Received from the British Ambassador (Makins), March 16, 1955, in *FRUS, 1955–1957*, vol. 2, Document 157.

71. Accinelli, *Crisis and Commitment*, 208.

72. Letter from General Alftred Gruenther to President Eisenhower, April 3, 1955, Seely G. Mudd Library, Princeton University, John Foster Dulles Files, Dulles-Herter Series (D-HS), AWF, MC172, Box 4, Folder 3.

73. Cable from the Australian Embassy (Tokyo) to the Department of External Affairs, March 12, 1955, in NAA, A1209, 1957/5035, 9.

74. Summary of remarks of the Honorable John Foster Dulles, March 18, 1955, AWF, D-HS, Box 5, DDEPL.

75. Dwight D. Eisenhower, *Mandate for Change, 1953–1956: The White House Years* (Garden City, NY: Doubleday, 1963), 478.

76. Garry Woodard, "Australian Foreign Policy on the Offshore Island Crisis of 1954–5 and Recognition of China," *Australian Journal of International Affairs* 45, no. 2 (1991): 256. The claim that Australian public opinion would not support a defense of the offshore islands conflicts with opinion polling from that time; see Woodard, 257. However, as this chapter has shown, the Australian government worked consistently to reduce the likelihood of such a conflict.

77. Memorandum of Discussion at the 211th Meeting of the National Security Council, August 18, 1954, in *FRUS, 1952–1954*, vol. 14, pt. 1, Document 256.

78. National Intelligence Estimate 100-4-55, March 16, 1955, in *FRUS, 1955–1957*, vol. 2, Document 158.

79. As quoted in Clubb, "Formosa and the Offshore Islands in US Policy," 527.

80. National Intelligence Estimate 100-4-55, March 16, 1955, in *FRUS, 1955–1957*, vol. 2, Document 158.

81. Letter from President Eisenhower to Lewis W. Douglas, March 29, 1955, in *FRUS, 1955–1957*, vol. 2, Document 178.

82. Memorandum of a Conversation, March 30, 1955, in *FRUS, 1955–1957*, vol. 2, Document 179.

83. Memorandum from the Director of the Executive Secretariat (Scott) to the Secretary of State, March 31, 1955, in *FRUS, 1955–1957*, vol. 2, Document 182.

84. Accinelli, *Crisis and Commitment*, 218.

85. Accinelli, *Crisis and Commitment*, 219.

86. Letter from Ernest Weir to President Eisenhower, April 1, 1955, AWF, D-HS, Box 5, DDEPL.

87. As quoted in Brands, "Testing Massive Retaliation," 143–144.

88. Memorandum from the Undersecretary of State (Hoover) to the Secretary of State, April 1, 1955, in *FRUS, 1955–1957*, vol. 2, Document 185.

89. Memorandum from the President to the Secretary of State, April 5, 1955, in *FRUS, 1955–1957*, vol. 2, Document 189 (emphasis added). For Eisenhower's previous arguments see, for example, Letter from President Eisenhower to Lewis W. Douglas, March 29, 1955, in *FRUS, 1955–1957*, vol. 2, Document 178.

90. Memorandum from the President to the Secretary of State, April 5, 1955, in *FRUS, 1955–1957*, vol. 2, Document 189.

91. Memorandum from the President to the Secretary of State, April 5, 1955, in *FRUS, 1955–1957*, vol. 2, Document 189 (emphasis in the original).

92. Memorandum from the President to the Secretary of State, April 5, 1955, in *FRUS, 1955–1957*, vol. 2, Document 189 (emphasis in the original).

93. See Draft Policy Statement Prepared in the Department of State, April 8, 1955, in *FRUS, 1955–1957*, vol. 2, Document 194.

94. Memorandum from the Director of the Policy Planning Staff (Bowie) to the Secretary of State, April 9, 1955, in *FRUS, 1955–1957*, vol. 2, Document 200.

95. Director of Central Intelligence, "Morale on Taiwan," National Intelligence Estimate (NIE) 100-4/1-55, April 16, 1955, CIA Freedom of Information Act Electronic Reading Room, https://www.cia.gov/readingroom/docs/CIA-RDP79R01012A006300040016-3.pdf.

96. See Accinelli, *Crisis and Commitment*, 223.

97. Memorandum of a Conversation Between the President and the Secretary of State, April 17, 1955, in *FRUS, 1955–1957*, vol. 2, Document 207.

98. Accinelli, *Crisis and Commitment*, 224.

99. Accinelli, *Crisis and Commitment*, 228.

100. Message from the Assistant Secretary of State for Far Eastern Affairs (Robertson) to the Secretary of State, April 25, 1955, in *FRUS, 1955–1957*, vol. 2, Document 219.

101. Accinelli, *Crisis and Commitment*, 229. On the question of China in US domestic politics, see Rosemary Foot, *The Practice of Power: U.S. Relations with China since 1945* (Oxford: Oxford University Press, 1995), chap. 4.

102. Telegram from the Secretary of State to the Embassy in Australia, April 30, 1955, in *FRUS, 1955–1957*, vol. 2, Document 233.

103. Memorandum of a Conversation, May 3, 1955, in *FRUS, 1955–1957*, vol. 2, Document 235.

104. Accinelli, *Crisis and Commitment*, 229.

105. As quoted in Editorial Note, in *FRUS, 1955–1957*, vol. 2, Document 319.

106. Eisenhower, *Mandate for Change*, 474.

107. Manila's 1909 to Washington, January 23, 1955, NARA, CDF, 1955–1959, RG 59, Box 3915, 793.00/1-2355.

108. State's 3856 to Manila, April 26, 1955, NARA, CDF, 1955–1959, RG 59, Box 3917, 793.00/4-255.

109. Manila's 2606 to Washington, April 2, 1955, NARA, CDF, 1955–1959, RG 59, Box 3917, 793.00/4-255. For the cable which requests Manila's view of five listed scenarios, see State's Circular 576 to various U.S. Embassies in Asia, March 30, 1955, NARA, CDF, 1955–1959, RG 59, Box 3916, 793.00/3-3055.

110. Manila's 2606 to Washington, April 2, 1955, NARA, CDF, 1955–1959, RG 59, Box 3917, 793.00/4-255.

111. Manila's 2642 to Washington, April 6, 1955, NARA, CDF, 1955–1959, RG 59, Box 3917, 793.00/4-655.

112. Memorandum from Comiskey to McConaughy, April 12, 1955, NARA, CDF, 1955–1959, RG 59, Box 3939, 793.5/4-1255.

113. Manila's 2772 to Washington, April 22, 1955, NARA, CDF, 1955–1959, RG 59, Box 3939, 793.5/4-2255.

114. Manila's 2799 to Washington, April 25, 1955, NARA, CDF, 1955–1959, RG 59, Box 3917, 793.00/4-2555.

115. See Manila's 2811 to Washington, April 27, 1955, NARA, CDF, 1955–1959, RG 59, Box 3917, 793.00/4-2755.

116. Seoul's 869 to Washington, February 4, 1955, NARA, CDF, 1955–1959, RG 59, Box 3939, 793.5/2-455.

117. Seoul's 1078 to Washington, March 30, 1955, NARA, CDF, 1955–1959, RG 59, Box 3916, 793.00/3-3055.

118. Seoul's 283 to Washington, September 10, 1954, NARA, CDF, 1950–1954, RG 59, Box 4209, 793.00/9-1054.

119. Seoul's 1186 to Washington, April 30, 1955, NARA, CDF, 1955–1959, RG 59, Box 3917, 793.00/4-3055.

120. Memorandum from the Director of the Policy Planning Staff (Bowie) to the Secretary of State, February 7, 1955, in *FRUS, 1955–1957*, vol. 2, Document 97.

121. Brands, "Testing Massive Retaliation," 127.

122. Memorandum of a Conversation, March 28, 1955, NARA, CDF, 1955–1959, RG 59, Box 3976, 794a.5/3-2855.

123. As quoted in Accinelli, *Crisis and Commitment*, 234.

124. Memorandum of a Conversation, Department of State, January 20, 1955, in *FRUS, 1955–1957*, vol. 2, Document 22.

5. Revision of the U.S.-Japan Alliance, 1955–1960

1. Interview with Douglas MacArthur II, December 16, 1966, JFD OHP.

2. George Packard, *Protest in Tokyo: The Security Treaty Crisis of 1960* (Princeton, NJ: Princeton University Press, 1966), 35.

3. Schaller, *Altered States*, 129. For accounts that emphasize the 1957–1960 period, see Schaller, *Altered States*, chap. 8, and LaFeber, *The Clash*, 314–324.

4. Security Treaty Between the United States and Japan, September 8, 1951.

5. The Ambassador in Japan (Allison) to the Department of State, August 14, 1954, in *FRUS, 1952–1954*, vol. 14, pt. 2, *China and Japan*, Document 790.

6. The Ambassador in Japan (Allison) to the Department of State, August 25, 1954, in *FRUS, 1952–1954*, vol. 14, pt. 2, Document 796.

7. As quoted in Schaller, *Altered States*, 77.

8. John M. Allison, *Ambassador from the Prairie or Allison Wonderland* (Boston: Houghton Mifflin, 1973), 274.

9. Roger Buckley, *US-Japan Alliance Diplomacy 1945–1990* (Cambridge: Cambridge University Press, 1992), 85–86.

10. LaFeber, *The Clash*, 314.

11. Tokyo's 954 to Washington, February 11, 1955, NARA, CDF, 1955–1959, RG 59, Box 2574, 611.94/2-1155.

12. Tokyo's 2202 to Washington, March 9, 1955, NARA, CDF, 1955–1959, RG 59, Box 3939, 793.5/3-955.

13. Tokyo's 2202 to Washington, March 9, 1955, NARA, CDF, 1955–1959, RG 59, Box 3939, 793.5/3-955.

14. Tokyo's 2202 to Washington, March 9, 1955, NARA, CDF, 1955–1959, RG 59, Box 3939, 793.5/3-955.

15. Tokyo's 2508 to Washington, April 4, 1955, NARA, CDF, 1955–1959, RG 59, Box 3917, 793.00/4-455.

16. National Security Council Report 5516/1, April 9, 1955, in *FRUS, 1955–1957*, vol. 23, pt. 1, *Japan*, Document 28.

17. Memorandum of Discussion at the 244th Meeting of the National Security Council, April 7, 1955, in *FRUS, 1955–1957*, vol. 23, pt. 1, Document 26 (emphasis in the original).

18. Tokyo's 13 to Washington, July 6, 1955, NARA, CDF, 1955–1959, RG 59, Box 2575, 611.94/7-655.

19. Interview with John M. Allison, April 20, 1969, JFD OHP.

20. Letter from the Ambassador in Japan (Allison) to the Director of the Office of Northeast Asian Affairs (McClurkin), July 19, 1955, in *FRUS, 1955–1957*, vol. 23, pt. 1, Document 36.

21. Tokyo's 201 to Washington, July 25, 1955, NARA, CDF, 1955–1959, RG 59, Box 3968, 794.5/7-2555.

22. Tokyo's 201 to Washington, July 25, 1955, NARA, CDF, 1955–1959, RG 59, Box 3968, 794.5/7-2555.

23. Memorandum from the Assistant Secretary of State for Far Eastern Affairs (Robertson) to the Secretary of State, July 28, 1955, in *FRUS, 1955–1957*, vol. 23, pt. 1, Document 37.

24. Tokyo's 378 to Washington, August 10, 1955, NARA, CDF, 1955–1959, RG 59, Box 3968, 794.5/8-1055.

25. Tokyo's 400 to Washington, August 12, 1955, NARA, CDF, 1955–1959, RG 59, Box 3968, 794.5/8-1255.

26. Mr Sebald to the Secretary, August 23, 1955, NARA, CDF, 1955–1959, RG 59, Box 3968, 794.5/8-2355.

27. Memorandum of a Conversation, August 24, 1955, in *FRUS, 1955–1957*, vol. 23, pt. 1, Document 42.

28. Memorandum of a Conversation, August 30, 1955, in *FRUS, 1955–1957*, vol. 23, pt. 1, Document 45.

29. Interview with Ichiro Kono, September 30, 1964, JFD OHP.

30. Memorandum of a Conversation, August 30, 1955, in *FRUS, 1955–1957*, vol. 23, pt. 1, Document 45.

31. Telegram from the Department of State to the Embassy in Japan, September 2, 1955, *FRUS, 1955–1957*, vol. 23, pt. 1, Document 50, footnote 4.

32. Memorandum from the Secretary of State's Special Assistant for Intelligence (Armstrong) to the Acting Secretary of State, October 10, 1955, in *FRUS, 1955–1957*, vol. 23, pt. 1, Document 57.

33. Tokyo's 942 to Washington, April 16, 1956, NARA, CDF, 1955–1959, RG 59, Box 2577, 611.94/4-1656 (emphasis added).

34. Tokyo's 276 to Washington, September 21, 1956, NARA, CDF, 1955–1959, RG 59, Box 2578, 611.94/9-2156.

35. Tokyo's 221 to Washington, September 7, 1956, as quoted in Parsons to Robertson, 24 January 1957, NARA, CDF, 1955–1959, RG 59, Box 3969, 794.5/1-2457.

36. Tokyo's 280 to Washington, September 24, 1956, NARA, CDF, 1955–1959, RG 59, Box 3968, 794.5/9-2456.

37. Tokyo's 587 to Washington, December 11, 1956, NARA, CDF, 1955–1959, RG 59, Box 2578, 611.94/12-1156.

38. Memorandum from Parsons to Sebald, December 21, 1956, NARA, CDF, 1955–1959, RG 59, Box 3968, 794.5/12-2156.

39. Memorandum from Parsons to Sebald, December 21, 1956, NARA, CDF, 1955–1959, RG 59, Box 3968, 794.5/12-2156.

40. Memorandum from Parsons to Sebald, December 21, 1956, NARA, CDF, 1955–1959, RG 59, Box 3968, 794.5/12-2156.

41. Memorandum from the Assistant Secretary of State for Far Eastern Affairs (Robertson) to the Secretary of State, January 7, 1957, in *FRUS, 1955–1957*, vol. 23, pt. 1, Document 106.

42. Tokyo's 2256 to Washington, April 10, 1957, NARA, CDF, 1955–1959, RG 59, Box 2578, 611.94/4-1057. Two other issues—territorial problems and trade restrictions—were also listed.

43. Tokyo's 2256 to Washington, April 10, 1957, NARA, CDF, 1955–1959, RG 59, Box 2578, 611.94/4-1057.

44. Tokyo's 2257 to Washington, April 10, 1957, NARA, CDF, 1955–1959, RG 59, Box 2578, 611.94/4-1057.

45. Tokyo's 2305 to Washington, April 13, 1957, NARA, CDF, 1955–1959, RG 59, Box 2578, 611.94/4-1357.

46. Tokyo's 2305 to Washington, April 13, 1957, NARA, CDF, 1955–1959, RG 59, Box 2578, 611.94/4-1357.

47. Buckley, *US-Japan Alliance Diplomacy*, 82.

48. Interview with Nobusuke Kishi, October 2, 1964, JFD OHP.

49. Telegram from the Embassy in Japan to the Department of State, April 17, 1957, in *FRUS, 1955–1957*, vol. 23, pt. 1, Document 126.

50. See Telegram from the Department of State to the Embassy in Japan, April 18, 1957, in *FRUS, 1955–1957*, vol. 23, pt. 1, Document 127.

51. Memorandum of a Conversation, June 19, 1957, in *FRUS, 1955–1957*, vol. 23, pt. 1, Document 183.

52. Memorandum of a Conversation, June 20, 1957, in *FRUS, 1955–1957*, vol. 23, pt. 1, Document 187. See also Memorandum of a Conversation, June 20, 1957, in *FRUS, 1955–1957*, vol. 23, pt. 1, Document 186.

53. Memorandum of a Conversation, June 21, 1957, in *FRUS, 1955–1957*, vol. 23, pt. 1, Document 191.

54. See Memorandum of a Conversation, June 23, 1957, in *FRUS, 1955–1957*, vol. 23, pt. 1, Document 193.

55. US Department of State, *Department of State Bulletin* 37, no. 941 (July 8, 1957): 52.

56. Packard, *Protest in Tokyo*, 58.

57. Letter from Horsey to Parsons, June 20, 1957, NARA, CDF, 1955–1959, RG 59, Box 3969, 794.5/6-2057.

58. State's 1623 to Tokyo, January 31, 1958, NARA, CDF, 1955–1959, RG 59, Box 2579, 611.94/1-3158.

59. Telegram from the Embassy in Japan to the Department of State, February 12, 1958, in *FRUS, 1958–1960*, vol. 18, *Japan; Korea*, Document 3.

60. Memo from Martin to Parsons, January 22, 1958, NARA, CDF, 1955–1959, RG 59, Box 2579, 611.94/1-2258. In the report, against the second part of this quote there is a handwritten notation: "This is only one aspect. I think this is too strong." It is not clear whose handwriting it is, nor to which aspect of the paragraph it specifically objects.

61. Letter from the Ambassador to Japan (MacArthur) to Secretary of State Dulles, February 18, 1958, in *FRUS, 1958–1960*, vol. 18, Document 4 (emphasis in the original).

62. Letter from Robertson to Secretary of State Dulles, March 28, 1958, NARA, CDF, 1955–1959, Box 2579, 611.94/3-2858.

63. Letter from the Ambassador to Japan (MacArthur) to Secretary of State Dulles, April 18, 1958, in *FRUS, 1958–1960*, vol. 18, Document 11.

64. Memorandum from MacArthur to Dulles and Robertson, March 8, 1958, NARA, CDF, 1955–1959, RG 59, Box 3969, 794.5/3-858 (emphasis added).

65. Letter from CINCPAC's Political Adviser (Steeves) to the Assistant Secretary of State for Far Eastern Affairs (Robertson), July 18, 1958, in *FRUS, 1958–1960*, vol. 18, Document 17.

66. Telegram from the Commander in Chief, Pacific (Felt) to the Joint Chiefs of Staff, August 19, 1958, in *FRUS, 1958–1960*, vol. 18, Document 22.

67. Telegram from the Embassy in Japan to the Department of State, August 1, 1958, in *FRUS, 1958–1960*, vol. 18, Document 20.

68. Memorandum of Conversation, September 8, 1958, in *FRUS, 1958–1960*, vol. 18, Document 23.

69. Schaller, *Altered States*, 138.

70. Memorandum of Conversation, September 9, 1958, in *FRUS, 1958–1960*, vol. 18, Document 24.

71. Memorandum of Conversation, September 9, 1958, in *FRUS, 1958–1960*, vol. 18, Document 24.

72. Report Prepared by the Joint Chiefs of Staff, September 10, 1958, in *FRUS, 1958–1960*, vol. 18, Document 25.

73. State's 206 to Tokyo, July 31, 1958, NARA, CDF, 1955–1959, RG 59, Box 2579, 611.94/7-3158.

74. Memorandum of Conversation, September 11, 1958, in *FRUS, 1958–1960*, vol. 18, Document 26.

75. Memorandum from the Assistant Secretary of State for Far Eastern Affairs (Robertson) to Secretary of State Dulles, September 12, 1958, in *FRUS, 1958–1960*, vol. 18, Document 27. This formula was directly based upon a communiqué issued by President Truman and Prime Minister Churchill in 1952.

76. Telegram from the Department of State to the Embassy in Japan, September 29, 1958, in *FRUS, 1958–1960*, vol. 18, Document 28.

77. The name is derived from Article III of the San Francisco Peace Treaty, which gave the United States administrative rights over the Ryukyus and Bonins. The Ryukyu Islands group comprises the Osumi, Tokara, Amami, Okinawa, and Sakishima Islands. See John

Swenson-Wright, *Unequal Allies? United States Security and Alliance Policy toward Japan, 1945–1960* (Stanford, CA: Stanford University Press, 2005), 111.

78. See Telegram from the Embassy in Japan to the Department of State, October 13, 1958, in *FRUS, 1958–1960*, vol. 18, Document 32.

79. Telegram from the Embassy in Japan to the Department of State, November 28, 1958, in *FRUS, 1958–1960*, vol. 18, Document 35.

80. See Memorandum for the Record, November 25, 1959, NARA, CDF, 1955–1959, RG 59, Box 3970, 794.5/11-2559.

81. Another issue, which was subject to political debate in Tokyo, was that if the new alliance covered the Article III islands, this could effectively create a "NEATO" (Northeast Asia Treaty Organization). This fear was due to the fact that Article III islands were mentioned in the US-ROC and US-ROK treaties. Inclusion of the Article III islands would mean that "Japan runs the risk of becoming entangled in hostilities involving the GRC or ROK if the Ryukyus and Bonins. . . . were included in the treaty area." This quote is from Tokyo's 583 to Washington, November 25, 1958, NARA, CDF, 1955–1959, RG 59, Box 3969, 794.5/11-2558. See also Tokyo's 815 to Washington, January 26, 1959, NARA, CDF, 1955–1959, RG 59, Box 3970, 794.5/1-2659.

82. Tokyo's G-199 to Washington, August 29, 1958, NARA, CDF, 1955–1959, RG 59, Box 2579, 611.94/8-2958.

83. Tokyo's 507 to Washington, September 2, 1958, NARA, CDF, 1955–1959, RG 59, Box 2579, 611.94/9-258.

84. Schaller, *Altered States*, 139.

85. Dean Acheson and Shigeru Yoshida, "Notes Exchanged between Prime Minister Yoshida and Secretary of State Acheson at the Time of the Signing of the Security Treaty between Japan and the United States of America," September 8, 1951, "The World and Japan" Database Project, University of Tokyo, http://www.ioc.u-tokyo.ac.jp/~worldjpn/documents/texts/docs/19510908.T3E.html.

86. Telegram from the Embassy in Japan to the Department of State, October 13, 1958, in *FRUS, 1958–1960*, vol. 18, Document 34.

87. Telegram from the Embassy in Japan to the Department of State, November 28, 1958, in *FRUS, 1958–1960*, vol. 18, Document 35.

88. See Telegram from the Embassy in Japan to the Department of State, May 8, 1959, in *FRUS, 1958–1960*, vol. 18, Document 55.

89. Telegram from the Department of State to the Embassy in Japan, June 8, 1959, in *FRUS, 1958–1960*, vol. 18, Document 71.

90. Telegram from the Embassy in Japan to the Department of State, June 10, 1959, in *FRUS, 1958–1960*, vol. 18, Document 72.

91. Telegram from the Embassy in Japan to the Department of State, June 10, 1959, in *FRUS, 1958–1960*, vol. 18, Document 72.

92. State's 2014 to Tokyo, June 19, 1959, NARA, CDF, 1955–1959, RG 59, Box 3970, 794.5/6-1959.

93. State's 2022 to Tokyo, June 20, 1959, NARA, CDF, 1955–1959, RG 59, Box 3970, 794.5/6-2059.

94. Tokyo's 2751 to Washington, June 21, 1959, NARA, CDF, 1955–1959, RG 59, Box 3970, 794.5/6-2159.

95. State's 2059 to Tokyo, June 24, 1959, NARA, CDF, 1955–1959, RG 59, Box 3970, 794.5/6-2459.

96. See State's 2059 to Tokyo, June 24, 1959, NARA, CDF, 1955–1959, RG 59, Box 3970, 794.5/6-2459.

97. State's 2126 to Tokyo, June 30, 1959, Personal for Ambassador, NARA, CDF, RG 59, 1955–1959, Box 3970, 794.5/6-2659.

98. Tokyo's 43 to Washington, July 6, 1959, NARA, CDF, 1955–1959, RG 59, Box 3970, 794.5/7-659.

99. Tokyo's 95 to Washington, July 10, 1959, NARA, CDF, 1955–1959, RG 59, Box 3970, 794.5/7-1059.

100. Tokyo's 509 to Washington, August 24, 1959, NARA, CDF, 1955–1959, RG 59, Box 3970, 794.5/8-2459. See also State's 656 to Tokyo, August 24, 1959, NARA, CDF, 1955–1959, RG 59, Box 3970, 794.5/8-2459.

101. Tokyo's 509 to Washington, August 24, 1959, NARA, CDF, 1955–1959, RG 59, Box 3970, 794.5/8-2459.

102. Tokyo's 1946 to Washington, December 19, 1959, NARA, CDF, 1955–1959, RG 59, Box 3970, 794.5/12-1959.

103. Schaller, *Altered States*, 129. Authors such as Swenson-Wright have argued that Shigemitsu's goal for the 1955 visit was primarily to strengthen his own political position in Tokyo: the US ambassador also regarded this as the main motivation for Shigemitsu's trip to Washington. See Swenson-Wright, *Unequal Allies?*, 208. See also the Memorandum of a Conversation, August 24, 1955, in *FRUS, 1955–1957*, vol. 23, pt. 1, Document 42, footnote 2. Here, Allison assessed that while Shigemitsu's trip was "primarily [an] internal political move," it would also "of course be intended at same time to serve Japanese policy purposes, which he sincerely pursues except where his personal ambitions conflict."

104. Memo from Parsons to Sebald, December 21, 1956, NARA, CDF, 1955–1959, RG 59, Box 3968, 794.5/12-2156.

105. Memo from Martin to Parsons, January 22, 1958, NARA, CDF, 1955–1959, RG 59, Box 2579, 611.94/1-2258.

106. Memorandum of Conversation, September 9, 1958, in *FRUS, 1958–1960*, vol. 18, Document 24.

107. US Department of State, *Department of State Bulletin* 37, no. 941 (July 8, 1957): 52.

108. Telegram from the Embassy in Japan to the Department of State, November 28, 1958, in *FRUS, 1958–1960*, vol. 18, Document 35.

6. Negotiating the Reversion of Okinawa, 1967–1969

1. Meyer, *Assignment Tokyo*, 33.

2. State's 44757 to Seoul, March 22, 1969, NARA, Subject-Numeric Files (SNF), 1967–1969, RG 59, POL 19 RYU IS, Box 2459.

3. See, for example, Kei Wakaizumi, *The Best Course Available* (Honolulu: University of Hawai'i Press, 2002); Meyer, *Assignment Tokyo*; U. Alexis Johnson, *The Right Hand of Power* (Englewood Cliffs, NJ: Prentice-Hall, 1984); and I. M. Destler et al., eds., *Managing an Alliance: The Politics of U.S.-Japanese Relations* (Washington, DC: Brookings Institution, 1976). See also Edwin O. Reischauer, *My Life between Japan and America* (New York: Harper and Row, 1986); Frank Langdon, *Japan's Foreign Policy* (Vancouver: University of British Columbia Press, 1975); Buckley, *US-Japan Alliance Diplomacy*; Schaller, *Altered States*; and LaFeber, *The Clash*. For more contemporary analysis, see Akikazu Hashimoto, Mike Mochizuki and Kurayoshi Takara, eds., *The Okinawa Question and the U.S.-Japan Alliance* (Washington, DC: George Washington University, 2005).

4. Johnson, *Right Hand of Power*, 465.

5. This "homeland" nomenclature is often used to refer to all of the Japanese islands except those covered by Article III of the 1951 Security Treaty, that is all islands except for the Ryukyu and Bonin Island chains.

6. Reischauer, *My Life between Japan and America*, 257.

7. Tokyo's Airgram 2109 to Washington, October 8, 1968, NARA, SNF, 1967–1969, RG 59, POL 12-1 JAPAN, Box 2245.

8. Morton Halperin, "American Decision Making on Reversion of Okinawa: A Memoir," in *Commemorative Events for the Twentieth Anniversary of the Reversion of Okinawa*. (Tokyo: Japan Foundation Center for Global Partnership, 1994), 53. The chapter appears in the proceedings of a seminar on Okinawa reversion and its long-term significance in US-Japan relations held in Tokyo, May 13–14, 1992.

9. Halperin, "American Decision Making on Okinawa," 54.

10. Halperin, "American Decision Making on Okinawa," 54–55. See also Destler et al., *Managing an Alliance*, chap. 2.

11. See Taipei's 3977 to Washington, June 28, 1967, NARA, SNF, 1967–1969, RG 59, POL 19 RYU IS, Box 2456.

12. See Taipei's Airgram 639 to Washington, March 24, 1967, NARA, SNF, 1967–1969, RG 59, POL 19 RYU IS, Box 2456; and Taipei's 3977 to Washington, June 28, 1967, NARA, SNF, 1967–1969, RG 59, POL 19 RYU IS, Box 2456.

13. See Taipei's Airgram 639 to Washington, March 24, 1967, NARA, SNF, 1967–1969, RG 59, POL 19 RYU IS, Box 2456.

14. Taipei's Airgram 786 to Washington, May 24, 1967, NARA, SNF, 1967–1969, RG 59, POL 19 RYU IS, Box 2456.

15. Taipei's 3977 to Washington, June 28, 1967, NARA, SNF, 1967–1969, RG 59, POL 19 RYU IS, Box 2456.

16. Taipei's 3977 to Washington, June 28, 1967, NARA, SNF, 1967–1969, RG 59, POL 19 RYU IS, Box 2456.

17. State's Airgram 39 to Taipei, July 27, 1967, NARA, SNF, 1967–1969, RG 59, POL 19 RYU IS, Box 2456.

18. Intelligence Note 729, September 12, 1967, NARA, SNF, 1967–1969, RG 59, POL 19 RYU IS, Box 2456.

19. See Destler et al., *Managing an Alliance*, 30.

20. Johnson, *Right Hand of Power*, 468–469.

21. For Okinawa's importance in the Vietnam War, see Schaller, *Altered States*, 196.

22. Tokyo's 818 to Washington, August 9, 1967, NARA, SNF, 1967–1969, RG 59, POL 23 JAPAN, Box 2248.

23. Memorandum of Conversation, Part III of V, Ryukyu and Bonin Islands, September 14, 1967, NARA, SNF, 1967–1969, RG 59, POL JAPAN-US, Box 2249.

24. Tokyo's 1917 to Washington, September 21, 1967, NARA, SNF, 1967–1969, RG 59, POL 19 RYU IS, Box 2456.

25. Tokyo's 2155 to Washington, September 29, 1967, NARA, SNF, 1967–1969, RG 59, POL 19 RYU IS, Box 2456.

26. Tokyo's 2417 to Washington, October 11, 1967, NARA, SNF, 1967–1969, RG 59, POL 19 RYU IS, Box 2457.

27. State's 65117 to Tokyo, November 5, 1967, NARA, SNF, 1967–1969, RG 59, POL JAPAN-US, Box 2249.

28. State's 66921 to Taipei and Tokyo, November 9, 1967, NARA, SNF, 1967–1969, RG 59, XR POL 7 JAPAN, Box 2244. See also Taipei's Airgram 258 to Washington, October 6, 1967, NARA, SNF, 1967–1969, RG 59, POL 15-1 JAPAN, Box 2246.

29. Memo from Shoesmith to Bundy, November 7, 1967, NARA, SNF, 1967–1969, Lot Files, ROC, Container 4. See also Tokyo's Airgram 364 to Washington, December 9, 1967, NARA, SNF, 1967–1969, RG 59, POL 7 CHINAT, Box 1983.

30. State's 66921 to Taipei and Tokyo, November 9, 1967, NARA, SNF, 1967–1969, RG 59, XR POL 7 JAPAN, Box 2244. Bundy followed through on his commitment: see State's 71419 to Taipei, November 18, 1967, NARA, SNF, 1967–1969, RG 59, XR POL 19 RYU IS, Box 2457. See also Taipei's 1410 to Washington, November 17, 1967, NARA, SNF, 1967–1969, RG 59, XR POL 19 RYU IS, Box 2457.

31. Eisaku Satō and Lyndon Baines Johnson, "Joint Statement of Japanese Prime Minister Sato and U.S. President Johnson" (a.k.a. Johnson-Sato communiqué), November 15, 1967, "The World and Japan" Database Project, University of Tokyo, http://www.ioc.u-tokyo.ac.jp/~worldjpn/documents/texts/JPUS/19671115.D1E.html.

32. Tokyo's 3414 to Washington, November 17, 1967, NARA, SNF, 1967–1969, RG 59, POL 7 JAPAN, Box 2244.

33. Tokyo's Airgram 647 to Washington, November 24, 1967, NARA, SNF, 1967–1969, RG 59, POL 7 JAPAN, Box 2244.

34. Tokyo's 4035 to Washington, December 16, 1967, NARA, SNF, 1967–1969, RG 59, POL 19 RYU IS, Box 2457.

NOTES TO PAGES 149–152

35. Tokyo's 8245 to Washington, May 15, 1967, NARA, SNF, 1967–1969, RG 59, POL 23 JAPAN, Box 2248.

36. Taipei's Airgram A-364 to Washington, December 9, 1967, NARA, SNF, 1967–1969, POL 7 CHINAT, Box 1983.

37. Destler et al., *Managing an Alliance*, 31.

38. Tokyo's 4035 to Washington, December 16, 1967, NARA, SNF, 1967–1969, RG 59, POL 19 RYU IS, Box 2457.

39. Letter from the Secretary of State to the Secretary of Defense, January 5, 1968, NARA, SNF, 1967–1969, RG 59, POL 19 RYU IS, Box 2457.

40. Memorandum from Sneider to Bundy, February 12, 1968, NARA, SNF, 1967–1969, Lot Files, Japan, Box 4. See also Cha, *Alignment despite Antagonism*, chap. 3.

41. Memorandum from Sneider to Bundy, February 17, 1968, NARA, SNF, 1967–1969, RG 59, POL 17 JAPAN-US, Box 2250.

42. Tokyo's 5638 to Washington, February 15, 1968, NARA, SNF, 1967–1969, RG 59, POL 33-6 KOR N-US, Box 2267.

43. Telegram From the Department of State to the Embassy in Japan, February 16, 1968, in *FRUS, 1964–1968*, vol. 29, pt. 2, *Japan*, Document 115.

44. State's 104284 to Tokyo, January 25, 1968, NARA, SNF, 1967–1969, RG 59, POL 15-1 KOR S, Box 2279.

45. Letter from Ambassador Johnson to Richard Sneider, February 23, 1968, NARA, SNF, 1967–1969, RG 59, POL 1 JAPAN-US, Box 2250.

46. Memorandum of Conversation, May 10, 1968, NARA, SNF, 1967–1969, RG 59, POL JAPAN-US, Box 2249. See also Schaller, *Altered States*, 206–207.

47. Interview with Ural Alexis Johnson, June 14, 1969, Association for Diplomatic Studies and Training, Foreign Affairs Oral History Project.

48. Telegram from the Embassy in Japan to the Department of State, June 5, 1968, in *FRUS, 1964–1968*, vol. 29, pt. 2, Document 123.

49. See Schaller, *Altered States*, 194. It is not perfectly clear whether this threat was intended to have the implication of nuclear coercion.

50. Memorandum of Conversation, Security Subcommittee: Second Session, June 7, 1968, NARA, SNF, 1967–1969, RG 59, POL JAPAN-US, Box 2249.

51. This odd situation—where Japan simultaneously feared both abandonment and entrapment—is also implicitly noted in Schaller, *Altered States*, 207. While this scenario might seem illogical, it makes sense when Japan's unique circumstances are considered. At various points Japan has had strong preferences for an ideal level of US involvement in Asia, with any position stronger than this ideal prompting fears of entrapment but any weaker position sparking fears of abandonment. See, for example, Intelligence Note 595, August 14, 1969, NARA, SNF, 1967–1969, RG 59, POL JAPAN-KOR S, Box 2248, which explains how Japan would welcome a partial withdrawal of US forces from the Korean Peninsula but only under certain conditions.

52. Memorandum of Conversation, June 6, 1968, NARA, SNF, 1967–1969, RG 59, POL JAPAN-US, Box 2249.

53. Tokyo's 9924 to Washington, July 5, 1968, NARA, SNF, 1967–1969, RG 59, POL 19 RYU IS, Box 2458.

54. Tokyo's 10835 to Washington, August 6, 1968, NARA, SNF, 1967–1969, RG 59, POL 15-1 JAPAN, Box 2246.

55. Seoul's 9594 to Washington, September 4, 1968, NARA, SNF, 1967–1969, RG59, XR POL JAPAN-KOR S, Box 2248.

56. Tokyo's Airgram 2177 to Washington, October 29, 1968, NARA, SNF, 1967–1969, RG 59, DEF 1 JAPAN-US, Box 1562.

57. Tokyo's Airgram 1965 to Washington, September 9, 1968, NARA, SNF, 1967–1969, RG 59, POL 1 JAPAN, Box 2250.

58. Tokyo's Airgram 2329 to Washington, December 13, 1968, NARA, SNF, 1967–1969, RG 59, POL 19 RYU IS, Box 2458.

59. Tokyo's Airgram 2109 to Washington, October 8, 1968, NARA, SNF, 1967–1969, RG 59, POL 12-1 JAPAN, Box 2245.

60. Taipei's Airgram 472 to Washington, February 7, 1968, NARA, SNF, 1967–1969, RG 59, POL 19 RYU IS, Box 2457.

61. As quoted in Shinkichi Eto, "Attitude of Peking and Taiwan Governments on Okinawa Issue," Enclosure 9 to Tokyo's Airgram 119 (date unknown), NARA, SNF, 1967–1969, RG 59, POL 19 RYU IS, Box 2458.

62. State's 251745 to Taipei, October 8, 1968, NARA, SNF, 1967–1969, RG 59, POL 19 RYU IS, Box 2457.

63. Taipei's 4872 to Washington, October 17, 1968, NARA, SNF, 1967–1969, RG 59, POL 19 RYU IS, Box 2457. See also Taipei's 4778 to Washington, October 9, 1968, NARA, SNF, 1967–1969, RG 59, POL 19 RYU IS, Box 2457.

64. Cha, *Alignment despite Antagonism*, 64. The three provocations were the guerilla attack on the prime minister's "Blue House," the capture of the USS *Pueblo*, and the shooting down of an unarmed American EC-121 reconnaissance aircraft in April 1969.

65. Cha, *Alignment despite Antagonism*, 63.

66. Memo from Sneider to Bundy, February 12, 1968, NARA, SNF, 1967–1969, Lot Files, Japan, Box 4.

67. Tokyo's 33 to Washington, January 3, 1969, NARA, SNF, 1967–1969, RG 59, POL 15-1 JAPAN, Box 2246.

68. Tokyo's 126 to Washington, January 8, 1969, NARA, SNF, 1967–1969, RG 59, POL 19 RYU IS, Box 2458.

69. State's 14473 to Tokyo, January 29, 1969, NARA, SNF, 1967–1969, RG 59, POL 19 RYU IS, Box 2458.

70. See Seoul's 11389 to Washington, November 25, 1968, NARA, SNF, 1967–1969, RG 59, DEF 4 PATO, Box 1610.

71. See Seoul's 599 to Washington, February 6, 1969, NARA, SNF, 1967–1969, RG 59, DEF 4 PATO, Box 1610.

72. Seoul's 1001 to Washington, February 27, 1969, NARA, SNF, 1967–1969, RG 59, DEF 4 PATO, Box 1610.

73. Seoul's 1111 to Washington, March 7, 1969, NARA, SNF, 1967–1969, RG 59, POL 19 RYU IS, Box 2459.

74. Memo from Bardach to Brown, January 14, 1969, NARA, SNF, 1967–1969, Lot Files, Korea, Box 2.

75. Intelligence Information Cable, March 1, 1969, NARA, RG 319, History of the Civil Administration of the Ryukyu Islands (HCARI), Box 3.

76. Taipei's 617 to Washington, March 3, 1969, NARA, SNF, 1967–1969, RG 59, POL 7 CHINAT, Box 1983.

77. State's 39611 to Taipei, Seoul, Saigon, and Bangkok, March 14, 1969, NARA, SNF, 1967–1969, RG 59, DEF 4 PATO, Box 1610.

78. Seoul's 1295 to Washington, March 18, 1969, NARA, SNF, 1967–1969, RG 59, DEF 4 PATO, Box 1610.

79. Seoul's 1289 to Washington, March 17, 1969, NARA, SNF, 1967–1969, RG 59, POL 19 RYU IS, Box 2459.

80. See State's 48425 to Seoul, March 28, 1969, NARA, SNF, 1967–1969, RG 59, POL 17 KOR S–US, Box 2283.

81. Memorandum of a Conversation, March 27, 1969, NARA, SNF, 1967–1969, Lot Files, Korea, Box 3.

82. Tokyo's 2170 to Washington, March 21, 1969, NARA, SNF, 1967–1969, RG 59, DEF 4 PATO, Box 1610.

83. Tokyo's 2170 to Washington, March 21, 1969, NARA, SNF, 1967–1969, RG 59, DEF 4 PATO, Box 1610.

84. State's 44757 to Seoul, March 22, 1969, NARA, SNF, 1967–1969, RG 59, POL 19 RYU IS, Box 2459.

85. Seoul's 1548 to Washington, March 28, 1969, NARA, SNF, 1967–1969, RG 59, POL 19 RYU IS, Box 2459.

86. Memorandum of a Conversation, April 1, 1969, Richard M. Nixon Presidential Library (RMNPL), Yorba Linda, California, White House Special Files, President's Office Files, President's Meeting File 1969–1974, Box 73.

87. Memorandum of Conversation, April 1, 1969, NARA, SNF, 1967–1969, RG 59, POL KOR S–US, Box 2282.

88. Memorandum of a Conversation, April 4, 1969, NARA, SNF, 1967–1969, RG 59, POL 7 KOR S, Box 2277.

89. Seoul's 1671 to Washington, April 4, 1969, NARA, SNF, 1967–1969, RG 59, POL 19 RYU IS, Box 2459.

90. Tokyo's 2818 to Washington, April 12, 1969, NARA, SNF, 1967–1969, RG 59, POL 19 RYU IS, Box 2459.

91. Seoul's 1731 to Washington, April 9, 1969, NARA, SNF, 1967–1969, RG 59, POL 19 RYU IS, Box 2459. See also Seoul's 1748 to Washington, April 9, 1969, NARA, SNF, 1967–1969, RG 59, POL 19 RYU IS, Box 2459, for the full text of the aide memoire.

92. See Seoul's 1848 to Washington, April 14, 1969, NARA, SNF, 1967–1969, RG 59, POL 19 RYU IS, Box 2459.

93. See Seoul's 1822 to Washington, April 14, 1969, NARA, SNF, 1967–1969, RG 59, ORG 7 EA, Box 107. See also Taipei's 1234 to Washington, April 18, 1969, NARA, SNF, 1967–1969, RG 59, ORG 7 EA, Box 107. Green's discussions with the ROC focused on the issue of Vietnam, and Okinawa was not mentioned in the record.

94. A. D. Horne, "Bases Are Stakes of Okinawa Game," *Washington Post*, May 11, 1969.

95. During this period, an alignment of interests between the ROC and Japan was also of concern to Communist China. See Evelyn Goh, *Constructing the U.S. Rapprochement with China, 1961–1974: From "Red Menace" to "Tacit Ally"* (Cambridge: Cambridge University Press, 2005), 176–178.

96. Henry Kissinger, *The White House Years* (London: George Weidenfeld and Nicolson, 1979), 328–329.

97. See Tokyo's 3156 to Washington, April 23, 1969, NARA, SNF, 1967–1969, RG 59, POL 19 RYU IS, Box 2459

98. Tokyo's 3511 to Washington, May 3, 1969, NARA, SNF, 1967–1969, RG 59, POL 19 RYU IS, Box 2459.

99. Memorandum from Richard Finn to Marshall Green, May 15, 1969, NARA, SNF, 1967–1969, RG 59, ORG 7 EA/J, Box 107 (emphasis added).

100. Tokyo's 4221 to Washington, May 27, 1969, NARA, SNF, 1967–1969, RG 59, POL 19 RYU IS, Box 2459.

101. Memorandum of Conversation, June 2, 1969, NARA, SNF, 1967–1969, RG 59, POL 7 JAPAN, Box 2244.

102. Memorandum of Conversation, June 5, 1969, NARA, SNF, 1967–1969, RG 59, POL 19 RYU IS, Box 2459.

103. Tokyo's 5907 to Washington, July 18, 1969, NARA, RG 319, HCARI, Box 19.

104. Tokyo's 4643 to Washington, June 10, 1969, NARA, SNF, 1967–1969, RG 59, POL 3 AS-PAC, Box 1854.

105. Seoul's 3343 to Washington, June 23, 1969, NARA, SNF, 1967–1969, RG 59, POL JAPAN-SAUD, Box 2248.

106. Tokyo's 5478 to Washington, July 3, 1969, NARA, SNF, 1967–1969, RG 59, POL 19 RYU IS, Box 2459.

107. Seoul's 4174 to Washington, August 2, 1969, NARA, SNF, 1967–1969, RG 59, ORG 7 S, Box 118. The US embassy in Seoul believed that these two memos had probably not been cleared with the ROK prime minister. The two memos are in Seoul's Airgram 271 to Washington, August 7, 1969, NARA, SNF, 1967–1969, RG 59, ORG 7 S, Box 118.

108. Tokyo's 6352 to Washington, August 3, 1969, NARA, SNF, 1967–1969, RG 59, ORG 7 S, Box 118.

109. Cha, *Alignment despite Antagonism*, 74.

110. See Memo from Shoesmith to Bundy, November 7, 1967, NARA, SNF, 1967–1969, Lot Files 1967–1968, ROC, Container 4; and Taipei's Airgram 364 to Washington, December 9, 1967, NARA, SNF, 1967–1969, RG 59, POL 7 CHINAT, Box 1983.

111. Intelligence Note 746, September 20, 1967, NARA, SNF, 1967–1969, RG 59, POL 7 CHINAT, Box 1983.

112. State's 137408 to Tokyo, August 15, 1969, NARA, SNF, 1967–1969, RG, 59, POL 7 JAPAN, Box 2245.

113. State's 138353 to Tokyo, August 16, 1969, NARA, SNF, 1967–1969, RG 59, POL JAPAN-US, Box 2249.

114. Tokyo's 6935 to Washington, August 23, 1969, NARA, SNF, 1967–1969, RG 59, POL 19 RYU IS, Box 2459; and Eisaku Sato, "Address to National Press Club," November 21, 1969, *US Security Agreements and Commitments Abroad*, Senate Committee on Foreign Relations, 91st Congress, 1428–1430.

115. Tokyo's 6935 to Washington, August 23, 1969, NARA, SNF, 1967–1969, RG 59, POL 19 RYU IS, Box 2459.

116. Eisaku Sato, "Address to National Press Club."

117. For more detail on the evolution of Sato's speech, see Tokyo's 6935 of August 23, 1969, NARA, SNF, 1967–1969, RG 59, POL 19 RYU IS, Box 2459; Tokyo's 7128 of September 1, 1969, NARA, SNF, 1967–1969, RG 59, POL 19 RYU IS, Box 2460; and Marshall Green to Secretary Rusk, September 13, 1969, NARA, SNF, 1967–1969, RG 59, POL 19 RYU IS, Box 2460.

118. Seoul's 4291 to Washington, August 8, 1969, NARA, SNF, 1967–1969, RG 59, POL 15-1 KOR S, Box 2279.

119. Memorandum for the President, August 16, 1969, NARA, SNF, 1967–1969, RG 59, POL 7 KOR S, Box 2277.

120. Tokyo's 7172 to Washington, September 2, 1969, NARA, SNF, 1967–1969, RG 59, POL 19 RYU IS, Box 2460.

121. Memorandum of Conversation, September 3, 1969, NARA, SNF, 1967–1969, RG 59, POL CHINAT-US, Box 1985.

122. State's 161203 to Tokyo, September 23, 1969, NARA, SNF, 1967–1969, RG 59, POL 19 RYU IS, Box 2460.

123. Seoul's 5327 to Washington, September 24, 1969, NARA, SNF, 1967–1969, RG 59, POL 19 RYU IS, Box 2460. The statement that "Japanese Government has taken into consideration ROK views" is presumably a reference to the ministerial conference conducted earlier in September.

124. Taipei's 3752 to Washington, September 24, 1969, NARA, SNF, 1967–1969, RG 59, POL 19 RYU IS, Box 2460.

125. Taipei's 4306 to Washington, October 28, 1969, NARA, SNF, 1967–1969, RG 59, POL 19 RYU IS, Box 2460. Interestingly, the Japanese embassy in Taipei found out about this meeting and requested that the American embassy brief them on it. See Taipei's 4305 to Washington and Tokyo, October 28, 1969, NARA, SNF, 1967–1969, RG 59, POL 19 RYU IS, Box 2460.

126. State's 191895 to Taipei, November 14, 1969, NARA, SNF, 1967–1969, RG 59, POL 19 RYU IS, Box 2460.

127. Seoul's 6290 to Washington, November 17, 1969, NARA, SNF, 1967–1969, RG 59, POL 19 RYU IS, Box 2460.

128. Seoul's 6287 to Washington, November 17, 1969, NARA, SNF, 1967–1969, RG 59, POL 19 RYU IS, Box 2460.

129. See Seoul's 6329 to Washington, November 19, 1969; State's 195056 to Seoul, November 20, 1969; and Taipei's 4799 to Washington and Tokyo, November 26, 1969: all in NARA, SNF, 1967–1969, RG 59, POL 19 RYU IS, Box 2460.

130. Johnson, *Right Hand of Power*, 545.

131. State's 196651 to all East Asian and Pacific diplomatic posts, November 22, 1969, Nixon Presidential Materials (NPM), National Security Council Files (NSCF), VIP Visits, Box 925, RMNPL.

132. State's 195884 to various U.S. Embassies in Asia, November 21, 1969, NARA, RG 319, HCARI, Box 26.

133. Taipei's 4761 to Washington, November 24, 1969, NARA, SNF, 1967–1969, RG 59, POL 19 RYU IS, Box 2460.

134. GRC Position on Ryukyuan Reversion, December 8, 1969, NSCF, Henry A. Kissinger Office Files, Country Files–Far East, Box 81, RMNPL.

135. Seoul's 6359 to Washington, November 22, 1969, NARA, SNF, 1967–1969, RG 59, POL 19 RYU IS, Box 2460.

136. Text of Joint Communiqué, November 21, 1969, Department of State Bulletin, December 15, 1969, 556.

137. Wakaizumi, *The Best Course Available*, 236.

138. Seoul's 6359 to Washington, November 22, 1969, NARA, SNF, 1967–1969, RG 59, POL 19 RYU IS, Box 2460.

139. State's 44757 to Seoul, March 22, 1969, NARA, SNF, 1967–1969, RG 59, POL 19 RYU IS, Box 2459.

140. State's 44757 to Seoul, March 22, 1969, NARA, SNF, 1967–1969, RG 59, POL 19 RYU IS, Box 2459.

141. Tokyo's 5907 to Washington, July 18, 1969, NARA, RG 319, HCARI, Box 19.

142. Interview with Marshall Green, December 13, 1988, Association for Diplomatic Studies and Training, Foreign Affairs Oral History Project.

Conclusion

1. Pentagon Papers, Part V. A, vol. 2.

2. State's 44757 to Seoul, March 22, 1969, NARA, SNF, 1967–1969, RG 59, POL 19 RYU IS, Box 2459.

3. It is crucial to note that from 1969 onward, two key themes can be observed in some of Washington's alliances in Northeast Asia: these allies doubted US reliability and they moved to improve their own security through the development of nuclear weapon programs. See Alexander Lanoszka, *Atomic Assurance: The Alliance Politics of Nuclear Proliferation* (Ithaca, NY: Cornell University Press, 2018).

4. This is consistent with Glenn Snyder's finding that states less dependent on an alliance for security have greater power in intra-alliance bargaining. See Snyder, *Alliance Politics*, chap. 9.

5. Cha, *Alignment despite Antagonism*, 61.

6. See, for example, the sources listed in the Introduction, endnote 13.

7. For a general analysis of the ROC nuclear program, see David Albright and Corey Gay, "Taiwan: Nuclear Nightmare Averted," *Bulletin of the Atomic Scientists* 54, no. 1 (1998): 54–60.

8. See Kogan, "Proliferation among Friends," 10.

9. Taipei's 3310 to Washington, June 6, 1977, National Security Archive, George Washington University.

10. Cha, *Alignment despite Antagonism*, 71.

11. Cha, *Alignment despite Antagonism*, 176.

12. Kadura, *War after the War*, 26.

13. Henry Kissinger, "The Viet Nam Negotiations," *Foreign Affairs* 47, no. 2 (1969): 219.

14. As quoted in Kadura, *War after the War*, 122. It is fascinating to note that Kissinger—the cold and calculating advocate of realpolitik—thought of credibility along the same lines as the morally minded and religious John Foster Dulles.

15. Kadura, *War after the War*, 153.

16. David Lange, *Nuclear Free: The New Zealand Way* (Auckland: Penguin, 1990), 61.

17. As quoted in Hensley, *Friendly Fire*, 267.

18. Hensley, *Friendly Fire*, 56.

19. Hensley, *Friendly Fire*, 266.

20. Edward Olsen, "Antinuclear Posturing: New Zealand vs. Japan," *Christian Science Monitor*, March 19, 1985.

21. Oberdorfer, "U.S. Withdraws New Zealand's ANZUS Shield."

22. On the Laotian civil war, see Arthur J. Dommen, *Conflict in Laos: The Politics of Neutralization* (London: Pall Mall, 1964); Bernard B. Fall, *Anatomy of a Crisis: The Laotian Crisis of 1960–1961* (Garden City, NY: Doubleday, 1969); and William J. Rust, *Before the Quagmire: American Intervention in Laos, 1954–1962* (Lexington: University Press of Kentucky, 2012). See also Tommy Sheng Hao Chai, "Smaller-State Autonomy Enhancement through Alignment Strategic during Great-Power Competition," MSS thesis, Australian National University, 2020. On SEATO military issues, see Damien Fenton, *To Cage the Red Dragon: SEATO and the Defense of Southeast Asia, 1955–1965* (Chicago: University of Chicago Press, 2011). On SEATO more generally, see Cheng Guan Ang, *The Southeast Asia Treaty Organisation* (London: Routledge, 2021); Robb and Gill, *Divided Allies*, chaps. 6–7; and Leszek Buszynski, *SEATO: The Failure of an Alliance Strategy* (Singapore: Singapore University Press, 1983).

23. Southeast Asian Collective Defense Treaty (Manila Pact), September 8, 1954.

24. As quoted in Fred I. Greenstein and Richard H. Immerman, "What Did Eisenhower Tell Kennedy about Indochina? The Politics of Misperception," *Journal of American History* 79, no. 2 (1992): 575.

25. Fredrik Logevall, *Choosing War: The Lost Chance for Peace and the Escalation of the War in Vietnam* (Berkeley: University of California Press, 1999), 23.

26. Bangkok's 1068 to Washington, December 20, 1960, NARA, CDF, 1960–1963, RG 59, Box 1757, 751J.00/12-2060.

27. State's 2760 to Paris, January 1, 1961, NARA, CDF, 1960–1963, RG 59, Box 1758, 751J.00/1-161.

28. See Bangkok's 827 to Washington, November 9, 1960, CDF, 1960–1963, RG 59, Box 703, 379/11-960.

29. Bangkok's 1240 to Washington, January 13, 1961, NARA, CDF, 1960–1963, RG 59, Box 703, 379/1-1361.

30. State's 1222 to Moscow, January 27, 1961, NARA, CDF, 1960–1963, RG 59, Box 1759, 751J.00/1-2761.

31. Bangkok's 1234 to Washington, January 12, 1961, NARA, CDF, 1960–1963, RG 59, Box 703, 379/1-1261.

32. Bangkok's 1508 to Washington, February 25, 1961, NARA, CDF, 1960–1963, RG 59, Box 704, 379/2-2561.

33. The aide memoire of April 3, 1961, is quoted in Background Paper: Recent U.S. Security Assurances to Thailand, May 1961, Papers of President Kennedy (PPK), National Security Files (NSF), Trips and Conferences (TaC), Box 242a, John F. Kennedy Presidential Library (JFKPL), Boston.

34. Bangkok's 1306 to Washington, January 26, 1961, NARA, CDF, 1960–1963, RG 59, Box 703, 379/1-2661.

35. State's 1312 to Bangkok, March 4, 1961, NARA, CDF, 1960–1963, RG 59, Box 704, 379/2-2561.

36. Bangkok's SECTO 25, March 28, 1961, 379/3-2861; and Bangkok's SECTO 29, March 29, 1961, 379/3-2961: both in NARA, CDF, 1960–1963, RG 59, Box 704.

37. Logevall, *Choosing War*, 25.

38. Bangkok's 2047 to Washington, May 13, 1961, NARA, CDF, 1960–1963, RG 59, Box 1763, 751J.00/5-1361.

39. Bangkok's 1954 to Washington, May 1, 1961, NARA, CDF, 1960–1963, RG 59, Box 1762, 751J.00/5-161.

40. Position Paper: Impact of the Lao Crisis on Thailand, undated, PPK, NSF, TaC, Box 242a, JFKPL.

41. Bangkok's 2096 to Washington, May 19, 1961, PPK, NSF, TaC, Box 242a, JFKPL.

42. Thai-U.S. Bilateral Defense Agreement, May 1961, PPK, NSF, TaC, Box 242a, JFKPL.

43. Bangkok's 2346 to Washington, June 29, 1961, PPK, NSF, Thailand, Box 163, JFKPL.

44. Bangkok's Airgram 24 to Washington, July 26, 1961, PPK, NSF, Thailand, Box 163, JFKPL.

45. Bangkok's 237 to Washington, August 16, 1961, NARA, CDF, 1960–1963, RG 59, Box 704, 379/8-1661.

46. See Memorandum for Mr. Rostow, September 28, 1961, PPK, NSF, Thailand, Box 163, JFKPL.

47. Memorandum for Mr. Rostow, September 11, 1961, PPK, NSF, SEATO, Box 230, JFKPL.

48. President Kennedy's Meeting with Thai Foreign Minister Thanat Khoman, Position Paper, October 3, 1961, PPK, NSF, Thailand, Box 163, JFKPL.

49. See State's 738 to Bangkok, November 17, 1961, PPK, NSF, Thailand, Box 163, JFKPL.

50. State's 470 to Bangkok, October 5, 1961, PPK, NSF, Thailand, Box 163, JFKPL.

51. Memorandum of Conversation, October 3, 1961, PPK, NSF, Thailand, Box 163, JFKPL.

52. See State's 476 to Bangkok, October 6, 1961, PPK, NSF, Thailand, Box 163, JFKPL.

53. Bangkok's 911 to Washington, December 23, 1961, PPK, NSF, Thailand, Box 163, JFKPL.

54. State's 949 to Bangkok, January 4, 1962, PPK, NSF, Thailand, Box 163a, JFKPL.

55. State's 1055 to Bangkok, January 23, 1962, PPK, NSF, Thailand, Box 163a, JFKPL.

56. Bangkok's 1076 to Washington, January 26, 1962, and Bangkok's 1101 to Washington, January 31, 1961, both in PPK, NSF, Thailand, Box 163a, JFKPL.

57. Bangkok's 1098 to Washington, January 31, 1962, PPK, NSF, Thailand, Box 163a, JFKPL.

58. State's 1134 to Bangkok, February 4, 1962, PPK, NSF, Thailand, Box 163a, JFKPL.

59. Bangkok's 1167 to Washington, February 10, 1962, PPK, NSF, Thailand, Box 163a, JFKPL.

60. Bangkok's 1177 to Washington, February 12, 1962, PPK, NSF, Thailand, Box 163a, JFKPL. South Vietnam was not a full member of SEATO but a protocol state.

61. Bangkok's 1299 to Washington, February 27, 1961, NARA, CDF, 1960–1963, RG 59, Box 705, 379/2-2762.

62. State's 1230 to Bangkok, February 16, 1962, PPK, NSF, Thailand, Box 163a, JFKPL.

63. Memorandum of Conversation, March 2, 1962, PPK, NSF, Thailand, Box 163a, JFKPL.

64. Department of State Press Release 145, March 6, 1962, PPK, NSF, Thailand, Box 163a, JFKPL.

65. Bangkok's 1794 to Washington, May 17, 1962, NARA, CDF, 1960–1963, RG 59, Box 2137, 792.00/5-1762.

66. See, for example, Jeremy Pressman, *Warring Friends: Alliance Restraint in International Politics* (Ithaca, NY: Cornell University Press, 2008); Patricia A. Weitsman, *Dangerous Alliances: Proponents of Peace, Weapons of War* (Stanford, CA: Stanford University Press, 2004); Gene Gerzhoy, "Alliance Coercion and Nuclear Restraint: How the United States Thwarted West Germany's Nuclear Ambitions," *International Security* 39, no. 4 (2015): 91–129; and Or Rabinowitz and Nicholas Miller, "Keeping the Bombs in the Basement: U.S. Nonproliferation Policy toward Israel, South Africa and Pakistan," *International Security* 40, no. 1 (2015): 47–86.

67. See the sources listed in the Introduction, endnote 13.

68. See Cha, "Powerplay Origins of the U.S. Alliance System in Asia"; and Cha, *Powerplay*.

69. Cha, *Powerplay*, 4.

70. Interview with Leslie Munro, September 10, 1964, Wellington, JFD OHP, Mudd Library, Princeton University.

71. Cha, *Powerplay*, 4.

72. Walt, "Credibility Addiction."

73. Walt, "Pay No Attention to that Panda behind the Curtain."

74. Seoul's 283 to Washington, September 10, 1954, NARA, CDF, 1950–1954, RG 59, Box 4209, 793.00/9-1054.

75. Beckley, "Myth of Entangling Alliances," 9.

76. Beckley, "Myth of Entangling Alliances," 12. On entanglement, see also Kim, "Why Alliances Entangle but Seldom Entrap States."

77. Beckley, "Myth of Entangling Alliances," 48. For Beckley's summary of the literature arguing against alliances on grounds of entanglement, see 7–12.

78. See Mercer, *Reputation and International Politics*, 226–228.

Bibliography

Books

Accinelli, Robert. *Crisis and Commitment: United States Policy toward Taiwan, 1950–1955.* Chapel Hill: University of North Carolina Press, 1996.

Allison, John M. *Ambassador from the Prairie or Allison Wonderland.* Boston: Houghton Mifflin, 1973.

Ang, Cheng Guan, *The Southeast Asia Treaty Organisation.* London: Routledge, 2021.

Bell, Coral. *Dependent Ally: A Study in Australian Foreign Policy.* Melbourne: Oxford University Press, 1988.

Benson, Brett. *Constructing International Security: Alliances, Deterrence and Moral Hazard.* Cambridge: Cambridge University Press, 2012.

Buckley, Roger. *US-Japan Alliance Diplomacy, 1945–1990.* Cambridge: Cambridge University Press, 1992.

Buszynski, Leszek. *SEATO: The Failure of an Alliance Strategy.* Singapore: Singapore University Press, 1983.

Cha, Victor D. *Alignment despite Antagonism: The US-Korea-Japan Security Triangle.* Stanford, CA: Stanford University Press, 1999.

Cha, Victor D. *Powerplay: The Origins of the American Alliance System in Asia.* Princeton, NJ: Princeton University Press, 2016.

Christensen, Thomas. *Worse than a Monolith: Alliance Politics and Problems of Coercive Diplomacy in Asia.* Princeton, NJ: Princeton University Press, 2011.

Cumings, Bruce. *The Origins of the Korean War.* Vol. 2, *The Roaring of the Cataract, 1947–1950.* Princeton, NJ: Princeton University Press, 1981.

Destler, I. M., Priscilla Clapp, Hideo Sato, and Haruhiro Fukui. *Managing an Alliance: The Politics of U.S.-Japanese Relations.* Washington, DC: Brookings Institution, 1976.

Dobbs, Charles M. *The Unwanted Symbol: American Foreign Policy, the Cold War, and Korea, 1945–1950.* Kent, OH: Kent State University Press, 1981.

Dommen, Arthur J. *Conflict in Laos: The Politics of Neutralization*. London: Pall Mall, 1964.

Dower, John. *Empire and Aftermath: Yoshida Shigeru and the Japanese Experience, 1878–1964*. Cambridge, MA: Harvard University Asia Center, 1979.

Eckstein, Harry. "Case Study and Theory in Political Science." In *Case Study Method: Key Issues, Key Texts*, edited by Roger Gomm, Martyn Hammersley, and Peter Foster, 118–164. London: Sage, 2009.

Eisenhower, Dwight D. *Mandate for Change, 1953–1956: The White House Years*. Garden City, NY: Doubleday, 1963.

Fall, Bernard B. *Anatomy of a Crisis: The Laotian Crisis of 1960–1961*. Garden City, NY: Doubleday, 1969.

Fenton, Damien. *To Cage the Red Dragon: SEATO and the Defense of Southeast Asia, 1955–1965*. Chicago: University of Chicago Press, 2011.

Foot, Rosemary. *The Practice of Power: U.S. Relations with China since 1945*. Oxford: Oxford University Press, 1995.

Foot, Rosemary. *The Wrong War: American Policy and the Dimensions of the Korean Conflict, 1950–1953*. Ithaca, NY: Cornell University Press, 1985.

Garver, John. *The Sino-American Alliance: Nationalist China and American Cold War Strategy in Asia*. London: M. E. Sharpe, 1997.

Gaddis, John Lewis. "Korea in American Politics, Strategy, and Diplomacy: 1945–1950." In *The Origins of the Cold War in Asia*, edited by Yonosuke Nagai and Akira Iriye, 277–298. New York: Columbia University Press, 1977.

Gaddis, John Lewis. *The Long Peace: Inquiries into the History of the Cold War*. Oxford: Oxford University Press, 1987.

Gaddis, John Lewis. *Strategies of Containment: A Critical Appraisal of Postwar American National Security Policy*. Oxford: Oxford University Press, 1982.

George, Alexander, and Bennett, Andrew. *Case Studies and Theory Development in the Social Sciences*. Cambridge, MA: MIT Press, 2005.

Goh, Evelyn. *Constructing the U.S. Rapprochement with China, 1961–1974: From "Red Menace" to "Tacit Ally."* Cambridge: Cambridge University Press, 2005.

Gomm, Roger, Martyn Hammersley, and Peter Foster, eds. *Case Study Method: Key Issues, Key Texts*. London: Sage, 2009.

Harvey, Frank P., and John Mitton. *Fighting for Credibility: US Reputation and International Politics*. Toronto: University of Toronto Press, 2016.

Hashimoto, Akikazu, Mike Mochizuki, and Kurayoshi Takara, eds. *The Okinawa Question and the U.S.-Japan Alliance*. Washington, DC: George Washington University, 2005.

Hastings, Max. *The Korean War*. New York: Simon and Schuster, 1987.

Heer, Paul. *Mr. X and the Pacific: George F. Kennan and American Policy in East Asia*. Ithaca, NY: Cornell University Press, 2018.

Hensley, Gerald. *Friendly Fire: Nuclear Politics and the Collapse of ANZUS, 1984–1987*. Auckland: Auckland University Press, 2013.

Hong, Sung Gul. "The Search for Deterrence: Park's Nuclear Option." In *The Park Chung Hee Era: The Transformation of South Korea*, edited by Byung Kook-Kim and Ezra Vogel, 483–510. Cambridge, MA: Harvard University Press, 2011.

Hoopes, Townsend. *The Devil and John Foster Dulles*. London: Andre Deutsch, 1974.

Hopf, Ted. *Peripheral Visions: Deterrence Theory and American Foreign Policy in the Third World, 1965–1990*. Ann Arbor: University of Michigan Press, 1994.

Immerman, Richard H., ed. *John Foster Dulles and the Diplomacy of the Cold War*. Princeton, NJ: Princeton University Press, 1992.

Immerwahr, Daniel. *How to Hide an Empire: A History of the Greater United States*. London: Vintage, 2019.

Jervis, Robert. "Domino Beliefs and Strategic Behavior." In *Dominoes and Bandwagons: Strategic Beliefs and Great Power Competition in the Eurasian Rimland*, edited by Robert Jervis and Jack Snyder, 20–50. Oxford: Oxford University Press, 1991.

Jervis, Robert. *Perception and Misperception in International Politics*. Princeton, NJ: Princeton University Press, 1976.

Jervis, Robert, and Jack Snyder, eds. *Dominoes and Bandwagons: Strategic Beliefs and Great Power Competition in the Eurasian Rimland*. Oxford: Oxford University Press, 1991.

Johnson, U. Alexis. *The Right Hand of Power*. Englewood Cliffs, NJ: Prentice-Hall, 1984.

Kadura, Johannes. *The War after the War: The Struggle for Credibility during America's Exit from Vietnam*. Ithaca, NY: Cornell University Press, 2016.

Kaufman, Burton L. *The Korean Conflict*. Westport, CO: Greenwood, 1999.

Kertzer, Joshua D. *Resolve in International Politics*. Princeton, NJ: Princeton University Press, 2016.

Khong, Yuen Foong. *Analogies at War: Korea, Munich, Dien Bien Phu and the Vietnam Decisions of 1965*. Princeton, NJ: Princeton University Press, 1992.

Kim, Byung-Kook, and Ezra F. Vogel, eds. *The Park Chung Hee Era: The Transformation of South Korea*. Cambridge, MA: Harvard University Press, 2011.

Kissinger, Henry. *The White House Years*. London: Weidenfeld and Nicolson, 1979.

LaFeber, Walter. *The Clash: US-Japanese Relations throughout History*. New York: W. W. Norton, 1997.

Langdon, Frank. *Japan's Foreign Policy*. Vancouver: University of British Columbia Press, 1975.

Lange, David. *Nuclear Free: The New Zealand Way*. Auckland: Penguin, 1990.

Lanoszka, Alexander. *Atomic Assurance: The Alliance Politics of Nuclear Proliferation*. Ithaca, NY: Cornell University Press, 2018.

Liska, George. *Nations in Alliance: The Limits of Interdependence*. Baltimore, MD: Johns Hopkins Press, 1962.

Logevall, Fredrik. *Choosing War: The Lost Chance for Peace and the Escalation of the War in Vietnam*. Berkeley: University of California Press, 1999.

Lowe, Peter. *The Origins of the Korean War*. Edinburgh Gate: Addison Wesley Longman, 1997.

Lupton, Danielle. *Reputation for Resolve: How Leaders Signal Determination in International Politics*. Ithaca, NY: Cornell University Press, 2020.

Mandelbaum, Michael. *The Nuclear Revolution: International Politics before and after Hiroshima*. Cambridge: Cambridge University Press, 1981.

May, Ernest R. *"Lessons" of the Past: The Use and Misuse of History in American Foreign Policy*. New York: Oxford University Press, 1973.

McIntyre, W. David. *Background to the ANZUS Pact*. Christchurch: University of Canterbury Press, 1995.

Mercer, Jonathan. *Reputation and International Politics*. Ithaca, NY: Cornell University Press, 1996.

Meyer, Armin H. *Assignment Tokyo: An Ambassador's Journal*. Indianapolis: Bobbs-Merrill, 1974.

Meyer, Milton. *A Diplomatic History of the Philippine Republic*. Honolulu: University of Hawai'i Press, 1965.

Miller, Gregory D. *The Shadow of the Past: Reputation and Military Alliances before the First World War*. Ithaca, NY: Cornell University Press, 2012.

Nagai, Yonosuke, and Akira Iriye, eds. *The Origins of the Cold War in Asia*. New York: Columbia University Press, 1977.

Packard, George. *Protest in Tokyo: The Security Treaty Crisis of 1960*. Princeton, NJ: Princeton University Press, 1966.

Press, Daryl G. *Calculating Credibility: How Leaders Assess Military Threats*. Ithaca, NY: Cornell University Press, 2005.

Pressman, Jeremy. *Warring Friends: Alliance Restraint in International Politics*. Ithaca, NY: Cornell University Press, 2008.

Reischauer, Edwin O. *My Life between Japan and America*. New York: Harper and Row, 1986.

Robb, Thomas K., and David James Gill. *Divided Allies: Strategic Cooperation against the Communist Threat in the Asia-Pacific during the Early Cold War*. Ithaca, NY: Cornell University Press, 2019.

Rust, William J. *Before the Quagmire: American Intervention in Laos, 1954–1962*. Lexington: University Press of Kentucky, 2012.

Sartori, Anne E. *Deterrence by Diplomacy*. Princeton, NJ: Princeton University Press, 2007.

Schaller, Michael. *Altered States: The United States and Japan since the Occupation*. New York: Oxford University Press, 1997.

Schaller, Michael. *The United States and China: Into the Twenty-First Century*. Oxford: Oxford University Press, 2002.

Schelling, Thomas C. *Arms and Influence*. New Haven, CT: Yale University Press, 1966.

Schonberger, Howard. *Aftermath of War: Americans and the Remaking of Japan, 1945–1952*. Kent, OH: Kent State University Press, 1989.

Sebald, William. *With MacArthur in Japan: A Personal History of the Occupation*. New York: W. W. Norton, 1965.

Spender, Percy. *Exercises in Diplomacy: The ANZUS Treaty and the Colombo Plan*. Sydney: Sydney University Press, 1969.

Swenson-Wright, John. *Unequal Allies? United States Security and Alliance Policy toward Japan, 1945–1960*. Stanford, CA: Stanford University Press, 2005.

Snyder, Glenn H. *Alliance Politics*. Ithaca, NY: Cornell University Press, 1997.

Snyder, Glenn Herald, and Paul Diesing. *Conflict among Nations: Bargaining, Decision Making, and System Structure in International Crises*. Princeton, NJ: Princeton University Press, 1977.

Stueck, William. *The Korean War: An International History*. Princeton, NJ: Princeton University Press, 1995.

Stueck, William. *Rethinking the Korean War: A New Diplomatic and Strategic History*. Princeton, NJ: Princeton University Press, 2002.

Tucker, Nancy Bernkopf. "John Foster Dulles and the Taiwan Roots of the 'Two Chinas' Policy." In *John Foster Dulles and the Diplomacy of the Cold War*, edited by Richard Immerman, 235–262. Princeton, NJ: Princeton University Press, 1992.

Tucker, Nancy Bernkopf. *Strait Talk: United States–Taiwan Relations and the Crisis with China*. Cambridge, MA: Harvard University Press, 2009.

Tucker, Nancy Bernkopf. *Taiwan, Hong Kong, and the United States, 1945–1992: Uncertain Friendships*. New York: Twayne, 1994.

Wakaizumi, Kei. *The Best Course Available*. Honolulu: University of Hawai'i Press, 2002.

Walt, Stephen M. *The Origins of Alliances*. Ithaca, NY: Cornell University Press, 1987.

Waltz, Kenneth. *Theory of International Politics*. Long Grove, IL: Waveland, 1979.

Weitsman, Patricia A. *Dangerous Alliances: Proponents of Peace, Weapons of War*. Stanford, CA: Stanford University Press, 2004.

Yarhi-Milo, Keren. *Who Fights for Reputation: The Psychology of Leaders in International Conflict*. Princeton, NJ: Princeton University Press, 2018.

Journal Articles, Conference Papers, Dissertations

Albright, David, and Corey Gay. "Taiwan: Nuclear Nightmare Averted." *Bulletin of the Atomic Scientists* 54, no. 1 (1998): 54–60.

Ang, Cheng Guan. "The Domino Theory Revisited: The Southeast Asia Perspective." *War and Society* 19, no. 1 (2001): 109–130.

Altfield, Michael. "The Decision to Ally: A Theory and Test." *Western Political Quarterly* 37, no. 4 (1984): 523–544.

Beckley, Michael. "The Myth of Entangling Alliances: Reassessing the Security Risks of U.S. Defense Pacts." *International Security* 39, no. 4 (2015): 7–48.

Bleek, Philipp, and Eric Lorber. "Security Guarantees and Allied Nuclear Proliferation." *Journal of Conflict Resolution* 58, no. 3 (2013): 429–454.

Brands, H. W., Jr. "Testing Massive Retaliation: Credibility and Crisis Management in the Taiwan Strait." *International Security* 12, no. 4 (1988): 124–151.

Cha, Victor D. "Powerplay Origins of the U.S. Alliance System in Asia." *International Security* 34, no. 3 (2009–2010): 158–196.

Chai, Tommy Sheng Hao. "Smaller-State Autonomy Enhancement through Alignment Strategic during Great-Power Competition." MSS thesis, Australian National University, 2020

Chang, Gordon H. "To the Nuclear Brink: Eisenhower, Dulles and the Quemoy-Matsu Crisis." *International Security* 12, no. 4 (1988): 96–123.

Choi, Lyong. "The First Nuclear Crisis in the Korean Peninsula, 1975–1976." *Cold War History* 14, no. 1 (2014): 1–90.

Christensen, Thomas, and Jack Snyder. "Chain Gangs and Passed Bucks: Predicting Alliance Patterns in Multipolarity." *International Organization* 44, no. 2 (1990): 137–168.

Clubb, O. Edmund. "Formosa and the Offshore Islands in American Policy, 1950–1955." *Political Science Quarterly* 74, no. 4 (1959): 517–531.

Cohen, Warren. "Symposium: Rethinking the Lost Chance in China." *Diplomatic History* 21, no. 1 (1997): 71–75.

Copeland, Dale. "Do Reputations Matter?" *Security Studies* 7, no. 1 (2007): 33–71.

Crawford, Timothy. "Preventing Enemy Coalitions: How Wedge Strategies Shape Power Politics." *International Security* 35, no. 4 (2011): 155–189.

Dobbs, Charles M. "The Pact that Never Was: The Pacific Pact of 1949." *Journal of Northeast Asian Studies* 3, no. 4 (1984): 29–42.

Duffield, John. "Why Is There No APTO? Why Is There No OSCAP? Asia-Pacific Security Institutions in Comparative Perspective." *Contemporary Security Policy* 22, no. 2 (2001): 69–95.

Dulles, John Foster. "Security in the Pacific." *Foreign Affairs* 30, no. 2 (1952): 175–187.

Fearon, James. "Signaling Foreign Policy Interests: Tying Hands Versus Sinking Costs." *Journal of Conflict Resolution* 41, no. 4 (1997): 68–90.

Fuhrmann, Matthew, and Todd Sechser. "Signalling Alliance Commitments: Hand-Tying and Sunk Costs in Extended Nuclear Deterrence." *American Journal of Political Science* 58, no. 4 (2014): 919–935.

Gerzhoy, Gene. "Alliance Coercion and Nuclear Restraint: How the United States Thwarted West Germany's Nuclear Ambitions." *International Security* 39, no. 4 (2015): 91–129.

Gibler, Douglas. "The Costs of Reneging: Reputation and Alliance Formation." *Journal of Conflict Resolution* 52, no. 3 (2008): 426–454.

Greenstein, Fred I., and Richard H. Immerman. "What Did Eisenhower Tell Kennedy about Indochina? The Politics of Misperception." *Journal of American History* 79, no. 2 (1992): 568–587.

Halperin, Morton. "American Decision Making on Reversion of Okinawa: A Memoir." In *Commemorative Events for the Twentieth Anniversary of the Reversion of Okinawa*, 53–58. Tokyo: Japan Foundation Center for Global Partnership, 1994.

Hemmer, Christopher, and Peter Katzenstein. "Why Is There No NATO in Asia? Collective Identity, Regionalism, and the Origins of Multilateralism." *International Organization* 56, no. 3 (2002): 575–607.

Henry, Iain D. "What Allies Want: Reconsidering Loyalty, Reliability, and Alliance Interdependence." *International Security* 44, no. 4 (2020): 45–83.

Huth, Paul. "Reputations and Deterrence: A Theoretical and Empirical Assessment." *Security Studies* 7, no. 1 (2007): 72–99.

Izumikawa, Yasuhiro. "To Coerce or Reward? Theorizing Wedge Strategies in Alliance Politics." *Security Studies* 22, no. 3 (2013): 498–531.

Izumikawa, Yasuhiro. "Network Connections and the Emergence of the Hub-and-Spokes Alliance System in East Asia." *International Security* 45, no. 2 (2020): 7–50.

Jervis, Robert. "Deterrence Theory Revisited." *World Politics* 31, no. 2 (1979): 289–324.

Jervis, Robert, Keren Yarhi-Milo, and Don Casler. "Redefining the Debate over Reputation and Credibility in International Security." *World Politics* 73, no. 1 (2021): 167–203.

Kang, David. "Getting Asia Wrong: The Need for New Analytical Frameworks." *International Security* 27, no. 4 (2003): 57–85.

Kim, Seung-Young. "Security, Nationalism and the Pursuit of Nuclear Weapons and Missiles." *Diplomacy and Statecraft* 12, no. 4 (2001): 53–80.

Kim, Tongfi. "Why Alliances Entangle but Seldom Entrap States." *Security Studies* 20, no. 3 (2011): 350–377.

Kissinger, Henry. "The Viet Nam Negotiations." *Foreign Affairs* 47, no. 2 (1969): 211–234.

Kogan, Eugene. "Proliferation among Friends: Taiwan's Lessons from 1970s–1980s." Paper prepared for the Nuclear Studies Research Initiative Conference, Austin, TX, October 2013.

Krebs, Ronald R., and Jennifer Spindel. "Divided Priorities: Why and When Allies Differ over Military Intervention." *Security Studies* 27, no. 4 (2018): 575–606.

Leeds, Brett Ashley. "Alliance Reliability in Times of War: Explaining State Decisions to Violate Treaties." *International Organization* 57, no 4 (2003): 801–827.

Leeds, Brett Ashley, Andrew Long, and Sara Mitchell. "Reevaluating Alliance Reliability: Specific Threats, Specific Promises." *Journal of Conflict Resolution* 44, no. 5 (2000): 686–699.

Leeds, Brett Ashley, Jeffrey Ritter, Sara Mitchell, and Andrew Long. "Alliance Treaty Obligations and Provisions, 1815–1944." *International Interactions: Empirical and Theoretical Research in International Relations* 28, no. 3 (2002): 237–260.

Mabon, David W. "Elusive Agreements: The Pacific Pact Proposals of 1949–1951." *Pacific Historical Review* 57, no. 2 (1988): 147–177.

McDevitt, Michael. "Taiwan: The Tail that Wags Dogs." *Asia Policy* 1 (2006): 69–94.

Mercer, Jonathan. "Emotion and Strategy in the Korean War." *International Organization* 62, no. 2 (2013): 221–252.

Miller, Gregory D. "Hypotheses on Reputation: Alliance Choices and the Shadow of the Past." *Security Studies* 12, no. 3 (2003): 40–78.

Moravcsik, Andrew. "Active Citation: A Precondition for Replicable Qualitative Research." *PS: Political Science and Politics* 43, no. 1 (2010): 29–35.

Moravcsik, Andrew. "Active Citation and Qualitative Political Science." *Qualitative and Multi-Method Research* 10, no. 1 (2012): 33–37.

Morrow, James. "Alliances and Asymmetry: An Alternative to the Capability Aggregation Model of Alliances." *American Journal of Political Science* 35, no. 4 (1991): 904–933.

Morrow, James. "Alliances, Credibility, and Peacetime Costs." *Journal of Conflict Resolution* 38, no. 2 (1994): 270–297.

Morrow, James. "Alliances: Why Write Them Down?" *Annual Review of Political Science* 3 (2000): 63–83.

Park, Junghyun. "Frustrated Alignment: The Pacific Pact Proposals from 1949 to 1954 and South Korea-Taiwan Relations." *International Journal of Asian Studies* 12, no. 2 (2015): 217–237.

Rabinowitz, Or, and Nicholas Miller. "Keeping the Bombs in the Basement: U.S. Nonproliferation Policy toward Israel, South Africa and Pakistan." *International Security* 40, no. 1 (2015): 47–86.

Snyder, Glenn H. "The Security Dilemma in Alliance Politics." *World Politics* 36, no. 4 (1984): 461–495.

Stolper, Thomas. "China, Taiwan, and the Offshore Islands Together with an Implication for Outer Mongolia and Sino-Soviet Relations." *International Journal of Politics* 15, no. 1/2 (1985): iii–xiii, 1–162.

Tang, Shiping. "Reputation, Cult of Reputation, and International Conflict." *Security Studies* 14, no. 1 (2005): 34–62.

Tucker, Nancy Bernkopf, and Bonnie Glaser. "Should the United States Abandon Taiwan?" *Washington Quarterly* 34, no. 4 (2011): 23–37.

Walt, Stephen M. "Alliances in a Unipolar World." *World Politics* 61, no. 1 (2009): 86–120.

Walt, Stephen M. "Why Alliances Endure or Collapse." *Survival* 39, no. 1 (1997): 156–179.

Weisiger, Alex, and Keren Yarhi-Milo. "Revisiting Reputation: How Past Actions Matter in International Politics." *International Organization* 69, no. 2 (2015): 473–495.

Woodard, Garry. "Australian Foreign Policy on the Offshore Island Crisis of 1954–5 and Recognition of China." *Australian Journal of International Affairs* 45, no. 2 (1991): 242–263.

Yarhi-Milo, Keren, Alexander Lanoszka, and Zack Cooper. "To Arm or to Ally? The Patron's Dilemma and the Strategic Logic of Arms Transfers and Alliances." *International Security* 41, no. 2 (2016): 90–139.

Government Publications, Speeches, and Miscellaneous Documents

Acheson, Dean. "Speech on the Far East." Speech delivered to the National Press Club. January 12, 1950. https://www.cia.gov/readingroom/docs/1950-01-12.pdf.

Acheson, Dean, and Shigeru Yoshida. "Notes Exchanged between Prime Minister Yoshida and Secretary of State Acheson at the Time of the Signing of the Security Treaty between Japan and the United States of America" (referred to as "Acheson-Yoshida Notes"). September 8, 1951. "The World and Japan" Database Project, University of Tokyo. http://www.ioc.u-tokyo.ac.jp/~worldjpn/documents/texts/docs/19510908.T3E.html.

Director of Central Intelligence. "Morale on Taiwan." National Intelligence Estimate (NIE) 100-4/1-55, April 16, 1955. CIA Freedom of Information Act Electronic Reading Room. https://www.cia.gov/readingroom/docs/CIA-RDP79R01012A00 6300040016-3.pdf.

Eisenhower, Dwight. State of the Union Address. February 2, 1953. https://www.eisenhowerlibrary.gov/sites/default/files/file/1953_state_of_the_union.pdf.

Mutual Defense Treaty between the United States and the Republic of the Philippines; August 30, 1951. Avalon Project. http://avalon.law.yale.edu/20th_century/phil001.asp.

Office of the Secretary of Defense Vietnam Task Force. *United States–Vietnam Relations, 1945–1967* (a.k.a. Pentagon Papers). Part V. A, Vol. 2, *Justification of the War—Public Statements: D. The Johnson Administration*. Washington, DC: National Archives and Records Administration, 2011. http://www.documentcloud.org/documents/205536-pentagon-papers-part-v-a-volume-ii-d.html.

Sato, Eisaku. "Address to National Press Club," 21 November 1969. *US Security Agreements and Commitments Abroad*, Senate Committee on Foreign Relations, 91st Congress, 1428–1430. https://play.google.com/store/books/details?id=Mtp JAQAAIAAJ&rdid=book-MtpJAQAAIAAJ&rdot=1.

Sato, Eisaku, and Lyndon Baines Johnson. "Joint Statement of Japanese Prime Minister Sato and U.S. President Johnson" (a.k.a. Johnson-Sato Communiqué), November 15, 1967. "The World and Japan" Database Project, University of Tokyo. http://www.ioc.u-tokyo.ac.jp/~worldjpn/documents/texts/JPUS/19671115.D1E.html.

Security Treaty between the United States and Japan; September 8, 1951. Avalon Project. http://avalon.law.yale.edu/20th_century/japan001.asp.

Security Treaty between the United States, Australia, and New Zealand (ANZUS); September 1, 1951. Avalon Project. http://avalon.law.yale.edu/20th_century/us mu002.asp.

Taipei's 3110 to Washington, June 6, 1977. National Security Archive, George Washington University. http://nsarchive.gwu.edu/nukevault/ebb221/T-16b.pdf.

Treaty of Mutual Cooperation and Security between Japan and the United States of America, January 19, 1960. Ministry of Foreign Affairs of Japan. http://www.mofa.go.jp/region/n-america/us/q&a/ref/1.html.

United Nations General Assembly Security Council. Memorandum on Security Assurances in Connection with Ukraine's Accession to the Treaty on the Non-Proliferation of Nuclear Weapons, December 5, 1994. United Nations A/49/765 and S/1994/1399, December 19, 1994. http://www.securitycouncilreport.org/atf/cf/%7B65BFCF9B-6D27-4E9C-8CD3-CF6E4FF96FF9%7D/s_1994_1399.pdf.

United States Department of State. *Department of State Bulletin* 20, no. 517 (May 29, 1949).

United States Department of State. *Department of State Bulletin* 20, no. 520 (June 19, 1949).

United States Department of State. *Department of State Bulletin* 28, no. 729 (June 15, 1953).

United States Department of State. *Department of State Bulletin* 31, no. 807 (December 13, 1954).

United States Department of State. *Department of State Bulletin* 32, no. 818 (February 28, 1955).

United States Department of State. *Department of State Bulletin* 37, no. 941 (July 8, 1957).

United States Department of State. *Department of State Bulletin* 61, no. 1590 (December 15, 1969).

United States Department of State. *Foreign Relations of the United States, 1949*. Vol. 7, Pt. 2, *The Far East and Australasia*. Edited by John G. Reid and John P. Glennon. Washington, DC: Government Printing Office, 1976. https://history.state.gov/historicaldocuments/frus1949v07p2.

United States Department of State. *Foreign Relations of the United States, 1950*, Vol. 1, *National Security Affairs; Foreign Economic Policy*. Edited by Neal H. Petersen, John P. Glennon, David W. Mabon, Ralph R. Goodwin, and William Z. Slany. Washington, DC: Government Printing Office, 1977. https://history.state.gov/historicaldocuments/frus1950v01.

United States Department of State. *Foreign Relations of the United States, 1950*. Vol. 6, *East Asia and the Pacific*. Edited by Neal H. Petersen, William Z. Slany, Charles S. Sampson, John P. Glennon, and David W. Mabon. Washington, DC: Government Printing Office, 1976. https://history.state.gov/historicaldocuments/frus1950v06.

United States Department of State. *Foreign Relations of the United States, 1950*. Vol. 7, *Korea*. Edited by John P. Glennon. Washington, DC: Government Printing Office, 1976. https://history.state.gov/historicaldocuments/frus1950v07.

United States Department of State. *Foreign Relations of the United States, 1951*. Vol. 6, Pt. 1, *Asia and the Pacific*. Edited by Paul Claussen, John P. Glennon, David W. Mabon, Neal H. Petersen, and Carl N. Raether. Washington, DC: Government Printing Office, 1977. https://history.state.gov/historicaldocuments/frus1951v06p1.

United States Department of State. *Foreign Relations of the United States, 1952–1954*. Vol. 14, Pt. 1, *China and Japan*. Edited by David W. Mabon and Harriet D. Schwar. Washington, DC: Government Printing Office, 1985. https://history.state.gov/historicaldocuments/frus1952-54v14p1.

United States Department of State. *Foreign Relations of the United States, 1952–1954.* Vol. 14, Pt. 2, *China and Japan.* Edited by David W. Mabon and Harriet D. Schwar. Washington, DC: Government Printing Office, 1985. https://history.state.gov /historicaldocuments/frus1952-54v14p2.

United States Department of State. *Foreign Relations of the United States, 1955–1957.* Vol. 2, *China.* Edited by Harriet D. Schwar. Washington, DC: Government Printing Office, 1986. https://history.state.gov/historicaldocuments/frus1955-57v02.

United States Department of State. *Foreign Relations of the United States, 1955–1957,* Vol. 23, Pt. 1, *Japan.* Edited by David W. Mabon. Washington, DC: Government Printing Office, 1991. https://history.state.gov/historicaldocuments/frus1955 -57v23p1.

United States Department of State. *Foreign Relations of the United States, 1955–1957,* Vol. 23, Pt. 2, *Korea.* Edited by Glenn W. LaFantasie. Washington, DC: Government Printing Office, 1993. https://history.state.gov/historicaldocuments/frus1955 -57v23p2.

United States Department of State. *Foreign Relations of the United States, 1958–1960.* Vol. 18, *Japan; Korea.* Edited by Madeline Chi and Louis J. Smith. Washington, DC: Government Printing Office, 1994. https://history.state.gov/historicaldocuments /frus1958-60v18.

United States Department of State. *Foreign Relations of the United States, 1964–1968,* Vol. 29, Pt. 2, *Japan.* Edited by Karen L. Gatz. Washington, DC: Government Printing Office, 2006. https://history.state.gov/historicaldocuments/frus1964-68v29p2.

Media Articles and Blog Posts

Cooper, Helene, and Martin Fackler. "U.S. Response to Crimea Worries Japan's Leaders." *New York Times,* April 5, 2014.

Cooper, Helene, and Jane Perlez. "White House Moves to Reassure Allies with South China Sea Patrol, but Quietly." *New York Times,* October 27, 2015.

De Luce, Dan. "Hagel: The White House Tried to 'Destroy' Me." Foreign Policy, December 18, 2015. http://foreignpolicy.com/2015/12/18/hagel-the-white-house -tried-to-destroy-me/.

Friedberg, Aaron. "Will We Abandon Taiwan?" *Commentary,* May 1, 2000. https:// www.commentarymagazine.com/articles/will-we-abandon-taiwan/.

Gerzhoy, Gene, and Nick Miller. "Donald Trump Thinks More Countries Should Have Nuclear Weapons: Here's What the Research Says." *Washington Post,* April 6, 2016.

Horne, A. D. "Bases Are Stakes of Okinawa Game." *Washington Post,* May 11, 1969.

Kelly, Robert. "My Expanded Lowy Post on Moral Hazard in US Alliances: Explaining Japan-Korea (and Greece-Turkey?)." Asian Security blog, January 28, 2014. https://asiansecurityblog.wordpress.com/2014/01/28/my-expanded-lowy-post -on-moral-hazard-in-us-alliances-explaining-japan-korea-and-greece-turkey/.

Mearsheimer, John. "Say Goodbye to Taiwan." *National Interest,* February 25, 2014. http://nationalinterest.org/print/article/say-goodbye-taiwan-9931.

Oberdorfer, Don. "U.S. Withdraws New Zealand's ANZUS Shield." *Washington Post,* June 28, 1986.

Olsen, Edward, "Antinuclear Posturing: New Zealand vs. Japan." *Christian Science Monitor*, March 19, 1985.

Sachs, Natan. "Whose Side Are You on? Alliance Credibility in the Middle East and Japan." *Order from Chaos* (blog of the Brookings Institution), May 31, 2016. https://www.brookings.edu/blog/order-from-chaos/2016/05/31/whose-side -are-you-on-alliance-credibility-in-the-middle-east-and-japan/.

Shanker, Thom, and Lauren D'Avolio. "Former Defense Secretaries Criticize Obama on Syria." *New York Times*, September 18, 2013.

Walt, Stephen M. "The Credibility Addiction." Foreign Policy, January 6, 2015. http://foreignpolicy.com/2015/01/06/the-credibility-addiction-us-iraq -afghanistan-unwinnable-war/.

Walt, Stephen M. "Pay No Attention to that Panda behind the Curtain." Foreign Policy, April 23, 2014. http://foreignpolicy.com/2014/04/23/pay-no-attention-to -that-panda-behind-the-curtain/.

Index